"Clint Willis' lively writing and his reporting elan lend *The Boys of Everest* a gripping, you-are-there quality. Your limbs ache, your toes freeze, you feel the burn of the icy wind. A wonderful read for both mountaineers and armchair adventurers."
—MIKE SAGER, contributing writer, *Esquire*,
author of *Scary Monsters and Super Freaks*

"*The Boys of Everest* is a captivating story and read. It's very, very good."
—ED WEBSTER, author of
Snow in the Kingdom: My Storm Years on Everest

"*The Boys of Everest* takes us deep inside the hearts and minds of men at once quixotic and genuinely noble. Willis has an extraordinary gift for conveying states of mind *in extremis*, particularly those moments for a climber when all the comfortable assumptions about himself fall away. The reader feels a powerful shock of recognition, whether or not he or she has ever been anywhere *near* a mountain."
—JOHN MANDERINO, author of *Reasons for Leaving*
and *The Man Who Once Played Catch with Nellie Fox*

"This book, with its vivid evocation of high-altitude derring-do, is so breathtaking, you may need to read it with supplemental oxygen."
—MICHAEL FINKEL, author of
True Story: Murder, Memoir, Mea Culpa

The Boys of Everest

Chris Bonington and the Tragedy of Climbing's Greatest Generation

CLINT WILLIS

**ROBSON
BOOKS**

First published in Great Britain in 2006 by
Robson Books
151 Freston Road
London
W10 6TH

An imprint of Anova Books Company Ltd

Published in the United States by Carroll & Graf Publishers

ISBN 1 86105 980 9

10 9 8 7 6 5 4 3 2 1

Printed and bound by MPG Books Ltd, Bodmin, Cornwall

This book can be ordered direct from the publisher
Contact the marketing department, but try your bookshop first

www.anovabooks.com

For Jennifer and Harper and Abner

Contents

SELECTED CHARACTERS
IN ORDER OF APPEARANCE

Chris Bonington

Hamish MacInnes

Don Whillans

CHRIS BONINGTON, CHRIS BONINGTON PICTURE LIBRARY

Ian Clough

CHRIS BONINGTON, CHRIS BONINGTON PICTURE LIBRARY

John Harlin

CHRIS BONINGTON, CHRIS BONINGTON PICTURE LIBRARY

Dougal Haston

Mick Burke

Nick Estcourt

Martin Boysen

Doug Scott

Peter Boardman

Joe Tasker

Dick Renshaw

Al Rouse

Selected Climbs and Expeditions

1958
Petit Dru, Bonatti Pillar (French Alps)

1960
Annapurna II, West Ridge (Nepal)

1961
Nuptse, South Face (Nepal)
Mont Blanc, Central Pillar of Freney (French Alps)

1962
Grandes Jorasses, Walker Spur (French Alps)
Eiger, North Face (Swiss Alps)

1963
Central Tower of Paine, West Face (Patagonia)

1966
Eiger, North Face Direct (Swiss Alps)

1970
Annapurna, South Face (Nepal)

1972
Everest, Southwest Face (Nepal)

1974
Changabang, East Ridge (India)

1975
Everest, Southwest Face (Nepal)
Dunagiri, South Ridge (India)

1976
Changabang, West Wall (India)
The Ogre, West Ridge (Pakistan)

1978
K2, West Ridge (Pakistan)

1979
Kangchenjunga, North Ridge (Nepal)
Gauri Sankar, West Ridge (Nepal)

1980
K2, West Ridge and Abruzzi Spur (Pakistan)
Kongur, reconnaissance expedition (China)

1981
Kongur, West Ridge (China)

1982
Everest, Northeast Ridge (Tibet)

1985
Everest, Southeast Ridge (Nepal)

AUTHOR'S NOTE

V IRGINIA WOOLF SAID that we read to "leave behind the tether of a single mind . . . and deviate into the minds and bodies of others." We also read (and write) to examine the stories other people tell about themselves and each other, and to repair or rethink those stories as well as our own.

Those motives informed my methods in reporting and writing this book. I conducted extensive interviews and correspondence with climbers and their friends and families. I made close and repeated readings of scores of primary and secondary sources, including articles, biographies, diaries, expedition books, letters, memoirs, poems and other published or unpublished work. I also drew upon all of those sources as well as my own experience to imagine what climbers might have thought or felt at certain moments. It occurs to me that in doing so I have taken in public the sort of liberty that readers and writers ordinarily take in the privacy of our imaginations.

THE SUMMIT OF Everest surprised them. Tenzing Norgay and Edmund Hillary had been climbing for five hours; the last hour or so they had lost themselves in toiling up the undulating ridge of snow that ended here, at 29,028 feet. They looked up and saw the view and understood.

The Sherpa and the young man from New Zealand looked at one another, smiling behind their black oxygen masks. They shook hands and then embraced, clumsy in their heavy boots and layers of clothing. They were awkward in their mutual shyness—partners in an arranged marriage, aware of their differences now that they had this in common.

They didn't stay long. They knew what lay ahead—the descent to the others, the journey back to their respective civilizations—and they thought of this with a mixture of exhilaration and curiosity and fear and the beginnings of grief.

Sherpa Tenzing buried some food as a gift to the mountain's gods. Edmund Hillary buried with the food a small crucifix. He was conscious that he had been singled out in some astonishing way—that he was a mere instrument in some enormous work, some new wonder of the world. After thirty-two years and sixteen expeditions—and at the cost of twenty-two lives—men had finally reached the summit of the world's highest peak.

Hillary and Tenzing left the summit just before noon—still

the morning of May 29, 1953. The news appeared in the *London Times* four days later, Coronation Day for the young Queen Elizabeth. The history of mountaineering was over.

What next?

A SMALL, CLOSE-KNIT band of roughly a dozen climbers spent the next three decades answering that question. They emerged from the villages, slums and middle-class suburbs of postwar Great Britain. Together, they formed the core of climbing's greatest generation. Their leader was the boyish but driven Chris Bonington. His chief lieutenants and collaborators included such legends in the making as Mick Burke, Nick Estcourt, Dougal Haston, Doug Scott and Don Whillans. The group, which came to be known as Bonington's Boys, took on handpicked reinforcements from the ranks of emerging prodigies. Their recruits included young superstars such as Dick Renshaw and Al Rouse as well as the two young men who by the end threatened to outshine them all: ex-seminarian Joe Tasker and his immensely strong partner and rival Peter Boardman.

Bonington and his companions began their adventures during the 1950s, setting new rock- and ice-climbing standards on crags and mountains in England, Scotland and Wales. Deprived of a shot at mountaineering's Great Problem—the first ascent of Everest—they took on the most difficult routes in the Alps, first copying and then surpassing the Continent's most advanced alpinists. The group eventually turned their attention to the Himalayan ranges, where they attempted a series of incredibly dangerous and difficult routes on the world's biggest mountains. Bonington and his comrades during the '70s and early '80s made legendary expeditions to more than a dozen high peaks, including Annapurna, K2 and—above all—Everest itself. The world's highest mountain became the scene of their most glorious achievements as well as their most bitter defeats. Their story in a sense begins on Everest, and it ends there.

The previous generation had taken more than thirty years to climb Everest in part because they were unwilling to take certain chances. Most of them would turn back from a summit attempt rather than risk a night out on the mountain's slopes. A few British climbers—George Mallory was one—took such risks, but their peers judged them daredevils, irresponsible and unsporting.

The climbers in Bonington's circle had a decided tendency to press on—to cross the avalanche-prone snow slope, to climb higher as daylight waned or a storm blew in. They took extreme risks; when their luck held, they pushed it still further. Their acceptance of such risks created new possibilities. It encouraged them to attempt more difficult routes on bigger mountains, most famously Annapurna's towering South Face and Everest's Southwest Face. Their targets grew more spectacular even as the teams grew smaller and their hierarchies grew more vague—so that by the end, each new expedition amounted to a small group of close friends moving fast and light up some enormous unclimbed mountain ridge or face.

Bonington and his comrades made climbing a mountain a more spontaneous and a more creative act—less a mission—than it had been. They paid a heavy price. Only a few men survived the great climbs the group undertook in the 1970s and '80s.

The dead left behind careers, friends, parents, wives and children. The survivors went on climbing. It's possible to generalize—to say that Bonington and his comrades climbed for thrills or for friendship or because they were ambitious or self-destructive or to prove their worth or courage—but the climbers' motives are buried in their story.

—Clint Willis

Those who travel to mountaintops
are half in love with themselves,
and half in love with oblivion.

—ROBERT MACFARLANE,
Mountains of the Mind (2003)

PART ONE

Boys

*They were young and did not
leave much behind them and need
someone to remember them.*

—NORMAN MACLEAN,
Young Men and Fire (1992)

The Eiger, North Face.

CHRIS BONINGTON, CHRIS BONINGTON PICTURE LIBRARY

T HE CLIMBERS WENT to bed early and rose in the dark to stuff ropes and pitons, stove and sleeping bags, tea and scraps of food into their tattered rucksacks. They struggled into boots and crampons and emerged from the relative warmth of the alpine hut to cross the glacier under a sky pocked with stars. The mountains looked to young Chris Bonington like black velvet cutouts against the starlit sky.

Chris and his companion, Hamish MacInnes, shivered as they walked with their burdens. They were silent for the most part. They saw the route—the Southeast Spur of the Pointe de Lépiney, a series of overhangs; it looked impossible to Chris.

He reminded himself that he was becoming a seasoned alpinist; at twenty-three, he'd been climbing for seven years. This season, the summer of 1958, was his second in the French Alps. He was a superb natural climber, and he was ambitious. He didn't look it, though; he looked young, even soft. He was a gangly, brown-haired boy. He had a long face with high cheekbones, full lips and smallish blue eyes. He had a baby's complexion. He was a graduate of the Royal Military Academy at Sandhurst; he commanded a British tank troop stationed in Germany—still, those overhangs looked hideous.

Hamish was older; he was twenty-seven, just back from his second Himalayan expedition. He didn't seem worried about the overhangs—but then that was the problem with Hamish: he never worried about anything. He was a lean-faced fellow with hollow cheeks and deep-set eyes, an eccentric who insisted on eating brown bread and who slept on the floor for his health. He had an interest in mountain rescue, but he was himself horribly accident-prone. He'd fractured his skull falling from a climb the previous summer; that same evening he'd gotten drunk and tried to climb a church; he'd fallen again, breaking a leg.

The two climbers roped up and moved across the easy terrain at the bottom of their route. There was something spectacular about these first moments of a day in the mountains. You began walking with a sour stomach, your body cold and stiff. Soon you would start to sweat and wake up. The difficulties lay well ahead and now you were keenly alert to the beauty of this place, of your surroundings; you pitied the people who slept in the valley. Chris was afraid of what might happen, and yet pleased with how things had turned out—he felt as though his story had come to its happy conclusion. And all the while he knew that the range of the day's possible outcomes included his own death, a death that he understood vaguely as a merging with the inky shapes of mountains, discernable in this earliest morning only because their forms blotted out the stars.

They entered a gully next to the face; it let them bypass the worst overhangs. Chris thought they should simply follow the gully to the summit. Hamish brushed this notion aside and led back out onto smooth rock slabs, which required slow and painstaking work.

They climbed until it was nearly dark and spent the night on a ledge under an overhang. Chris tucked himself into a nook in the rock. He had brought a sleeping bag and he wrapped it in plastic sheeting, but he was too cold to sleep.

He was eager to move in the morning, and he led the first pitch.

He tied one end of the rope to his waist and began to climb. As he moved higher, he looked for cracks in the rock or other spots where he could place protection, mostly metal pitons or wooden wedges. He hung a sling from each new piece of gear, and clipped a carabiner—a gated metal oval—to the sling; that done, he clipped his trailing rope to the carabiner.

The rope now ran from Chris down through each protection point, all the way to Hamish at the start of the pitch. Hamish had passed the rope around his waist. He fed out slack as Chris moved higher; he would hold the rope if Chris fell. The length of the fall would depend upon how far Chris had climbed past his most recent protection; assuming his gear held, he would fall roughly twice that distance.

The climbing here was difficult. Chris was forced to resort to artificial techniques; he tied long slings to wedges and stood on the slings to gain height. That's what he was doing when one of the wedges came out.

He hurtled through sky, utterly disoriented, and then stopped. He was intensely relieved—his lower wedge had held—but dimly aware of a mindless, a physical, disappointment, as if his body had wished to keep falling. He dangled upside down over the glacier. The rope had twisted itself around an ankle and his foot went numb for a moment.

He wrangled himself back onto the rock and climbed again to his high point. He continued past an overhang to finish the pitch, but the next overhang looked harder still. Worse, the weather was turning. The clouds moving toward the climbers looked threatening enough to deter even Hamish, who suggested that it was time to go down.

They moved left and descended easy rock for a time. It brought them to the top of a steep gully. They prepared a rappel, placing a piton for an anchor and feeding their rope through the eye of the piton until they reached the rope's midpoint. Hamish tossed the ends of the rope into the gully. Chris straddled the doubled rope and reached back with his right hand to bring the rope up across his chest and over his left shoulder so that it ran down his back. He took the rope in his right hand—his brake hand—and backed down into the gully's invisible depths.

Once in the gully, they couldn't climb out. The walls were too steep. They could not climb down, either; they could only rappel. This meant they must find sites for rappel anchors every 80 feet or so. Otherwise they would be stuck, and they would freeze to death. Dying wouldn't take long; as the day progressed, the gully was turning into a sort of vertical riverbed for a torrent of melted snow.

Hamish rappelled one rope-length to a tiny stance, where he placed a single piton as an anchor. Chris followed him. Both men were wet to the skin. They moved quickly, both reaching to pull on one end of the doubled rope to bring it down for the next rappel. The rope wouldn't budge; it was stuck somewhere over their heads.

A stuck rappel rope is a mountaineer's nightmare. A stuck rappel rope in an alpine waterfall is worse. Hamish tried to climb a slab in the torrent to retrieve the rope, and failed; it was too slippery—a fall here would be fatal. Chris tried, and sheer desperation got him up the slab and out of the main flow of meltwater. He still couldn't free the rope, but now he could think. He stood shaking with cold and anxiety, and realized that he'd have to climb the rope itself.

He wrapped two bits of cord around the doubled rope, using prusik knots. The prusik when weighted will grip a rope, but otherwise will slide easily up it. Chris clipped himself to both knots and then—shifting his weight from one prusik to the other, each time sliding the unweighted knot a bit higher—climbed the rope to the point where it was wedged. He quickly freed it, and carefully climbed back down to Hamish.

The climbers set up one last rappel, past a bulge of rock. The doubled rope didn't reach the ground; it dangled over the jaws of an enormous bergschrund—a yawning crevasse between the base of the route and the snowfield that lay below. They would have to cross the crevasse somehow. They considered the problem for a moment and concluded that they would have to use the rope to swing across—a sort of Tarzan maneuver—and hope to clear the gap.

Chris balked. He imagined letting go of the rope at the wrong instant, and falling forever into the black, frigid depths of the glacier. Hamish went first, and managed to land on the crumbling edge of the snowfield and maintain his balance. Chris was now even more afraid but he rummaged and came up with what felt like the ghost of a memory—it might have been an old dream—of himself pursued, in flight. He gathered himself and leaped.

He landed well clear of the gap and fell forward into the snow, skidding downhill, scattering chips of half-melted ice so that bits of it got into his eyes. He picked himself up. Hamish was already moving and Chris followed as quickly as he could, feeling suddenly light, almost weightless; he wondered for a moment if he had somehow left his rucksack on the other side of the bergschrund. The bedraggled pair walked downhill for what seemed a long time and at last came to the hut where they had spent the previous night. The caretaker was a young woman; she had made much of the two young climbers—in particular, Hamish.

They were too ashamed to face her. They carried on past the shelter as daylight faded, picking their soaking-wet way down to the empty shepherd's hut they'd occupied for the season; the hut was at Montenvers, still 3,000 feet above Chamonix. They shivered as they walked; the mouths of crevasses loomed beneath them in the shadowed glacier. Chris's weariness now rose in him like night itself, a deep and inexorable tide so that moving even downhill was like trying to run in deep snow. He walked stiffly, almost staggering; once his knees gave way under the weight of his rucksack, and he collapsed in a momentary heap. He noted from time to time that he was horribly thirsty.

He didn't mind any of it—the shame, the weariness, the thirst. He could barely make them out. He was listening, enthralled, to the high-pitched buzzing of his happiness, to the joy that fairly sang in his bones.

THE TWO YOUNG climbers had met almost six years earlier, when Chris hitchhiked up from London for a taste of Scotland's famous winter climbing. He'd come across Hamish and several of the Scotsman's mates at a climbers' hut. Chris was eighteen. He had quit school after failing an examination, and was awaiting his call-up papers from the Air Force.

Hamish was a different story; at twenty-two, he already cut a figure in British mountaineering circles. Like other young climbers of the day—in particular Scottish ones—he was a troublemaker. He'd done his national service in Austria, climbing in the Alps and learning to use pitons for aid: hammering pegs into the rock and clipping slings to them; standing in the slings to reach up and hammer another peg in. He had brought the technique home to Scotland, where he pegged his way up difficult climbs over the objections of traditionalists, who thought such devices were a form of cheating. Their complaints—they dubbed the young man Hamish MacPiton—served mainly to encourage him.

He often plucked his partners from the ranks of newcomers to the climbing scene. Such innocents didn't yet know better than to accept his invitations, which typically involved them in some absurdly ambitious and perilous venture. Hamish would adopt a wistful manner; he would gaze stoically into the middle distance and speak as if to himself, describing some soul-destroying route as *a plum, a real beauty; it's nothing too hard, really, barely worth the bother, but still* . . .

Hamish saw the young Chris Bonington as a potential recruit. The other Scots drinking tea in the climbing hut that day in the winter of 1952 regarded the English boy in quite another light—as an object of mild contempt. They were part of climbing's emerging elite, a club-centered culture composed largely of working class lads who were terrible snobs; they despised any climber with a new pair of boots, let alone an expensive education. They certainly weren't inclined to befriend this young Englishman with his rosy cheeks and his upper-class accent; as one climber remarked, the poor lad looked like he'd been raised in a fucking doll's house.

In fact, he'd grown up in boarding schools, and with women. His father had left when Chris was an infant. His mother and his maternal grandmother fought over the boy after that; between schools, he lived with one or the other, depending upon his mother's mental state. He'd emerged from those difficulties as the sort of earnest and self-absorbed young person, slightly fussy, who sometimes gets himself disliked.

He seemed vulnerable—even a bit fearful—but he was a bold climber. He was self-conscious and ambitious; he carried in his head a picture of himself and he wished to live up to it. He wanted to be accomplished and he wanted to behave well. He wanted his way, and he wanted to be liked—admired—by men he respected. The complexity of his agenda set him apart and made him hard to understand.

He had discovered climbing almost by accident. He was already sixteen when he traveled to Ireland to visit his paternal grandfather near Dublin for two weeks. The old man had run off to sea as a boy and had seen the world, finishing his career working with

Aborigines as a member of the British forestry service. Chris's journey to Ireland offered the teenager a glimpse of the mountains that lined the Welsh coast. He stopped on his way home to visit an aunt who happened to own a book of mountain photographs, and the pictures of Great Britain's various ranges impressed the boy deeply. He returned to school that fall and talked a friend into hitchhiking to Wales that Christmas. The two of them floundered around in the snow on Snowdon, eventually triggering an avalanche that might easily have carried them both off a cliff.

Chris found it all enthralling—the danger, the weather, the mountains themselves. He convinced a family friend to take him rock climbing near London. Chris loved that as well. Something— an interior buoyance as mysterious as gravity itself—rose up in him when he climbed.

He was soon seeking out more serious partners for harder climbs. He was still a teenager, and he had a talent for playing the protégé, finding and enlisting mentors who could teach him what he needed to know. Chris by the time he met Hamish MacInnes was a climber of sorts, one well-suited to the Scotsman's purposes: eager and talented, surprisingly bold but still willing to let the more experienced man take the lead.

The two young men roped up together for the first time a week or so after their initial meeting. The climb was a terrifying experience for Chris—the first of many he was to endure under his new mentor. Hamish had a frightening enthusiasm for new and difficult routes, and he often climbed long distances without placing protection. He had impressive powers of endurance, and seemed impervious to cold. Chris on one occasion that winter followed his new friend up a gully, emerging soaked from a torrent of melting snow. Hamish, holding the rope, stood in the snow in his socks; he'd taken his boots off to climb a difficult bit of iced-over rock. Chris, through chattering teeth, asked Hamish if his feet weren't cold.

No, replied Hamish. *I can't feel them.*

They made several climbs that first winter in Scotland. Chris left to report for his military service with the Air Force. He spent roughly a year with the RAF, including a stint at the Royal Air Force College, Cranwell, during the autumn of 1953. His Air Force experience ended in disappointment when he washed out of pilot training the following spring. He had terrible trouble trying to land the plane; strangely enough, he couldn't tell how far away the ground was.

He transferred to the army. The transition period left him free to spend the summer in Wales, where he climbed a series of increasingly difficult rock routes. He entered the Royal Military College, Sandhurst in the fall of 1954. He had always had an interest in military games and history, and he liked Sandhurst. He polished his accent and bought a bowler hat and umbrella for trips to London. He also became a leading figure in the Sandhurst Mountaineering Club. He put up new routes in the Avon Gorge in Bristol—a 200-mile round trip from school—and made more trips to Wales. He was becoming a fluent climber; he would take his time to sort out a route, and then climb it with a minimum of fuss. He wasn't what you'd call a rock athlete, but he was very smooth.

He finished the eighteen-month Sandhurst course in early 1956, and the army sent him to Germany to take command of a troop of tanks. He made his first foray to the Alps in the summer of 1957. The idea—Hamish's, of course—was to climb the North Face of the Eiger, a 6,000-foot wall of crumbling black rock, punctuated by huge, steep fields of ice and snow; by most accounts, it was the most dangerous climb in Europe.

Chris was vastly relieved when the weather turned bad low

on the route, forcing Hamish to admit defeat. Hamish had other wild ideas, though. For starters, he wanted Chris to join him on the almost equally daunting Walker Spur of the Grandes Jorasses. Bad weather again came to the rescue; the Walker remained plastered with fresh snow. The two friends waited three days at their campsite before snatching the first ascent of a minor route, a rock buttress some 1,500 feet high. The descent, unroped, frightened Chris; still, he had completed his first route in the Alps. He returned to his tank troop the next day, glad to have escaped his first alpine adventure with his life.

And now, a year later, he was back for his second alpine season. He'd met Hamish in Chamonix in early July. The two of them had immediately moved up to occupy their rickety but rent-free shepherd's hut at Montenvers. Chris was growing tired of army life after another winter of training and military routine. Hamish was lean and tan; he'd spent part of the winter searching for the Yeti in India's Valley of the Gods.

The two climbers were utterly broke, living mainly on stolen tank rations and figs—and once again, Chris was in fear of his life. The failure on the Pointe de Lépiney—with its hideous overhangs and near-fatal waterfall gully—had been only the start of their season. Their horrifying epic had been a warm-up, a mere exercise.

Hamish had big plans.

2

C HRIS WAS LEARNING that memories of the fear and discomfort endured on a difficult climb fade quickly. Each climb was a blur of intensity that he carried until the colors died away to leave a picture like a Japanese wall hanging; the picture carried an abstract beauty that made him long for the real thing.

He wanted to climb. A greed for it grew in him when he was away from the mountains. Chris and also Hamish were riding this particular kind of momentum, beginning to live in it like addicts. Their clothes were still wet from their epic on the Pointe de Lépiney when Hamish announced his intention to try another first ascent. This time, he had his eye on a 2,000-foot wall of ice known as The Shroud.

Chris, suffering from a nasty head cold, declared that he would not participate in such madness. The climbers spent three rainy days more or less happily debating the issue. They eventually reached an agreement: Chris would climb anything—if someone else had climbed it before. Hamish saw his opening and at once proposed the formidable Southwest Pillar of the Dru, known to climbers as the Bonatti Pillar.

Like many of his ideas, this one was ridiculous. The Bonatti Pillar was a 3,000-foot spur of sheer granite: the hardest rock climb in the entire Mont Blanc Massif, the center of world mountaineering for almost a century. The massif is a complex of stupendously beautiful peaks, glaciers and sheer rock outcroppings where France, Italy and Switzerland converge; it culminates at the summit of Mont Blanc itself (4,807 meters; 15,771 feet).

The great Italian climber Walter Bonatti had made the first ascent of the pillar just three years earlier, in 1955. He had climbed the route alone, relying on a cumbersome belay system that often offered little or no protection from a fall. Other climbers had rightly hailed his ascent as one of the great achievements in mountaineering history. The Bonatti Pillar had seen four subsequent ascents by strong parties, but several groups had been forced to retreat—and no British climber had yet done the route.

It was perfect.

IN TRUTH, BRITISH climbers during the first half of the century had fallen behind their counterparts on the Continent. The British obsession with Everest was largely to blame. Great Britain had sent a series of official and unofficial expeditions to the mountain over a period of thirty-two years, beginning in 1921 and culminating in the first ascent of Everest in 1953. The quest for Everest had been an overriding mission—and an enormous distraction—for Britain's strongest mountaineers, drawn from the upper ranks of their class-bound society.

Their attempts on Everest had been very serious affairs, due to the mountain's remote position, powerful winds and extremely high altitude. The early climbers on Everest had all they could do merely to survive the frigid winds and thin air above 20,000 feet. The British expeditions took on the shape and aura of military campaigns, laying siege to the mountain. That suited a generation of privileged climbers often drawn from the military itself—men accustomed to giving and taking orders.

A typical expedition would establish a well-stocked base camp at the bottom of the route. The climbers—supported by scores or even hundreds of porters—would spend weeks or months ferrying supplies to a series of higher camps. The top camp would serve as a launching pad for one or more attempts on the summit. Ultimately, success or failure boiled down to logistics. The actual climbing—most of it, anyway—consisted of low angle snow slopes and rock slabs that would have been considered easy ground in the Alps.

Mountaineering meanwhile became a popular sport on the European Continent, where millions of young students and workers—Austrian, French, Italian, German—lived within easy reach of the Alps. The range provided challenges and opportunities very different from those the British found on Everest. The Alps' major peaks (the Matterhorn was the most famous) had all been climbed in the last decades of the nineteenth century, mostly by well-off British adventurers, who enlisted local guides to help them find the easiest routes to various summits. But the young continental Europeans who escaped to the Alps after the nightmare of World War I brought a new intensity to the sport of mountaineering. They pioneered more difficult routes, often targeting subsidiary pinnacles, ridges or buttresses that posed extreme difficulties. The new generation developed new techniques and better gear to meet those challenges; they also took greater risks.

The British climbing establishment—epitomized by the stuffy Alpine Club, founded in 1857—held itself aloof from such practices. But a small vanguard of British climbers, mostly drawn from the working and middle classes, eventually began to develop the sport of extreme rock climbing on crags in Wales and England; they also explored the more difficult ice and snow gullies in Scotland's mountains. Most of these climbers—who eventually included young men like Chris Bonington and Hamish

MacInnes—were a far cry from the Oxbridge elite who had gone to Everest. The new generation had grown up in a Great Britain where class identity was losing some of its power to define a man's career or social position. They brought their personalities and their ambitions on their climbs, and carried a very different set of experiences.

Earlier generations of British climbers had been led to the mountains by way of childhood trips to the Alps or membership in the Oxford or Cambridge mountaineering clubs. Many climbers who emerged in Great Britain during the years before and after World War II discovered climbing on their own—traversing the stone embankment walls of polluted rivers near industrial centers such as Manchester or exploring abandoned mineshafts in the nearby Peak District. Their climbing retained a makeshift quality even when they ventured into the mountains. They made do with the barest necessities—gym shoes, old ropes or even clotheslines, plastic bags for ponchos and shelters. They had little or no formal instruction, so they took terrible risks—first out of ignorance and later from a growing sense that risk was essential to their pursuit.

By the early 1950s—a few years before Chris and Hamish took up residence in their alpine shepherd's hut—this new generation was at last venturing across the English Channel to come to grips with difficult routes in the Alps. The mountains they encountered were much bigger than those they knew in Great Britain, and presented new risks and challenges. Many climbs required long approaches over difficult and dangerous terrain, including glaciers laced with hidden crevasses, cold and seemingly bottomless, that lay in wait for the incautious or unlucky climber. The weather was severe, and subject to sudden changes, so that you might be moving on warm, sunlit granite and suddenly find yourself in the midst of a terrific blizzard or thunderstorm or both. Such storms often smeared the rock with a thin coating of ice known as verglas, perhaps making it impossible to move higher. You might try to retreat, but the sheer scale and difficulty of many alpine climbs sometimes made retreat impossible. Young climbers stranded by storms often froze to death on their exposed perches.

There were other hazards. The Alps were an old range, and the mountains were falling apart. The snow that fell year-round melted during the afternoon. The meltwater pooled in the cracks that riddled the stone, only to refreeze at night. This process gradually split the rock. As the day advanced, warmer temperatures melted the ice that held together disparate pieces of stone. The rocks fell apart. The fragments fell hundreds or thousands of feet to smash into gullies, snowfields, other rocks and on occasion climbers.

The Alps also called for new techniques. The young British climbers who made their first forays into the Alps during the '50s found that the hardest routes required them to ascend sheer or overhanging walls. This required artificial aids. The British copied the Continentals, who carried wooden wedges or iron pitons to shove or hammer into cracks; a climber would use the pegs as handholds or footholds, or clip slings to the pegs and use the slings as awkward steps.

The British climbing establishment had long snubbed such techniques as unsporting, and shunned climbs that required them. Such scruples were lost on the new generation, who recognized them as empty snobbery, an attempt to preserve an order and an elite whose time had passed. The younger British climbers, having missed both world wars, had no patience for nostalgia. They had little interest in the failures of the past—and indeed, British mountaineering during the past half-century had been defined by its more or less heroic failures to climb the world's highest mountain. Edmund Hillary and Tenzing Norgay's ascent of Everest when it finally occurred in 1953 struck many young climbers as an achievement of the past, an echo from a world that had never concerned itself with the likes of them. The new climbers had their own battles to fight; they needed no instruction or inspiration from their elders or betters.

The emerging vanguard included a pair of young plumbers, Joe Brown and Don Whillans. Brown, born in 1930, was the youngest of seven children who lived with their parents in a tiny, four-room house in a Manchester suburb. Their father died when Joe was six months old. Whillans, three years younger, was raised in slightly better circumstances; his father had a white-collar job at a grocer's shop, also near Manchester.

The two boys began their climbing careers in the late '40s on the gritstone outcroppings of the nearby Peak District, where workers and their families escaped Manchester and its suburbs on weekends and holidays. They met at a crag in 1951, and soon teamed up to astonish their peers. They were built like gymnasts, broad-shouldered and short of stature; both men stood about 5' 3", with Joe perhaps a hair taller than Don. The mountaineering establishment's bias against artificial climbing meant that Joe and Don knew little of such techniques, which would have been familiar to them if they had grown up as climbers on the Continent. Otherwise, the precedents of the older generation of British climbers did not trouble the two boys; they routinely climbed routes that men more familiar with current standards wrote off as impossible. Joe and Don spent their long hours on gritstone developing ways to get up the hardest sections of a route without sling steps or similar devices. They learned how to place a fist or a foot in a crack and twist the wrist or the ankle just so, floating up terrain that baffled everyone else.

They climbed when they could. Joe had become a plumber's apprentice at age fourteen. Don had waited until age fifteen to take a similar position—only because the authorities had increased the minimum age for leaving school. The two young apprentices were careful with their money. They lived at home and hitchhiked to climbs, sleeping with other climbers in barns or tents. They read books about Everest and other Himalayan peaks with the understanding that such expeditions weren't for the likes of them: Everest climbers and their sort wouldn't have much to say to a plumber's apprentice, would they? Anyway, who could afford to take three months off work to go off on a climb? You'd get the sack for certain.

The Alps were a different matter. Don and Joe and their mates had followed. The Everest climbers didn't figure in those stories, which were populated by daring young Continental climbers. The Alpine Club branded such routes as unsporting, fit only for fools and circus performers—in short, too hard. A few of the boldest climbers from the Oxbridge and Cambridge mountaineering clubs and begun to venture onto different alpine routes. Even so, Don and Joe and their mates knew you wouldn't find many of the old Everest climbers in a punch-up in a pub; likewise, with a few exceptions, you wouldn't find them on the hardest alpine routes.

That was all right, though. These new alpine climbs offered a way to outstrip the old toffs. Don and Joe had jobs; they could imagine—if only barely—paying their way across the Channel and coming to grips with the big mountains that waited there. It meant scrimping and saving the rest of the year—living at home and even skipping some of their climbing weekends in the Lake District or Wales—but the pictures in the books and in their heads drew them on; there was another world, and they meant to go there.

Whillans made his first trip to the Alps in 1952, in the company of friends from Manchester's Rock and Ice Club. The party didn't

accomplish much, but the size and beauty of the mountains staggered the young plumber's apprentice. He wrote later that he had
discovered his life's purpose upon arriving at the Montenvers train
station above the French mountain village of Chamonix, where
he had his first sight of the Grandes Jorasses—the huge, black,
snow-plastered wall that towers above the surrounding peaks.

Don returned to England determined to hone his artificial
climbing techniques. He and Joe spent many hours pegging their
way up steep cracks in the Peak District; it became the thing
to do on wet winter days. They visited Chamonix together in
1954. That season they made the third ascent—the first British
ascent—of the intimidating West Face of the Dru, adjoining the
still virgin Southwest Pillar.

They were surprised; it was easier than they had expected. They
had climbed it much more quickly than previous parties. It was
beginning to dawn on Don and Joe that they were far better climbers
than many of the Europeans. The two young British climbers' raw
ability on rock, honed on British gritstone before they had learned
artificial climbing techniques, gave them an immense advantage
over Continentals who relied more heavily on aid. The Continentals
tended to hammer their laborious way up sections that the British
could climb free—without aid—and that made a huge difference.

Four years on, Don was back for the Southwest Pillar—now
known as the Bonatti Pillar—itself. He knew other British climbers had their sights on the route. He didn't know that Hamish
MacInnes and young Chris Bonington were among them.

CHRIS MEANWHILE COMFORTED himself with the fact
that the Pillar had been done—not once but five times, including
Bonatti's epic solo. His fears receded a bit when two young Austrian climbers—Walter Phillip and Richard Blach—showed up at
the hut. Blach was only nineteen, but both men were experienced

climbers; they were friendly sorts, here for their own attempt on the Pillar. The four climbers resolved to tackle the route together, which reassured Chris. A party of four felt safer, and there was the chance that the Austrians would help him to manage Hamish.

The spell of bad weather came to an end. The climbers spent the first fine morning packing, and then left their hut to stroll up a long ridge of broken rock and other glacial debris. They set up camp at the base of the climb to allow an early start the following morning.

Darkness was falling when Bonington spotted two more climbers coming up the ridge toward his own little party. One of the new pair was Paul Ross, a well-known English climber. Ross had grown up in Keswick, in the heart of England's Lake District; like Hamish, he was willing to place a piton when the occasion demanded it. The second man was short and broad-shouldered, his pack bristling with loaves of French bread. Chris and Hamish recognized Whillans at once—any climber who spent time in Wales or the Peak District knew Don by sight as well as by reputation.

Chris was delighted to see these newcomers. He liked the idea of having such a formidable pair on hand in case of trouble. The encounter also presented an opportunity of sorts. Chris had managed to make second ascents of some routes that Whillans had put up with Joe Brown in England. He knew that Don—though his senior by only a year or so—had much to teach him.

Not that the prickly Whillans seemed likely to take much interest in the still boyish Bonington. Don already had a frightening reputation as a hard-drinking, blunt-spoken customer. Chris was uncomfortably aware that Don's punch-ups in pubs and elsewhere—buses, climbing huts—had become as much a part of his growing legend as his climbs.

Whillans was indeed pugnacious—quick to take offense, and

willing to use his fists. He was cheap; he hated to pay for his own beer, let alone anyone else's. He was lazy, often refusing to share camp chores or cooking with his climbing partners, and he was stubborn. His peers tolerated him for his strength and his skill and his entertainment value; also because he was hugely contemptuous of outsiders and fiercely loyal to his own kind. The climbing establishment—including the Everest crowd—found him terrifying, and not at all amusing. That suited Whillans, who relied on his reputation for violence to frighten men who might otherwise be inclined to snub him.

Don's reputation worried the young Bonington. Still, Chris understood that this small, scary man might prove a useful companion on a route as daunting as the Bonatti Pillar.

Ross and Whillans reached Chris and his little group. The two parties spoke briefly: six climbers, ambitious and more or less afraid, more or less glad to see one another. Each character sized up the rest, making comparisons and tentative judgments. Whillans recognized young Bonington from Wales; he'd once seen Chris come off a rappel in something of a state, fussing about rope burns. He wondered now if Chris and this crowd belonged on the Bonatti Pillar—whether they might get themselves in trouble. Don at any rate was a man of few words. He and Ross soon carried on up to make camp just above the others.

Chris and Hamish and the young Austrians retired to their sleeping bags. The party hoped to be high on the route before the sun's warmth set off the rockfall they could expect on the lower sections. Someone set an alarm for two o'clock but when it woke them the climbers convinced themselves and each other that the weather looked doubtful. Chris had slept poorly; now he relaxed and nodded off. Hamish woke him three hours later. The weather was fine; the climb was on.

Don Whillans and Paul Ross had already left, crossing a snowfield to a 1,000-foot rock gully that would take them to the base of the Pillar itself. Chris and Hamish and the Austrians walked across the snowfield to the bergschrund, a two-foot gap where snow had melted away from the rock at the start of the gully.

Walter Phillip, the older of the two Austrian climbers, suggested that the party should solo the lower part of the climb. They would move much more quickly without ropes, and perhaps regain some of the ground their late start had cost them. Walter crouched to leap across the gap, and the snow collapsed under him. He managed to throw himself backward, away from the gap, which was now slightly wider. He gathered himself again and this time made the leap. He moved quickly up the gully. His companions followed, with Chris bringing up the rear.

There were now six climbers in the gully. Chris, looking up at Don Whillans and Paul Ross, noted wistfully that they were roped together. He would have been happy to trade speed for safety, since the climbing in the gully—clinging to dubious handholds and skating on loose pebbles—was not entirely casual. The Austrians and Hamish moved quickly, but Bonington did not; he climbed cautiously, and soon fell behind his group. Walter Phillips meanwhile passed Don Whillans—and promptly fell, landing on Don, who took it surprisingly well. Chris caught the rest of the climbers at the bottom of an ice slope. He was relieved to note that Hamish and the Austrians were at last uncoiling their ropes.

Whillans and Ross were putting on crampons. Chris and his three companions had brought only a single pair between them; the idea was to save weight. Hamish wore the crampons, and cut steps for Chris and the Austrians—a painstaking process that devoured time as well as energy. Hamish stopped every 100 feet or so to chop out a stance and establish a belay for his three companions. They moved up one at a time, careful to stay in his steps.

The two parties climbed for hours in the shadow of rock, the sunlit sky reduced to a faraway strip of light. They could see the sky only if they craned to look up. They couldn't manage such contortions while teetering across Hamish's freshly cut steps, but they could look for the sky when they arrived at each anchor; or else they could watch the next climber or review their own efforts on the pitch. They could gaze up at the route or down and across at the view. All of it served the same purpose; it reminded them of their whereabouts.

They knew that each step took them further from what felt like the safety of the glacier; that they were in a place where a stray rock or an awkward step could kill them. No one in the valley would be surprised or even much distressed to hear that a young climber had fallen to his death in the gully that led to the Bonatti Pillar. People would shrug, grimace, shake their heads—and go about their business.

Chris considered various possibilities: that the weather might change when they were high on the face, that he might fall or be hit by a falling rock, that one of the other climbers might kill him—Walter in his haste that morning had nearly knocked Whillans from the cliff. The climbers bunched together at each stance regarded one another with fascination, like soldiers who stare across a river at opposing pickets: innocents like themselves, each side on the brink of something dark, incomprehensible. They drew comfort from each other. The great Walter Bonatti had done this climb alone. Chris for a moment tried to imagine what that might have been like. A dizzy nausea flickered in him; he veered away.

They arrived at the top of the gully in the late morning. They moved left, emerging from shadow into sunlight to the base of the Pillar itself. It was a relief to feel the light on their bodies and faces. They touched the warm rock and remembered with a wary surprise that some 2,000 feet of difficult rock climbing lay ahead.

The two parties agreed to join forces. They would tackle the route in three roped pairs. Whillans proposed that the two Austrians, Walter and Richard, set off first. Whillans and Ross followed. Chris led the third rope. Hamish seconded him, removing the pitons the Austrians placed; the party would need them again higher up.

The rock was steep, laced with cracks that called for sophisticated jamming techniques. Chris sized up each crack as he came to it, and then wedged some body part—hand, forearm, foot or knee—into it. He knew to relax his hand completely before slipping it in; only then did he flex the muscles between the thumb and forefinger, perhaps twisting his lower arm to create a particular torque. He relied on those handholds primarily for balance, using foot-jams or other footholds to move higher. Even so, his arms began to tire after the first 200 feet.

The climbing was exposed, offering views both spectacular and appalling. He fought off the feeling that came with such exposure: dread, a growing sense that he had been foolish to come here. He wanted to go down—down—before God or some equivalent force took annoyed note of his foolishness. He told himself the exposure wasn't dangerous; it was just a view. And he knew that given time he would begin to feel that some part of him belonged as high as this. He could only arrive at such a feeling if he rode out the dread; the dread would enter the new feeling, would give it power.

The party arrived in their pairs at a ledge protected by a huge roof. The Austrians tackled the roof, nailing pitons and hanging from them in sling ladders—etriers. It was infuriating and terrifying work, but the frustration and fear blurred into exhilaration at moments. The Austrians disappeared over the roof, and now

Whillans in his turn led the pitch. He did it in fine style, moving with little apparent effort across the bottom of the roof and vanishing over its lip to climb a difficult groove.

Chris, still leading the third rope, climbed the roof and arrived at the base of the groove. The exposure—the vastness of the space that had opened up around and beneath him—was again tremendous. He continued to climb and his momentum soon took him 50 or so feet past his highest piton. His forearms shook with fatigue. His position was too precarious for him to pause. He continued to climb higher in the dwindling hope of finding a crack or other weakness—a place to drop a nut or place a piton, a decent hold, some reprieve from the fall that would otherwise come. He found nothing, and still his inclination was to move higher and now it was too late to retreat.

He knew that he had made a mistake he might not be able to fix, that he was staking everything on the outcome of the next few moments. He struggled higher; at one point he tried and failed to thread a sling around a stone that had lodged in a crack. Even now, he found that he was too proud to ask the others to drop him a top-rope. This view of his own stubbornness gave him access to an unfamiliar strength and he tapped this new resource with a deftness that surprised him. He was able to cling to a sloping hold with one hand while he reached up and over a shelf; there he found a better hold that allowed him to heave himself onto a ledge and sit gasping next to Paul Ross—who casually informed him that he'd followed Don up the wrong groove; the one next to it was much easier.

The climbing became still more exposed. The space opened out until its tug came from every direction; they might sail into space as easily as fall to the glacier. Falling might come as a relief; they were partly convinced that the real danger was above and behind them; they might disappear into this yawning distance. They could not protect themselves; they must try to be inconspicuous; they must hope to creep unnoticed past this great void.

They came to an enormous ledge in the waning hours of the day. It was a fine site for a bivouac. The four British climbers stopped, and the ledge was soon littered with their gear and their sprawled or crouching bodies. The Austrians moved higher, placing pegs as they went, making use of the light that remained; they established their bivouac at a slightly higher point.

The British settled down to make tea, melting snow on their portable gas stove. Chris and Hamish had brought along some of Bonington's stolen survival rations. Don and Paul contributed real food—bread and sausage and bacon. The climbers had leisure to contemplate the view. They were comfortable enough on their broad ledge to enjoy their position as darkness came on. They were tired, and they could savor the pleasure of doing nothing for a time. The day had gone well. The climb was no longer entirely a mystery or a choice that lay ahead as it had been the night before.

Hamish gazed at the lights of Chamonix and Montenvers. He took pleasure in the contrast between the earthbound villagers' situation and his own lofty perch. He lifted his eyes to stare across at the Grépon and the Charmoz. He'd soloed both peaks during his alpine apprenticeship. His rappel anchor had failed on the Charmoz. He'd plunged 40 feet to a ledge. The impact had damaged both of his feet, and his knees had slammed into his eye sockets, blinding him for a time. Raymond Lambert—the great Swiss guide—had been climbing nearby; he had rescued the foolish young man. Hamish thought back to that now. He thought of the climbing that lay ahead tomorrow.

A roar of falling rocks—an enormous avalanche of stone-fall far below—interrupted the climbers' thoughts and conversation. The torrent of rocks clattered and rumbled across the gully they had climbed to reach the Pillar; the rocks struck sparks in the dim light and sent up a tower of dust that stank of brimstone.

Don spoke first, noting the obvious: the avalanche had it occurred that morning would have killed them all. They were silent for a moment in contemplation of this fact and what it implied, and so they all heard the high-pitched whine of a rock falling through space. It hit Hamish in the head, gashing his scalp and fracturing his skull, and knocking him off the cliff.

He had clipped into an anchor for the night. He hung from it half-senseless, blood pouring from his head. He was able to gather what was left of his wits, and he struggled back onto the ledge. The others, horrified, stared at him; even Whillans seemed concerned. Chris had the group's first-aid supplies—a single dressing—and he dug the bandage out and set to work wrapping the wound. The dressing turned black with blood, but the bleeding slowed and then stopped.

The climbers' next concern was to get out of the line of fire. Whillans found a spot that suited him, and the other three Brits hunched together in a niche in the wall. Hamish spent the night in a haze, occasionally losing consciousness and slumping against Bonington, threatening to dislodge him from his precarious stance.

Chris was tired but he didn't sleep. He lay hunched against the rock; he was cramped and cold. He watched the lights flicker in the valley. He shivered in his down jacket and yearned for sunrise even as he dreaded the trials of the coming day; he wished himself down in the village, having dinner with people who slept in beds.

Retreat would not be possible now. The party had made several long rising traverses during the day. It would be too difficult and dangerous to reverse that ground on this steep terrain. Also, they did not wish to try to down-climb the gully at the bottom of the

Pillar—not after watching the rockslide that had wiped out their tracks of the morning. They would have to try to finish the climb. The route was a difficult and uncertain endeavor even under the best of conditions; they would have to do it with a climber who had a fractured skull.

They all knew such moments, when matters took on a new degree of seriousness. A climber trudging across a snowfield might glance down and recognize that a fall would kill him and his partner. Or he might top out on a high ridge and look west to see thunderheads advancing rapidly across the sky. At such times one's options narrowed; ambition and preference and other trivia fell away. The climber was left to determine what the situation required of him and to try to do it.

The six young men on the Bonatti Pillar of the Dru had the night to consider their predicament. They knew they couldn't carry Hamish. He must try to climb. If he couldn't, the group must split into two parties. One party would try to finish the route and go for help. The other would stay with Hamish, knowing that a rescue was unlikely and that a change in the weather—snow or rain—might strand them with the injured man. Hamish, slumped against Chris, was not fit to contemplate such contingencies. Chris was alive to them.

Dawn came at last. The four British climbers pottered about on their ledge; they moved stiffly and uncertainly, like old men. They were glad that the day had come, but the sun did not warm them much; their cliff faced west and so they rose in shadow. Hamish suffered from bouts of dizziness, and he looked terrible: black sheets of dried blood streaked the right side of his gaunt, white face. Young Richard Blach peered down from his perch at the Austrian's bivouac site and turned pale himself at the sight of the Scotsman.

Chris didn't think he could get Hamish up the climb. He asked

Hamish MacInnes and Paul Ross on the Bonatti Pillar
CHRIS BONINGTON, CHRIS BONINGTON PICTURE LIBRARY

Whillans to rope up with the injured man. Don accepted the proposal as a sort of tribute and as an example of Bonington's good sense. It was the beginning of an understanding between them.

The Austrians started up the face, hammering in a ladder of pitons that led up a series of grooves. Don followed with Hamish. Chris led the third rope, with Paul coming up behind him to remove pitons. Don, after leading each pitch, clipped to an anchor and hauled on the rope as Hamish climbed. Hamish's strength came and went; he lost consciousness from time to time and simply hung on the rope that snaked down from Whillans. The pair made slow but reasonably steady progress. Chris, whose periodic funks alternated with fits of optimism, began to imagine a happy ending to this adventure.

The party reached a ledge around midday and stalled there. The sun by now was very strong; the climbers forgot how they had suffered from cold during the night. Hamish, looking up from the ledge in a haze of fatigue and pain—craning his neck made his headache worse—could see the Austrians working their way up a smooth wall. Walter from time to time called down for more pitons. Whillans, resting from his own labors, watched for a time and decided that the Austrians had wandered off Bonatti's original route.

Don took a belay from Hamish, and moved around a corner to discover an enormous overhang of dark rock split by cracks that bristled with rotting wooden wedges. He had found the right way, but it would require strenuous aid climbing. Hamish clambered awkwardly over and inspected the overhang, privately doubting his own ability to climb it.

The Austrians came down and followed the others across to Whillans' overhang. Don meanwhile set off. The work consisted of hammering in a piton and clipping a sling to it, then standing awkwardly in the sling to hammer in another piton. The other climbers, reduced to bystanders, clustered at the base of the over-hang. They watched Whillans work his way across the ceiling of rock and reach up over the lip of the overhang and heave himself out of sight. Time slowed down for the climber and his watchers, but the sun tracked through the sky at its usual pace, spending the day. The weather had changed; the cliff was swaddled in swirling cloud, and it was cold again.

Chris took a picture of Hamish. The injured man sat with his back to the rock, craning his neck to stare upward, the blood-soaked bandage wound around his jaw and over the top of his head like a sort of scarf—the sort of bandage that once indicated a toothache. His tousled dirty-yellow hair escaped in front and covered most of his forehead; his dark blood covered the side of his face. Hamish's short, blond beard made him look a little like someone's idea of a saint or a sprite, gaunt and mischievous. Chris recognized in his friend something of his own youth, of the ignorance and shaky glamour of leaving childhood.

It was seven o'clock. The party wouldn't all get up the overhang that evening. Whillans shouted down that there were no decent ledges above it. He anchored a rope and descended it to rejoin his companions. Five of the climbers retreated to a convenient series of ledges to establish a bivouac. Hamish remained on a smaller ledge 50 feet higher than the others. He didn't want to give up height that he would have to regain the following morning. He lowered a rope for his supper—a pair of sausages. The climbers had nothing to drink; the rock up here was too steep to hold snow or ice, so there was nothing to melt for water.

The party had climbed only a few hundred feet today, their second day on the route. They were weary and dehydrated. Hamish seemed worse now; it seemed unlikely that he would have the strength to get past the overhang Whillans had climbed that afternoon.

Chris shared Don's shelter—a large plastic bag, which the two men draped over their heads. Don chain-smoked much of the night. Chris was not a smoker, and his throat was raw from thirst and from the dry mountain air. He worried out loud that he might suffocate under the plastic. Whillans replied that suffocation wasn't such a bad way to die—*better than bloody freezing*—and continued to smoke.

The climbers' ropes and boots froze during the night. The five men on the lower ledges awoke and untangled the mess and made breakfast: a lump of oatmeal. Don proposed that the Austrians resume the lead. Don himself would follow with Hamish, but he knew that it would be impossible to haul the injured man up the overhang. Hamish himself would have to do much of the work, and it would be better for him to try it now, before he grew even weaker.

The Austrians climbed the pitch, and Don went up after them. He put Hamish on belay, and the Scotsman started up the roof, clipping a sling to a peg and hanging from it; reaching up for the next peg to clip his second sling; moving up onto the high sling; reaching behind to retrieve the first sling and repeat the process.

Chris followed just behind. He broke tiny icicles off the rock and sucked on them as he hung from the pegs low on the pitch; he could only watch. Hamish every few minutes sagged on the rope, breathing in great rasps and recovering to glance down at his boots and find that he was swimming in 2,000 feet of empty air. He felt himself to be trapped in some odd and uncomfortable dream; someone had granted him powers sufficient to come to this alien place but not to survive here, and not to leave.

Hamish somehow got past the overhang, which led to another. This one was less difficult, but it was in the sun. The heat made the climbers miserable. The Austrians carried on higher, followed by Don and Hamish. The four of them disappeared up the seemingly endless Pillar. Chris and Paul fell behind as Paul worked to collect the party's pitons for use again higher on the climb. Chris in his growing weariness felt the solitude and a sense of abandonment.

Chris led a ramp and then a short wall to the beginning of a slab—sweeping, low-angle rock featuring tiny holds and halfway across a single piton. The slab called for delicate climbing. He moved very slowly, aware again of his fatigue. He stopped to rest on a good foothold and allowed himself to try to remember the feeling of standing on the earth, on a field or a road or a floor. It was a mistake. Thoughts arose, among them the thought that he would never leave this place. He was again aware of the exposure; it gave him to understand that he was stuck in a universe that operated by implacable laws, that circumstances and outcomes did not reflect his wishes, that he was alone and mortal. The climbing on the slab wasn't near his limit; even so, Chris was frightened almost to tears. He reached the peg at the center of the slab and gripped it fiercely and called out to the climbers who stood on a ledge just above him. Someone dropped him a top rope, and he finished the pitch in safety.

Whillans had found some dirty ice in a crack and he was melting it on his stove. He added tea leaves to make a gravelly drink—the climbers' first fluid in more than thirty-six hours—and they swallowed it and set off again. The paltry drink intensified their thirst and made them suddenly eager to be done with all of this. The Austrians made their way up to the shoulder of the Pillar, where the angle relented, and now the three roped pairs moved quickly until in the gathering dusk they reached the top.

They stood stunned, self-conscious at finding themselves inside of this view, specks in this beauty—huge shapes and spaces in every direction. They peered up at the dome of sky as if for relief from the vast clutter of the range and found themselves peering into the seats of some empty arena. They were at once relieved and cast down to find that no audience awaited them, that they stood alone on this high and desolate platform.

They had done the climb but there was still the descent to make—it would have to wait until morning—and the weather had changed. The wind blew hard and cold, and clouds filled the sky from the south. Snow flurries skittered down like handfuls of rice flung across their bleak pinnacle.

They had escaped from the route just in time—they could not have finished it in this storm—but they were not out of trouble. The six men had been climbing for three days on short rations. Their food was almost finished, and they were cold and wet. Hamish in particular seemed likely to collapse at any time. Chris was tired and hungry, and he was frightened at the prospect of a long descent. He'd nearly died getting down the Pointe de Lépiney with Hamish, and this descent posed far greater difficulties.

The climbers shared their last food, a single packet of soup that yielded each man a few swallows. They clipped into anchors and climbed into their bivouac sacks in the dark. They listened between snatches of sleep to the wind and the ominous patter of snowfall on plastic. The snow found its way into their sacks, where their body heat melted it; the water refroze into ragged ice sheaths as the night grew colder.

It was still snowing at dawn. The ropes were frozen. The climbers untangled them and set up the first rappel. Walter Phillips, the more experienced of the two young Austrians, had been in this place the previous year, when he'd climbed the Dru by its West Face. He offered to lead the descent.

Four rappels later, Walter and the teenaged Richard Blach stood on a tiny ledge a rope's length below the others. The Austrians in their haste to escape the storm had descended the wrong gully without realizing their mistake; if the climbers carried on much further, they might not have the strength to climb back out and find the right way down.

Don Whillans saved them. He was known already for his mountain sense—his uncanny ability to find a path through difficulties or to judge when to turn back. He decided that the party had veered off route, and he shouted his opinion down through the storm to the Austrians on their ledge.

Walter and Richard accepted Whillans's word on the matter—his tone was convincing, not to say intimidating. The Austrians struggled back up through drifts of new snow to the others, drawing deeply on their fading strength. Don and Chris by this time had set off down a line that Don liked better. Paul Ross followed them. Hamish had rallied; he waited for the Austrians. They arrived and the three men started down after the others. Walter slipped on the snow and barely managed to stop his slide, using his axe as a brake in the snow. Hamish noted mechanically that

Richard Blach was near the limit of his endurance. The teenager staggered and lurched through the snow, his eyes at once empty and stricken.

The snow stopped and the wind fell. The climbers could see now. They were back on the proper descent route. Walter, shaken by his slip, seemed nervous as he helped set up a rappel anchor at the top of a steep section. He threw a sling over a sharp spike of rock and threaded his doubled rope through the sling. Hamish watched and suddenly knew what was going to happen. He was too slow to stop it. Walter leaned back on the rope, the rock sliced through the anchoring sling, and Walter fell.

His body careened through the gray air. He smacked into a snow bank 20 feet below and came to a halt at the brink of a cliff that overhung the storm-shrouded void. He was unhurt, but a sloppy fatalism that had briefly settled over the climbers left them as they continued their descent. They were no longer philosophical about their chances; they understood as their ordeal drew to a close that they had a say in their survival—they were more likely to live if they were careful.

They made more rappels, checking and rechecking anchors and knots, until at last they could pick their way wearily down snowfields and across wet rock slabs to an easy snow-filled gully. It led them past a hut where they might have spent the night in safety but they staggered on to arrive at the Hotel Montenvers in time for red wine and spaghetti. They ate their meal and got a little drunk, and stumbled outside in the cold darkness to find their way to their hut on the outskirts of the town. They unrolled their sleeping bags on the wooden floor and crawled into them and lay at ease, consumed by the pleasure of lying prone on the flat hard wood. It was behind them; they had climbed the Bonatti Pillar.

Chris and his three compatriots in particular were struck by this fact. They were the first of their countrymen to make this climb or one like it, and they knew this counted for something, but didn't know quite what that might be. Chris felt the fear of the past days leave him—or rather, he felt himself leave his fear, as a spirit might cheerfully depart a corpse. He enjoyed for a moment a sense that he would never again be afraid. He fell asleep with the others; above them, the mountains remained wrapped in storm.

3

CHRIS BONINGTON, NOW twenty-seven, arrived in Chamonix at the start of July 1961. He had come directly from Kathmandu, making the 5,000-mile overland journey in a rickety van with two other members of a successful expedition to Nuptse (7,861 meters; 25,790 feet), one of Everest's satellite peaks. Chris had climbed the mountain, but he hadn't enjoyed the expedition. The various climbers hadn't known each other well going into the expedition, and the team had never really taken shape. Chris was looking forward to seeing Don Whillans again.

Chris had approached the Bonatti Pillar three years before afraid of what might happen. Trouble had come, and he had survived it. The experience had reassured him; had drawn him further along a path that led to more ambitious and more dangerous climbs. It had also made him eager to learn what he could from a climber like Whillans.

Don in turn had been impressed by Bonington's performance. Chris *was* young—and fussy about a bit of cigarette smoke—but he had not fallen apart when his friend Hamish got hit on the head. He had stamina; he was surprisingly bold on rock; he was no fool—he'd had the sense to let Don take charge when things looked bad on the Bonatti. He had that posh accent, but he wanted to know things; he would take direction.

Don also knew that Chris knew something of the climbing

establishment, that other world with its school ties and its accents, its lists and invitations, its committees and grants. Don needed that crowd—they still ran most trips to the Himalaya. But he didn't like them or their ways, and they didn't appear to think much of him, either.

Don's old partner, Joe Brown, was another story. Joe was a diligent, low-key character, quiet but fiercely intelligent; he had become an establishment favorite. Joe knew how to make the right impression—was willing to do it. He'd had his first chance to break into that circle—they both had—in 1954. Joe and Don were just down from their triumphant ascent of the Dru's West Face when former Everest climber Tom Bourdillon dropped by their campsite to congratulate them. Tom mentioned plans for an expedition to Kangchenjunga, the world's third-highest peak. A trip might be in the works for 1955; would Joe or Don be interested?

Don had treated the inquiry—it wasn't quite an invitation—as a joke, half-believing it was. He told Bourdillon that he'd heard Himalayan climbing was all hard work. And anyway, Don couldn't imagine what his father would think if Don threw up a steady job to climb some mountain halfway around the world.

Joe kept quiet; he didn't say much to Bourdillon, but apparently he made the right impression. A few months later, he received his official invitation to join the Kangchenjunga expedition. Joe had gone on the trip and he'd enjoyed himself, getting along fine with the educated lads who made up the rest of the climbing team and getting himself to the summit. They'd asked him on another trip, to Mustagh Tower in the Karakoram. Joe had climbed that one, too.

Don had been furious at missing the Kangchenjunga trip. He resented the climbing establishment for passing him over, and he was jealous of Joe. And Don was angry with himself for turning away from what he suddenly feared was the opportunity of a lifetime. He knew very well the difference that chance could make in a workingman's life. His knowledge traced back to memories of his first encounters with climbers, when he'd gone as a schoolboy to the Peak District for solitary weekend rambles. He'd seen the fellows who rode the bus to Derbyshire and back with their ropes and their rucksacks. He'd forgotten their faces—he had no memory for faces—but he would remember for all of his life certain pairs of nailed boots. He'd gone later with his Scout troop to the Lake District, and he'd seen more climbers there. Never in all of that time did he think of becoming a climber himself. He believed—without knowing he believed it—that it wasn't for him to imagine such a life.

He quit school to clean and fix and haul boilers for forty-six hours a week. And then one weekend out walking alone in the Peak District, he bumped into a school friend, a boy named Eric Worthington. Eric wanted to climb, so the two of them found a rope and tried one of the easy routes and somehow survived it, and that was the start of the life Don knew now.

The regulars had taken them up and taught them rudiments of mountaineering: how to manage the rope, how to place protection, how to rappel from a climb. Don found himself climbing serious routes almost immediately, without trouble or fanfare. He was a natural climber, strong and centered. He was decisive; he didn't ask himself questions that most new climbers ask. It helped that he knew nothing of climbing tradition or history. He soon acquired information, but he wasn't daunted; descriptions of a climb's difficulty were just language—he had no context for the words, and he left them on the ground when he climbed.

He had loved the climbing and his own easy mastery of it. Here was something new, something free of family and neighborhood and school. It was a stunning surprise, one at odds with the bleak future that had begun to unfold for him. He had no words for it, but setting off up a hard new route he felt like a wingless angel—apart from ordinary things, off into something fresh and distant.

His love for climbing had taken him where he wished to go until that morning in 1954, down from the Dru with Joe. And then the climbing establishment in the person of Tom Bourdillon—as tactful and gracious an emissary as Don could have wished—had offered him another new world, and Don had retreated out of clumsiness or fear. He understood that this retreat was his choice and it shamed him. He worked at his plumbing job that winter, but he quit in the spring of 1955. That was right before he got word that Joe and the others had climbed Kangchenjunga.

Don climbed in the Alps that summer. He worked during the following winter as a laborer on a hydroelectric project near Glencoe in Scotland. He earned enough money to buy a motorcycle, and rode south to look for plumbing work in Manchester. He found none, so he wandered back up to Scotland; after a time he went south again to England with a bricklayer friend named Pete Whitell. They were hard up—utterly broke—when they finally found work in the Lake District, signing on as laborers on an excavation for the Manchester Water Board. The work was wet, dark and dangerous; it was loud too, with incessant drilling and blasting in the freezing, muddy tunnel. The rock cut their hands, and the cuts became infected from dust and chemicals.

Whillans was twenty-two. He could leaf through his memories of climbs or walks or bivouacs: his first sight of the Grandes Jorasses towering above Montenvers, or the fields of Derbyshire, where he had walked away much of his solitary childhood. And yet he was attached to the darkness and the difficulty of his work in the tunnel. He shared his labor with men who were like

men he'd known all of his life. He would later recall those men
and their circumstances—how they lived—and his recollections
would help set him apart from climbers who were younger or
more privileged. For now, the tunnel offered him a vision of his
life without climbing. He did not exactly fear it, but he felt it as
a possibility that could claim him.

He waited almost two more years for his first Himalayan expedition. He did a few routes with a Cambridge-educated climber
named Bob Downes. They hit it off, and Downes got Whillans
invited on a 1957 trip to Masherbrum (7,821 meters; 25,660 feet)
in Pakistan. Don performed well, but no climbers reached the
summit—and Don's friend Bob Downes died of high-altitude
pulmonary edema.

Don's second chance at the big mountains didn't come until
1960, two years after his meeting with Chris and Hamish on the
Bonatti Pillar. He'd joined an expedition to Trivor (7,577 meters;
24,859 feet), an obscure but challenging peak, also in Pakistan.
This time, he'd gotten sick himself on the mountain—he suspected
an attack of polio. Once again, he failed to summit.

Don's failure on Trivor had been followed by still another disappointment. He'd traveled back to England on his motorcycle—a
grueling six-week journey—and immediately plunged into planning for another expedition, this one to Nuptse. He'd managed to
wangle an invitation for Bonington, who had climbed Annapurna
II (7,937 meters; 26,040 feet) the previous year with an army-
sponsored expedition.

One night in January of 1961, Don left Manchester for nearby
Stockport to help pack some gear for the Nuptse trip. He was
riding his motorcycle with his wife, Audrey Whittal, on the back.
Audrey was a plainspoken young woman, two years older than
Don. She'd left school at fourteen to work as a cutter in the rag
trade. She was a climber herself, and they'd been together since

meeting at the crags in 1952, the day before Don's nineteenth birthday. They'd been married since 1958.

It was raining this night, and they were both cold and wet on the motorcycle. A lorry turned right without signaling, and the couple went under the truck. They survived the accident, but Audrey broke a leg and so did Don. His injury kept him off the Nuptse trip. Chris would be going without him.

The leg healed quickly. Don managed a few rock climbs near home when the weather turned warm. He'd arranged to meet Bonington in the Alps at the start of July. Meanwhile, his mind at odd moments—before sleep, upon waking—turned to the route that would be their principal objective: the North Face of the Eiger.

IT HAD BEEN three years since Chris and Don had met on the Bonatti Pillar of the Dru. Both men had changed. Chris in particular had become more experienced, narrowing the gap between them. He had stood on two Himalayan summits—Annapurna II and Nuptse—while Don had failed on both of his trips to the high mountains.

Don may have counted on running things between them, but Chris had his own notions. Bonington was growing into his own ideas of how to be a British mountaineer. His insecurities stayed with him as he accumulated these early achievements; at moments, he could be a bit of a snob. All of this—especially the younger man's growing success—galled Whillans and brought out the crank and the bully in him. Chris wanted to climb several low-key routes to get in condition for the Eiger. Don waved his objections aside, insisting that Chris could do his training on the Eiger itself.

Don needed a success. He needed something to keep him on the lecture circuit and out of the daily grind of manual labor.

He needed something to compete with Joe Brown's success on
Kangchenjunga and elsewhere—something to impress the mountaineering establishment, which still handed out invitations to
the major expeditions. The North Face of the Eiger was the most
notorious route in Europe, and no British climber had yet made
the ascent. Whillans was not the type to advertise his wishes—he
would go without something rather than ask for it—but he badly
wanted to accomplish the first British ascent of the Eiger's North
Face. It would make up for a lot.

Chris meanwhile looked back on his own early attempt on the
Eiger—his first-ever alpine climb, with Hamish back in 1957—
with dismay. He now had a more sophisticated understanding of
the route's dangers, and he knew the face's reputation: eighteen
men had died there, four of them since Chris and Hamish had
visited the lower reaches of the wall four years earlier.

The Eiger's hazards included its sheer size—some 6,000 feet of
rock, snow and ice—and sustained technical difficulty. The rock
was mostly loose, so that holds were unreliable and the North
Face often showered climbers with rockfall. Worse, the place
was a magnet for sudden and severe storms. Many climbers had
frozen to death on the route waiting for conditions to improve
so that they could retreat or climb higher.

The face was notorious even among nonclimbers in Great
Britain and on the European continent. Readers on both sides
of the English Channel had an appetite for newspaper features
about the so-called "Wall of Death." German, Austrian and Italian climbers had climbed the face. British climbers had stayed
clear of it—but by 1961, a handful of them were at last ready to
attempt the route.

Whillans was a leading candidate—but he knew there were
others, and it was important to be first. Chris was less committed.
This summer was to be his last big fling in the mountains. He

had resigned from the army to accept the invitation to Nuptse, but giving up the security of his military career had frightened him. He had immediately signed on as a management trainee at Unilever, where his job would involve selling margarine to various accounts. He would begin his work as a corporate trainee in September; after that, climbing would become a mere hobby.

It was not simply that his courage had failed him. He saw something of himself in the men who wore suits to work in London office buildings. He believed he was willing to join them in exchange for what they could teach him about their world and for a share in that world's business. But this belief existed alongside a vague notion that getting up the Eiger might save him from such a life. If it didn't, it might at least prove that he wasn't leaving the mountains because he was afraid of them.

Chris and Don made camp about 100 yards from a small hotel in the village of Alpiglen, near the base of the climb. They needed a period of good weather to bring the climb into condition. They didn't get it. Rain—it would be snow high on the face—would give way to a day or two of sun, but more rain would follow.

Chris did most of the cooking. Don simply left it to him; Whillans's selfishness around camp was becoming part of his lore. The menu consisted largely of potatoes and vegetables (curried, fried or boiled), with large quantities of cheese. The two young men after supper would stroll across to the tourist hotel to split a single beer in the bar.

Chris felt his strength return. He put on some of the weight he'd lost on Nuptse. Once again, he proposed tackling an easy climb or two. Why not get in some routes while they waited for the Eiger to come into shape? Whillans refused, maintaining somewhat pompously that he wished to climb only routes that appealed to his imagination. Don did tend to be choosy about the lines he'd climb at a particular crag; others, including Joe Brown, would plaster a wall with routes of wildly different quality. Still, Chris thought Don in the present case was simply being lazy and stubborn. This was to be Bonington's last fling in the mountains; in a matter of weeks, he'd be stuck in England trying to learn to sell margarine. They were in the Alps to climb. Why not climb?

They waited. The weather improved—a little. A party of four Polish climbers arrived and camped near them. The weather and the Poles' presence and their own growing boredom convinced Don as well as Chris that it was time to take a stab at the face, if only to have a closer look at the difficulties.

They left camp on the first clear morning and walked up through pasture, and Chris as he walked realized that he was not afraid. His visit to the Eiger with Hamish four years earlier had been a terrifying experience; he'd known that he wasn't ready. But he'd since survived the Bonatti Pillar and two Himalayan expeditions—and this time he was going on the face with Whillans.

The two men climbed easily up the Eiger's lower rocks. They encountered hard-packed snow, and stopped to put on crampons. They set off again, moving quickly, unroped, and were soon a thousand feet above the start of the route. The valley, still in shadow, seemed far away.

The difficult climbing began at a band of overhanging rock. Here they roped up. The leader climbed while his second belayed from an anchor. Bonington led the first pitch, using his axe to chip at the ice that coated the rock, clearing tiny slots for the front-points of his crampons. He found no protection—no ice deep enough for a screw, no crack that would take a piton, no place to slot a stone or pebble or a knotted piece of webbing. If he fell, he'd fall past Don, tumbling twice the length of the rope he'd run out. He didn't think Don's rudimentary anchor would hold.

He kept his head and reached the bottom of a section known as the Difficult Crack, and built an anchor and put Don on belay.

Don followed him and then led through. He took more than an hour to climb the next 80 feet—he had to use his piton hammer to clear ice from handholds. Chris followed, and the climbers moved across a snowfield to the base of a chimney below a steep wall. They had reached the famous Hinterstoisser Traverse—a point-of-no-return in Eiger lore.

The feature was named for Andreas Hinterstoisser, the first climber to lead it. He had been twenty-three years old in 1936, one of a party of four, the second group to make a serious attempt to climb the face. The other three climbers followed Hinterstoisser across the traverse, but then a falling rock injured Willy Angerer—at twenty-seven, the oldest member of the party. The climbers retreated. They weren't able to get Angerer back across the traverse, so they roped up and attempted a more direct descent. Hinterstoisser fell to his death. Edi Rainer became tangled in the rope and died; the same rope strangled the already injured Angerer. Only Toni Kurtz, twenty-three, survived the fall. The accident left him hanging from a sling, some 150 feet above a ledge.

A party of would-be rescuers eventually reached the ledge, but they couldn't get to Kurtz. The young man hung there throughout one horribly cold night; the next morning, he took five hours to rig a rappel with his half-frozen hands. His rappel came to a halt when a knot jammed in a carabiner. He dangled just out of reach of the rescue party and eventually spoke two words—*I'm finished*—and died.

It was a gruesome story. Chris and Don had it in mind as they gazed at the wall, now plastered with snow and ice. Someone had fixed a rope across the traverse; the rope was mostly buried in snow—there was no point going higher in such conditions. The two climbers turned and made their way back down to the grassy slopes that led to their campsite.

A Swiss journalist phoned the hotel in Alpiglen the next day, looking for the English climbers. He turned up at their campsite the following morning for an interview. The man's rugged good looks and new climbing togs made Chris uncomfortable. Whillans despised the visitor—*soft as shit*, he called him. But the encounter gave Chris an idea; maybe a newspaper would sponsor their climb in exchange for exclusive rights to interview them if they got up the face. Don wasn't enthusiastic, but it didn't matter; more bad weather followed. The Eiger was out for now.

Chris and Don returned to Chamonix. One of the Poles—a bespectacled climbing instructor named Jan Dlugosz—went with them. The North Face of the Eiger would have to wait, but meanwhile the trio had their eye on another prize: Mont Blanc's Central Pillar of Freney.

THE FRENEY PILLAR had a fearsome reputation of its own. It had killed fewer climbers than the Eiger, but far fewer climbers had attempted it—and none had climbed it. It stood on the south side of Mont Blanc at the head of one of the Alps' most inaccessible glaciers; this remote position helped account for the fact that the Freney Pillar was one of the Alps' last great virgin features.

Walter Bonatti had tried to climb it with Andrea Oggioni two years before, in 1959. They had tried again recently, not long before Whillans and Bonington had explored the lower reaches of the Eiger's North Face. The Italians' second attempt on the Pillar had led to a spectacular epic—one of the worst disasters in the history of alpine climbing. Bonatti, Oggioni and a third climber, Roberto Gallieni, had joined forces with four Frenchman making their own attempt. A storm had stranded the entire group near the top of the Central Pillar for four days. They had at last retreated, but four of Bonatti's six companions had collapsed and died during the descent.

Chris and Don and their new Polish friend, Jan Dlugosz, arrived in Chamonix just weeks after Bonatti's ordeal. They knew a disaster had occurred on the Freney Pillar, but didn't know the details. Their only guide to the route was a photograph taken at a good distance from it.

They needed a fourth climber, and they soon found him. Ian Clough, a dark-haired Yorkshireman in his midtwenties, was in town. He was just back from climbing a spectacular route in the Dolomites; he had made his way up 700 feet of overhanging rock, spending two nights dangling in slings. Clough eked out a living as a climbing instructor back home, and had done a number of hard climbs in the Alps. Neither Don nor Chris knew him well, but they knew his reputation. He seemed an easygoing sort, quiet and self-deprecating, and he was eager to try the Freney Pillar.

The four men packed their gear and took the telepherique to the top of the Aiguille du Midi. They walked down to the Vallée Blanche, and spent the night in a crowded hut. The ground outside the hut offered a view of the long gully leading up to the Col de Peuterey at the base of their route. Chris eyed the gully with dismay. It looked like a major climb in itself. His eye was drawn to the huge Eckpfeiler Buttress, which stood in the foreground. He watched horrified as a silent torrent of rock and dust swept down it. He had never seen such rockfall. The avalanche roared across ground he and his friends meant to cross that very night.

The climbers retired early. Chris found it hard to get to sleep. Some time before midnight the door of the crowded hut swung open, and a big man wearing a climbing helmet walked in. The visitor shone a light on the hut book and read Don's entry, which declared the party's intentions to climb the Freney Pillar. He bent to make his own entry in the book and left. Chris was impressed by the man's size and rugged good looks, and by his air of lordly self-confidence. Don got up to check the inscription—the climber was Walter Bonatti himself, out with a client. It was as if Chris and Don had seen a ghost, a revenant of the tragedy that had begun its unfolding in this very room not long before.

The alarm would go off in an hour or so. Bonington lay awake, brooding. The hut came alive as various parties collected their gear and brewed drinks. Chris and the others rose and dressed, sorted their gear and stepped outside. They put on crampons—the snow was frozen at this early hour—and set off into the darkness. Don took note of two lights on the Brenva Face: Bonatti with his client, at work on one of Mont Blanc's less serious routes.

The sky was still ink-black, with no clouds or wind. The morning was on the warm side. Chris heard the trickle of melting snow. He worried that the high temperature might herald a front that would bring a storm. He wondered aloud whether the party should consider a less committing route. Don dismissed the suggestion. They'd come this far; they'd climb the Pillar or go home.

Chris by now knew not to waste his breath in argument. And Don's determination was reassuring—the conditions didn't trouble him. The party roped up to cross the glacier. They moved past the base of the Eckpfeiler Buttress, anxiously picking their way through debris from the rockslide Chris had witnessed the previous evening. They reached the bottom of the 2,000-foot snow gully that would take them to the Col de Peuterey and the Freney Pillar itself. They began to climb, kicking steps in frozen snow, finding their way by the light of headlamps—it was still only two o'clock in the morning.

Chris and Don took turns at the front. It grew much colder as they climbed, and their hands and feet lost feeling. Chris led the final pitch in the gully. The pitch was steeper than the rest. Snow gave way to rock. Chris somehow dislodged a boulder; it missed Don and the others and disappeared into the darkness that loomed below them.

Chris turned to watch, and his headlamp went out. The dark enveloped him; it occupied the void at his feet so that he felt at once frightened and oddly safe—as though he could float in this blackness. He was aware that his position was precarious, but he felt he could manage it; this was climbing he enjoyed. He finished the gully still in darkness, his hands and feet feeling for holds. He climbed up and over a mound of snow to arrive at the Col de Peuterey.

The rest of the party joined him there: Don arrived first, followed by Ian and Jan. The climbers had spent almost four hours in the gully; it was 5:30 in the morning. They melted water for tea and sat shivering on rocks. They stood and paced, waiting for the sun to rise and warm the rock on the Pillar.

Ian pointed down to a pair of climbers in the gully. Many of the best climbers in the Alps had their eye on the Freney Pillar; Bonatti's recent disaster had given the route new status. The three British climbers and their Polish companion shouldered their rucksacks and crossed a snow slope to the gap at the base of the Pillar. One by one, they leaped across the gap, lurching under packs and landing clumsily on the far side, standing heavily to approach and examine the rock itself. Don took a moment to inspect the view and the ground they had crossed. Retreat would be difficult. Fortunately, the day had dawned fair; if they climbed well, they might get up the route before the weather changed.

He took the first rope with Chris. They set off up the warm, brown rock. They saw no signs of previous climbers. This freed them to make their own way up the climb—through awkward chimneys, up cracks, out onto wide, steep slabs. They could look across peaks to the Italian foothills or look down to the base of the Pillar. The two unidentified climbers had reached the top of the gully and two more had joined them; the four newcomers had pitched tents. Still another pair of climbers arrived late in the afternoon to make camp at the start of the Pillar.

Don and Chris by now were 1,500 feet up the route. Ian and Jan had fallen far behind. The Pole was moving too slowly. Chris volunteered to rope up with Jan and hurry him along. Don agreed and the two of them waited for the slower pair. The four men made the switch and climbed on. They came upon gear left behind by retreating parties: pitons, carabiners, even a pair of fixed ropes. Whillans left the ropes in place; they'd come in handy if the party had to descend in a hurry.

The climbers arrived at the route's last major obstacle—a slender rock tower—at around four o'clock in the afternoon. They had been moving for fifteen hours. The tower was roughly 500 feet tall, split by cracks that petered out in smooth and sometimes overhanging rock. They climbed a 50-foot column at the base of this final tower; on top of the column, they came upon debris—a cooking pot, wooden wedges, a gas cylinder. This was the gear abandoned by Bonatti and his companions after their nightmarish four-day bivouac in the storm.

Don and Chris roped up again. Don set out to lead a crack festooned with pitons. He occasionally clipped his etriers to the pegs and stood in the slings to move higher. He soon lost any sense of the others; craning his neck to look up, he saw that the tower disappeared into mist. The mist soon sank to envelop him, so that he felt entirely alone. He was climbing into clouds. The climbing was precarious. He arrived at a constellation of pitons that led in no particular direction—certainly not up.

Don moved left to look for a crack, but didn't find one. He moved back right across rock that was even steeper; past bent pitons some previous climber had hammered a bare quarter-inch into the cliff. Chris shouted up questions and received no reply. Don was cold and his prodigious strength was fading. There was still a chance that the route would appear around a corner to his right, but for the moment he was too tired to pursue the possibility. He found a place to bash in a piton, and rappelled from this tenuous anchor to rejoin his comrades for the night.

Ian had the stove going to melt water for tea and soup. The climbers carried no sleeping bags. They wrapped themselves in their down jackets and sat on the ledge. Their legs soon grew numb. Bonington shivered and his teeth chattered. He considered the isolation of their position, and thought of what would happen if they couldn't get past this final tower. He thought of Bonatti and his party, stuck in their storm for four long days on this very spot—the seven men growing weaker as their food ran out; losing strength and hope as they grew colder; disappointed as the summit slipped from their grasp; and then frightened as they weighed their diminishing chances of survival. They had gathered their courage and their failing strength for the descent into the blizzard. They had struggled through the drifts on the glacier, four of them dying in their tracks, leaving three to tell the story and to try to live with it.

The morning came. Chris and the others moved stiffly about their perch. They were now very high on the south side of Mont Blanc; their view was spectacular, and the sun reached them early. Chris climbed Don's last pitch from the evening before. Don came up and led past him. He traversed out of sight around a corner, but Chris at his horrifyingly exposed belay stance—they were now some 3,000 feet above the glacier—could hear his partner's hoarse breathing and the singing of Don's hammer on iron.

Don slowly edged right, toward a corner where the tower met a wall. He now believed that he could make out a route; it would take him up cracks and through overhanging rock, some of it rotten. He climbed 50 feet or so to the corner, and hammered in some decent pitons. He set up a hanging belay and clipped into it and dangled in slings as he brought Chris up.

Don had taken two hours on the pitch. He had climbed into shadow; it was cold. He envied Ian and Jan—he imagined them napping in the sun down at the bivouac site. He eyed the crack overhead; it looked as though it would take small wooden wedges, but he had none. Four of the anonymous climbers from below had reached Ian and Jan. The new arrivals were French. Two other climbers—Americans—had turned back. Don hollered down to Ian, asking him to borrow wedges from the French; after some confusion, the French refused. They argued that Don had taken a wrong turn. They believed the true route lay to the left, and they would need all of their wedges to follow it.

Don cursed and carried on to the top of his corner, then into a chimney that cut through the roof. He jammed his shoulders into the chimney but found nothing for his feet. There was a place for a piton, but he couldn't work himself into position to place it—he suddenly realized that he was going to fall. He shouted to Chris to watch the rope, and resumed his struggle. Chris had a moment to wonder whether the pitons Whillans had placed for protection would hold; if not, Don would fall more than 100 feet. The impact would blow out the belay anchor.

Don spent a final moment suspended from a fist jam. He felt his fist ooze from the crack, and he went—limbs flailing, hardware jangling like a rack of huge keys. His piton held. He hung upside down, hatless and hammerless, while Chris, wide-eyed, stared up at him. Don was unhurt, and he managed to gain a stance on the rock. Chris—cold and sick of waiting—volunteered to try the pitch himself.

He couldn't compete with Don on rock; almost no one could. But Chris felt surprisingly strong this morning, and in any case he planned on aiding the crack. He did so by taking pebbles from the back of the crack and wedging them into place, then threading slings around the pebbles. That done, he clipped his etriers—the loops of webbing that could serve as awkward steps—to the slings and then stood in the steps to gain height.

Chris reached the bottom of the chimney and moved into shadow, dangling over thousands of feet of empty air. At some point he leaned back and lifted a leg, and his wallet—it held all of Don's money, as well as his own—fell from his pocket. It took a long time to waft and tumble its way to the glacier. The crack narrowed and filled with ice, forcing Chris out of the chimney onto tiny handholds that at last brought him to a ledge. A simmering joy that he carried at all times—he hadn't known it until now—bubbled up in him as he rummaged through his rack of gear for pitons to build an anchor. He brought Don up; they had overcome the climb's main difficulties.

They dropped a rope to the others, who used prusik knots to climb the rope itself. Ian went first. He spun in circles as he clung to the rope. He prayed briefly that the rope overhead didn't lie across a sharp edge.

The French by now had given up on their alternate route. They asked Jan to trail one of their ropes and fix it in place for them to climb in the morning.

Don and Chris and Ian and Jan spent the night on a ledge. The next morning they climbed two easier pitches to the top of the Central Pillar. They made a short rappel to a snow slope, and followed the snow to a ridge that led to the summit of Mont Blanc. A French journalist met them there. He had come in a helicopter, bringing tinned fruit juice and red wine.

THE BRITISH AND their Polish friend had snatched the Freney Pillar from Bonatti and his crowd, further evidence that British climbers had arrived at the forefront of alpine mountaineering.

They had done so in part because they were simply better all-around climbers. The past decade had shown that it was easier for the British to adopt artificial climbing techniques than it was for the Continentals to learn how to climb large stretches of difficult rock without such aids. The Continental climbers' tendency to rely too heavily on artificial climbing was turning out to be a major disadvantage in a venue where speed often meant success.

Chris had five days to report to his new employers in London. He couldn't imagine going in his current state, giddy with excitement, filled with a sense of possibility. He wanted to do one more stupendous climb before starting his life as a sales trainee. The weather had been good for two weeks; it occurred to him that the Eiger must at last be in condition.

He bumped into an Australian reporter down in Chamonix, and struck a deal with him. Chris and Don would try to climb the Eiger's North Face. The reporter's newspaper would finance the bid—and the paper would fly Chris home afterward, so that he could report to work on time.

Chris had struck up a romance with a girl named Anne. She gave the climbers a ride to Grindlewald. Chris and Don walked up to Alpiglen and then up through alpine pastures to the base of the North Face, a photographer panting in their wake. They were glad to leave him behind and get onto the face itself.

They climbed without a rope up long easy slabs with an occasional steeper section. The snow they'd encountered three weeks earlier was mostly gone. They moved quickly. They hoped to spend the night at the foot of the First Ice Field so they could cross it in the morning, before the heat of the afternoon exposed it to severe rockfall.

They were both happy to be here, on ground that was becoming familiar. They roped up at the foot of the Difficult Crack, and moved quickly up to and then across the Hinterstoisser

Whillans at the Swallow's Nest

Traverse, now largely free of snow. Another pitch brought them to their bivouac site—the Swallow's Nest—some 1,500 feet up the 6,000-foot face.

They were pleasantly tired. They kicked ice from a ledge, clearing just enough room to sit down. They brewed tea and dozed through the night. They were chilly, but this was nothing like the cold they had experienced on the Freney's Central Pillar; they heard water running on the rock.

Don by midnight was convinced that the weather was too warm; that rockfall would continue through the night and grow worse as soon as the sun rose. He resolved to descend at first light. Chris objected—they could climb higher and then decide—but Don had made up his mind: he was getting off the mountain.

Their descent was uneventful. They spent the night at the Alpiglen hotel; in the morning they made preparations to leave. A German tourist arrived, shouting that he'd seen a climber fall from the North Face. Bonington and Whillans accompanied him to the foot of the face, and came upon the corpse with its twisted, bloody limbs. The long, tumbling fall had torn the climber's clothing from his body. The tourist was excited; he was making a fool of himself. Chris and Don covered the corpse with a blanket, and left the arrangements to the local guides.

Chris said good-bye to Anne at the Geneva airport the next morning; six hours later, he arrived at the entrance to a black skyscraper—his employer's London headquarters. He stood for a moment looking up the city street, past rows of glass and stone. The buildings put him in mind of mountains, of what he was leaving as he stepped inside.

4

B ONINGTON SPENT SIX months as a management trainee. He began his work as a sales representative early in 1962. He visited grocers' shops in London's Hampstead district, where he took orders, closed six existing accounts—and failed to open any new ones.

He went to a party at someone's flat with a young freelance illustrator named Wendy Marchant, the daughter of a clergyman-turned-illustrator. Wendy was physically slight, unconventional and quietly determined. She had told friends she meant to marry an explorer and was a bit surprised to find herself dating a margarine salesman. She figured it wouldn't last. Chris took her climbing; she didn't like it, but the couple meanwhile had fallen in love. They married in May, five months after their first encounter.

Chris was by now fed up with his job. He received an invitation to join an expedition to the unclimbed Towers of Paine in Patagonia and asked for a leave of absence. His superiors responded as he had assumed they would: Bonington must choose between margarine and mountaineering. Chris talked it over with Wendy and resigned his job with the vague notion that he might go to teacher training college when he returned from Patagonia.

The Patagonia expedition wasn't scheduled to leave England until the autumn. Chris immediately began preparations for another summer in the Alps. Once again, he meant to go with

Don—and once again, they meant to try to climb the North Face of the Eiger.

Chris was short of cash, and Don had spent more than he could afford on an expedition the previous winter. The trip had been a success. He had stood on the summit of an unclimbed needle in Patagonia's Fitzroy Group. He had balanced that success against the news that Audrey wasn't able to bear children. Don had shrugged off the news; he told Audrey he wasn't bothered—but it was another defeat, and it weighed upon him. He had admired his father, had wanted a chance at being a father himself.

At any rate, Whillans was as broke as Bonington. Chris thought back to his encounters with journalists the previous summer; clearly, an English attempt on the Eiger was still a big story. He asked London's *Daily Express* to support the venture in return for exclusive coverage. The editors agreed to contribute some funds, and the paper ran a photograph of the two climbers departing London on Don's latest motorbike.

They arrived at the cliff in late July. They climbed the lower sections through torrents of meltwater. Chris dropped his axe at a chimney below the Hinterstoisser Traverse. His heart sank as he listened to the tool clatter down the face. Don vetoed any notion of retreat; he was sick of trooping up and down the slabs at the bottom of the route. They continued to climb. They reached the Swallow's Nest, below the First Ice Field, and spent a wet night there.

Nothing froze. The risk of rockfall was even greater than on their last attempt—but they were both losing patience with the climb; they wanted it done. Morning came and they set off up the 50-degree slope of the ice field. Stones bounded down the face, smacking into the ice that surrounded them. The two climbers moved quickly. They didn't stop to chop steps. The risk of fall-

Chris Bonington and Don Whillans depart for the Eiger

ing frightened them less than the thought of spending more time exposed to this bombardment.

They reached the top of the ice field and Chris took the lead. He was now climbing rock, working his way up on small holds slick with ice. He could find no cracks or other features that would take protection, and he soon ran out 150 feet of rope. He climbed in a state of growing fear until he reached the start of the Second Ice Field; here he found a crack for a piton. Don climbed up to join him, and something—seeing each other's faces—broke their momentum. They eyed the gray ice that loomed skyward and listened to stones whistle past. It wouldn't do. They turned to retreat—and saw two climbers approaching their stance from below. One of the men was shouting at them in German.

The new climbers had come to rescue two Englishmen who were in difficulties higher on the route. Chris and Don agreed to accompany the rescuers, and started back up the face. They forced themselves to stop and cut steps as they made their way across the Second Ice Field amid the whistle and shriek of falling stones; they might need the steps to bring down an injured climber. A single figure in red came into view and made its way slowly down toward them; after a time, the figure seemed to collapse. The rescuers continued to climb until another sound made them look up.

Chris saw a body falling—sliding across steep ice and gathering speed, flailing through air and tumbling over rocks like a cooking pot some clumsy person might have dropped. Chris held a wordless understanding that these passing moments were more real for the falling body than any mere observer could imagine. Chris couldn't believe what he was seeing; he couldn't acknowledge what was happening to flesh—to a state of awareness and being—so much like his own.

He froze for a moment. It was tempting to turn over in his mind this new event—this horror—but he knew better. He fixed his attention on his next step and carried on. He felt his mind recede and he was intensely aware of his body. He was not going to fall. He looked up. The weather had turned; clouds filled the sky. The second climber, the figure in red, was still there.

Chris and Don continued to climb the Second Ice Field. The barrage of stones and ice went on: sharp cracks and softer thumps, muted by the sheer expanse of the face and the blanket of sky. A rock—a very small one—slammed into Bonington's shoulder and bounced off to clatter on. His arm went numb but he could move his fingers.

The other two would-be rescuers turned back. Chris and Don climbed on—a seemingly endless series of pitches—and at last reached the figure in red. He was a young Englishman named Brian Nally. His partner—a student named Barry Brewster—had been hit by a rock the day before while leading a pitch at the start of a wall known as the Flatiron. The blow had knocked Brewster from his perch, and he had taken a very long fall. Nally had carved out a ledge for his injured partner, but Brewster had died some time in the early morning. His corpse had somehow fallen from the ledge, perhaps swept from it by falling rock or ice; Chris had watched it tumble past.

Nally's eyes were blank and his face wore an expression of dull shock. He asked Chris and Don whether they were going to the summit—and if so, could he come with them? They stared at him for a moment. Don broke the silence with an uncharacteristically gentle suggestion—perhaps it was time to get down to the valley for a cup of tea—and he and Chris quickly set to work.

They tied into opposite ends of the rope and put Nally in the middle. Chris helped him navigate the steps down the Second Ice Field. Nally performed surprisingly well—he was a competent climber—but a falling rock struck a glancing blow to his bare head; he had given his helmet to Brewster. The blow staggered him, but Nally shook his head and went on with the descent. He moved more slowly now. The weather grew steadily worse and a hailstorm broke around them as they left the ice field. Don placed a single piton and the three men hung from it until the squall blew past; then they continued down.

They descended the Ice Hose, the gully leading down the First

Ice Field. They were approaching the Hinterstoisser Traverse. It would be difficult if not impossible to cross with an injured climber. Young Tony Kurtz and his three partners had died in 1936 because they couldn't find a way to reverse this section of the route. Whillans the previous day had noticed a spot where a simple rappel would bypass the traverse altogether. He guided the others to it now.

The rappel behind them, it was a simple matter to shepherd their charge to the Stollenbach Window—an entry to the train tunnel that burrows through the Eiger. Here they turned Nally over to an official rescue party. A pair of Swiss journalists had hired a special train to come up to the tunnel and get the story before their competitors. The journalists immediately accosted the climbers—including Nally, who answered their questions in a state of shock.

Chris and Don left for Innsbruck the next morning. Wendy and Audrey joined them there. The men climbed on limestone cliffs while the story of the dramatic rescue on the Eiger played in newspapers and on television in England and abroad. The party ran short of money near the end of August. Wendy and Audrey set out to hitchhike home; Don and Chris took the motorcycle. They stopped for a route—the imposing North Face of the Badile—and found it easy. They were climbing extremely well. They made one last stop in Chamonix, where Bonington saw blue sky over the mountains and realized he wasn't ready to leave.

He proposed one more climb to Whillans. Don refused. He had made up his mind to go home—he had a lecture to give—and he wasn't going to change it to suit circumstances or his partner's whim. *I'll meet any bugger halfway*, he'd often told Chris. *Don't ask me to go further.*

So Don left Chamonix alone. The two oddly matched friends would climb together again, but their dealings with one another were becoming difficult now. Chris had come to see himself as Don's peer in the mountains. And he had begun to weary of Don's stubborn streak; Whillans sometimes seemed a young man old before his time.

Chris understood that Don was a kind of genius. They were bound together by what they could give or teach one another. Even so, Chris that night felt relief at being free of his crotchety partner. He was in effect single again—but only for a few hours. He saw Don off and went to the Bar National to drink, and ran into Ian Clough.

IAN HAD PERFORMED well on the Central Pillar of Freney the previous year, and he quickly fell in with Bonington's latest brainstorm: an assault on the 4,000-foot Walker Spur of the Grand Jorasses. Hamish MacInnes had convinced a much younger Chris to join him for a run at the route five years before, but weather had fortunately stopped them. Chris now felt far more prepared to tackle what remained a serious alpine test-piece. He was like anyone who has been afraid and is now less afraid: he was eager to put his new freedom to work. He wanted to run things—no need for a Hamish MacInnes to manipulate him into tackling hard climbs, no need for a Don Whillans to protect him.

Chris and Ian found the Walker Spur crowded with climbers—Italians, French, Austrians. The two young British climbers passed them all, and continued to climb when the other parties retreated in the face of threatening weather. A route-finding error forced them to make an airy traverse across a blank wall, but the detour only added to their sense of exhilaration. Chris was perhaps the stronger climber, but there was no one in charge. Each climber existed in the thrilling state of solitude that comes when you can't be found or caught or told what to do. They swapped leads, climbing with the economy and pleasure that occurs when a person stops holding back, stops burying what he knows. Chris was happy.

They climbed from the base of the Walker Spur to its top in thirteen hours, emerging into the teeth of a north wind. The weather had an ugly aspect, and the pair began their descent—but the weather improved as darkness approached. Chris had long entertained the notion that a strong team might crown an ascent of the Walker Spur with a traverse of the Jorasses Range. It had seemed a wild notion, but now he put the idea to Ian. Ian was willing, even eager; there was nothing about him of Don's pinched and stubborn nature. The pair settled down for the night, and in the morning turned and set out across the ridge.

They moved from pinnacle to pinnacle. The views shifted and opened across seemingly endless vistas. The climbing wasn't difficult—they moved unroped for most of it—and they were aware of something more perfect than a glorious future; what opened before them was rather an endless present composed of emptiness and beauty.

They climbed all day, seeing no one, hearing no voices but their own. Their boots chafed their feet and the climbers felt their growing weariness. They struggled up and over the last high point on their ridge, and began their descent. Bonington felt his happiness swell within him as he set off down the last snow slope. Here he slipped and slithered on the snow, gathering speed and rolling to bury the pick of his axe in the slope to stop his slide.

Ian gently urged him to take care. The great Lake District climber, Arthur Dolphin, had died in almost the same spot not long before—a ridiculous, sliding fall on snow on this easy ground. The two friends carried on down, legs leaden, minds lit by a flickering gray—adrenaline and fatigue and mountain light—and by an interior swirl of feeling that they understood comes only at such times; it would rest in memory until recalled by another such experience.

They'd been moving for sixteen hours when they reached the Torino Hut. Bonington drank some Chianti and found his bed in a room filled with bodies. While the other climbers slept he watched a kind of interior film of seemingly random moments and views; he allowed his mind to roam and it did so, calming and settling him. The Eiger's North Face arose in this vision and he knew that he could do the route with Ian. He lay awake until dawn and at the first sign of day he woke his friend. They agreed to make the attempt together.

THEY ARRIVED AT Alpiglen two days later. Chris by now had experienced one of his characteristic mood swings. His exalted state of two days before had departed; he was partly convinced that he had come to the Eiger to die.

They shouldered their gear and set off for the climb in the late afternoon, planning to spend a night low on the route. An Austrian trying to solo the face had fallen to his death two days before. This news had further blackened Chris's mood—and now in the fading light his eyes fell upon bits of clothing and fragments of flesh or bone clinging to rock. Ian saw them too, but neither man spoke of these artifacts; each was unsure whether his partner had seen them.

Darkness was nearly upon them as they reached their bivouac ledge. They had only a little time to look around—out across the sky, down at the valley unfolded beneath them, up at the mountain whose bulk opposed the space that otherwise surrounded them. There was a sense that they had run out of room, that the universe had borders and the climbers were pressing themselves against one of them.

They didn't know what was most frightening. There was the

silent space that forced itself upon them and into their eyes and mouths, like murky water. There was the yawning expanse of black rock, as real as a geometry theorem; it conjured a wringing and emptying anxiety in the two young men. They felt a sudden wish to hide, as if from the eye of some huge winged being. But they knew that this desire might give way to an equally irrational joy—and that any hiding place they chose would be easy to find.

Their solitude fell away as the last light left the sky. Two figures climbed toward them from lower on the face. The newcomers were a Scot and a German, near-strangers to one another, who had roped up after their respective partners had gone home. They made an odd pair, two more among the growing ranks of climbers, most of them outmatched, who had begun to clutter the slopes of the Eiger. Chris and Ian had come to know each other on the Freney Pillar and on the Walker Spur. They felt afraid, but also strong and engaged. The newcomers didn't interest them—they were a distraction; worse, they might get in the way.

The night was going to be a cold one. Chris realized that he was hungry; he proposed a feast. Chris and Ian set about cooking and eating all of their canned food, leaving only tea and soup for the rest of the climb. They spread their gear across the ledge, which was protected from stray stones by an overhang. They talked about the spot—how cozy and safe it seemed—and settled into their bivouac bags to sleep.

Dawn woke them. They hurried their breakfast and their packing in order to get on the rock ahead of the other pair. They were at the start of the Difficult Crack, and Chris prepared to lead it. He remembered being here with Don. The recollection gave him pause. He knew that Don would find this hard to forgive.

They climbed the Difficult Crack quickly, and crossed the Hinterstoisser Traverse. The First Ice Field had shrunk in the weeks since Chris's previous visit, and they climbed on the exposed rock at its periphery. They climbed the Second Ice Field in crampons. There was no need to cut steps. The sky was clear. By nine o'clock in the morning they were very high on the face, with many of the route's difficulties behind them.

Their momentum carried them into a gully that led to surprisingly difficult rock climbing. Bonington climbed more than 100 feet without placing any gear—and suddenly a fall seemed likely. He felt his courage leave him, a flock of birds leaving a tree. He took a breath and felt the air enter his lungs and fill him. His fear settled and grew still without vanishing. It was enough, and he reached higher for a nubbin of rock that allowed him to move his feet higher. The climbing became not easy but obvious and in a general sense familiar. He recognized it as work he loved. He had run out almost all of the rope when he at last clambered onto a ledge where he could build an anchor. Ian followed, and now the two of them moved together across more ledges until they came to a dead end; they had wandered off the route.

They retreated to the top of the Second Ice Field. They had lost an hour of daylight, but they were back on route now— and the climbing again seemed easy. Bonington took the lead and spotted a badly twisted piton in a crack; it was the peg that had anchored Brian Nally when Barry Brewster had fallen. That was five weeks ago, fantastically distant.

They moved up a steep section and then across easy slabs. This was the Flatiron, where climbers could expect to encounter heavy rockfall by the middle of the day; the rock they stood upon was pitted from it. Chris, looking down the face to a spot some 150 feet below, could make out a patch of darkness—perhaps clothing or equipment—at the ledge where Brewster had died. The Scot and the German had fallen far behind; they seemed likely to reach the Flatiron just in time for its afternoon bombardment.

Chris and Ian finished the Flatiron, and set off up the Third Ice Field. The ice was steep here; it required them to cut steps, which took them up to a sheltered rock gully known as the Ramp. This was cozier. The world narrowed down to a chimney of rock and then to a steep, ice-glazed pitch that on a warmer day would carry torrents of water; climbers knew it as the Waterfall Pitch.

Ian led it smoothly, and led another pitch past an ice bulge. The climbing was difficult but not terribly so. Soon they were up the Ramp and across the ice field that served as its exit, searching for the stupendously exposed Traverse of the Gods. This passage would bring them back across to the center of the enormous face.

The Traverse was not easy to find. Chris was aware that a route-finding mistake here might be hard to fix. Ground that could be traversed in one direction might prove difficult or even impossible to reverse. They couldn't rappel sideways, so they would have to retrace their steps. This might prove impossible if a storm blew in suddenly, or if one of the climbers suffered an injury.

A thick haze had materialized during the late morning. They were climbing in cloud. Chris noticed that the rock-studded ice that clung to the face was very dirty. This dirty ice defined their world. The cloud masked the climbers' exposure, hiding the depths so that below their feet was only a kind of invisible tunnel; it would draw a falling climber to the bottom of all things. They imagined this tunnel and also the vastness that lurked at every angle. The earth had disappeared; it was unknown to them, as mysterious as the surface of another planet's moon. They were obscurely glad of this.

They had reached the most remote part of the face. Here they looked up and were amazed to see more climbers, as if the face had become a path upon which pilgrims encountered ghosts and visions from every realm—or perhaps merely stumbled across one another. Chris and Ian climbed to this new pair and a strange conversation ensued. The two climbers, both Swiss, had gained just 300 feet that day. They were settled in for the night; it was only four o'clock, but they were very tired. Bonington invited them to climb with him and Ian. The two Swiss smiled and refused. They repeated that they were very tired.

Chris and Ian left them and hurried on. They found the Traverse of the Gods and moved across ledges. They heard sounds from the valley—a cow horn and a train—and knew that no one could help them now. They came to the White Spider, a patch of steep ice that clings to the upper reaches of the face; dark stone surrounded it to form a tilted amphitheatre in the sky. A stone ripped past Chris. The sound of it cutting the air near his head brought him up short.

It was five o'clock. There was time to reach the summit before dark, but the risk from rockfall at this hour was too great. They stopped on a narrow, sheltered ledge—it was just large enough to sit on—and made a sort of camp. They slept and dreamed in fits and starts, waking to brew tea. The night was dry and cold; they felt the face grow hard and still around them. They accepted this good fortune as due to them in their weariness.

Chris in the morning led into the entrance of the White Spider; the place seemed simply to hang above the valley that lay now some 4,000 feet below. It was possible to imagine the ice tipping forward, the climbers teetering backward to spin and plunge into the spectacular distance. The view that hovered just between their boots as they climbed the steep ice was strangely distant grass.

The green of it sickened them at first and then brought them to the brink of silent tears. They had spent two nights and parts of three days on the climb, and seeing this vision of grass they were like satellites, or like the long-dead remembering the earth. The sight of grass and the recollection of it gave them pain. They regretted their life on earth; they regretted not living it with less clumsiness, more quietly. Their lives began and ended in each breath. They no longer climbed toward the summit of the Eiger; they only climbed.

They climbed through the quiet of morning, impossibly far above alpine pastures. They climbed past stones half-buried in the ice, and Chris was again afraid. He moved slowly—too slowly, cutting deep steps that provided a beguiling but false sense of security. There was no safety here; his safety lay in speed. He knew this, and gathering himself he quit cutting steps and climbed instead on the front-points of his crampons, a more tenuous but more efficient approach. He ran out a full rope-length of 150 feet and gazed upward, stricken and quieted by what he saw. The ice field seemed vast. Ian followed, equally subdued: they were inside the Spider.

They set themselves to their task. They kept their eyes and their minds on the work of movement, taking comfort in the grip of their hands on their axes and the press and bump of their stiff boots on the flesh of their toes and feet. They visited their various discomforts, their blisters and aches, as if gathering evidence of their own actuality—and still they felt eaten, insignificant. They might be climbing toward some vast and ancient dome, up endless, narrow stairs that led to some final result: an ushering into Paradise or a banishment to some overcrowded hell. Chris felt some of the hollow discomfort, the longing of an unbeliever who visits a huge and beautifully frescoed cathedral; creation itself threatens to compel belief, makes belief almost unbearably attractive.

The climbers did not speak except to perform tasks at their belay anchors. A sense of urgency carried Chris forward. He lost track of time, and was surprised when he looked up from the snow at his feet and saw that they were at last finished with the Spider.

Their hearts lifted—now there were only the Exit Cracks and the summit ice slopes to climb. Chris started up rock and the climbing seemed too easy; it didn't seem to match the route description. He descended to try a different way. He found something that looked right—it looked hard enough—and set off in his boots, slipping on patches of verglas. The pitch was nearly vertical, with no cracks for pitons. He had committed himself; retreat was impossible.

He took an hour to climb 60 feet. Ian from time to time peered up at him and saw the rope still hanging free. They both knew that a slip here would kill them, but Chris knew this like a piece of news or history he couldn't manage to believe. He put it well aside and got on with standing just so or tugging cautiously at a hold; his mortality shrank to a concept. And still his knowledge of the risk colored every action he performed, lending his movements and the stillness between them a deliberate and serious quality that awoke his desire for peace, for clarity. He made a series of awkward moves that required almost perfect balance, becoming aware of his body, of his hands and his feet. He experimented with positions and shifts of posture and found that he knew what to do. He wedged his right foot in a crevice and used tiny fingerholds to stay in balance as he stood; he let go with a hand and reached for a better hold as his body stood vertical, suspended over his foot and inclined to fall backward. The hold he found was good and he was able to pull up and onto a small ledge.

He made an anchor and Ian followed him, calling for tension on the rope. The slow-moving Swiss climbers now appeared at the foot of the pitch. Bonington dropped them a top rope—they would never be able to lead this section—and they struggled up.

Chris meanwhile studied the rock above his perch and realized that he had lost the route; he could find nothing to climb from here. The four climbers reversed the pitch; incredibly, Chris had to teach the two Swiss how to rappel.

Chris returned to the section he'd dismissed as too easy. These were in fact the Exit Cracks. They would be difficult in icy conditions, but today they were dry. Ian and Chris unroped for a time, and quickly reached the summit ice field. Here the face swept out beneath them. A rope seemed necessary again. They finished the climb in the orthodox way, building anchors and moving one at a time.

They came onto the Eiger's Mittellegi Ridge and walked into a different view—there were mountains in all directions. The climbers felt their breathing change. They unroped once more and descended the ridge; the two Swiss were still climbing, but would be off the face soon. The descent took a mere two hours.

The innkeeper at Kleine Scheidegg had news: two climbers—the Scot and the German they'd met at the first bivouac—had fallen from the face. The dead men had been near-strangers to Chris and Ian. The news troubled them but it was jostled by increasingly rambunctious thoughts: that they had done the climb; that they had accomplished the first British ascent of the Eiger's North Face. Chris in particular knew that he had done something people outside of mountaineering circles might notice; that this might be useful to him in some way; and also that he could carry this achievement with him forever, like winning a famous prize. It reassured him and unearthed hopes that had eluded his notice until now. He had lived through five attempts on the North Face. He'd seen other men die there, and had returned to finish the route. He had done all of this, and he felt dimly that in doing it he had created for himself the possibility of a life different from the one into which he'd been born.

5

C HRIS AND IAN returned to England as minor celebrities in the fall of 1962. The newspapers and television newscasts were filled with their exploits, which dimly echoed the Everest triumph, now almost a decade old. Harold Macmillan, the Conservative Prime Minister, sent a telegram of congratulations to the young men. Chris traveled the country giving lectures about the Eiger, and signed a contract to write a book—a memoir of his climbing career.

He used much of the money to pay his share of costs for the Patagonia expedition. The invitation to go to Patagonia had given Chris the excuse he needed to give up his career as a margarine salesman; he had expected to be entirely broke by now. As it was, there was just enough money for Wendy to come. Chris, having cast aside his plans for a conventional career, felt a powerful need for her presence. Wendy's unconventional notions, her accepting and serene temperament, were reminders that life could take a form warmer and more exciting than the alternative he had rejected. Expedition leader Barrie Page was bringing his wife and the Page's small son. The two women would stay at a nearby ranch; they could look after the boy and keep each other company while the men climbed.

Page had explored the area two years earlier as a member of a scientific expedition. He had come away with a vision of three granite spires: the Towers of Paine. Page and two of his companions from that 1960 expedition—Derek Walker and Vic Bray—believed that a strong team might manage to climb the spectacular Central Tower. They had invited John Streetley and Ian Clough as well as Chris. The _Daily Express_, which had covered Chris and Ian's ascent of the Eiger, had put up money for this trip and Chris would act as expedition correspondent.

Don Whillans was coming, too. Don had written letters to Chris and others in their circle, deriding the commercial elements surrounding Bonington's Eiger climb. His disappointment was searing. He knew he might have stayed with Chris and done the climb. Once again, he had somehow fended off an opportunity that he believed he'd earned. He saw Bonington's ascent of the Eiger as an act of infidelity—much as he continued to regard Joe Brown's decision to go to Kangchenjunga seven years before. Don was wounded. The pain of it surprised and frightened him, made him angry.

He had begun to inhabit a complex response to his disappointments. He had become more assertive; he couldn't bear to be thwarted. He wasn't a thief, but he wouldn't ask or negotiate for what he wanted. He would forgo it—or simply take it—rather than risk a rebuff.

Chris and some others understood and tolerated his behavior—to a point—because he was a genius in the mountains and because he was an old friend of the sort difficult to love but nearly impossible to abandon. He knew how to behave himself as part of a team when it mattered most. And Don's anger was authentic; it made other climbers' lives more difficult, but they sometimes admired him for it. Whillans sometimes reminded them that they were angry, too.

The Patagonia Expedition departed England on November 11. The climbers traveled by passenger liner to the city of Valparaiso in Chile. A plane carried them down the length of the Andes to

Punta Arenas, a small town on the Straits of Magellan. They had been traveling for three weeks when they boarded a truck for the final leg of their trip to the Paine Massif.

They huddled among boxes in the back of the truck, rumbling through a wilderness of dead trees, the carcasses sun-bleached, buffed by the wind. The world seemed to grow larger and emptier; one afternoon a single pink flamingo rose from a lake. The jolting of the truck colored this vision; Chris watched the creature rise into the empty sky and felt something give way within him. This feeling was accompanied by another feeling, which he recognized as envy. He felt stuck in his mind, in his ambition.

The expedition established Base Camp at a small ranch, a two-story stone house amid a scattering of sheep-pens and primitive outbuildings. The climbers that first night got drunk with the ranch owner—a tall, heavy man whose brother managed the place. The brother was a lean, sad-faced cowboy who cooked for them, roasting lamb on an open fire. They ate under the stars—there had been a long spell of fine weather—and drank wine from skins. They slept late, and one by one awoke to hideous hangovers.

They aimed to establish Camp One at the start of a glacier that ran almost to the base of the Towers. This morning they packed slowly, talking in low voices, beginning now to suspend their ordinary ways of thinking—their ordinary beliefs—so that the route could become the center of all that mattered.

Three of them had seen the Central Tower, and they had told the others what they'd seen. It was huge and sheer, a monster with no obvious weakness; it might not be possible to climb it. The climbers had heard about the weather, too. The winds here appeared without warning and seemingly from nowhere; they swept like a wall of water across the earth, their power evidence of God or of his absence.

This morning as they prepared to approach the route some of

the climbers came into the presence of their fear; it edged over the horizon like the fiery rim of some anxiously awaited dawn, spilling its hue on the landscape. Chris was learning that his version of fear was patient. It didn't lurk or cast shadows; it took its ease or went about its hidden business as conditions unfolded, allowing him to forget that it lived in him at every moment, and then it arose to sicken him.

They set off. The weather was hot; the sky was still. The wind's utter absence pressed at them. They were physically miserable as they trudged uphill with their burdens of tents and gear. The wine and the lamb were sour in their stomachs; sweat ran down their foreheads, and flies buzzed at their faces. This unpleasantness and the uncertainty of their position made them still more anxious. Each man from time to time asked himself with a half-authentic, momentary despair whether any of this was necessary or even in any way useful.

They came to the top of a rise and stared down at acres of scree: a shambles of rock fragments, good ground for twisting an ankle. The slope led down to a forest of low, wind-tortured trees. Three previous expeditions had been here to climb or explore but it occurred to Chris that this ground remained innocent of men and their doings, their foolishness.

The climbers dumped the day's carry at the base of the glacier and stared up and across to the Central Tower. The monolith rose 3,000 feet from the start of the real climbing. They looked away and found shade and sat for a time, feeling better for their walk. Their talk died and someone stood up; the others rose and the party returned to Base Camp. The walking was easier and very different, moving downhill without loads—Chris was pestered by a dim sense that he'd forgotten something—and they talked as they moved, discussing plans for their campaign. They would establish Camp Two above the glacier, at the foot of the Tower, and take turns making the route.

Don and Barrie went first, taking three days to establish Camp Two and work their way above it to a notch between the Central and North Towers; this gave a view of the Central Tower's West face. They descended to Base Camp with news that a crack seemed to run most of the way up the face. There was a gap, but they believed that a person might cross it by delicate climbing across a blank-looking slab.

Chris and Ian left Base Camp on December 5. They passed Camp One and struggled up through dense, low forest and then across a wilderness of boulders and rock fragments to Camp Two at the foot of their Tower. They woke the next morning to a gray world: the weather had turned. They made the final approach to the climb across rocks damp with new snow; big wet flakes slapped gently at their cheeks and a sharp wind brought tears to their eyes. They reached ledges that led across the bottom of the North Tower, and moved carefully across them to a gully that rose to Don and Barrie's high point.

The gully spared them the wind's full impact, but only until they reached the col between the two towers, with its view out to the Central Tower's West Face. Here they emerged into a hideous gale; it forced them to crouch, and they lost their balance and fell to their knees, surprised when even this posture of supplication was barely sufficient to keep them from toppling and rolling across the rock and over some edge to a fall that would kill them. The view to the other side of the col was spectacular and alien—a great expanse of green, set with lakes of different colors: blue, gray and brown. It appeared to Chris and Ian as a wind-scoured map of itself. They shivered squinting into the wind to inspect their wall: soaring sheets of brown and yellow granite, seeming as wide as the sky behind them.

The Towers' sheer size made them something beyond monsters. Their shapes seemed manifestations of something impersonal and dark, beyond judgment or seeing. Chris and Ian felt the cold sap their strength and with it their ability to smother their fear. Their ambition rose to counter their anxiety, taking shape as a commitment to a task that might be beyond them. They had traveled weeks to reach this place and now they gazed upon ground that no one had touched and the idea thrilled them. It appealed to their wish to be set apart, as if traversing virgin ground would restore their own purity, would make them part of this beauty. They felt afraid, but they felt that they must climb the Central Tower or else suffer and risk so much in their efforts that turning back would not shame them.

It was too cold to climb today. Ian put Chris on belay, and Chris climbed 12 feet and hammered in a piton: a gesture. He lowered himself from the peg, and the climbers descended to Camp Two for the night. They carried on down to Base Camp in the morning. This ugly turn in the weather might last; there seemed no point in spending days at their cramped and windy high camp. It was better to go down, leaving the supplies intact for the next pair of climbers.

The weather kept the climbers off the mountain for almost a week. The wind tore through the heights above Base Camp; it was wicked in its constancy, and strong enough to rip a tent to pieces. The climbers made brief forays to the Tower later in the month, but the breaks in the weather were too brief to allow real progress.

Christmas came. The climbers had been away from home for almost two months. The pile of empty beer bottles near Base Camp grew daily, a sort of living monument to the expedition's futility. Chris had almost nothing to report to the *Daily Telegraph*, a fact that made him increasingly anxious. He had begun to entertain the notion of making a career as a photojournalist covering climbing and other adventures, and he had hopes that this assignment would lead to others.

A group of Italian climbers arrived. They established their Base Camp a half mile from the British, who sauntered over to greet them. The Italians were slightly older men. They wore matching sweaters and shared an air of single-minded purpose that annoyed and worried the British, who found themselves slightly ashamed of their own shabby clothing and casual approach to camp chores and expedition strategy. The Italians spoke little English and the British had virtually no Italian. Nonetheless, it was soon evident that the Italians had come to make their own attempt on the Central Tower of Paine.

The British returned to their Base Camp for a council of war. For all of their contempt for traditional standards and rules, they were patriots; they took it more or less on faith that a single British climber was worth any number of foreign ones. Don especially was appalled at the idea of losing the route to a bunch of bloody Italians. He snapped out of his beer-induced stupor and proposed a strategy: the British would build a windproof hut to install at their high camp and would maintain a pair of climbers there. Those climbers could then go to work on the route as soon as the wind died, stealing a march on the snooty and (contrary to all appearances) decadent Italians.

Don went to work on New Year's Eve. He enlisted Ian Clough, John Streetley and Vic Bray as helpers. They built the hut at Base Camp, then took it apart and carried the pieces to the foot of the Tower; all told, the structure's components weighed roughly 250 pounds. The hut once assembled was some seven feet long and five feet wide, with a four-foot ceiling. This was the first version of the Whillans Box—the squat, ugly and near-indestructible shelter that would play a crucial role on this climb as well as future ones. They called it the Hotel Britannico, and they posted a sign over the door: *Members Only*.

They still needed a break in the weather. The wind continued to frustrate their attempts to climb higher on the Tower. Chris and Don until now had avoided climbing together, but both were increasingly impatient with the team's lack of progress. One night, drinking at Base Camp with the others, the two men rose and left the mess tent together to have a piss. They had been drinking for hours. The talk had been the usual—other climbs, women, food, the Italians, the weather. Chris and Don emerged into the night from the smoky fug of the mess tent, and stood in the bright, moonlit darkness. They were woozy from the liquor, and the air felt clean and cold on their faces. Chris felt a curious drunken lightness of being, a sense that what mattered wasn't obvious—that he had missed some critical point. He experienced this as good news; he felt in a kind of drunken clarity that it was better to be lost than to believe in a world of trivial and heavy consequence. The clouds sailed across a backdrop of bottomless sky as each man gazed up, gauging the weather. Don remarked on the wind pushing those clouds; it meant another day would pass with no progress on the Tower.

They stood for a moment longer, growing cold in the night air. Chris, acting on impulse, suggested that maybe it was time the two of them took a turn together out front. Don agreed, said he'd been thinking the same thing.

Chris felt enormous relief. He had become a figure by climbing the Eiger, and he knew what Don had missed: a chance to become someone who had less to prove. Chris half-believed that he had colluded in Don's loss. He was aware of his own losses and regrets and failures. This shared affliction—this melancholy—made the connection between them more difficult to sever.

They walked up to the Whillans Box the next day. John Street-ley and Barrie Page went with them. The wind had dropped, and the climbers were able to pitch a tent next to the Box. They watched a spectacular sunset; Bonington, taking it in, was a little ashamed of the rivalry with the Italians. The climbers went to bed and listened to black silence, the sound of no wind. Chris and Don were to start up first in the morning; John and Barrie would follow in support. The silence allowed the four men to pursue their thoughts about the coming day and then to sleep.

Bonington put his head outside just before three o'clock. He found what he only half-hoped to find—winking stars in an inky sky, a cold and windless quiet. He woke the others, and the party made breakfast and finished their preparations for the Tower. They trudged to the foot of the fixed ropes, and began to climb.

Whillans went first. He pulled himself hand-over-hand up the fixed rope that led to the expedition's current high point. Chris belayed him on a separate rope, but Don placed no gear to stop a fall. He simply hauled himself up the rope that crossed the blank slab near the bottom of the route. He had climbed some 90 feet when the rope snapped.

He should have toppled over backward and fallen past Chris, pulling Bonington from his unanchored stance and killing them both. Instead he clutched at both pieces of the broken rope and teetered on a pair of small footholds—tiny features on the vast slab—long enough to regain his balance. He stood for a moment and tied the two frayed pieces of rope together and continued to climb.

Bonington had watched all of this from below. He was momentarily frightened but near misses of this sort were becoming familiar to him; he was learning to file them away quickly. And this reminder of Don's resourcefulness, his sheer ability to stay alive, heartened Chris. He followed his partner up the fixed ropes to the start of new ground. It was his turn to lead. He looked up and found a groove that led to an overhanging roof. The rock was warm and dry and he started up the groove toward the roof, placing pitons for aid as he went.

The Italians meanwhile arrived at the base of the route and took note of Chris and the others, already high on the wall. Appalled, the latecomers gave chase, rushing up the fixed ropes that the British had left to create a line of retreat. John and Barrie, following Don and Chris, had intended to leave ropes in place all the way up the route. Now they began pulling the rope up at the end of each pitch. The Italians would have to climb the pillar for themselves.

Chris was still making his way up to his roof, taking more than two hours to climb 150 feet. He could conceive of no other line up the face—he saw nothing but steep, blank granite to either side. He reached the overhang and stood and searched for a crack that might take a piton. He found a suitable slot and rummaged through the gear that hung from a sling looped across one shoulder until he found a piton that seemed the right size. He fitted the tip of the piton into the crack and reached for the hammer that hung from his waist. He found the tool and hammered at the piton until the metal sang; when the tone reached a certain pitch he knew that the placement was solid.

He placed a second piton as insurance and clipped slings to both of the pegs and stood in the slings to reach for holds that would take him past the roof. He moved too quickly and his feet came out of the slings. He tumbled through emptiness to finish upside down, some 15 feet below the roof, not unhappy but surprised, as if awakened roughly from a dream or born full-grown into an unfamiliar world.

He rested for a moment. His body spun slowly at the end of the gently swaying rope. He was sore and queasy and winded, but curiously at peace. The world moved far below in empty, quiet circles; he was afloat. His fear rose up in him and he swallowed it; he hung for another moment, and the aftertaste of his fright blended with a muffled jubilation. He was aware of the sky that loomed in all directions.

He was trembling and at first he couldn't get his breath but he was not hurt. He reached across and pulled himself back onto the rock and went back to work. He tapped in an extra peg and this time clambered up and past the roof to finish the pitch; it wasn't difficult. The size of everything—the Tower itself; the Patagonian Ice Cap that receded into the distant west; the immense vault of the sky, still windless—made the climbing seem at once effortless and irrelevant. Chris lost any sense of himself, any notion that what he said or did mattered. Such foolishness fell from him like guilt from the newly baptized. His self-importance spun at first like a leaf, gained heft as it traveled, and clattered stonelike across slabs so far distant that the echoes of its clatter faded instantly to nothing.

John Streetley's voice came floating up from below, where he and Barrie Paige had come to a halt. They had decided to turn back, figuring Chris and Don could move more quickly as a single team. The Italians came into view, but Chris had lost any sense that they mattered. He was alone with this place and with Whillans, who followed him up and over the roof. Don took the lead now, bridging up an imposing corner—an acrobat at work, a precarious, strenuous dance.

The two men climbed on as daylight faded. They were struck by this alteration and by how this vast change did not in any way disturb the stillness in which they labored. They came two hours before sunset to a prominent shoulder on the Tower. The shoulder marked the beginning of a long ridge that led toward the summit. The climbing here looked easier, but they would have to move quickly to reach the top before dark. They could instead bivouac now and try to finish the route in the morning, but the weather might change overnight; they might have to retreat without finishing the route. The possibility had become almost unthinkable.

They dropped their bivouac gear at the shoulder and carried on quickly up lower-angled rock. The cracks here were filled with ice, and ledges were piled high with snow. They had crossed a line; they must finish their work here and skitter back across as soon as they could. Don led a pitch up ice-smeared rocks, placing no pitons and moving at a speed that astonished Chris, who followed at a more deliberate pace; he saw that he would take a long, pendulum-like fall if he lost his footing on the rock, which in spots was slick with ice.

They came to a gap in the ridge and rappelled onto the face below it. They moved across snow past the gap and then climbed back onto the crest and climbed another pillar as light bled from the sky. This metamorphosis bathed them in beauty but they were unaware of it; they moved still more quickly now, intent upon their goal. They climbed two more pillars, and then Don led across a short wall to disappear around a corner. He shouted and Chris followed to find his friend sitting on a block the size of a table; there was nothing else to climb.

Night drifted up at them like smoke from some enormous distant fire. Each man considered the possibility that he had stumbled into a trap; that some force had arranged things to puzzle him and draw him onward. It was possible. They had come here to satisfy their curiosity, and in doing so had uncovered precise and secret patterns. The patterns blurred and faded into mystery even now; fear and grief leaked into the enterprise.

The sun had sunk almost into the ice cap. There was still—by what seemed a miracle—daylight. They looked upon glaciers and peaks that seemed new to the world. They knew there was nowhere to keep this; it would never again be as real to them. Even now their awareness sputtered and lapsed between moments of astonishment. The wind had dropped entirely away. It was as if the wind had died in a literal sense; as if the wind would not return. All around them was the peace they had sought without knowing they sought it.

Chris understood that it was time to leave. Don knew it, too. They had been on the summit for ten minutes and already the tide of unthinking courage that had brought them here had begun to ebb. They must get down to their bivouac gear; otherwise they would die if the wind returned during the night.

They made a series of rappels to the shoulder that marked the bottom of the summit ridge. They found the gear where they had left it. The light grew yet thicker and still there was no sign of storm or wind. They were thirsty—John and Barrie had descended with the stove, so it wasn't possible to melt snow for drinks. Don found matches, though, and happily smoked his cigarettes into the night.

The wind did not return. The two climbers slept some and woke early to a pink dawn, and began their descent of the steep face. They were tired, and they were distracted—by memories of the climb; by their wish to preserve certain of those memories, by their relief at having it done. Chris reminded himself to be afraid. He reviewed the risks: a rappel anchor might fail; a sharp edge might saw through a rope; he might let go of the rope with his brake hand; the rope might dislodge a rock or jam behind a flake. They passed the Italians two rope-lengths down from the shoulder; the party had spent the night on the route and would finish the climb today. The climbers exchanged wry looks and greetings, and the British continued down.

Ian and Derek and Vic were waiting at the col between the North and Central towers. Don tossed the doubled ropes down for another rappel, which deposited him and then Chris on a pedestal some 15 feet above their friends, who were shouting and waving a bottle of whisky at them. Don tugged on the rappel rope one last time; it plummeted past to slither into a crack below his stance. It was stuck there; he couldn't work it free quickly enough to suit his impatience. He picked up the fixed rope—the rope that had broken under his weight at the start of the climb—and lowered his body the last few feet. Chris followed and as his weight came onto the rope it broke again. He fell like a stone and hit snow that didn't stop him and slid onto rock; here he began to tumble, rolling and snatching at passing bits of ground as his friends looked on in horror. His body skidded to a stop at the brink of a 500-foot drop.

He took some time to find his feet. He felt guilt at his unforgivable foolishness. He had in his haste trusted to luck and luck had nearly failed him. He realized as he stood that he had sprained his ankle or perhaps broken it.

Ian and Derek lingered for a few moments and left to make an attempt on the North Tower. Chris and Don made their way down to Camp Two. Bonington, still in a state of near-shock, wrote a report for the *Telegraph*. Don asked him to make spaghetti. Chris set about the task as mindless for the moment as a weary child.

The peace he had found on the Central Tower soon dissipated. He took another two days to hobble down to Base Camp. Ian and Derek had climbed the North Tower. The rest of the team was now planning an attempt on the South Tower in hopes that the fine weather would persist. Chris and Wendy left for a hospital in Punta Arenas, where Chris learned that his ankle had suffered a hairline fracture. He spent a boring and uncomfortable week in the hospital, a plaster cast on his ankle. He played Scrabble with Wendy. She often beat him at the game; once he threw the board out of the window.

One day a quiet, silver-haired character poked his head through the doorway of the hospital room. Chris recognized the man at once. He was the great English explorer and mountaineer Eric Shipton, still lean and vigorous in his late fifties. He had just returned from two months of grueling exploration in South Patagonia.

That sort of thing was routine for Shipton, who had made path-breaking expeditions in the '30s, often in the company of another great explorer, Bill Tilman. The two of them had explored huge tracts of difficult ground in Asia and Africa, and had climbed high peaks on both continents. They planned their expeditions on the backs of envelopes, subsisting for months on tea and dried meat, accompanied by tiny teams of porters. Shipton also had climbed with several Everest expeditions, and he had been the original choice to lead the 1953 trip to the peak—the one that finally climbed the mountain. He'd lost out on that job, in part because he was more interested in exploration than in summits. He had since faded from the scene. He'd had financial problems, and had become a rather sad character in the eyes of his contemporaries.

The young Chris Bonington and others of his generation saw Eric Shipton differently—as a shining figure, an exemplar of a simpler and cleaner approach to mountain exploration. Chris and his comrades would rediscover Shipton's lightweight approach in the years to come. They would help to redefine its limits, once they had exhausted the potential of the traditional siege-style expedition.

All of that lay ahead. Chris for now was struck by the older man's apparent happiness; Shipton seemed well content with the unsettled life he'd pursued. He told Bonington of his most recent adventure. He'd gone off to investigate a volcano—wanted to know if it was active—and had spent seventeen days on the move in appalling weather, circumnavigating the peak without finding a way to its summit, living mostly on porridge and meat bars. Someone had forgotten to bring salt for the porridge but Shipton told Chris it hadn't really mattered—he proposed to leave it behind on the next trip as well.

Chris and Wendy returned to England as winter ended. Chris continued to lecture, traveling the countryside in his van. His fame had not entirely faded. Audiences were still eager to hear about the Eiger, and the Patagonia venture had made a small stir. He enjoyed the attention and he was glad of the money the lectures brought in. But he felt at certain moments swamped by his ambition and troubled by the nature of it. He understood that he wished to achieve great things so as to be beyond the world's reproach, and this seemed a poor motivation.

His thoughts at times returned to his encounter with the aging explorer. Eric Shipton had sacrificed the greatest opportunity of his generation—the chance to lead the first successful assault on Everest. He had maintained his integrity and his appreciation for the joys of exploration. Chris increasingly felt his own wish to be happy. This wish allowed him to enjoy his connection to his intelligent and gifted young wife, to climbing and climbers, to his stories and the memories that sustained them, to the mountain landscapes near his Lake District home. He awoke some mornings in bed with Wendy as if in a fog-shrouded meadow, unsure of where or who he was and blissful in his ignorance. And then, as thoughts formed, he would feel a sense of exposure, of all there was to lose.

6

B ONINGTON DIDN'T KNOW it yet, but he wasn't through with the Eiger and its notorious North Face—although this time, he would encounter it on very different terms. The ascent of Patagonia's Central Tower of Paine had marked a step in climbing's accelerating evolution toward smaller teams on harder routes. That movement had taken on another dimension in recent years. The best young climbers in Europe looked to climb the hardest alpine walls by the most direct routes possible: they spoke of climbing the line followed by a drop of water falling from the summit. This uncompromising stance stood as a rebuke to anyone who merely meandered up a wall's weak spots, as Chris and Ian had done on the Eiger.

As it happened, the Eiger's North Face was an obvious candidate for a more direct ascent. The existing route snaked its way up and across the face from the right side to the left, detouring around a series of difficulties and hazards. Climbers now began to search in earnest for a line that would run directly from base to summit. This new challenge became the latest in a series of Last Great Problems for mountaineers in the Alps.

Two Polish climbers made the first attempt on the Eiger Direct during the winter of 1963, only months after Chris and Ian had made their ascent of the North Face. The Poles chose to climb in winter, when the cliff's features were frozen, to reduce the risk of rockfall. The Poles turned back in bad weather. Other mountaineers continued to ponder the potential for a Direct Route—the *Direttissima*—on the Eiger. The most determined of those climbers was a handsome young American by the name of John Harlin.

HARLIN HAD MADE the first American ascent of the Eiger's North Face in 1962, barely a week before Chris finally climbed the route. Like Bonington, the American was ambitious and insecure, a gifted, moody, self-involved young man—but there were differences. Harlin had a more urgent need to be admired; he inhabited a more ramshackle myth of himself. Harlin's moods went deeper; his bouts of manic enthusiasm were more intense, more likely to get him into trouble.

His qualities were appealing to some men and women; they also could be dangerous to John and the people who relied upon him. The myth he created was a romantic one; he saw himself as someone in pursuit of experience and truth. He wanted to think of himself as an extraordinary man connected to other extraordinary men. He wrote in his journals of wanting *a certain oneness, a penetration of one life into another.* These visions distracted him, made him careless at times.

Harlin—like Bonington—had a touch of boyishness, but no one took Harlin for frail. Other climbers called him the Blond God. He could be imperious and demanding, and he looked like someone's notion of a Nordic deity—yellow hair and piercing eyes, square jaw and sturdy bearing. It often seemed that he wished to become a god of sorts: an irreproachable version of himself.

He was born in Kansas City, Missouri in 1935, and spent his first seven years there. He was—again like Bonington—an only child, and a woman raised him. He was named for his father, an airline pilot who bought him a shotgun and took him on hunting and fishing trips. But the boy spent most of his time with his mother, Sue Harlin. She was a tall, strong-willed woman with artistic tendencies—she was a talented amateur painter.

The family lived in Paris for several years after the war. They moved back to the United States when John was a young teenager. He finished high school in Redwood City, California. He was good at sports, and he was proud of his body and his looks. He wore shorts and tight T-shirts; he tried to get his cowlick to stay flat. He took his two dogs for long walks in the hills near home. He wasn't popular, but people noticed and remembered him. He had lovely manners. He surprised his mother's friends by talking to them about interior decoration and women's fashions—he'd learned about clothes on shopping trips with his mother in Paris.

John finished high school in 1953. He spent the summer at a military school designed to prepare him for the Naval Academy— his father's idea. John didn't like the drilling or the uniforms, so he came home and enrolled at Stanford. He was taking shape as a character. His behavior became flamboyant and even erratic. He joined a fraternity and played on the Stanford football team; meanwhile, he posed for nude photographs that ended up in a magazine, causing a minor scandal. He learned to climb with the Stanford Alpine Club, doing some routes in Yosemite. The Club suspended him for using unsafe climbing techniques, and he brushed aside the rebuke. They were merely playing at climbing; John told people that he meant to be a real mountaineer.

His father's airline job provided the family with free plane tickets. John flew to Europe in the summer of 1954 with the idea of climbing the Eiger's notorious North Face. He arrived in Switzerland and made his way to Kleine Scheidegg, where he pondered the face through the hotel telescope. He came home without doing the route, but he had managed to rope up with the newly famous Sherpa Tenzing Norgay—touring Europe after his Everest ascent—to inspect the lower reaches of the Eiger's North Face.

He went back to school and met a girl, a Stanford junior named Marilyn Miler. He courted her with flowers and stories of his Eiger visit. He confided that a thug with a knife had tried to rob him that summer, and told Marilyn that he'd responded by killing the would-be thief—put a wrestling hold on him and broke his neck. He returned to the Alps in the summer of 1955, roping up with an American law student for a failed attempt on the Matterhorn's North Face. John wrote Marilyn a postcard claiming that he'd climbed the route; he would later include this fictional ascent on his application to the American Alpine Club.

John meanwhile had decided to study fashion design. He stopped in Paris on his way home from Europe and managed to meet the designer Pierre Balmain, who invited the young man up to his country house for the weekend. One afternoon, young Harlin surprised Balmain and two other guests—the three were playing cards at a table outside—by entering the garden dressed only in a pair of tight red shorts. John would later claim that he'd worked as a designer for both Balmain and Christian Dior.

He was very young—still twenty years old—but his story was picking up speed. He returned to Stanford in the fall of 1955 and married Marilyn. He changed his major to fine arts—with a con-centration in dress and costume design—and joined the Air Force ROTC. He took to sleeping with a gun under his pillow.

He finished school in 1957, and spent the next two years in pilot training. The Air Force in 1959 approved his request for assignment to Germany's Rhineland, within easy driving distance of the Alps. The Harlins by now had two small children, John III and Andrea.

Harlin would spend another four years in the military, flying out of Hahn Air Force Base. He made a certain reputation as a climber, making repeated attempts on many of the Alps' most serious routes. He got up a handful of impressive climbs with his Stanford friend Gary Hemming and one or two others. The Eiger's North Face remained his great ambition. He was successful on his fifth attempt, reaching the summit on August 22, 1962.

John's success on the Eiger, the first ascent by an American, made him a figure in climbing circles. He left the Air Force in 1963 to take a teaching position at the American School in Leysin, Switzerland—a short drive from Kleine Scheidegg and the Eiger. Harlin by now had his eyes on the Eiger Direct. He made three reconnaissance trips to the face: one in the summer of 1963, two more the following winter. Those forays confirmed that the route should be climbed during the winter to reduce the risk from rockfall —and that it would require a team of very strong climbers.

JOHN HARLIN FOUND one of those climbers during the summer of 1964, when he came across a Scottish climber named Dougal Haston. Haston, twenty-four, had made a series of hard winter climbs in Scotland and the Alps. His Eiger credentials were good; he'd made the first Scottish ascent of the North Face. He was a formidable character, another talented misfit with outsized ambitions and an erratic temperament. Unlike John Harlin, Dougal didn't court or seduce people. Still, certain types were drawn to him, saw in him something they recognized or lacked. He was lanky, oddly attractive: people noticed his long, gaunt face with its deep-set eyes, all of it framed by an unruly mop of hair. He cultivated a kind of coldness. He was prone to long silences and occasional outbursts of drunken violence. He dressed like a beatnik's idea of a Romance poet. He kept a journal filled with accounts of his climbs and with philosophical ramblings; he quoted Nietzsche and at moments imagined himself a philosopher *Ubermensch.*

Like Harlin, he'd noted the potential for a Direct Route on the Eiger. All those acres of rock, and only one route—it seemed wrong to him. And he *liked* the Eiger. Other climbers did the route and moved on, vastly relieved to have it done. They were drawn back to their lives and their homes; Dougal felt himself drawn back to the face.

He had come to climbing from a working-class background. His father was a baker in Currie, six miles from Edinburgh. Dougal's mother worked as a domestic servant. Currie had a tannery and a couple of paper mills. The countryside during Dougal's childhood—he was born in 1940—was mostly farmland, with grazing for sheep and cattle. The village lay on a ridge near a river: the Water of Leithe, filthy from the tannery and the mills. Dougal made his first climbs there in the early '50s, traversing the walls along the river's bank—much as Don Whillans had done a decade earlier on the Irwell near Manchester. He climbed Currie's stone church one night with two other boys—James Moriarty and Jim Stenhouse. The three of them called their wall the Currie Eiger. They made their first real rock climb together in 1954, when the Currie Youth Club ventured to Glencoe. The three friends continued to practice on railroad bridges, and passed around mountaineering books—their favorite was *Nanga Parbat Pilgrimage* by Herman Buhl, the great Austrian mountaineer.

Dougal's friends by now knew him as a daredevil and something of a loner: a long-limbed, pigeon-toed eccentric. He often strode off ahead of his companions during trips to the local hills. He began a journal of his mountain experiences when he was sixteen—he made his first entry in July 1956—and maintained it for the next twenty years.

He outgrew his mentors in the Currie Youth Club, moving on to other teachers. A young Edinburgh shipwright named Ronnie Marshall—brother of Jimmy Marshall, a leading Scottish climber—taught him rope skills. Marshall also recruited Dougal—together with Moriarty and Stenhouse—to the Junior Mountaineering Club of Scotland, which ran trips to the country's various ranges.

Dougal knew already that he liked to drink. He was a mean drunk. He would start fights and let his friends step in to finish them; the hulking Moriarty, known to his mates as Big Eley, was very good at this work. Dougal's behavior stood out even in the Scottish climbing scene, increasingly populated by informal clubs of students and workers that could seem as much street gangs as recreational clubs.

These young Scottish climbers—like their counterparts at English clubs such as the famous Rock and Ice—brought to mountaineering a knee-jerk antiestablishment attitude. They backed up their bad attitude with a violent streak and the ambition to reinvent their lives through climbing. Dave Agnew, a member of Glasgow's famous Creagh Dhu—a club known for boozing and brawling almost as much as for climbing—later recalled his first day in the mountains. He had looked out across to the smog over Clydebank and seen blue sky for the first time—he hadn't known such a thing existed.

Dougal and his friends spent many nights at a ramshackle Creagh Dhu hut near Glencoe. Dougal meanwhile found another mentor in Robin Smith. Smith, the son of a naval architect, was nineteen, two years older than Dougal. He was pursuing a philosophy degree at Edinburgh University, where his studies came easily to him; schoolwork was only a minor distraction from the climbing that had absorbed him for three years. Smith had an appetite for extremely difficult climbs undertaken in all conditions, and a reckless grace that appealed to both men and women. His boldness was different from Dougal's, which was often clumsy, as if reflecting a wish to forget or to bludgeon. Dougal was a striking figure, with his melancholy, his hunger, his edgy vulnerability—but his version of recklessness was something to look away from; it betrayed desperation.

He joined Robin Smith at Edinburgh University, enrolling in the philosophy program in the fall of 1959. Robin suggested the move; they could do their reading at night, leaving days free to climb. Dougal grew his hair long and cultivated an image as a hard-drinking philosopher—he took to wearing tight moleskin trousers and a scarf—but he was still a teenager, troubled and self-centered, and he didn't fit in at Edinburgh. There were snobs who wanted to know where he'd been to school, young women who wanted to talk to him in clubs and bars, tutors and school-work. He stuck with his old climbing friends. Robin had friends in the philosophy department, and went to their parties. Dougal remained aloof.

He continued to climb. He read his Nietzsche. He drank with intensity and purpose; people noticed and remembered his drink-ing. He would drink in pubs with other climbers; he would con-tinue with girls and loud music at the rooms kept by the Scottish Mountaineering Club; long after midnight, he would wander into the Club library to read mountaineering journals until he fell asleep on the floor—he wouldn't stop drinking or go home. Some nights, the climbers would box or wrestle; Dougal might choose an opponent and try to hurt him. He was still starting fights with strangers, still leaving Eley Moriarty to finish them. Dougal would go off to drink himself to sleep, awaking baffled and ashamed.

He was ambitious and talented. There still was the possibility that climbing would not always be necessary to him, that it was merely a bridge to the rest of the world—but two things happened to make climbing still more a matter of urgency, of need.

The first occurred in 1962. Robin Smith joined a British-Soviet expedition to the Russian Pamirs. Dougal stayed home to work nights at a frozen food warehouse in Maidstone, earning money for the Alps. He planned to meet Robin there; they'd talked of climbing the Eiger together. Dougal finished his shift one morning and picked up a newspaper to come upon the news that Robin was dead at twenty-three.

The details came later. Smith had been descending an easy snow slope, roped to Everest veteran and scholar-poet Wilfred Noyce. One of the climbers had slipped—the rest of the party had agreed not to say which man—and the pair had fallen some 4,000 feet.

Dougal found that he couldn't bring any reasonable feelings to bear on Robin's death; what surfaced was mostly a familiar blurred shame. He made a stab at the Eiger that summer with Andrew Wightman, another Edinburgh climber and a friend of Robin's. The climbers retreated in a storm; Wightman slipped on wet rock and broke an ankle.

Dougal did almost no schoolwork that fall. He thought of quitting university altogether. He returned to the Eiger the following season, the summer of 1963. This time, he roped up with Rusty Baillie, a young climber from Rhodesia. They climbed iced-over rock and green icefalls to reach the top in three days. The ascent made headlines at home. Dougal finally quit school later that year, with the idea that he might somehow make a career out of climbing.

He headed for the Alps again in 1964, and bumped into a London climber named Bev Clark at a Chamonix campsite. They climbed the West Face of the Dru, the route that had sealed the reputations of Joe Brown and Don Whillans a decade earlier. Dougal and Bev were celebrating their accomplishment in a subsidized workers' cafeteria—they were turning over a plan to tackle the Walker Spur—when a big, blond American approached their table.

Bev Clark knew John Harlin slightly, and he introduced him to Dougal. The American and the Scot eyed one another appraisingly. John didn't waste time; he'd come to invite the two Brits to join him on the Shroud—the huge unclimbed ice field to the left of the Walker Spur. Clark had relatively little experience on ice, and he bowed out. He understood at any rate that he wasn't in the same league as these two. John and Dougal made the attempt on the Shroud. A storm forced them to retreat, but they agreed to climb together again.

Dougal ran out of money and went back to England. Bev Clark had family money, and he bankrolled an informal climbing school, with Dougal and Big Eley Moriarty as instructors. The teaching was sporadic. Dougal did odd jobs on the side, mostly painting rich Londoners' apartments with Eley. When he had a little cash, he returned to the Alps. He took up residence in John Harlin's concrete basement in Leysin, subsisting on Leysin School leftovers. He got his first taste of winter climbing in the range: extreme cold, high winds, deep snow, brutal approaches. The nature of the climbing made sense to him, made him feel briefly clean.

John told Dougal of his plans for a Direct Route on the Eiger. Dougal agreed to join him. Dougal was now far along in the task of inventing himself. His posturing protected him from anyone who might judge him for his background or identify some weakness. His need for such protection led him into various kinds of disguise and retreat, but he wanted the mountains to be real—and the Eiger was very real to him.

John for his part felt the Eiger's pull partly as the lure of fame and the romance of risk and death. But he also carried an authentic desire to know what the mountain could tell him about the nature of things apart from his mixed-up and occasionally childish emotional life. The Eiger's glamour seduced him but he saw that something deeper was at stake, and this helped to draw him on.

John and Dougal visited the lower reaches of the North Face together in the winter of 1965. They floundered in snow that came to their waists to arrive at the start of a low band of rock—the first real obstacle for climbers attempting the new route. It looked hard. They resolved to return the following winter.

They fell out soon after. Dougal had grown sick of John's basement and fed up with the American's big talk. He returned to Scotland and went to work in a climbing shop. He went climbing with friends on Easter Saturday. Eley Moriarity was with him. Rain drove them off the rock and into a pub. They drank for a time and decided to make the thirty-five-mile trip to Glencoe—there was a party at Ian Clough's house; there was a dance somewhere; there were more bars to visit.

A small group piled into the van Bev Clark had lent to Haston and Moriarty for their climbing school. Moriarty drove. The group dropped a couple of friends in Glencoe, and the main party stopped to drink at a climbers' bar. They left that bar and traveled another ten miles to the Clachaig Inn, and drank there until closing time. Dougal was still learning to drive, and when the party left the bar and went out to the van he insisted on taking the wheel, fending off the protests of Moriarty and another friend.

He set off in the dark down the winding, single-track road. He had been drinking most of the day; it was raining. The walkers were invisible until he was upon them—James Orr, eighteen, a student from Glasgow, took most of the impact, suffering severe head and chest injuries.

Dougal got out of the van and drifted away from the horrible scene. He wandered through the rain to a friend's cottage and spent the night there. Moriarty, his friend and protector, stayed behind with two of the van's other passengers—one was a nurse—and tried to help the injured teenagers. Moriarty tracked Dougal down the next day, and convinced him that he must turn himself in to the police.

James Orr died of his injuries the following week. Jimmy Marshall, who with his brother Ronnie had played a role in Dougal's climbing development, believed that Dougal was essentially unmoved by the consequences of his carelessness; that he cared only about himself and the trouble the accident brought upon him. But something had changed in the moments after the collision. Dougal's wish to hide had blossomed in him as though some vessel had ruptured. He surrendered to his need to make up stories, to retreat, to fend off the real.

Even so, his shame gained traction and momentum. Dougal fled through the wet dark and his mind filled with notions he couldn't contemplate. He saw things from a distance during the weeks that followed: the blurry fact that he had killed another young person, that he had cut himself off from the community of men who had not done murder. He felt his claims to happiness or success permanently compromised. He was young, not far removed from the newness and sheer surprise of childhood, but now these disasters: Robin Smith, and now this young stranger; loss, and now this sin.

His early dealings with death would define Dougal's future relationships. His loss and guilt drew him deeper into a life of extreme climbing even as he drew apart from other ties and pursuits. His confusion and shame helped draw him to certain other climbers; he recognized their wish to be clean, to be insignificant; to leave the web of desire and consequence in exchange for a life that promised absolutes, clarity. He told himself that certain climbers wanted to know the nature of things; that they kept each other company in this. And he nursed the whispering fear that such a life wasn't possible; that he and his chosen companions were in retreat from life, not in pursuit of it.

Dougal was sentenced to sixty days in jail for his crime. He entered Glasgow's Barlinnie Prison in July of 1965. He served his time quietly, working in the prison library. He left prison in September, and almost immediately got drunk and wrecked a Ferrari that belonged to Jimmy Marshall's business partner. Harlin called to patch things up—they hadn't spoken since parting the previous winter. He wanted to know if Dougal still wanted to climb the Eiger Direct.

HARLIN'S TEAM BY now included Chris Bonington. Chris had returned from Patagonia in early 1963 with his vague notions of building a career as an adventure photojournalist. He still had his memoir to write—he was far behind schedule—but the advance had been modest, and his financial prospects seemed hazy at best. Meanwhile, he needed a place to live with Wendy; something cheap but cozy, near good climbing. They went looking for a cottage in England's rural Lake District and were dismayed at the rents.

One Sunday they stopped at a pub for a meal, and Chris chatted with the bartender—a young climber named Mick Burke. Mick knew something about living on the cheap; he made a living at manual labor and tending bar, jobs that left him time to climb. He had spent the previous winter in a room over a farmer's garage. He suggested that the Boningtons might wish to drop by and speak to the farmer.

They did so. The room had bare plaster walls and rotten linoleum floors; the toilet was an earth closet set behind a pigsty—but the door to the room opened upon a view of fields and hills and forest. Chris and Wendy lived there for three months; in early

1963, they became tenants of a small lodge on another Lake District farm. They stayed friendly with Mick Burke. Chris did some routes with him, and the two climbers got on well. Mick was a bit like Whillans; he had a sharp, down-to-earth wit, and he had ambitions. But there was more warmth and less violence in Mick; then again, he didn't climb as well as Don.

Chris had begun to chip away at his book; he also continued to pick up income from lecturing on the Eiger climb. He spent part of the summer in Zermatt with his old friend Hamish MacInnes. The pair planned to make a low-budget film about climbing the Matterhorn's North Face; they hoped to sell the film to television. The weather didn't cooperate. They managed to climb the normal route on the peak, but the film came to nothing.

Wendy by now was pregnant. She gave birth to the couple's first child, Conrad, during the final hours of 1963. She had strong domestic instincts, and settled in to mother the new child. Chris was amazed at the strength of his own attachment to Conrad. Fatherhood also intensified his wish to make some sort of career.

He was now thirty. He had accomplished little as a climber the previous year, and 1964 was no better. He made a few minor climbs that summer in the Alps, with Joe Brown and the Scottish climber Tom Patey. He returned home that fall to give still more Eiger lectures, and to try to finish his book; the manuscript was now more than a year overdue. He still had no clear sense of how he would support himself and his family. He suffered bouts of anxiety; the possibility of outright failure frightened him deeply.

Things began to look up during the first weeks of 1965. A young television producer invited Bonington to participate in a climbing documentary. Chris starred that spring in a televised ascent of a new rock climb in Somerset's Cheddar Gorge. The I TV paid him a little money; meanwhile, he managed to finish his book.

Chris and Wendy celebrated by moving again, this time to an unfurnished cottage in the northwest of the Lake District. Tom Patey had invited Chris to a conference of international climbers in Chamonix, and Chris left in July. Wendy followed a bit later with Conrad, arriving at the end of the conference. The party drove to Leysin to meet Rusty Baillie, the young Rhodesian who had climbed the Eiger with Dougal Haston two years earlier.

The three climbers composed a list of potential objectives for the season. The list included a Direct Route on the Eiger's North Face. Patey knew of John Harlin's designs on the route, and suggested that as long as they were in the neighborhood, they should pay the Blond God a visit. John had left his position at the American School to found his own establishment, the grandly named International School of Modern Mountaineering. He had recruited several prominent climbers—including Don Whillans and the American big wall expert Royal Robbins—to work with him as part-time instructors.

Bonington didn't expect to like Harlin. He had heard—by way of Whillans, among others—that the American was an insufferable poser. Chris also saw Harlin as a potential rival for the Eiger Direct. But John surprised him; Chris was struck by the American's vitality and by his impulsive generosity. Harlin proposed joining forces on the Eiger Direct, and Chris, acting on impulse, agreed.

Harlin was in fact finding it hard to assemble a team of first-rate climbers for the route. His resumé was impressive, but at least some of the credit belonged to his partners. There was some feeling among other alpinists that Harlin's vision and his promotional talent exceeded his considerable abilities as a mountaineer. This latest venture, the Eiger Direct, sounded extremely ambitious and potentially very dangerous.

Chris and John agreed it would be wise to postpone the Eiger attempt until the end of the season, in hopes that cooler nights would reduce the risk of rockfall. Meanwhile, Chris and his party set up camp on the grounds of the climbing school. John taught Chris to use jumars—handheld devices that would slide up a rope and then grip it when weighted; they made it easier for a climber to ascend a fixed rope. The weather grew cooler, but it wasn't settled enough for the Eiger. The Boningtons departed for home, with Chris promising to return for an attempt on the Eiger Direct during the coming winter.

Chris and Wendy settled in back at their cottage in the Lake District, where Chris soon began to worry about the wisdom of his promise to Harlin. The American's relentlessly demanding presence had worn on Bonington. One incident in particular rankled. John had neglected to mention that climbers who use jumars to climb a free-hanging fixed rope generally tie a knot in the bottom of the rope; the knot prevents the climber from sliding off the end if the jumars slip. Chris in his ignorance had failed to take this simple precaution—a potentially fatal mistake. The incident bothered him.

He worried about the weather, too. John had estimated that climbing the Eiger Direct could take ten days. There was every chance that a winter storm would catch the climbers high on the face, where retreat might be difficult or impossible.

Chris shared his doubts with Wendy; having done so, he felt compelled to withdraw from the venture. The decision threw him into one of his periodic funks. His climbing career had stalled, and so had his writing—apart from his book, he'd written only one short piece for the *Daily Telegraph* magazine. But now the magazine's editor called with another assignment. The *Telegraph* had negotiated exclusive rights to cover John Harlin's Eiger Direct climb. They had assigned a reporter—a young fellow named Peter Gillman—but wanted Bonington to go along as photographer.

It seemed the perfect compromise. He would take part in the venture, but as an independent observer. Chris flew to Zurich on February 8, and took the train to Kleine Scheidegg. John Harlin was already there, with Dougal Haston and an American rock climber, Layton Kor; the three climbers were installed in the attic of a hotel outbuilding.

Chris knew Dougal Haston slightly, but they had not climbed together. The Scot somehow put him in mind of a cowboy. Layton Kor—a gangly 6' 4" bricklayer from Boulder, Colorado—made Chris think of a puppy. John had met Layton during a visit to the United States, and had invited him to join the Eiger Direct Team after Chris backed out.

The young men seemed barely adequate to their task. For starters, there were just the three of them. Dougal had a strong record in Scotland and the Alps, and had made a few winter alpine climbs. Layton was famous back in Colorado for climbing hard rock routes (sometimes at night), and he had made a handful of hard alpine ascents in Colorado and the Alps. Still, he had limited winter climbing experience, a considerable handicap given the party's objective. Harlin had significant alpine experience, but was by most accounts a less gifted climber than the other two.

John had designed the expedition to make the most of limited manpower. His initial plan ruled out fixed ropes and established camps. He believed that the team could expect several ten-day windows of settled conditions during the winter. He meant to wait for such a window, and take advantage of it to power up the face in good alpine style; the three climbers would carry all of their gear and shelter on their backs.

That vision began to fade almost immediately. The team had accumulated huge amounts of gear—far too much to lug up through the deep snow on the Eiger's lower slopes. Dougal and Chris caught a train up to the Eiger Station, where the track tunneled into the North Face. They left the train, and lowered bags of food and ropes out of the window to the snow below the first Rock Band. That done, they took the train back down to Kleine Scheidegg and retired to their rooms to wait for better climbing conditions.

The weather improved, but John—showing off on skis— dislocated his shoulder. The three official expedition members retreated to Leysin. Chris agreed to stay and keep an eye on things at Kleine Scheidegg. He was having breakfast at the hotel one morning when a waiter called his attention to a group of tiny figures in the distance. The figures were engaged in some sort of activity at the bottom of the face.

A TEAM OF eight Germans had begun a siege-style assault on the Eiger Direct—a huge threat to Harlin's hopes for a first ascent of the route. The new team's size would allow them to stock a series of camps, linked by fixed ropes. They could use the ropes to ferry gear and climbers up and down the steep face—in effect borrowing the tactics of Himalayan climbers, adapting them to much steeper ground. It made sense: the Germans could make steady progress during brief periods of good weather, and use the fixed ropes to beat a temporary retreat at the onset of a storm. They might even be able to ride out bad weather on the face, leaving them in position to resume the climb from their high camp as soon as conditions improved.

Chris telephoned the news to John and the others, who rushed back from Leysin the next morning. Already, the Germans had fixed rope on the first 1,500 feet of the route. It was obvious that John's team must change their tactics or give up their dreams of a first ascent. They would need to establish their own camps on the face, fixing ropes between them. That meant they would need at least four climbers—one pair to push out the route and create the line of fixed ropes; another pair to ferry more ropes and gear up behind them.

Chris was an obvious candidate to join the expedition as its fourth climber. He hesitated. His concerns about climbing under Harlin's direction had deepened. John on one or two occasions had struck him as unstable. There had been one moment in particular, with Chris jammed into a phone cubicle, on the line with his editors at the *Telegraph*, trying to relay to them John's increasingly unreasonable demands. John had loomed over him, growing increasingly angry; the American had used his physical presence as a weapon, a threat.

Bonington set aside his doubts. The climb was taking shape as something that mattered. He had a notion that the Eiger Direct was a sort of next step for climbers. He wanted to be part of that, whatever his doubts about Harlin. He told himself he'd be better able to photograph the expedition if he joined the climbing team. It made sense, and it made him a climber again.

He wasn't happy, though. He was scared.

DOUGAL HASTON AND Layton Kor left the hotel at three o'clock in the morning on February 20. They reached the bottom of the route and climbed the German's fixed ropes for two pitches before abandoning them. The climbing here was easy, and they needed to come to grips with the face itself. They soon passed the German high point, and climbed more ice and snow to reach the slopes below the Eiger station window. Here they dug a platform, made tea and studied their next problem: the First Rock Band, a 300-foot rock wall laced with thin cracks.

Layton spent the next four hours building a ladder up the wall's lower reaches—tapping knife-blade pitons into shallow cracks; hanging etriers from the pitons; stepping cautiously up to gain a few feet; reaching high into the next crack to hammer in another knife-blade. It was delicate, painstaking work, entirely absorbing. He felt the cold and the exposure and the knowledge that a piton could pop and send him sprawling through the air to weight the next peg. He knew that such a fall might create a zipper effect as his momentum grew, multiplying the forces on each successive piton until he hit a ledge or his weight came directly onto the perhaps dubious anchor that held his belayer to the cliff. Layton did not fall; he made some 90 feet of progress, then drilled a hole and placed a bolt. He clipped a carabiner to

the bolt, threaded a rope through the carabiner and rappelled from the new anchor.

The wind rose and snowflakes drifted past the climbers' faces; there were black clouds building to the north. Dougal and Layton spent an uncomfortable night on their sloping ledge beneath the Eiger Station window. They fended off powder avalanches, and listened to the wind; it gusted up to 100 miles per hour. They retreated to Kleine Scheidegg in the morning with a sense that they had undertaken something very difficult.

The storm continued for two days. John Harlin meanwhile talked things over with the leaders of the German Expedition: Peter Haag, twenty-eight, and Jörg Lehne, thirty. The American and the Germans agreed that their respective expeditions would follow slightly different routes to the top of a feature known as the Second Rock Band. The two routes might converge after that, since there might be only one way to the top of the face.

Chris had decided that he needed a climbing partner who could serve as a photographer's assistant. Don Whillans, teaching at John's school in Leysin, accepted the job; he arrived at Kleine Scheidegg on February 27. Chris and Dougal and Layton set off for the fixed ropes at the base of the route early the next morning. John and Don followed later with supplies. The team spent a week digging and improving a snow cave at the base of the First Band and ferrying food and ropes and other gear to the cave. They made more progress on the route, fending off the constant powder avalanches that poured down the face—the powder flowed or trickled soundlessly across the ice, reminding Chris of sand in an hourglass.

Chris and Dougal reached the top of the First Band on March 4. They retreated to the snow cave to rest and to brew tea. John and Layton came up with more supplies that afternoon, and the four climbers plotted their next move—up a gully to the start of the

Second Rock Band. It grew dark and it began to snow; the snow
blew into the crowded cave, making it impossible to stay dry.

Peter Gillman, the *Telegraph* reporter, had become the expedition's unofficial Base Camp manager down at the hotel. The
climbers made radio contact with him in the morning. Gillman
informed them the weather forecast called for two days of snow.
Chris and Layton retreated to Kleine Scheidegg to sit out the
storm. Don meanwhile had quit the expedition after suffering
a bout of vertigo on the face; the ailment, probably caused by a
condition involving his inner ear, had troubled him before. At
any rate, he'd hated the circus atmosphere that had grown up
around the climb—too many gawking tourists, too much rub-
bish in the press.

John and Dougal stayed up at the snow cave so that they could
go back to work on the route as soon as conditions improved.
They spent much of the day fighting off spindrift—particles of
windblown snow that accumulated on their clothes and sleeping bags and gear, melting in the stale air of their cave so that
everything became more or less wet. The two climbers stuffed
socks and other debris in gaps at the cave entrance to block the
wind, and tried to sweep out the snow that made its way into their
shelter. They cooked and ate, and maintained radio contact with
Gillman. A group of German climbers arrived at the ledge around
lunchtime. There was an exchange of greetings—courteous but
reserved—before the Germans retreated to their own snow hole,
less than 10 feet away. The hours passed; between tasks, John
and Dougal rested and talked.

Their snow hole was deathly quiet and surprisingly warm, in
spite of the storm. The climbers enjoyed a sense that the world
of bustle and confusion was far away. They lay in the quiet and
thought about what was coming, but any urgency that arose with
such thoughts quickly faded; they were left to contemplate some

mysterious but harmless puzzle. John felt himself invited to come
into some knowledge, but the invitation was gentle. He listened to
the whisper of snow falling on snow. He watched Dougal sleep,
and felt the rise and fall of his own breath.

The snow stopped during the night. John and Dougal left the
cave in the morning; it was Sunday, March 6. The ground looked
a fantastic distance away, but the face felt almost safe to them.
They had been up here before; each man felt himself on familiar
terrain. They climbed the fixed ropes that led to the top of the First
Band. Dougal took the first lead above the ropes. He climbed on
thin ice across sketchy, low-angle rock slabs, kicking tiny holds
with the front-points of his crampons. There were few cracks for
pitons or other protection. He dragged his trailing rope across
the slabs and around corners, and the friction from this created
rope drag that threatened to pull him from his stance. He had to
use one or both hands to haul up slack before he took each new
step. He created a makeshift anchor out of no fewer than seven
dubious piton placements, and brought John up.

Dougal led another difficult pitch to a snowfield, where the
climbing became easier. John led the next pitch, and stumbled on a
natural snow cave at the top. The two climbers went to work with
their axes to expand the shelter, and then settled in for the night.
They told each other that the Second Rock Band looming just
ahead looked reasonable—easier than the First Rock Band.

The night was cold but they were comfortable. They slept well
and awoke to clear skies. They quickly set out again, moving
higher on firm snow; they kicked steps easily and made good
progress. This was one of the pleasures of a bivouac: you woke
up to the climb; no approach to the mountain; less time to worry
or fret. You left sleep and entered the climb like swimmers wading through shallow mud to the bank of a river and stepping

ashore. Here there was no waiting for your life to begin; here
you awoke to it.

Dougal had the dreamy notion that he had lived in some mystery while he slept; also that the mountain had him in its protection. This idea and this feeling made him unafraid. He would
later recall the happiness that possessed him this morning as he
moved up the snow. The mountains awoke his fear but swept it
up into something bigger so that he understood that his fear was
a mere feeling; it meant nothing.

He found a good stance and put John on belay. He glanced
up to see one of the Germans, Karl Golikow, climbing a pitch
just overhead. The two young men exchanged greetings. Another
moment passed and Karl came off, pitching 30 feet amid a heavy
rattling of gear that ended—a strange, backward interruption,
sound broken by silence—when he landed in a snow bank. A beat
or two passed and Golikow picked himself up, brushing snow
from his clothes. The German looked up to smile at Dougal from
a sun-glazed, oddly blurry tangle of fabric and metal and flesh.
Dougal hesitated and returned his smile.

John arrived. Dougal led on to the foot of a gully and into
it. The German and his partner also entered the gully. The two
roped pairs climbed almost together up several pitches of snow
and then onto steeper ice. The climbers fixed ropes at the top of
the difficult pitches. They did this work carefully. A poorly built
anchor could fail; a rope laid over a sharp edge could fray and
part under the weight of a climber. They had all imagined it.
The climber would fall thousands of feet, his legs tangled in the
rope, gathering speed, the falling man spinning and wondering
until a blow set off a last bright explosion; what remained would
continue to bounce and slide and tumble and disintegrate. These
visions flickered at unguarded moments in a kind of brown light,
as if lit by a moon in eclipse.

The Germans turned around at dusk to head down to their snow cave. Dougal and John carried on. They came to a ledge near the top of the Second Band as the night gathered itself. A staring red sun slipped behind a sky half-filled with mountains; the mountains seeming fragments of the void that rose up to meet the higher emptiness of space. Dougal set out to lead a traverse. The night grew still and cold; in the silence he was aware of his position. The sheer immensity of the face was apparent even as he understood that it was very small, a fleck on the face of being. He felt dimly that his knowledge of this could swallow him.

Dougal stood for a moment on good holds and experimented even as the remaining light fled the sky. He scraped his understanding back to what he knew. He was one of two confused young men on a high mountain wall in late winter. He stared at the sunset in his ignorance and felt himself on the verge of happiness; he was alive, inhabited.

He made himself move. The traverse brought him to the top of the Second Band as the face grew entirely dark. John followed him across and the climbers rummaged for a spot to dig a new cave. They couldn't find a suitable snowbank. They scratched out a platform in the ice and pitched their tent near midnight. They crawled into the tent to crouch awkwardly and take off boots and lay out sleeping mats and bags. They went to sleep without eating.

They rose late to yet another fine day. The two Germans from the previous day arrived at the top of the Second Band. John and Dougal watched from their tent as the new arrivals stumbled on a perfect natural snow cave. The Germans took possession of the cave and departed, carrying on up a gully toward the Second Ice Field.

Dougal and John cursed the Germans' luck and rummaged around in the bright morning sun until they found a place to begin digging their own snow hole. Chris and Layton arrived, having climbed the fixed ropes with loads of food and gear. The cave wasn't yet big enough for four climbers, so Layton descended to Kleine Scheidegg, taking a list of items needed on the face: radio batteries, candles, chocolate.

He returned the next morning, making his way up the fixed ropes in the hours before dawn, arriving at the top of the Second Band as the others made ready for another day of climbing. Dougal and John would lead, fixing ropes as they went. Chris and Layton would follow on the ropes, carrying heavier loads. They hoped to climb 800 feet today, to the infamous Death Bivouac; this was the spot where in August of 1935 the first two climbers to attempt the North Face had frozen to death.

The four climbers followed a German fixed rope up a gully that led out of the Second Band. Dougal and John went first, followed by Chris and Layton. Dougal led carefully across the rock below the Flatiron and onto the Second Ice Field. He moved quickly now, kicking steps in the frozen snow; untroubled by the exposure or the Eiger's reputation—it was just climbing and he liked it. John led a pitch of rock above the Second Ice Field. Dougal followed him; the daylight ebbed and it began to snow.

Dougal set out to lead a final traverse that would bring him to the Death Bivouac. The traverse required a sort of sideways crawl across nearly vertical ground. He knew that if he fell he would sweep down and across the face like a pendulum, suspended from his belayer. He would gain momentum as he tumbled or swung; he would smack or brush rock; he might collide with a ledge or corner. His aversion arose in him, familiar, a kind of knowledge; he shook it off and forced himself to move.

The climbing grew harder. The ice was too thin for screws and he climbed without running belays, aware that each step made retreat more unlikely. The day was ending in a fog of snow and wind and darkness; it—the day itself—seemed to rise from the earth as if in departure. Dougal was partly bewildered—by his fear, by the shifts in the light and the view, by the strain of climbing on this ground and choosing not to fall. He was near tears when he finished the pitch, arriving at last at the Death Bivouac. He quickly found a heap of snow that would do for a cave site and began to dig. He had fixed rope across the traverse. The others—John, then Chris and Layton—followed the rope across to the new site.

They took turns digging until the cave was big enough for the four of them. They had left two loads at the start of the previous pitch, but no one volunteered to go back. Chris refused outright; he maintained that he was here to take photographs, not to climb the route for them. Dougal stood at midnight and left the others. He emerged into darkness and set off back across the traverse. He had the party's only working headlamp—even so, he was nearly blind from the wind and cold as he fumbled his way back across the fixed rope. He tripped once, sliding 30 feet in a tangle of limbs and fabric, inexplicably calm, until the rope caught him and he felt his heart lift, his loneliness abate. He finished the crossing and collected the party's stove and fuel and returned to the cave. John left the cave to retrieve the second rucksack while the others melted snow for tea.

John was back in an hour. The night was passing already. It was very early in the morning, still black inside the cave. Some-one lit a candle. Dougal unscrewed a gas cylinder, which wasn't quite empty. The canister caught fire and he hurled it at the cave entrance; it ricocheted off a wall and tumbled back in among the four men. Chris panicked and made a leap for the cave entrance; he was halfway out before he realized that he had nowhere to go—he clutched at snow as the darkness veered up at him.

The canister sailed by his head and disappeared, a flare falling into a night sea. John, the ex-ballplayer, had grabbed the thing on the rebound and thrown a flaming bullet: John Wayne hurling a stray grenade out of a foxhole. Harlin eyed Bonington with something like contempt as everyone settled back into the cave.

Chris was horrified. He blamed his ill-defined role on the mountain had made him fearful enough to behave badly. He was here on the face with the others, but he hadn't made his peace with what that implied. Ordinarily on a hard route he felt exhilaration, a freedom in courting danger. This freedom taught him the taste of life in his mouth, the weight of his body, the color of the light that pooled in his head. He felt nothing like that now; he was only tired and frightened and ashamed.

The climbers brewed drinks and at last settled into their sleeping bags, sprawled half across each other in their snowy lair. They slept fitfully and then more deeply into the light of midmorning. They woke to discover that they had dug their snow cave into a cornice in the darkness of the previous evening; the cave's outer wall overhung the lower reaches of the Third Ice Field. The terrifying view through the hole someone had punched in the bottom of the cave was part of a thicket of facts and possibilities to try to ignore.

The snow had stopped but they were tired; no one was eager to climb. Chris left to descend to the valley. He had film to get out to the *Telegraph*. The others spent the morning organizing the chaos of gear in the cave, and making and drinking more tea. They had climbed for twenty hours without liquid the day before; their thirst seemed unquenchable.

They needed to keep pace with the Germans. Dougal and Layton left the cave at midafternoon. They roped up and Dougal led two steep pitches to the top of the Third Ice Field. Layton led a mixed pitch of rock and ice. They caught the Germans at the base of an arête that led to the route's next major landmark, the Central Pillar. The Germans planned to climb a crack system to the right of the Pillar. Dougal thought it looked too hard. He had his eye on a traverse that led across to a chimney; the traverse looked difficult, but feasible. It was getting late, so he and Layton descended to John at the Death Bivouac.

Snow began to fall as the three men ate their evening meal. It continued to fall as they slept. They woke to overcast skies and made radio contact with Peter Gillman, who told them that more snow was likely. The three climbers conferred, and concluded that Layton should go down. John and Dougal would remain at the Death Bivouac to resume climbing when the weather improved.

Layton set off on his descent, glad to return to the comforts of Kleine Sheidegg. John and Dougal spent much of the day clearing spindrift from their cave, tinkering with their stove—the cold made it temperamental—and chopping ice chips from the back of the cave to melt for tea. The gray, worn light in their shelter oppressed them both. They went to sleep early.

Dougal awoke to find his sleeping bag covered in snow. He fumbled in the dark, cursing, waking John. It took more than an hour to clear the spindrift from their shelter. They settled down to sleep again, and woke in the morning to brew tea and eat dried meat. Every so often, one of them poked his head out of the cave entrance to check on the weather. The storm continued. The day passed in a dank blur. John and Dougal slept and talked between bouts of coping with the snow that continued to find its way into their shelter.

They had known each other for two years. They were both misfits in a world of misfits; even other climbers found them difficult—but they made themselves useful. John's dreams were in part dreams of virtue, as if dreamed in defense of some principle. He had his energy and his fits of manic enthusiasm; he planned and insisted until climbers found themselves engaged in some transformative project; it was as if he made himself partly ridiculous on their behalf. And Dougal had his need to do the work of climbing; once on the hill he had no interest in stopping. He didn't occupy space that other men wanted to occupy; he stayed silent and let them talk and argue and decide.

They both had glamour that was only partly faked. They were genuinely interesting, often attractive. They had violence in them, and imagination; they took chances and showed off. Other climbers responded to them as people respond to characters in certain stories. You could admire their mistakes and wonder why you were so much more careful than they were. You could wish to be more like them even as you understood that they were in some kind of trouble.

Here in the snow cave at the Death Bivouac they made an audience for each other. They talked about climbs. They made plans for Himalayan expeditions; John had his eye on Everest's huge and unclimbed Southwest Face. They talked about food. They fretted about the cornice that encompassed their snow cave; it might conceivably collapse. They listened to wind and to the intermittent hiss of powder avalanches.

They listened for five days and nights. Dougal dreamed three nights running of a third person in the snow hole. He awoke each time to find himself huddled against a wall of the cave, making room for this ghost. John developed a head cold and then a fever. The two of them worried about running out of food, and also about the four-man German party camped near them. John talked about the possibility of a joint summit push with the Germans. He was worried that there might be room for only one team to camp above the Death Bivouac, at a spot on top of the Central Pillar. It would be difficult to pass the Germans if they got there first.

The food ran out as the storm ended. Dougal and John left the snow cave on the morning of March 16. The world opened into something huge again. It was odd to be upright, bathed in daylight. The two men moved like prisoners stepping out of a cell into an empty landscape. Their time in the snow cave was already a dream.

They had been on the route for thirteen consecutive days. They were glad to go down; it took them only a half-hour to descend the fixed ropes. Chris had come up to watch the pair descend through the snowdrifts at the bottom of the route; Peter Gillman came with him. The two pairs greeted one another with shouts and then chatter in the brilliant sunshine.

Chris took a picture of John and Dougal standing in the snow. They posed for him, gripping ski poles and facing away from the mountain. The slopes behind them looked harmless, not steep. The mountain squatted in its own shadow, which stopped at a line not far behind the two men as they struck their respective poses. John peered at the camera through his small eyes; a white headband kept his hair from his face. He looked almost boyish even with the shadow of new beard on his jaw. Dougal with his oddly-shaped head, his thick hair and his deep-set eyes, squinted and grimaced, showing his teeth as he gazed up and off to his right, refusing to acknowledge the photographer. He looked tired, but certain lines had vanished from his face as if he had been relieved of some interior burden. He had lost for the moment the look of an orphan; he looked like someone's son or younger brother.

THE WEATHER HAD changed in a way that felt fundamental and permanent; it was cold but glorious—high, bright, blue skies—when Chris and Layton started up the route the next morning. They fought their way up the fixed ropes; it was awkward work and Chris grew frightened again as the exposure increased. He made an effort to ignore the view as it spun and shimmered at his back—he was practiced at this climber's game of

make-believe—but he was aware of the ropes themselves. They
were beginning to fray in places.

Chris and Layton reached the Death Bivouac that evening.
They woke the next morning to gray skies and very high winds.
They did no climbing that day. Chris lost himself in a comic novel,
Modesty Blaise. Layton napped. They scooped spindrift out of
the cave and talked about the weather.

The sky cleared overnight. They rose early and climbed the
fixed ropes to the bottom of the Central Pillar. Layton led left
and up across rock, smooth and brittle. He found shallow cracks
for piton placements; he clipped his etriers to the pitons to create
a wobbly bridge past the most difficult sections. The sky loomed
at his back; he would pause from time to time and stand in his
nylon steps and take note of the yawning drop at his feet. The
immensity of space seemed alternately to press him into the rock
and gently pluck or tug at him, its rhythms confusing yet comforting. He carried on with his work for three hours, and found
his way at last to a belay around a corner. He peered up into an
ice gully; it led up another 250 feet to the potential bivouac site
at the top of the Central Pillar.

Chris followed Layton across the traverse, dangling anxiously
from each peg as he groped for the next one. Layton's long arms
and legs had let him space the pitons well apart. It was difficult
for even the lanky Bonington to reach from one to the next.

Layton now set off to lead the first pitch of the ice gully. His
experience in Yosemite had taught him how to climb difficult rock,
but he had little technique on ice. He was very slow. He placed
three ice screws low on the pitch, thrashing and muttering and
scaring Chris, whose belay was by no means bombproof. Layton's
screws—no matter how many of them he placed—were next to
useless in the thin ice. A leader fall here would be disastrous,
perhaps fatal to them both.

Chris convinced the American to back off of the pitch, and set out to lead it himself. The ice was steep. Rock showed through it in places. This climbing—difficult, poorly protected—required precision. He cut handholds as well as footholds, careful not to shatter the ice with his chopping. He placed his crampons with particular care, and tested each handhold before weighting it. He understood that every move and judgment was critical—that he was dealing with information that was uncertain, that any mistake or bad luck might kill him.

He was entirely absorbed. He found that he had climbed 30 feet above his last gear. The ice here became even thinner, with no chance for another screw. The rock that lay beneath the ice offered no crack wide enough for one of his pitons. He was aware of his body and a thought rose like a muddy bubble to the surface of his thinking mind: his weight might peel the entire sheet of ice from the face.

The ice had melted out from the rock in places to form a blurry, see-through casing. He gently hammered two holes in it and clung to their fragile edges, which made him think of broken windowpanes. The holds and his purchase on them calmed him even as he knew that this sense of refuge was a lie. He would keep his grip even if it all collapsed; he would sail and tumble with the massive plates of ice. He brushed some switch as if with his elbow or body and the world went quiet. Whispered or even unspoken questions became briefly audible; abstractions were illuminated, visible. He rested on the brink of discovering or remembering some secret.

The silence stopped his thinking. He climbed on in a crystalline fog of concentration. An interior light occasionally flickered; this was his fear. His eyes seeking solace lit upon a snow slope some 20 feet away—the snow might mean he could kick steps. He glanced down between his feet. If he fell he would travel

160 feet before his weight came onto a piton. The piton would fail and he would fall another 40 feet and blow out the anchor. He continued to climb, each step seeming to yield itself to him. He reached the snow and found it was frozen sufficiently for crampons; he'd worried that the stuff would collapse beneath his weight. His relief at this reprieve seemed a betrayal: he had turned away from something. He cut steps in the snow, moving carefully across to a spot at the edge of the Pillar. He built an anchor and savored his rising elation. Layton followed him up the pitch, but it was very late. They descended to the Death Bivouac, reaching it in darkness.

Jörg Lehne approached Chris the next morning to propose that the two teams join forces. Chris hesitated. The Germans weren't making progress on their side of the Pillar. This meant the Harlin expedition would have first crack at establishing a campsite above the Death Bivouac, where the options for sites still appeared very limited. For the first time, Harlin's team had an edge on the Germans. Chris thought John might not want to share credit for the route—but a joint effort would free Chris to concentrate on taking photographs, since John would no longer need him for the actual climbing. Chris had climbed well the previous day; he could back away feeling that he'd contributed something. And he felt strongly that he'd pushed his luck far enough on this climb.

He accepted Lehne's proposal, subject to John's approval. Layton set off up the fixed ropes with one of the Germans—Karl Golikow. Chris would follow later; he stayed behind for the morning radio call and gave John the news. John was concerned about appearances: he didn't want the world to think that the larger German team had hauled his own party up the climb. He agreed to think over the proposal.

Layton and Golikow meanwhile surmounted a final barrier of

crumbling ice blocks to reach the top of the Central Pillar. The German was a big, cheerful man who claimed to have 750 meters of climbing falls to his credit. He took obvious pride in sharing this fantastic statistic with Layton, who watched horrified as his new partner led an entire pitch protected by a single, wobbly piton; at one point the German lost his footing, scrabbling and sliding for several meters before somehow stopping himself. The pair dropped a rope to Chris; he climbed up to take pictures as Layton led another pitch of loose, rotten rock.

The climbers were approaching the White Spider, with its ice field and its leglike gullies. Amid the politics and the climbing, the face retained its power, not merely as an icon but as an actual place. One climber or another would notice a smell or a sound and would enter a sort of spell and forget the others. He would emerge from his spell like a person cured of fever—his questions not answered but for the moment gone.

The day was ending. The climbers returned to the Death Bivouac. Chris continued down, descending the highway of fixed rope, checking and rechecking his set-ups at the top of each rappel. This was just routine, but he remained subject to a dim surprise at finding that a particular rope held him. The vast empty drop at his back seemed to add its burden of weight to the slender cord that supported his own. He knew that each rope—exposed to the elements and to the repeated stress of climbers jostling their way higher and lower—was an element in a system vulnerable to failure. He told himself that this was his last journey up or down the face.

John and Dougal, down at Kleine Scheidegg, had recovered from their five-day stay in the snow cave at the Death Bivouac. They meant to join Layton on the face for a final summit push—perhaps in company with a pair of Germans. Chris meanwhile laid his own plans. He had recruited his friend Mick Burke to replace Whillans as his climbing partner and photo assistant. Chris and Mick would climb the Eiger by its easy West Ridge; from there Chris would photograph Layton and the Germans as they reached the White Spider. Chris and Mick could then dig a cave near the top of the North Face and wait there to photograph a successful summit party.

John and Dougal left Kleine Scheidegg soon after midnight on March 20. They crossed the snow slopes to the fixed ropes in silence. They made good time to the first snow cave, and stopped there to brew tea. Harlin drank his gratefully; he had a persistent, racking cough, a relic of the bronchitis he'd developed at the Death Bivouac.

John was happy. He was living up to the image he had cultivated. The Eiger Direct would make him more difficult to ignore or dismiss. And there was something deeper. He was losing himself and his ambition in the intensity of this work, in these moments. The cold, the glint of moonlight on snow, the effort of coming up the ropes—all of it helped him to forget the man he thought he should become. He became instead something small and sweetly particular in this immensity.

He thought of his children—little blond creatures, more beautiful than himself. He had married young out of a vague but intense need. He had at times experienced the children and the marriage as distractions from what seemed the more important business of building and living inside of his notions of himself. Other times he had understood that Marilyn and the children were central to whatever meaning he might discover. A clumsy and intermittent pursuit of clarity had led him here to this mountain wall. The ache and intensity of the pursuit suggested possibilities of love, of happiness, of peace.

The children were such slight, perfect-looking creatures—he

was proud of their looks and their obvious intelligence. He took credit for them even as he loved them for the proof they offered that the world was beyond his understanding. He didn't know what to make of his children. He told himself that he was still young—he was thirty—and that he might come to know them. Meanwhile they were growing up in ways partly determined by his confusion. He had been too confused and too young to father them as he wished he might.

He had scribbled a note to his family from the Death Bivouac five days earlier. He had written that he hoped to reach the top of the climb in a few days; that he was being very careful, that he loved them all. He would write when this was finished—when there was this achievement to report.

Dougal went first on the fixed ropes above the first snow cave, sliding his jumars up the slender rope—they were using 7-millimeter cord. He dangled awkwardly over the abyss that in the dark felt empty and without boundary as if nothing would contain the void; it threatened to envelop the face and the climbers with it. He felt sorry for Harlin this morning; John's cough was getting worse as they climbed.

John waited at the bottom of each rope until Dougal reached the top and unclipped. Then John reached as high as he could to pull on the cord to get the stretch out of it. He clamped his jumars to the rope and heaved and shouldered his way up the pitch. The rope had held Dougal; it would hold him, too.

The two climbers arrived at the Death Bivouac in the late morning. The weather was still fine. The place had the alien but familiar quality of any abandoned shelter—forlorn and welcoming at once, as if their presence recalled it to being.

John and Dougal discussed their next move. They would climb the remaining fixed ropes the next day to put themselves in position to try for the summit. For now they could look up at the face and see Layton on the White Spider; he had climbed the gully that formed one of the spider's right legs.

Their immediate plans seemed to disintegrate during the next morning's radio call. Peter Gillman reported that a cold front was approaching the region, bringing a storm with it. John and Dougal decided to remain at the Death Bivouac in hopes of a better forecast. Layton left the Germans and descended from the Spider to spend the night with John and Dougal; the next morning, March 22, he continued down to Kleine Scheidegg for more supplies.

John and Dougal stayed put until the noon radio call. Gillman now reported that the Germans were making good progress overhead. They had reached the Fly, the small ice field above the Spider. The climbing must have been easier than expected. Better yet, the cold front had stalled. They probably could count on two more full days of good weather—perhaps just enough time to reach the summit.

John and Dougal prepared to set off up the fixed ropes. They could catch the Germans and make a joint summit attempt the next morning. Another German—Sigi Hupfauer—arrived at the Death Bivouac on his way up with supplies for his teammates. Hupfauer continued up the fixed ropes. Dougal, eager to be off, followed him. John would come last.

Dougal as he moved up the ropes thought of Layton; too bad he had gone down that morning, before this good news about the weather. He could come back with some of the other Germans to make a second summit party. Dougal reached the rope that hung down the side of the Central Pillar. He heaved his way up, hanging completely free of the rock for most of the pitch. The rope was badly worn by usage and weather—but he was going for the top; with any luck, he wouldn't have to climb this rope again. He was relieved to reach the lower-angled section that led to the Spider. He climbed it and found two of the Germans. A third German was already on the fixed rope that led to the Fly. An hour passed as Dougal waited for his turn on the rope. He began to wonder what had become of John.

PETER GILLMAN STEPPED onto the terrace of the team's hotel, the Villa Maria, where the proprietor kept a telescope for the benefit of curious guests. Peter peered through the lens, tracing the route from the Death Bivouac to the Spider, seeking blots of color. He wanted to know how quickly John and the others were moving up the face. A red figure fell past his line of vision; it turned slowly as it fell, and disappeared behind a buttress.

Peter crouched frozen for a moment and then stood, momentarily bewildered. He backed away from the telescope and shouted for Chris, whose room overlooked the terrace. The hotel's owner, a gentleman by the name of Fritz von Almen, ran to the telescope and quickly scanned the base of the route. His eye fell upon a dark heap in the snow, below the lowest of the fixed ropes. The snow held scattered bits of color: gear and clothing and a rucksack the same blue as John's.

Layton and Chris set out from Kleine Scheidegg a half-hour later on skis. They reached John's body just after 4:30 in the afternoon. They sat down near it in the snow. Chris radioed Peter Gillman at the hotel. Peter agreed to call Don Whillans, who had returned to his work at Harlin's mountaineering school in Leysin. Don would carry the news to Marilyn Harlin.

Chris sat in the snow and sobbed. It seemed to him that death might be forgiven for taking an interest in them. He had been afraid trusting his life to those ropes, and here it was—he had been entirely right to be afraid. He hadn't been comfortable with John, hadn't believed his stories, had found him wearing and even dangerous. Still, Chris knew that people invented themselves. Most people were simply less clumsy about it, more cunning than John.

THE GIRL ANDREA and her brother Johnny looked up when their mother entered the room full of children. The two of them saw the look on her face before she asked them a frightening question: *What's the worst thing that can happen to this family?*

The girl knew at once. The boy had to be told. Johnny already was an accomplished skier—better than his father. He wanted to know—but he didn't ask—if his father had made the mistake that had killed him.

The boy would remember that moment later, and also the funeral, where he stood holding his mother's hand and looking up at people standing in the snow that fell among the tombstones, everyone pale in dark overcoats, a scene of soothing white and gray and black except for the freshly cut flowers, piled everywhere in what struck the boy as huge mounds, strange and somehow cruel in the winter landscape. It was good to be outside after the ride to the cemetery in a car that followed the hearse that carried his father's body. The Germans, kind men, had made a wreath that hung on the back of the hearse; they had laid a banner across the wreath and Johnny had stared smitten at the words on the banner: *Good-bye John.*

The girl had believed that she was closest to her father. Her brother and the neighbors' children cried at the news; she pretended to cry but she was not sad. She was furious, filled with anger that felt like an inheritance, a souvenir of her bond with her father. He had understood this about her—the storms that rose in her, the sense of opposition to the others and to the world at large.

She would decide later that her father had faked his death. Her theory explained some of the mystery and surprise surrounding the event and also why no one had wanted her to look upon the body. Her father had always run off to the mountains. The family would ski up to see him at the base of a route—Andrea was frightened of the glaciers, afraid of falling into a crevasse as people sometimes did. And when the family arrived John would be glad to see them but he received them as visitors who would soon depart.

He had run off again, only this time for good—it made sense. Andrea waited seven years for her father to contact her—perhaps to invite her to visit him or to come to live with him in his new hiding place. She imagined it must be far away, perhaps in the Arctic or somewhere like that. She was sixteen years old—a junior in high school back in America—before she decided to believe that her father had after all fallen to his death on the Eiger's North Face in the winter of 1966. It was a painful decision not only because it meant she would not see him again but also because it meant she might never forgive him.

THE GERMANS ON the face got the news on their radio, and they told Dougal. He saw that they were moved. They had liked John—had perhaps seen him as he needed to be seen, a figure in a good story. Dougal didn't know what to feel. He had been just ahead of John, and he had noticed the rope's poor condition. He might have said something; instead, he had played the child's game—the climber's game—of pretending not to notice. He was surprised again by the irrevocable nature of things and by his own incompetence to countenance facts, endings. He thought of Robin Smith, and of the boy killed on the road in Scotland.

He spent the night on a ledge near the top of the Spider with two of the Germans, Roland Votteler and Karl Golikow. Three other Germans—Jörg Lehne, Sigi Hupfauer and Günther Strobel—were bivouacked higher, at the Fly. The climbers had resolved among themselves to finish the route; quitting now would be too dreary—unbearable.

Karl Golikow descended in the morning to inspect the remaining fixed ropes between the Death Bivouac and the Spider. He found them badly frayed in places. The Germans decided that only four of their team—the climbers who remained above those ropes—would continue to the summit. The rest would go down. Layton Kor had been making his way up the route to join Dougal; he retreated with Golikow and the other Germans.

Dougal couldn't imagine going down to the others. He climbed the fixed ropes that led to the Fly—an almost unbearable task, physically strenuous and utterly terrifying. It was like a punishment, like being forced to live John's penultimate moments. The Germans received him with bread and chocolate and tea. Dougal joined two of them to dig out platforms for the night. The other two Germans went up to climb further, fixing rope almost to the summit ice fields.

It snowed that night. Dougal felt himself flotsam on the surface of something vast and deep. He drifted past mud banks and forest. John's death was part of that dark scenery. Dougal felt a sense of urgent gratitude, almost painful in its intensity; he was alive with this task to perform. He fell asleep after a time and dreamed of himself as a man who leaped naked into a winter sea. He woke from this and drifted back into a sort of dream of John's death. Dougal had been on the rope a half-hour before John; he knew what that was like. The spinning; pushing the metal clamp higher on the rope, stepping awkwardly to stand in the loop; pushing the second jumar higher and stepping up into the second loop; feeling each dangling lurch of the rope as a shock. Dougal knew the moment when your weight and the weight of your rucksack came onto a bit of slack in the rope. You fell with no time to configure a question; the rope came tight, arrested the fall—but you carried now this unthinking impulse to know something more than you knew.

John as his death approached saw the sky they all saw. He fell when the rope broke. He turned upside down from the weight of his rucksack and continued to turn. He tumbled breathless, his mouth open. There was briefly a muffled wild joy at the speed, no surprise but rather a dazed acceptance, a new way to move through the world. The face came up to brush him and the first contact was fantastically odd—an explosion that drove any vestige of thought from his body so that only his naked awareness remained and that only for the instant before it collapsed to a point that winked and disappeared. The body continued to fall. It careened and slid from feature to feature of the Eiger's North Face, shedding gear and then clothing and finally flesh.

HARLIN'S EIGER DIRECT expedition had dwindled to Dougal Haston. Layton Kor had descended to Kleine Scheidegg. Chris Bonington and Mick Burke had gone up the West Ridge as planned, in hopes of photographing an eventual summit party. Don Whillans was in Leysin. John himself was dead.

Dougal felt his isolation on the face. He liked the Germans; they grieved for Harlin without falling apart or expecting anyone else to do so. But Dougal wasn't like them—or like Chris or Layton for that matter. He could ignore the cold as well as his own spasms of grief and fear and the odd and somehow unfinished fact of John's death. He would finish the climb whatever anyone else might choose to do.

He bivouacked at the Fly with three of the Germans. Roland Votteler descended to the Spider for the night. The weather turned while they slept. Dougal awoke in dim light to a world of fog and blowing snow and set about getting his boots on. Roland came up the fixed ropes not long after, and the five men set out for the summit.

The wind continued to rise. Their range of vision shrank to 30 feet. There was no sign of the world or even the climb—only movement that seemed almost to unfold of its own accord, as if to unknown ends.

Dougal had roped up with Jörg Lehne. The two of them carried light loads; their task was to make the new route, fixing rope as they went. The three other Germans followed with heavier loads, pulling up the ropes as they came—the party would need them for the route ahead.

Dougal and Jörg took turns in the lead, finding their way across mixed ground that required great care. The climbing was harder than Dougal had expected. He struggled to find piton placements in the ice-smeared rock. The hours melted away. The sun remained hidden, and even the half-light began to fade as Dougal stared through cloud up a ramp of iced-over rock that ran past a buttress. The storm had grown still worse, and the climbers were getting cold. They needed to find a place to spend the night.

Dougal had left his sleeping gear 400 feet lower, at the start of a difficult stretch of climbing. He descended to join Roland Votteler and Sigi Hupfauer; they had carved him a small platform in the ice. Jörg Lehne and Günther Strobel found a ledge near the new high point and cleared a space barely adequate for their tent. Dougal had no shelter apart from his bivouac sack. He wrapped himself in it and leaned back against the face; one of his legs dangled in space. He dozed occasionally, waking to bouts of violent shivering. He marveled at the force of the storm, and wondered how he and his companions would manage to climb in the morning.

Daylight came as a relief, but it was still snowing and still very cold. The climbers took hours to melt snow for tea and prepare to leave their cramped bivouacs, pulling on half-frozen gloves and gaiters. They had slept in their boots, and only Dougal had removed his crampons. He broke a crampon strap putting the things back on, and the work of repairing the strap was painfully slow in the cold. Roland and Sigi were also slow at their preparations. They fell in behind Dougal as he left camp. He set off up the fixed ropes and quickly lost feeling in his fingers.

There was no sign of Jörg or Günther at the top of the fixed ropes. They had already left their bivouac to set out for the summit. Dougal peered up into the clouds—nothing. He began climbing. Jörg and Günther had fixed ropes on some of the difficult sections, but they had neglected to leave a rope on one long pitch of thin ice was bare of rope. Dougal carried no ice axe and his jury-rigged crampons were wobbly; the newly repaired strap was too loose. He led the pitch anyway, using a single ice dagger, aware that his belay anchor probably wouldn't hold a fall; he would go all the way to the bottom of the face, taking Roland and Sigi with him.

He moved deliberately—he couldn't lose time in these conditions—until he drew near the bottom of the next fixed rope. It was 20 feet to his left, across very steep ground. He hammered his ice dagger an inch or so into the ice and tied a sling to it. He clipped a carabiner to the sling and clipped the rope to the carabiner. His notion was that the slight tension of the rope running through the carabiner behind him would help him stay in balance as he crossed to the fixed rope—unless the wobbly ice dagger came out.

Everything fell away. He cast off memory, ambition and any notion of loss in exchange for this. The world was white—the wind itself, the cliff, his hands raised to his task. He let go of his name; he was a being in a world of blowing snow.

He reached the fixed rope and hung from it in the wind, which rose still higher. He had trailed a rope and he tied it off for Sigi and Roland to follow. He carried on up the remaining fixed ropes, now hearing voices above him. He pulled up over the last bit of climbing and the world seemed to float up beneath him; the white sky rose to assume an ordinary shape, a familiar low dome, which he associated with the wing of some huge bird. He staggered like a voyager who steps onto a beach.

There were people here. Chris and Mick had given up on climbing the West Ridge; they had taken a helicopter up the mountain two days ago. The landing had been a precarious undertaking in the deteriorating weather. They had dug a snow hole near the summit and waited through the rising storm with growing doubts about the fate of the five climbers on the face. Members of the German expedition had meanwhile come up the West Ridge to join the greeting party or help form a rescue mission.

Jörg and Günther had already reached the summit and the others had come out to them. Dougal approaching the top of the face saw the figures of various young men; they appeared and disappeared in the blowing cloud that swathed the peak. The figures milled about pointlessly, calling to one another in their respective languages, their voices caught up and carried off by the wind even as the cold seeped into their gloves and boots and froze their fingers and toes; it was some hellish garden party.

Chris came across in the wind to greet Dougal and lead him to the snow hole, where he gave him a mug of coffee. Dougal had not seen Chris since before John's death—exactly when he couldn't remember. He sat shaking and staring at Chris out of a haggard, wind-burned face, his cheeks raw, his eyes red and tearing in the sudden quiet of the cave. His gaze brought to mind a wolf, a child raised by wolves.

Roland and Sigi arrived and so the five summit climbers were all off the face. Chris and Mick had dug their snow hole for four people; it now held eleven young men. They occupied it with hunched backs, limbs jumbled and shifting. The silence filled with their breathing and their shouting as they lifted their voices

in a blur of exhaustion and relief that held undertones of regret and also of fear: some of them were very worried about their partly frozen hands and feet. They spent the night in the cave; the storm made the descent via the West Ridge too dangerous. They ran short of air and poked shovels through the entrance to avoid suffocation. Some of the climbers slept.

Chris and Dougal talked. John's family—his parents, Marilyn, the children—had buried him that morning in the cemetery in Leysin. His death made him an outsider—he was missing this—and Chris and Dougal held it against him. Their own ruthlessness shocked them. They didn't talk about that. They exchanged stories of what they had endured and seen. Chris had been very worried that Dougal and the Germans would die in the storm. Their survival and their success made John's death seem less like a sign; perhaps it was simply an accident.

Harlin was at any rate gone. The loss made Chris aware of the others, those who remained. It was now some fourteen years since he'd come upon Hamish in that climber's hut in Scotland. A sort of fellowship had taken shape. Chris and Hamish were in the circle; so were Don Whillans and Ian Clough. Mick Burke and now Dougal Haston had made their way into it; the circle silently widened to encompass them, even as it closed to fill the space where John Harlin had briefly appeared. Others, acquaintances or strangers, haunted the periphery; circumstances might at any time exclude them or else enlist them in whatever work was ahead.

Chris, as he lay stormbound in the near-silence of the summit cave amid the other exhausted climbers, considered their shadowed, sleeping bodies with interest and a fierce affection, with gratitude for this moment and with longing for whatever was to come. It was as if they had arrived to pursue some purpose he cherished. The task remained invisible—it might be that these men or others like them would teach or deliver it to him.

PART TWO

Men

*In the curious playgrounds of their sport,
mountaineers learn what primitive people
know instinctively—that mountains are
the abode of the dead, and that to travel
in the high country is not simply to risk
death but to risk understanding it.*

—ROBERT REID, *Mountains of
the Great Blue Dream* (1991)

Everest, Southwest Face.
KEIICHI YAMADA, CHRIS BONINGTON PICTURE LIBRARY

8

CHRIS BONINGTON WENT from the Eiger to the London Hospital. Doctors there spent six weeks successfully working to save three toes that had turned black during his vigil at the Eiger's summit. Dougal Haston was a fellow patient, recovering from frostbitten fingers.

Both men had emerged from the Eiger ordeal with enhanced reputations and prospects. The Eiger story had been widely followed in Great Britain as well as on the Continent. Dougal was now famous as the only one of the Anglo-American party to complete the Eiger Direct—now known as the Harlin Route. He received scores of letters from fans, mostly females entranced by his brooding looks and modish clothes. He was now, in fact, established as a cult figure on the climbing scene: Jim Morrison in crampons. He had taken over John's mountaineering school in Leysin, and the publicity was good for bookings there.

Chris had received less publicity, but his work had given a strong boost to his hopes of making a career as an adventure photojournalist. *The Daily Telegraph* had offered him a new assignment—to explore and photograph a remote and highly active volcano in Ecuador. Bonington said good-bye to the London doctors, went home briefly to pack—and to say good-bye to Wendy and young Conrad, now a toddler—and was off again.

A month after his release from hospital, he was sorting through gear at Base Camp in Ecuador when he turned and saw an Indian enter camp at a surprisingly rapid trot. The Indian looked stricken. He had crossed the rain forest with a message for Bonington, whose first thought was that something had happened to Wendy. Chris was afraid to open the envelope; when he did, a collision occurred—his relief to discover that his wife was alive smashed, wavelike, into his horror at the news that their child was dead. He sagged and fell to his hands and knees on the muddy ground and sobbed as the messenger and the Indian porters looked on in sympathetic but alien silence. The expedition leader, an older man named Sebastian Snow, ran to Chris and held his shoulder and spoke to him. The kindness in his voice made Chris ache unbearably for home. He longed for Wendy and for the child he would never again see or touch.

He set out for home that afternoon, walking silently through the jungle alongside his Indian porters. The party hired horses at a way station, and rode on in darkness toward the nearest road. Chris understood that he would not sleep until he was with Wendy—he could not stop himself from trying to imagine her suffering during the week that had passed since the death of their child. Chris sat on his horse as the animal moved through the night; every moment brought him nearer to the world where this bewildering loss had occurred.

He reviewed the facts as he rode. The story seemed so unreal as to offer some hope that it was untrue; that this nightmare could be an elaborate mistake. Wendy and Conrad had been visiting Wendy's friend Mary Stewart near Glasgow. The little boy—he was two and a half years old—had wandered off to play with Mary's children near a stream. Children had played happily in the place for years; the stream was ordinarily a trickle—but on this day it was swollen from a recent rain. Conrad had fallen into the water and drowned. Wendy had been the one to find him.

She was waiting for Chris at Heathrow. They were very young, and each meant to survive their terrible loss. They understood that their salvation lay partly in how they behaved toward one another. Their family happiness—so different from what Chris had known as a child—had made them vulnerable to this great wound, but almost from the first days of their bereavement they hoped to invent and share some new version of joy. They drew upon this mutual desire for the strength to comfort one another.

Chris resumed his climbing after a time; he was drawn to it as to a balm for his unyielding pain. He thought to lose himself in movement and in the touch of rock and the smell and colors of gear and rope, the sight from some ledge or low Lake District summit of trees spread across the immediate world. He made one climb with Tom Patey that summer. Patey was a character. He was Scottish, a medical man in private life. He was the boldest of climbers—he specialized in making new winter routes under horrible conditions—and a cheerfully obnoxious companion. He was also a writer of satirical climbing ballads as well as surprisingly elegant semicomic essays for the climbing club journals. He knew as did everyone of the Boningtons' loss, and when a decent interval had passed he called and asked Chris to come along for the first ascent of the Old Man of Hoy, a crumbling sea stack in Scotland's Orkney Islands.

The Old Man was a spectacular feature, soaring out of the surf near the cliffs like a primitive, decaying monument to some forgotten god. Chris took pictures on the route—including a good one of Patey, cigarette dangling from cheerful, sneering lips—and led a pitch near the top, swimming smooth and fearless up a crack, the rope hanging free from his waist to the feet of his partners. His grief was still terribly new and immediate; he awoke to it not every morning but rather at each new hour. This awareness swept away certain fears. He felt not so much self-destructive as self-abandoned, as if he had left behind his identity as someone with something to fear.

The *Telegraph* sent him hunting with Eskimos on Baffin Island that winter. He returned home in time to be with Wendy for the birth of the couple's second child, Daniel, on April 25, 1967. The BBC had meanwhile agreed to broadcast a new assault on the Old Man of Hoy. The network arranged an extravaganza, engaging a platoon of Scots Guards to ferry tons of equipment to the top of the cliffs overlooking the column, and hiring six climbers to climb three different routes. Chris and Tom Patey would rope up on the original route. Joe Brown and Ian McNaught-Davis would attempt a new line up the South Face of the column. Pete Crew and Dougal Haston would try to get up the overhanging Southeast Arête. Hamish MacInnes came along, too; he would handle some of the camera work.

The broadcast, aired live in the summer of 1967, was a huge hit—perhaps the most widely watched climbing film since the one that documented the 1953 first ascent of Everest. Chris—with his youth, his upscale accent and his earnest desire to appeal to his audience—made an especially pleasing impression on the millions of viewers who tuned in. For the young climber, the broadcast was yet another step toward public recognition that could make it easier to attract support for further projects or expeditions. Tom Patey liked to tease Chris about his ability to attract valuable publicity; some climbers were starting to resent it.

Chris and Wendy had moved to a new home in the Lake District; the previous one held too many memories of Conrad. Chris now decided that the region itself was too remote. He needed to be closer to other climbers as well as editors and other potential clients. The couple looked in London, but they recoiled from the noise and the traffic as well as the high rents. Driving back up to the Lakes from the city after a depressing day of house hunting in early 1968, they stopped near Manchester to visit friends—a young climber named Nick Estcourt, and his wife, Carolyn. The Estcourts had recently moved up from London to the Manchester suburb of Cheshire. The neighborhood was attractive and affordable, especially compared to what Chris and Wendy had just seen in London. It wasn't terribly far from the city, and it was within striking distance of climbing in both Wales and the Lakes as well as the nearby Peak District.

The Boningtons were intrigued. They did some looking in the area, and that summer they settled on a modest fixer-upper in the South Manchester community of Bowden. Wendy was left to oversee renovations while Chris traveled to Africa for his latest assignment; he was to report on the Great Abbai Expedition's attempt to descend the Blue Nile.

The expedition was a terrifying experience. The explorers traveled 500 miles of unknown gorge, encountering huge rapids. Chris was thrown from his raft and nearly drowned during the first days of the trip. One team member—John McLeod—did in fact drown during a river crossing. The expedition also came under attack by local bandits, who fired rifles and hurled rocks at Chris and his companions.

The trip marked the end of Bonington's attempt to make a living by covering other people's adventures. He returned home badly shaken in the fall of 1968, firmly resolved that henceforth he would take his chances in the mountains, where he knew what he was doing. And he would go as a participant—a decision-maker—and not as a more or less helpless observer.

Builders were still at work on the Bowden house. The Estcourts invited the Boningtons to move in with them while the workmen finished. Chris, Wendy and Daniel crowded into the Estcourts' two-bedroom apartment in late October and stayed for two months. The arrangement worked surprisingly well; the two couples became very close.

Nick was almost a decade younger than Chris. He came from an upper middle-class background, unlike most of his contemporaries in the climbing community. Nick had climbed in the Alps as a schoolboy with his father, and had served as president of the Cambridge University Mountaineering Club. It was a background that might have gotten him invited on the Everest trips of the 1920s and '30s, but he didn't look the part of an aristocrat. He was a wiry character, with smallish eyes and vaguely impish features framed by a dark beard and a head of unruly hair. He was capable of astonishing flights of vulgarity. He had a wild, somewhat clownish streak, and his behavior at parties or pubs was at best unpredictable; for example, he often threw things.

And yet even at twenty-five, Nick was entirely reliable in certain ways. Unlike Chris, he had a conventional career: he'd started as an engineer before switching to computer programming. He was ambitious and self-confident; he was intelligent; he was fair-minded to a fault. And Nick was by nature a skeptic. He resisted Chris's patented flights of fantasy as well as his countervailing bouts of pessimism. He listened to Chris's ideas and meanderings, consistently asking the right sort of question.

The two of them spent the weekends climbing. They talked about mountains in the car on the way to the crags around Manchester. They continued their conversations at night after Daniel and the women had gone off to bed. They were soon deeply involved in plotting the most ambitious expedition in British mountaineering history.

CHRIS HAD NOT participated in a serious climbing expedition since the Eiger Direct, almost three years before. He now began to kick around ideas with Nick and another Cheshire climber, Martin Boysen. Martin was twenty-six, a superb rock climber—

better than Chris or Nick—but he'd never climbed in the Alps, let alone the Himalaya.

Chris by early 1969 had known Martin for almost a decade. They had met at Harrison Rocks near London. Boysen back then was a sixteen-year-old prodigy, ticking off the test-pieces of the previous generation. He'd been born in Germany during the war, and his earliest memories included a scene in an air raid shelter in his native Alsdorf—the adults and children huddled together while the Royal Air Force bombed the city. His father, a music teacher, had been drafted to serve in the Wehrmacht; the Russians had taken him prisoner. Martin's mother, a native of England, worked for the American occupation forces just after the war. She found her name and her children's names in a Gestapo file; they had been slated for the concentration camps. She took the children to England and worked as a teacher. Martin's father rejoined the family after his release from Russia, which came seven years after the war's end.

Martin was tall—6' 1"—and gangly and bespectacled. He had not done well in school sports; instead, he'd wandered the landscape on foot and bicycle. He'd taken up climbing almost by accident—he was watching some climbers one day and they invited him to rope up—but by his midteens he was following the great Joe Brown up some of the hardest routes in Wales, displaying a dazzling mix of drive and an almost lazy physical grace. Don Whillans allowed that young Martin Boysen, with his long arms and legs and his disgracefully shaggy haircut, was the nearest thing Don himself had to a peer on rock.

Martin as he grew older was also known for his low-key wit and his rare but impressive outbursts of temper. He was a bookish sort, a teacher. He generally held himself aloof from the climbing scene—the clubs and social gatherings where reputations were burnished or inflated—but other leading climbers knew and respected his abilities.

Chris and Nick and Martin agreed that they would try something big together. They wanted to do something hard, but their options were limited. Western climbers had been largely shut out of the Nepalese Himalaya for most of the 1960s, due to political tensions between countries that relied upon the mountains as military buffer zones. Tibet was off-limits, and so were many of the ranges in Pakistan and India. Such restrictions helped to explain why young British climbers like Nick and Martin had little or no experience at high altitude. Chris himself hadn't been to the Himalaya since the Nuptse expedition in 1961—now more than seven years ago. A British expedition had visited Nepal to attempt the remote Gauri Sankar (7,134 meters; 23,405 feet) in late 1964; the party had included Don Whillans and Ian Clough. Those two had accomplished some of the hardest technical climbing yet done in the Himalaya—but even that trip, now four years gone, seemed a rather distant episode.

Chris and Nick and Martin had turned their attention to Alaska when they got the news that Nepal had reopened its doors to climbers. Nepal's highest peaks had been climbed—and Chris, recalling his experiences on Annapurna II and Nuptse, wanted something that offered a greater technical challenge. He talked it over with the other two, and they considered an alternative. The winter ascent of the Eiger Direct had proved that the right team could climb a big mountain face in extreme conditions. What about trying something like that again—only this time in the Himalaya?

Chris recalled seeing a photograph of the South Face of Annapurna (8,091 meters; 26,545 feet). The mountain had been the first of the world's fourteen 8,000-meter peaks to be climbed—the French had done it back in 1950. Chris knew the

Annapurna region of Nepal from his 1960 expedition to the mountain's satellite peak Annapurna II.

More recently, a British expedition to Machapuchare (6,993 meters; 22,943 feet) had climbed directly across from Annapurna's South Face. Several of the expedition members had gotten a good look at the face, and Chris contacted them. Two of the climbers spoke of the face's awe-inspiring size—it was 12,000 feet high—and the near-constant barrage of avalanches that swept down it. Jimmy Roberts, the leader of Chris's 1960 expedition to Annapurna II, also had been on the Machapuchare trip. He had photographed the South Face of Annapurna, and he offered Chris a more measured response. Roberts maintained that the face would certainly be more difficult than the existing routes on Everest, and would require supplemental oxygen to support hard technical climbing above 24,000 feet. He didn't say it was impossible. Chris found his former mentor's comments encouraging—and he liked the notion of doing something harder than Everest.

Chris and Wendy by now had moved into their new home in Bowden. Nick and Carolyn Estcourt had bought a new home as well. It was the Estcourt's turn for renovations, so they moved in with the Boningtons. Someone had sent a color slide of Annapurna's South Face. Martin Boysen came over, and the three friends projected the slide onto six feet of the Boningtons' living room wall.

It looked immense.

They gazed at it, each climber responding to the image in ways at first impossible to organize or voice. They began to pick an imaginary line up the face, engaging the image before them; in doing so they began to commit to their notions of trying to climb it. Each man imagined possible outcomes—Chris saw himself climbing a snowfield or stepping onto a slab of rock. The climb no longer existed as merely one alternative among an almost infinite number of possible routes on possible mountains. It existed now as work to be taken up or left undone. They had in effect begun the climb. They felt dimly that they should continue; if they did not, this might become an opportunity they had glimpsed and rejected—it might torment them. The face was beautiful, too. There was only one reason to stay clear of it: They were afraid.

The photograph showed a glacier leading to a snow ridge—a buttress that leaned against the lowest reaches of the face. That led to a thinner, steeper ridge of ice; after that, a maze of ice cliffs reached to a towering rock wall, beginning at 23,000 feet. There was more steep snow above the wall. And then mixed climbing—a tattered quilt of rock and ice and fields of snow—to the summit. *There's a line*, said Boysen. *But it's bloody big.*

They had initially planned a small, alpine-style expedition—the three of them and perhaps one other climber. They saw immediately that the size and difficulty of Annapurna's South Face would require something of an old-style siege. They would need to establish a series of camps and stock them with gear and food, as well as oxygen for the hard climbing near the summit. They would need a bigger climbing team—Chris upon reflection figured that eight was the minimum number—with a huge supporting cast.

Dougal Haston's performance on the Eiger made him an obvious choice. He was still in Leysin running John Harlin's climbing school, where he employed Don Whillans and Mick Burke as instructors. Dougal occasionally guided clients himself; but he was more likely to drink with them. The drinking took place at the Club Vagabond, which housed the guides and students upstairs at priority rates. Dougal routinely remained in the bar until the place emptied, then struggled across the room and up the stairs—one careful step at a time—to his bed.

He still carried the aura of a pop star; in the three years since the Eiger Direct he'd settled into his role as a sort of pseudo-working class hero, mountaineering's version of the rock stars who dominated British and American pop culture. He dressed the part: sunglasses and scarves, pink shirts and tight trousers. His hard drinking, together with his moody silences and sullen good looks, completed the picture for the young climbers, star-struck girls and others who arrived in Leysin to sample the mountain lifestyle and drifted into the Club Vagabond. A pair of English nurses on holiday—their names were Annie Ferris and Beth Bevan—had wandered into the Vagabond one night in May of 1966 and paired up with Dougal and Mick Burke. Dougal had ended up marrying Annie, an intense, pixyish young woman; Mick had married Beth.

Dougal at moments tried to convince himself that he was indeed a kind of hero. His journals were laced with cutting and somewhat callow remarks about climbers who struck him as over the hill or unserious. He still sometimes cultivated the notion of himself as a kind of superman—someone who lived with a purpose and vitality that set him apart.

His passion surfaced in bouts of climbing. He climbed in Patagonia in 1968, with a group that included Don Whillans and Mick Burke as well as Martin Boysen. He made some difficult routes in the Alps—including a few winter climbs with Chris, who found he enjoyed climbing with Dougal. They had in common their single-mindedness, and Dougal's reserve interested the voluble Bonington. Chris also understood something of what his younger friend could do. He understood on some level that Dougal's ambition and selfishness endowed the Scot with a ruthless brilliance that might be useful on Annapurna's South Face.

Ian Clough, now thirty, was another obvious choice for the expedition, but for very different reasons. Chris still recalled with pleasure his early days with Ian in the Alps, leading up to their ascent of the Eiger's North Face. And Ian's 1964 trip to Gauri Sankar made him one of the few young British climbers with Himalayan experience. Ian still taught climbing in Glencoe, Scotland, where he occupied a small cottage with his wife and their young daughter. Ian liked teaching. He had in fact established a number of his new routes in Scotland with his climbing students. Chris liked and admired Ian, and trusted him to behave well—he was the furthest thing from a prima donna.

Chris also asked Mick Burke to come. Mick was a steady and cheerful companion, the kind who could be trusted to speak his mind and keep a bloke honest. Chris over the last few years had gotten to know a bit about his background. Mick had grown up working class in Wigan, an industrial town with not much to recommend it; he'd left school at fifteen to work in an insurance office, and soon quit that job to live and climb in the Lake District. He kept bar and did odd jobs during the winter, climbing when he could and putting aside money for annual trips to the Alps.

He was just back from a stint teaching at Dougal Haston's school in Leysin, where he'd spent much of his time drinking with Dougal and Don Whillans at the Club Vagabond. Mick liked to drink, and he was wildly funny. He was intensely argumentative; like Whillans, he was inclined to insist upon his rights. And yet there was something impressively normal about Mick. He was a talented climber—not a genius like Martin Boysen, but he worked hard at it. He'd done well on the Eiger, following Chris around in 85-mph winds at the top of the face, huddling for days in the summit snow hole with nothing much to eat while they waited for Dougal and the Germans to finish the climb.

Whillans was another candidate, but Chris hesitated to ask him. Don was now thirty-six, only a year or so older than Chris but badly out of shape; the old working-class hero carried quite a gut these days, and had done nothing much lately in Britain or the

Alps. The Gauri Sankar expedition four years before had marked his third trip to the Himalaya, and he'd yet to reach a summit there. His continued string of failures had made him more difficult than ever. He made fewer concessions to courtesy or tact. He was increasingly lazy and presumptuous; he was touchy and still on occasion violent. Chris knew all this, but he also believed that Don's stubbornness sometimes amounted to a kind of wisdom. The other climbers were young and had very little experience in the big mountains; perhaps Don could help protect them—as he had protected Chris and Hamish and the others twelve years before on the Bonatti Pillar. The photograph of the South Face was frightening. Chris knew that the reality would be worse. The picture of the face—strange in its two dimensions—occupied a towering place in his mind.

He invited Don for a day of winter climbing in Scotland. Don by now knew that something was up, but Chris didn't mention Annapurna; he just arranged to pick up his old friend on a Friday night. Don arrived home four hours late—2:30 in the morning—from a marathon at the local pub. It was precisely the behavior to set Bonington seething. And Don wanted to drive; Chris had to insist on taking the wheel.

Chris had made plans to meet up with Tom Patey in Glencoe that morning. The three climbers made their rendezvous and immediately set out for an unclimbed gully. Don lagged behind Chris and Tom, letting them lead the hard pitches until the party reached the last pitch: an awkward chimney choked with ice. Here Don came to life. He volunteered to lead the pitch and climbed it in impressive style, with a steady and deliberate power.

Chris was moved by this surprising, last-minute display of genius and grace—and also by his own sense of relief. He had dreaded leaving Don behind. It would end their friendship; and Chris had a sense that such a break would leave unresolved some chapter in his own story. That evening he asked Don to join the Annapurna expedition, offering him the post of deputy leader.

Don for his part had made his point; he had something to offer and was willing to offer it—on his own terms. Chris showed him a photograph of Annapurna's South Face. Whillans looked it over for a moment, concluded that it could be climbed, and agreed to come and help do the job.

That made seven climbers. Chris wanted one more. He chose a stranger, an American named Tom Frost. Frost was a practicing Mormon, who adhered strictly to his religious code—a strange bedfellow for the foul-mouthed, vice-riddled British. He'd made his name in Yosemite, refining techniques for climbing huge walls—techniques that might be useful on the South Face of Annapurna. And Chris had another reason to invite him. The expedition by now had an agent—one George Greenfield—who maintained that including an American would make it easier to raise money in the United States.

Such considerations mattered now. The proposed climb combined the scale and altitude of a Himalayan peak with the types of technical challenges encountered on the Eiger Direct. Once again, the climbers would borrow tactics from earlier mountaineers, mounting a siege on the peak. They needed sufficient funds to buy huge quantities of supplies—and also to pay the army of porters who would carry those supplies to the mountain.

The expedition also presented a huge logistical challenge, which brought into play Bonington's military background and his mania for organization—his sheer love of planning. He lost himself in contemplation of the expedition's future in all of its intricate potential. He asked and tried to answer questions about how many feet of rope they'd need; how many climbers would stay at Camp Four in support of a summit team; whether to send the gear by air or truck or ship; the number of porters required to ferry gear from Base to Advance Base Camp. He had begun work in late 1968, recruiting the team and seeking financial support; by the fall of 1969 the work of the expedition consumed his days—he spent his nights lecturing at various clubs and other venues within 60 miles or so of his Bowden home. There was food to plan and order, and travel to arrange; there were endless permits to pursue and appointments to schedule; there were donors to entreat and thank. Gear and equipment had to be begged or purchased and then packed—thousands of feet of rope for stringing between camps; hundreds of pitons and ice screws and carabiners; tents, ladders, flares, snow shovels, headlamps, a winch . . . all of it.

The others helped, but Chris did the lion's share of the work. He did it with a growing sense of elation. He was discovering a new aspect of his genius. He had found a task that engaged his peculiar qualities: his wish for certainty and his need to have that wish thwarted, his need to recognize that life was unmanageable and his urge to try to manage it. Thus engaged, he felt at moments that his life was at last unfolding without his interference.

He had found three support climbers to supplement the eight lead climbers. Mike Thompson, an old friend and climbing partner from Sandhurst and the army, agreed to help ferry gear on the mountain's lower reaches; meanwhile, he could help organize the food for the expedition. Dave Lambert, a thirty-year-old hospital resident, called to volunteer as team doctor. Chris liked Lambert well enough to accept his offer almost on the spot. Chris asked Kelvin Kent—an army officer stationed in Hong Kong, who understood wireless communications as well as logistics—to manage the flow of information and supplies out of Base Camp.

Chris planned to hire six climbing Sherpas to ferry supplies between camps on the face. George Greenfield managed to sell the expedition's television rights to Independent Television News and Thames Television, which planned to send a four-man film crew. That brought the main party to twenty-one members. The expedition ultimately would employ another half-dozen local porters on the route, as well as a motley collection of European and Asian trekkers and climbers—passers-through recruited on the spot to carry loads and perform camp chores. The climbers also would need to hire 140 porters to carry supplies to the bottom of the route.

Chris had never commanded more than twelve men and three tanks in the army—and this was not the army. His friends were difficult, most of them misfits with antisocial tendencies and refined or quirky sensibilities. Some of them had adopted the style and sensibilities of the booming counterculture; they had longish hair and beards, wore grubby bellbottoms, smoked grass and listened to rock and roll. The climbers who gathered at Heathrow airport in March of 1970 looked and sounded more like a traveling rock band—the Beatles on their way to visit Maharishi Mahesh Yogi—than a traditional British mountaineering expedition. These young men didn't look disciplined or ambitious or respectful of convention; they looked moody and painfully young and rather confused but also earnest, as though they were serious about something—or as though they wished for something to be serious about.

The ship carrying most of the gear had left England on January 23, 1970, but it was late arriving in Bombay—engine trouble. Ian Clough gamely agreed to wait for its arrival. The main party went on to Pokhara to hire porters and pack loads for the walk to the peak. Chris sent Don Whillans and Mike Thompson ahead with two high-altitude porters to find a site for Base Camp. The main party left Pokhara on March 22.

The approach was dreamlike. They walked for eight days. The cook boys woke the climbers each morning with tea and biscuits at six o'clock. The porters shouldered their loads and set off; the climbers followed in small groups or alone, chatting or watching the scenery unfold. The preparations were behind them; the actual climb lay in what seemed the remote future. The dangers ahead remained abstractions, just as the mountains to the north remained mysterious, glimpsed through haze or cloud. They were marching into the Annapurna Sanctuary, a fantastic amphitheater surrounded by a series of huge, exquisite peaks—fishtailed Machapuchare, the virgin Hiunchuli, massive Modi Peak. The march led past villages and terraced fields and into the shadowy gorge of the Modi Khola.

They encountered Mike Thompson on the third day. He'd come down to meet them after failing to get a glimpse of their peak—too many clouds, and a great deal of snow in the higher approaches. He'd come back to report, leaving Don and the two porters to finish the reconnaissance. The main party marched three more days and at last came upon Whillans himself, calmly sitting on a boulder at the entrance to a cave.

Don had seen the South Face. It was big and steep—but the avalanches stayed clear of the line of ascent they'd picked out in the photographs. He'd seen enough to believe that this original line or something close to it offered the most feasible way up the face. Chris was vastly relieved; he had during the past year fretted endlessly that the photographs would prove misleading, that the climbers' first view of the actual face would shatter their hopes of climbing it.

Don also had a story to tell. There had been a noise one afternoon, and he'd turned in time to glimpse a black figure drop behind a ridge. Don had lain awake that night with his head outside of his tent, and at some point he'd seen an apelike creature run on all fours across the snow to disappear in the shadows. Don had seen the Yeti, or so he believed.

The others were interested as well as amused; they let the

story pass. Don understood the dark figure as further evidence of the world's potential to surprise him. He had lived part of his youth working in shadows, moving pipes and appliances to and from cellars. He'd dug and blasted in the mud of new tunnels, subject to a civilization that would without remorse deprive him of the sun. The greater world meanwhile had shown itself to him in hills and then in mountains. He felt the gap between his different lives without adequate language to filter or explain it. He lay with his head outside of his tent and watched moonlight ricochet from snow to illuminate the night and this black creature and he thought he recognized the Yeti. The idea of such a creature seemed to him no stranger than the notion of a miner or a plumber's assistant.

Whillans was by reputation a surly, violent man with a quick wit and a talent for climbing. He also had an artist's vocation. He could glance at a slope and measure the risks. He could find the best way through the jumble of a glacier. He could lay eyes on a ridge and know whether to try to climb it. Chris understood Don's limits but he understood as well that Don was admirable and at this stage indispensable. Bonington's own artistry lay partly in knowing this—as he had known that John Harlin's demons made him dangerous, and that Dougal Haston in pursuit of salvation in the mountains would avoid certain mistakes and distractions.

The expedition established a temporary Base Camp on March 28. Chris sent Don and Dougal and Mick Burke ahead to establish the expedition's permanent Base Camp. Chris himself stayed behind to oversee the porters at their task of ferrying loads up through increasingly difficult terrain. Many of the men walked barefoot through the snow and frozen avalanche debris of the Sanctuary. They were saving their expedition-issue canvas gym shoes for barter. It was infuriating; the shoes were meant to protect the porters' feet so that they could climb further up the glacier.

And yet it was disturbing to try to imagine what these men must think of their employers, who were in a position to expend such vast resources on an enterprise of such dubious merit.

The advance party quickly found a site for a permanent Base Camp. Don and Dougal took two more days to pick their way past the glacier above the new camp. The glacier was a jumble of ice walls and bottomless slots that shifted under the heat of the sun, threatening to collapse and destroy the climbers. The creaking of the glacier sometimes escaped their immediate notice, and at such times their fear became blurry. Other times they heard the sound without fear of any sort, as if their futures were of no concern to them. They made their way across the glittering maze toward their first objective, an island of rock in what seemed a sea of snow.

The other climbers helped the high-altitude porters ferry loads up to the new Base Camp. They carried the tents, sleeping bags, stoves and other gear needed to stock higher camps. They carried the heavy bottles of oxygen for climbing the route's upper reaches; they also brought food and cooking fuel. The permanent Base Camp grew to include a two-man tent and two Whillans Boxes, improved versions of the shelter Don had designed to withstand the Patagonian winds.

Chris moved up to Permanent Base Camp on March 31. He roped up with Mick Burke the next day to consolidate the route through the glacier. Don and Dougal remained out front; they climbed an easy snow slope to the top of their rock island at 16,000 feet on April 1. This would serve as a site for Camp One. The two climbers dropped their loads and descended to Base Camp for a rest.

Chris and Mick moved up the next day to occupy the newly established Camp One and take over the lead. They were now at 16,000 feet, and the night was bitterly cold. They lingered in their sleeping bags on the morning of April 3, melting water for tea and waiting for the sun to warm their tent. They were old friends now. Mick's marriage had settled him down a bit; he'd begun film school. It was nice being up here together, away from the others.

The two of them crawled out of the tent. They could look down at Base, now three miles and 2,000 vertical feet below. They could look up into the cloudless sky, the dry perfect blue that seemed to draw the mountain itself toward heaven. The sun's rays fell with no indication of warmth on the half-frozen snow. No wind stirred. The sounds in the dazzling light were the crunch and squeak of their boots.

A ridge ran down the lower half of the center of the South Face, and continued down to divide the field of snow and ice that lay in their path. Chris and Mick roped up against the risk of falling into a crevasse, and set out toward the face. They left bamboo wands in the snow to mark their path through the maze. Chris felt dimly afraid—not of death but of his own unfathomable ignorance; the scale of this place suggested to him that he knew nothing. Mick felt unsettled as well.

They walked on into heat and searing light and what seemed a shimmering ageless emptiness. They could imagine a watcher who regarded them from the world to come. They would appear to him as tiny black figures like those that exist in some photographs, too small to offer a sense of intention or outcome. Their figures would flicker so that any such watcher would be required to fish for them as people fish for ghosts—for those who know nothing of us, who do not watch us in return, whose ignorance suggests that what is past is gone.

The climbers walked for two hours through a corridor that split the glacier. They passed features so enormous as to make them recoil from the scale of things. The terrain became more

threatening. They stood and shivered in the shadow of a creaking ice tower and debated their course. They climbed onto the
glacier itself and walked to the start of a new maze of towers. It
was midday; the sun had turned the snow heavy and soft so that
it was difficult to walk. Chris and Mick dropped their loads and
returned to Camp One. Don and Dougal, back already from their
brief rest lower on the mountain, were there to greet them.

Mick awoke exhausted the next morning. Chris and Dougal
and Don set off without him to find a site for Camp Two. They
reached the previous day's high point and continued up snow
toward the base of a cliff. Debris—fragments of ice and rock—
rained down from the ridge as they climbed. They entered a new
maze, this one made of angles and towers—dark unstable-looking
shapes that cast huge shifting shadows on the snow.

Chris and Dougal roped up and made their way across a shelf
that seemed to offer a way past the cliff. They stopped to build an
anchor, and Don caught up with them. He paused only long enough
to suggest that they hurry—this was not a place to linger—and
carried on higher without benefit of a rope. The three climbers
traversed a wall that had the feel of a vertical glacier, a slow-motion
riot of decaying ice. They climbed more steep ground above this
wall to a shelf protected by a rock overhang—the shelf would do
as a site for Camp Two.

They were now at an altitude of around 17,500 feet—roughly
2,500 feet below the col the climbers had designated as the route's
next major landmark. The col would serve as a starting point for
their attempt on the huge ice ridge that was a key to the face.

Chris carried a load from Camp One to Camp Two the next
day—April 6—and then descended all the way to Temporary Base
Camp to greet Ian Clough. Ian had made a difficult journey from
Bombay, where he had waited for the ship with their remaining
supplies. He arrived at the mountain worn out and dispirited from

the maddening work of collecting and supervising tons of supplies on bad roads with unreliable transport. He'd brought with him a small mob of porters who had carried the gear up into the glacier. Many of them had suffered from hypothermia during a snowstorm that occurred near the end of their approach march.

Don and Dougal spent the night of April 6 at Camp Two. They left the next morning to climb toward the col. They climbed steadily past hanging glaciers and towers of ice. Whillans understood this task of finding the route better than any of them. He knew how to balance one hazard against another—when to move quickly, when to slow down to avoid a careless mistake. Dougal watched him. Snow fell and both men grew cold. They reached a short rock wall that led to the col and at last turned around. They slept at Camp Two, and spent the next day fixing a line of ropes to the col before retreating to Base Camp for another rest.

The two of them had entered into a partnership of sorts. Dougal did the heavy work, breaking trail and leading most pitches. Don followed, still working off his beer gut. He gave Dougal a belay when Dougal wanted one, and made the hard route-finding decisions. There were ten years between them. Dougal took to calling the older man Dad.

They were coming to believe that the climb belonged to them—and so far it did. Chris and Mick had played a modest part in making the route to Camp Two. Nick Estcourt and Martin Boysen had been glorified porters to this point. Nick and Martin now moved up to Camp Two, and went to work to clean up the route to the col, digging the fixed ropes out from under new snow. The two of them erected a Whillans Box at the col—Camp Three—on April 11. That done, they descended to join the others at Base Camp.

The expedition was making good progress, but the most difficult work awaited them. The porters weren't trained to use fixed ropes or climb on steep ground. Mike Thompson and Ian Clough were down with influenza. Mick Burke was feeling poorly. Dave Lambert wasn't adjusting well to the altitude.

Chris saw how easily his expedition could fail—but he was increasingly hopeful that it would succeed. He began to see that he was playing for high stakes, that this route might be celebrated and remembered. And even as he allowed himself to glimpse such possibilities he felt a puzzling sorrow. He would lie in his sleeping bag at night and figures from his past would rise up—forlorn but somehow purposeful shapes—as if to attend him as he drifted into sleep.

He could remember the end of the war in Europe. He had gone with his mother on VE Day to watch the celebrations in Trafalgar Square. She'd taken him home but she had awakened him that evening to go with her to see the giant bonfire and the fireworks. He had been very sleepy standing there near her with his hands in his pockets. He could remember something of what it had felt like to be that boy—ten years old, drowsy and cold, seeing the lights, wondering what it all meant, having no one to trust for an answer.

9

CHRIS AND THE American, Tom Frost, moved up to Camp Three on April 13. The next morning they set out to come to grips with the Ice Ridge that towered above it. Don had urged Chris to follow a shelf that rose to the right of the ridge. Tom disagreed; he was determined to tackle the ridge directly. He set off alone, trailing a rope. Chris hung back long enough to wade through wet, heavy snow for a look at Don's proposed route. It looked frightening. Chris turned and waded back to rejoin his partner.

Tom meanwhile had given himself a scare, coming very close to falling into a hidden crevasse. The two climbers roped up and Chris took the lead. The ground quickly grew steep. The ice was rotten; it offered no purchase for screws, and his axe placements were tenuous. The world dwindled to his field of vision, a series of close-ups. He knew dimly that he was pressed against certain limits. He could not safely retreat; he stood almost parallel to the steep ice and he couldn't lean away from it to look down at the ground that fell away beneath his boots; if he tried to descend he would have to guess where to put his feet, and he would fall. He glanced quickly to his right and saw easier ground. He edged across to it and then found a way up to a ledge. He had climbed just 100 feet. He was shocked to discover that it had taken two hours.

Tom led now, moving up through deep snow. He used a shovel to make a path. Chris followed him. The snow was pocked and hollow; he thought of a honeycomb. The world seemed desolate and very quiet. Chris paused to breathe, and felt his breath deepen and steady him. He had been very frightened on that first pitch.

The two climbers retreated to Camp Three for the night. The next morning they followed the fixed ropes to their high point. The climbing up here did not relent; the snow conditions grew worse as they floundered slowly higher, seeking firmer ground.

Dougal and Don meanwhile arrived at Camp Three at mid-morning. They dumped their loads and set out up the shelf that Don had recommended to Chris—the route Tom Frost had rejected. They made good progress, and it was soon evident that Don's instincts had been right. The shelf offered an easy way to bypass the section of ridge where Chris and Tom had struggled for two days to little end. Chris up on the ridge saw the progress Don and Dougal had made, and was furious at himself. His decision to ignore Don's advice and follow the American's lead had cost the expedition two days of wasted effort—time that could easily cost them the summit. He resolved to keep Don out in front as much as possible.

Tom and Chris abandoned the ridge. The next day they joined the other two on Don's ramp. The four men climbed toward an enormous gully that had accumulated vast quantities of snow. They edged closer to the Ice Ridge. Huge overhanging cornices threatened the climbers here, but they were safer from the even greater threat of avalanche. Dougal led up the start of an arête, which the party hoped would regain the ridge above the difficulties that had defeated Chris and Tom.

They spent three days on the arête. Don suffered one of his attacks of vertigo, and sat out the second day. The third day found all four climbers struggling up a subsidiary gully, still short of regaining the ridge. They retreated amid blowing snow. Chris and Tom descended to Base Camp. Nick Estcourt and Martin Boysen had already arrived at Camp Three to take their place. Dougal and Don were staying.

Dougal was still doing most of the leading. The arrangement suited him as well as Whillans. Dougal had an almost physical need to see the mountain fall away beneath him. Each step kicked in the snow or chopped in the ice took him further from reproach or closer to some solution; he climbed at some moments in a panic of need that receded as he moved higher. Don was less impatient. The idea occurred to Dougal that Don knew what awaited them; that there wasn't much curiosity in Don—only a smoldering anticipation.

The four climbers woke at Camp Three on April 19. The view from the camp was spectacular—serrated peaks, endless fields and shadows, the sky. Don and Dougal felt by now that these sights belonged to them, had become a part of their strange routine. Nick and Martin, the new arrivals, weren't feeling well; the ascent to this altitude—20,100 feet —had given them bad headaches, and they decided to remain at Camp Three for the day. Dougal and Don melted snow for tea, and dressed and trudged once more to the fixed ropes. They followed the ropes to the small saddle that marked their high point of the previous day; here Dougal stood and considered his alternatives.

The climbers had exhausted the potential of their arête, which disappeared into a cornice before reaching the crest of the Ice Ridge. Dougal traversed a gully to the wall of the ridge, and carefully forced his way up 50 feet of rotten snow and fractured rock. He emerged at last on the crest of the ridge in the early afternoon. It was snowing. Dougal and Don retreated to Camp Three to find that Nick and Martin were feeling somewhat better after their day of acclimatization.

The four men sat out a snowstorm in their tents the next day, and climbed together on April 21. They regained the ridge crest and found that it led quickly to easier ground, low-angle snow that could accommodate Camp Four. They spent two days carrying loads to the new site and digging out a platform. Dougal and Don at last returned to Base Camp for another rest.

Nick and Martin remained at the newly established Camp Four. Their job was to find a way up or around the rest of the Ice Ridge, which still towered overhead. The two friends had been on the mountain for three weeks. They were happy to be out front making the route. They woke alone on the morning of April 24 and stepped into a world of sky and snow, feeling that this was what they had come here to do. This was the reason for all the talk, the planning and expense, the walking and the headaches, the worry and homesickness. It all fell away, meant nothing in the context of this beauty and this isolation.

They set off up a snow slope that quickly grew steep. They were climbers again after their weeks of hauling loads, and their relief was like a drug. They climbed into a gully that seemed to offer a way past a pair of ice towers blocking progress on the ridge. The snow here was rotten, so Martin moved to the right and set off up an overhanging wall of ice that required direct aid, which here meant hanging from ice screws. The ice was somewhat rotten, so the screws offered poor security.

Martin reached a sort of hole in the snow and burrowed for 20 feet, emerging over a 2,000-foot drop that seemed to lunge at him. He set himself to ignore the exposure and his task took possession of him. He reached up—he was like a man climbing out of an attic window onto a roof—and placed a screw in the wall that loomed overhead. He clipped a sling to it and clambered out to stand in the sling, swaying and creaking over what seemed a near-infinity of crystal air. He was in it; he'd gone through a hole and no one would know where to look for him. There was an incredible freedom—also terror—in his sense of the surrounding void, how it lapped at him. He forced himself to continue to move, reaching yet higher to chop holds in the ice, traversing toward easier ground. He stopped to place his ice screws and each time felt the fatigue in his arms but his physical and emotional limits seemed to back away, receding as he worked. He felt amazed and pleased by this, but he believed at each moment that this dispensation would end in the next one. He knew he would fall when it did.

Martin took a full two hours to cross the wall to a corner. He finished in a gully full of still more rotten snow. He was almost entirely exhausted. He sank into the sun-pocked snow and rested for what seemed a long time. Then he rose and looked up and picked out a route up an ice arête. He started up and it was like climbing the sun-drenched prow of some enormous barge at sea. He was 50 feet above his last protection when at last he stepped back onto the crest of the Ice Ridge.

He had never done harder ice climbing, not back in Scotland, not anywhere. He built an anchor and brought up Nick—who even with the top-rope took two hours to climb through the tunnel and cross the wall to Martin's stance, arriving worn out and deeply impressed.

Martin led one more pitch, and the climbers retreated to Camp Four. The next day they encountered still more hard climbing—complex route-finding, unstable snow, rotten ice. Each climber led entire pitches without finding any real protection, knowing that a fall would rip him and his partner from the mountain. They would drop into another world—sucked out of a window and into the sky itself; no one would have the faintest prayer of finding them or their remains. They had climbed some 700 feet of new ground when they turned to make their way back to

Camp Four. Their strength was ebbing, and with it the crisp and thoughtless nature of their awareness; anxiety welled up in them as they descended the fixed ropes.

Nick and Martin slept late the next morning. They rose and ascended the fixed ropes but the effort exhausted them both. They pushed the route a mere 30 feet higher, through difficult mixed ground. That was all they could do. They turned and set off down the mountain for a rest.

Chris and Ian had meanwhile arrived at Camp Four to take over the lead. They spent the next day—April 27—shoveling out sections of the route above the camp; they adjusted anchors and fixed ropes for climbers who would ferry loads up this ground during the coming weeks. High winds battered their Whillans Box that night. Chris woke at midnight, and the two friends went about their preparations clumsy from the altitude, taking their time, waiting for the wind to blow itself out. They left the tent at seven o'clock in the morning.

They made their way up the fixed ropes in the cold mountain light. Chris set off to lead an overhanging corner. He could not afford to fall and hurt himself; there was little chance of a rescue here. Each move echoed dimly in the folds of the mountain. He'd climbed a beanstalk to the anteroom of an empty palace; he was awestruck but prepared to act from what he knew.

He climbed to the foot of another steep groove in the rock. He placed a single piton for an anchor. Ian followed and then climbed past, moving steadily, hammering in more pins for protection. Chris watched clouds fill the vast mountain hollows like billows of snow. His sense of drama faded. He heard stones fall from the Rock Band overhead, and saw them bound past in the near distance to land in snowfields far below.

The falling rock threatened some of the fixed ropes. The route was festooned with them; climbers carrying loads higher or descending to lower camps swayed and dangled on the ropes for hours at a time. Chris thought of John Harlin; the knowledge of John's death was like a blurred woodcarving, half-shrouded in wishes and aversion, marked and worn by fumbling attempts to examine it. Chris owned his knowledge of the death in common with Dougal and the others who had been there.

Ian surmounted an overhang and took a full hour to improvise a belay anchor in the rotten ice. It was very cold. The partners retreated to Camp Four for the evening radio call, which gave the climbers at various camps a chance to communicate. Don came on the air to insist that Chris stop letting climbers retreat all the way to Base Camp to rest. Don argued that this practice disrupted the flow of supplies on the mountain. He went further, accusing Mick of spending too much time resting at Base Camp. Don proposed that none of the lead climbers should descend below Camp Three; they could leave the Sherpas to supply the lower camps. Mick, furious, broke in to argue that climbers didn't fully recover at the higher camps. Nick and some of the others agreed—but Chris shared Don's concern that the flow of supplies to the higher camps had dwindled. He tentatively agreed to Don's suggestion, leaving most of the other climbers in various states of unhappiness.

Chris and Ian spent part of the next day, April 29, improving the route above Camp Four. They climbed further in the afternoon, up bad snow and broken rock. Chris took three hours to lead a 60-foot traverse. The tremendous exposure at his back seemed to tug at him as bits of rock skittered from his footholds. Each move called for a precision difficult to muster at this altitude and in his growing fatigue.

Ian followed the traverse. Chris set off to lead another difficult section. He took off his gloves to grip the small handholds. His fingers grew cold. He couldn't feel the rock. He retreated to join

Ian, and the two of them descended to Camp Four in a rising snowstorm. They spoke for the first time of the possibility of failing on the route.

Ian was physically shattered. He wanted a rest. Chris asked him to stay for one more day. That would allow time for Dougal to arrive and replace him—they wouldn't lose a day of climbing. Ian agreed, but the next morning he was in no condition to climb. He sagged at the edge of collapse on the fixed ropes; still, he carried on above them so that he could hold a rope for Chris.

Chris led higher, climbing slowly and with great care as if afraid of disturbing some balance that held things in place. No person in the history or prehistory of the world had been here. He stepped into that empty flow of time and felt the crispness of solitude draw fear from him like a dry poultice. A huge mushroom of snow towered above him and he climbed cautiously out of its shadow, losing track of the scale of his surroundings even as he felt himself dwindle to a speck of awareness. He imagined sailing backward toward the sun—he would leave this tiny, four-limbed figure on this sky-sized wall.

These odd sensations passed; the wall became a mere obstacle. Chris moved with great effort, amazed at his own selfishness; he should have let Ian go down. There was nothing lighthearted or playful about this work; this was just fending off death in the shape of this menacing wall, which threatened to collapse or topple as he clung to it. The wall seemed big enough to sweep him from the planet and into the endless, slow spin of an infinite fall. Chris was aware of his body—cold and sweat and the awkwardness of joints and sinews, the pull of gravity and the tug of his muscles on bone. He forced his way up, every step new. He saw a chimney that might lead to easier ground. It was snowing. The climbers turned back—the snow fell every afternoon now.

It was May 1. The climbers had been at work on the Ice Ridge for eighteen days. They wouldn't finish the route at this rate. They were tired, and some of them were sick. The team doctor, Dave Lambert, was laid up with dysentery at Camp Two. Mike Thompson had a badly ulcerated mouth; he was too debilitated to carry loads. Nick Estcourt had chest pains. Ian was now truly exhausted; he must have a real rest at Base Camp.

Martin Boysen was still moving strongly, but he couldn't support the frontline climbers by himself. The carries between the upper camps were nightmarish. They began with the three-hour process of dressing and cooking in the bitter cold, all of it done in a fug of weariness and nausea. Then the slow plodding and heaving in a stupor of misery, the stupor pierced by terrifying moments of clarity on the fixed ropes, where a climber would in effect wake up dangling thousands of feet above the glacier, wondering how each lurch wore at the now-battered ropes.

Such moments of doubt soon sunk into fatigue. The climbers were far too miserable most of the time to consider hypothetical outcomes, however gory or profound. It was also true that other considerations distracted them from the danger. Each climber understood that a strong performance carrying loads between camps might earn him more time at the front, where he could compete for a spot on one of the summit teams. At the same time, each climber knew that too much load carrying might render him physically unfit to take advantage of such an opportunity.

They managed this knowledge in different ways. Dave Lambert and Mike Thompson had been recruited as support climbers. They did that work; still, they dreamed of the summit. Nick and Martin worked themselves to the point of exhaustion to carry loads between camps, and grew more or less resentful of the others—especially of Don and Dougal. Mick Burke complained—it was in his nature and in his history to resist any form of exploitation. Don and Dougal alternated bouts of lead climbing and resting, with not much time or inclination for carrying loads.

Dougal replaced the shattered Ian at Camp Four, joined Chris to at last reach the top of the Ice Ridge in two days of hard climbing. That effort left Chris exhausted; he descended to Camp Three to rest.

Don arrived to take Bonington's place, and roped up with Dougal to climb an ice cliff above the ridge. Dougal led, climbing into dazzling sunlight. He arrived at the top of the cliff and stared up at the enormous Rock Band, which towered above him across a patch of easy snow. He crossed the snow and hammered a ceremonial piton into the rock to mark the site of Camp Five. Don came up behind him, and the two climbers discussed their agenda. They would go down for a rest, leaving the Rock Band to Mick Burke and Tom Frost—and then they would return to finish off the mountain.

Mick and Tom spent two days carrying loads up to Camp Five, and occupied the camp on May 9. They arrived that evening weary but excited. Tom knocked over a pan of boiling water. The climbers were too tired to melt more snow so they went to sleep in a haze of thirst and fatigue and desire—all of it colored by their isolation and by the fear that smoldered in them like a low-grade fever.

They left their tent early on May 10, under perfectly clear skies. Their comrades at Base Camp could observe the two climbers through binoculars—the watchers almost like the tourists who peered up at Eiger climbers from the hotel balcony at Kleine Scheidegg; only here the scale was grander and the climbers more remote. The climbers had tentatively mapped out a route through the Rock Band. The route led through ice fields and up rock walls to a huge spur of rock—they called this landmark the Flatiron, after the feature of similar shape on the Eiger's North Face.

Tom and Mick climbed at first unroped on easy snow that seemed to lead past the first difficulties. Tom soon plunged into a slot in the snow, much as he had done at the start of the Ice Ridge. He hung wedged in the throat of the crevasse, his legs dangling over the darkness like limbs of some stubby insect. The easy snow slope lost its appeal; it menaced them now. They made their way back to their starting point, and set out across ice-glazed rock. Mick led, climbing on blunt crampons that offered precarious purchase on the thin ice.

He knew that a fall with crampons—even a short fall—would be serious. The crampon points might catch on ice or rock as his body continued to fall, tearing an ankle or a knee. The worry flickered at the periphery of his mind. He traversed left toward rock that looked like it would take a piton for a new anchor. He reached left with his axe, taking weight off his right crampon, which shifted beneath his boot. The ice was brittle and steep. Each time he lifted a foot he balanced carefully on the other as he moved the first foot sideways and kicked it back into the ice; sometimes when he kicked, a crampon skittered and when this happened he teetered on the brink, supported by the tip of his axe. He had in the intensity of his work forgotten to place screws; he would fall at least 100 feet if he came off now. Fear gripped him; he could barely shout to Tom to watch the rope.

Tom could see that a fall at this point would be catastrophic for him as well as Mick. He calmly advised Mick to try tapping in an ice piton; it would be easier than placing a screw. Mick had forgotten he had ice pitons. He managed to get one in—barely—and he began to climb again but now his right crampon had come loose. It dangled useless from his foot. He somehow retreated to the ice piton and struggled awkwardly to get the crampon back onto his boot; he thought of standing on a high stool to put on socks.

It took him ten minutes. He rested briefly and set off again, feeling a bit like an astronaut casting off for a space walk. He climbed further toward the rocks where he hoped to build a proper anchor. He reached them at last, standing on small holds in his crampons and sighing with relief as he laid hold of a giant flake—the rock moved and he saw it was going to come off and take him with it.

It didn't. The huge rock settled in again, some ancient stone creature disturbed in its long sleep. Mick had recoiled in fright but now he recovered his balance and commenced an awkward, one-handed struggle to place a piton. He managed to get something hammered into a crack, and clipped in and settled down to smoke while Frost followed him up the pitch.

The next pitches were mostly steep rock, slick with ice. Mick continued to lead, climbing in his heavy boots; he made steady progress. He placed occasional pitons for protection, and hung from each new pin to smoke his Gauloises. The intensity of the climbing hid the wider world from him, but Mick while he rested could look around and note the steepness of the ground. The sky was in front of him when he turned his face and body from the mountain to smoke. There was nothing directly above him but a narrow band of light that was as much a border as a river might be—it divided the mountain from the rest of the world.

They continued to climb. The sun warmed the mountain and rocks whistled past; one brushed Tom's pack with a muffled thump. The two men came to a ledge at the foot of huge ice fields. They studied the fields for a moment but they were too tired to draw conclusions. They turned and retreated to Camp Five.

The following morning dawned windless and clear. Mick and Tom carried 500 feet of rope to their new high point. Mick led again. He climbed rock slabs and traversed across the top of a huge snowfield—steep, engaging climbing with good protection. They were now some 8,000 feet above the glacier; the climbers felt a dim wonder only partly blunted by fatigue and altitude and concentration. Mick ran out of rope just below a spur of rock that obscured his view of the Flatiron, their next objective.

It was May 11. Chris and the others at Base Camp could see the tiny black figures of their two friends and the immense task that awaited them—Mick and Tom had made what seemed small progress on the towering mass of the Rock Band. Chris estimated that the expedition had perhaps three weeks to finish the route before the monsoon would arrive with heavy snowfall that would make climbing impossible. They wouldn't get up the wall at this rate.

Chris had this in mind when he made his next decision. The decision would define the careers and reputations of every climber on the expedition. Nick Estcourt and Martin Boysen were scheduled to go out front when Mick and Tom finished their work on the Rock Band. But Chris believed that Nick and Martin had worn themselves out carrying loads between camps. He wondered, too, if they were equal to the route finding that might be required high on the face. Meanwhile, Don and Dougal had finished a two-day rest at Base Camp; they were already moving back up the mountain.

Chris, taking up his mantle of official expedition leader, resolved to send Don and Dougal back into the lead, leapfrogging them past Nick and Martin. He knew those two would be upset, and he put off announcing his decision until Don and Dougal had made their way back up the route to the higher camps.

Mick and Tom meanwhile made further progress. Mick led yet again on May 12, climbing more difficult rock with very little protection. He climbed deliberately, a man who understood his job and its risks. He occasionally reached down to wipe snow from rock or to chip away patches of ice. He was entirely absorbed and the climbing drew him on into difficulties that weren't obvious until they were upon him. He led Tom up two frightening pitches to the foot of a gully that seemed to lead to a traverse, which Mick thought would bring them at last to the Flatiron. They retreated to Camp Five in a rising snowstorm.

They didn't climb at all the next day. Tom cleared huge drifts of snow from the campsite. Mick descended to meet Martin Boysen and Mike Thompson; they had come up with supplies for the high camp. Martin was still going surprisingly well. Mike was in desperate shape, very tired and still suffering from his ulcerated mouth. Mick took his load and sent him down and turned to hump his way back up the ropes to Camp Five.

THE CLIMBERS SCATTERED up and down the route had until now operated in a quasidemocratic mode. They had settled their differences as a kind of fractious family. This now changed—in part because more of them had begun to glimpse what was at stake.

They had all seen the television camera crew that haunted Base Camp (the crew had stayed off the glacier since a cameraman's run-in with a crevasse). The climbers knew that this expedition was in some ways a public undertaking, that it had the potential to make or cement or enhance reputations. At the same time, each man carried his desire to shrug off his greed for success or reputation. The climbers' competing wishes—for success and for virtue—led them on and helped account for what happened to them.

Chris knew that a success on Annapurna would give a major boost to his mountaineering career. It might also allow him to strengthen the narrative that was taking shape in his mind, the story he wished to inhabit. Don needed a success because he had failed too often, and because he needed reputation and the money that he assumed would follow. Dougal wanted admiration and forgiveness and also the oblivion of kicking steps in snow.

The others—Nick Estcourt and Martin Boysen, Mick Burke and Ian Clough and the American, Tom Frost—had their own ambitions. They wanted to behave well. They had done carries and some climbing, and each had imagined finding himself on the summit.

Don and Dougal reached Camp Four on May 13. Chris during that evening's radio call announced his plan to send them immediately into the lead, ahead of Nick and Martin. Nick objected; so did Mick Burke. They argued that Don and Dougal, fresh from Base, were needed to carry loads to Camp Five, which was very low on supplies. Don broke in to say that he and Dougal were needed up front; in his view, the other climbers had done a poor job of pushing out the route. His accusation infuriated both Nick and Mick.

The conversation veered into acrimony. Chris eventually shut it down, dictating a compromise. Don and Dougal would carry loads for one more day; that done, however, they would take over the climbing above Camp Five.

Mick and Tom, both of them stung by Don's criticism, covered 800 feet of new ground the next day. They descended the mountain on May 15. They had done the hardest climbing on the face during their five days in the lead. Mick in particular had delivered a spectacular performance. He felt a sense of release and fulfillment; the feeling came in waves as he followed the fixed ropes down. He passed other climbers struggling to haul loads up the face. They looked weary—downhearted and confused. He saw himself in them: they were children, ignorant optimists who had promised to make a stream run uphill—but children would have played at their task for a time and then wandered off.

Chris was making his own way up the mountain from Base

Camp, where he had gone to recover from a bout of chest pains. He reached Camp Three on May 17. Don and Dougal meanwhile joined Martin to carry loads up to Camp Five, where the three of them spent the night. The next day they followed the fixed ropes to Mick and Tom's high point. Martin turned back—his feet were very cold. Don and Dougal dropped their loads at the top of the Flatiron and carried on, fixing rope up a gully that Dougal thought might take them out of the Rock Band at last. They climbed another 400 feet before turning back to follow Martin back down to Camp Five, where Nick Estcourt had arrived with another load of supplies.

The night was hellish. Nick and Martin were nearly suffocated when a snow slide collapsed their tent. The snow also covered the Whillans Box, and all of the climbers' supplies. Don and Martin spent the next day digging out and relocating the shelters. Dougal and Nick descended to Camp Four to pick up more food and gear. The day was very cold and windy, but Dougal felt a mounting happiness. He was moving well; the conditions that had begun to overwhelm the other climbers had spared him.

Martin also had held up better than most of the other climbers—repeatedly making the long carry between Camp Four and Camp Five—but now he had reached the end of his tether. He left for Base Camp that day, knowing that he wouldn't be this high on the South Face again. Nick was suffering, too; coping with the avalanche the previous night had taken much of his fading strength.

Don and Dougal climbed the fixed ropes the following day to reach Mick and Tom's high point again. This time, they traversed across into a snow bank and began digging a platform for Camp Six. Nick followed with supplies, but couldn't finish the carry; he left his load in the snow beneath them. Dougal went down a few rope lengths to retrieve Nick's abandoned load and stopped.

He took off his own pack for a moment. His foot brushed it. The pack moved, and before he could react it was sliding and bouncing down the face. It took with it his personal gear and the food for the new camp.

A wave of self-pity welled up in him. He imagined Don going for the summit without him. He smothered the image, and turned away from the mountain in a half-amused rage, oddly pleased by this new turn. He knew what he must do and the fact that he had the strength to do it—when none of the others would have—made him happy. He would descend and scrounge a sleeping bag from one of the lower camps; that done, he would simply climb back up with it. He was in this moment the person he had wished to be, a kind of superman after all.

It took him a mere twenty minutes to descend to Camp Five. Chris had come up the ropes to the camp with more supplies, and he offered his own sleeping bag to Dougal. That would leave Chris without a bag, but he could radio down for someone to carry up a replacement the next day. Dougal meanwhile could rejoin Don at Camp Six.

Dougal agreed; he would leave the next morning—which meant he was stuck here with Nick and Chris for the night, with two sleeping bags between three men. Dougal put on all the down clothing he could scrounge and woke shivering every few hours to lay awake cursing his own clumsiness. He rose early the next morning and set off with Bonington's sleeping bag and some porridge—Don was living on cigars and melted snow up at Camp Six.

Dougal reached the camp in the early afternoon. The two men ate some of the porridge, and then they climbed two more rope-lengths up the gully they hoped would at last lead them out of the Rock Band. They returned to camp amid whirling snow and heavy gusts of wind. Chris arrived with more rope and a radio, and immediately turned around to head back down to Camp Five. Dougal, watching him leave, thought Chris seemed exhausted.

The tent here at Camp Six hung over the edge of its narrow platform. The site was tremendously exposed, with awe-inspiring drops on three sides and very little shelter from the wind. The tent shook and billowed. Dougal imagined it setting sail across the Himalayan sky with himself and Don in its belly, some hideous runaway kite. Don kept his boots on and advised his partner to do the same; they might need to make a quick exit. Still, they were content. They were where they had meant to be from the beginning—in position to try to finish climbing the face.

THEY SURVIVED THE night and set out in the morning in continued high winds and snow. It was a relief to be out in the weather after a night of damp cowering behind the tent's fabric walls. The cold seemed like a breath of heaven; it uplifted and protected them. They weren't afraid at all.

Each man climbed almost as if alone. Dougal strained to look across through blowing snow to where his companion stood or moved; at times he only felt Don's presence. It was possible in these conditions to acknowledge that the two of them were bound to one another by a mutual love of this solitude and the freedom it conferred upon them—by a love of the distance it put between them and their mistakes, their confusion. They reached their gully amid the continuing storm. Dougal led up through small avalanches, favoring one side of the gully to avoid being swept off his feet by the shin-deep torrents of snow. He found bare rock and placed a piton for an anchor, and at that moment a tide of snow pummeled and drenched him. He waited for it to stop, but the heavy white stuff continued to billow and press at him; there seemed no limit to the snow on this mountain. The climbers gave up and turned to make their half-blind way back to Camp Six, where they crawled inside their tent and listened to the wind shriek.

The sound died after a few hours and the climbers emerged to mottled sunlight. They were not tired, and they climbed back to their high point in the gully, reaching it early in the afternoon to swim upward once more through the heavy new snow. Don had brought an entrenching tool, and they used it to dig a path of sorts to the start of a chimney.

They were weary when they descended once again to their lonely camp. They were short of food and pitons. No one in the lower camps had ventured out to make a carry. The two climbers again felt their solitude. It seemed to them that the expedition was winding down; that they were left to climb the mountain themselves. The idea pleased and disoriented them; some tether had snapped. And they were very curious. They didn't know where their new gully was taking them. It might be a dead end or it might be the finish of the route's difficulties. They were afire to know.

They set out very early the next morning. This time it was astonishingly cold. The cold drove their wits from them. They were down to awareness, and after a time even that seemed to vanish so that the climber's identities blurred into the mountain or the cold itself. Dougal's experience near the finish of the Eiger Direct had been something like this—an almost hellish striving that he loved and that emptied him of memory and regret, made him useful and appropriate. He recognized this as an echo of the truth of things. He was stepping at dawn onto an empty stage where he could perform without witness.

They worked their way into the gully again. Don found a place to take off his boots and warm his feet; he was very concerned about frostbite. Dougal led up into the chimney they had reached the day before. The rock was slick with snow, offering poor holds and little protection. They were down to four pitons. They were now very high—over 24,000 feet—so that every move made it hard for Dougal to breathe. A part of his mind held a picture of something from school: a syringe taking fluid from a beaker. He made his way at last out of the chimney and once more into snow; there was still more of the gully to climb.

They had fixed almost all of their remaining rope, but they wanted to know what came next—in particular, whether they were at last approaching the end of the Rock Band. They untied from their last anchor and continued to climb, roped together but with no anchor to stop a fall. They had been on more dangerous ground many times but here the possibility of dying together was vivid to them; it awoke in them a sense that their living together—what was happening now—was no less profound. The intimacy of this moved them both. They held their understanding of the risk at a barely sufficient distance, aiming to diminish it toward its ordinary status as a kind of myth without losing the intimacy or the thrill of it; it was very thrilling. Tears rose in Don's eyes, not only because of his love for the younger man—what he suddenly recognized as his hopes for Dougal—but also because this view of his own vulnerability came as a relief. He was for the moment free of any notion that he could not die.

They moved in a dream of a narrative; the world had dwindled to a setting for a children's story. The gully led them to a view of a snowfield and of Annapurna's summit—it looked in reach. They could establish Camp Seven here, at the top of the gully; they believed this would put them within a day's climb of the summit. Death shrank to a mere enemy as they retreated in the snow; death was once again something that lay between them and some future—no longer with them, no longer part of each moment.

DON AND DOUGAL descended to the tent at Camp Six and crawled into their sleeping bags. Chris arrived from Camp Five with more rope. They needed a tent for Camp Seven, and he offered to go down to retrieve one the next day. Don and Dougal would take a rest day; there was no point in going back up without the tent. Dougal urged Chris to bring up a sleeping bag and personal gear along with the tent so that the three of them could go to the summit together.

Chris set out down the fixed ropes late in the day, promising to be back with the tent and his things the following morning. He spent the night alone at Camp Five, and in the morning rose and packed carefully: tent, movie camera, food, his own gear and sleeping bag and oxygen cylinder. The load came to more than sixty pounds—it was too much to carry. He would have to leave his own gear and his sleeping bag behind. Dougal and Don would go to the summit without him. He gave in to his fatigue and disappointment, slumping in the snow and sobbing—then stopped as suddenly, cursing himself for his weakness. His head cleared and he set out with his smaller load, struggling up the fixed ropes to Camp Six.

He delivered his load to Dougal and Don, and returned to Camp Five, where he came upon Ian Clough. Ian with his characteristic unselfishness had forced his way up through the snow with oxygen masks and food for the summit team. The two friends settled in for the night and Chris reviewed the situation. Dougal and Don were in position to establish Camp Seven the following day—April 24—and then try for the summit. Ian and Chris would meanwhile carry loads to Camp Six. They would move up to Camp Seven on April 25, and would make their own summit attempt the next day. Mick and Tom were at Camp Four now; they could be in position to make their summit bid on April 27.

It looked good on paper—but the next morning's weather was

bad, with clouds and high wind. Chris had now spent three days carrying loads to Camp Six at 24,000 feet. Those carries had been difficult, but this fourth day was nightmarish. He had several attacks of diarrhea while he was packing at Camp Five. Each attack meant dropping his wind pants and other layers to expose his bottom to the stinging cold; cleaning up each time was another ordeal. He had another attack on the fixed ropes later in the day; this time, he had to remove his waist harness and dangle from a make-shift chest harness—amid this struggle, a powder snow avalanche filled his pants and ran up his back. Ian had his own problems; his oxygen bottle didn't work properly. He discarded it, and was soon very cold. He reached Camp Six half an hour behind Chris.

The wind was bad all day. Ian thought back to his time with Chris in the Alps eight years before—their blissful day on the Walker Spur in 1962, just before they'd climbed the Eiger together. This place was darker; you could never manage to forget that it was dangerous. You had to think of your fear as a hiding place and refuse to go there; you had to force yourself to stay out in the open or you would be miserable every moment. It occurred to Ian that climbing protected him from being ordinary even as it threatened to take away everything—love and work, the joy that sometimes came to him at night so that he lay awake thinking of his sleeping wife and child. He brought them to mind briefly now. He did it like someone drinking whisky in the daytime—a quick swallow and put it away.

DON AND DOUGAL followed the ropes back up to the site for Camp Seven, carrying the tent that Chris had brought them. It was very foggy; they climbed in a near-whiteout. It was windy, too, and cold again. Don stopped twice to take off his boots and warm his feet. They reached the top of the ropes and Dougal peered up through the murk toward the top of the gully. He could make out the stretch they had climbed unprotected two days earlier. It was more frightening in these conditions. He stared through the crust of ice that had formed on his goggles and set out; this time Don gave him a belay.

Dougal was reminded once more of summit day on the Eiger Direct; only this was worse. There was no protection at all, and no sense of anyone through this white wind. He thought once of falling—he had run out almost 300 feet of rope—and the thought was like an escape; he felt the pull of speed, of departure. Abruptly he came upon the new campsite, desolate and alluring at once. The sight of it made him smile; he didn't know why.

Don followed. He took a long time and rose from the gloom like some Yeti; the sight of him startled Dougal. The two of them staggered about in the wind, looking for a flat spot to pitch the tent in this world of white. Don began digging in the snow but he soon struck hard ice. There was nowhere to dig a decent platform. Dougal took dazed notice of the absence of his own left hand. It had gone completely numb. They had run out of time; they would have to return to Camp Six for the night.

Dougal didn't know which way to go—but even as his fear arose in him the clouds parted long enough for the climbers to spot their gully. They descended 300 feet to the top of the gully and stopped; perhaps they could spend the night here. Dougal tried to hack out a platform for their tent, but once more the ice was too hard.

Don turned without speaking and walked across to the fixed rope. He set off into the gully and Dougal followed; soon they were piling into the tiny two-man tent at Camp Six. Chris and Ian had already moved in; they had expected Don and Dougal to establish Camp Seven and spend the night there. It was too late for anyone to go down to Camp Five—at any rate, Tom Frost and Mick Burke already occupied the only shelter there.

The four climbers at Camp Six settled in for the night. Chris had never spent a worse one in the mountains. The blowing snow made its way into everything, wetting the sleeping bags so that the climbers huddled in pools of snowmelt. Ian took the worst spot, in a corner. Dougal crouched nearest the entrance. He went outside once to clear snow from the tent so that the shelter wouldn't collapse. The four men brewed tea; they listened to the wind and they talked.

Chris and Ian decided to abandon their own summit plans. They were very tired; more to the point, Don and Dougal needed their support: there was no one else to do the carry from Camp Five to Camp Six. They began their descent in the morning. Chris felt low and fearful. Ian was better. He was taking his first steps toward home; his real work on the mountain was done. He could begin to look forward to friends and to family and work. He knew that he would carry something away from the mountain—he wondered how he would make use of it.

DON AND DOUGAL stayed put at Camp Six. It was snowing too heavily to climb. They had enough food left for two days. They spent the morning clearing new snow from the tent, and trying to dry their clothes inside the shelter. They kept the stove burning and eventually slept.

The storm continued through the night and into the following day. They rested at camp for a second day, dealing with the accumulations of snow on the tent and dozing off from time to time. Mick and Tom came on the air during the evening radio call and promised to try to carry food up to Camp Six the next morning. Dougal during the night poked his head out of the tent and saw stars—the storm had passed.

He woke Don up early. They left camp at seven o'clock, and reached their high point before midday. They had planned to establish Camp Seven here—but it was early; there seemed no reason to stop, so they picked up the tent they had left here and kept going. They had come to a place where the top of the mountain existed; it was no longer a mere concept. It occurred to them that today they might reach the summit. They gazed up at an ice field that led to a narrow, snow-covered ridge. The ridge in turn led to an 800-foot face, mixed ground. It didn't look like much, and after that—after that, there was nothing.

They considered for a moment. The weather was unsettled; gusts of wind whipped snow past them, and the sky held some clouds. They might have to bivouac on the ridge if the weather grew worse. They would have the tent—assuming they could manage to pitch it in the wind—but no stove or food or sleeping bags.

They climbed on. They reached the ridge and Dougal unpacked the tent and set it down in the snow. They continued up the ridge, feeling it under their feet, and set off up the final steep section, climbing without anchors. The terrain wasn't easy; steep patches of ice and sketchy rock slabs. Dougal was surprised to find that he wasn't suffering terribly from the altitude. He had a crampon that kept coming loose, and he made himself stop climbing and fixed it. He dug out the camera and shot some film of Don moving ahead of him toward the summit ridge; as the camera clicked and whirred, Dougal was aware of their spectacular position—the world, everything but this, gone.

Don continued to climb. The altitude was nothing to him. He climbed away from all that had blocked and stymied him—the pointless clutter of violence and difficulty and shame. He climbed toward snow and sky at 26,000 feet, drawn onward by the immense silent gravity of space. Dougal watched his solitary figure vanish into clouds of blowing snow and briefly reappear to disappear once more, this time on the final ridge.

Dougal followed. The climbing was still difficult. He scraped snow from wobbly rocks and moved deliberately; an ignorant observer might have suspected him of eyeing the ground for seashells or arrowheads. He was in no hurry. The climb was in his grasp, and he had only this time to enjoy the task itself, the unfinished work. He felt a familiar regret rise in him; he fended it off, exasperated. That passed and he came to the ridge and over it and was surprised by the calm; there was no wind on the north side of the peak.

He stared down and across into a world until now hidden. Snow slopes disappeared in cloud, a sea of it a thousand feet below—everything a dove gray, like staring from the bottom of a winterbound lake in, say, Scotland.

The two men barely spoke; they had their oxygen masks on and words were no comfort to them, were obvious lies in this context. Don had already set to work building an anchor for the first rappel. He was at once relieved and angry at the fact that it was done, that there was nothing left to climb. But here he corrected himself: the actual summit was hard to identify on the ridge and the climbers could see a point that looked perhaps 30 feet higher than the ground they occupied. Don finished with his anchor and crossed the snow to the high point. Dougal filmed him, and then followed. They stood together for a moment upon the summit, confused, without ceremony to orient them, and then walked back across to Don's rappel anchor.

They rappelled 150 feet of steep ground, and then disengaged from the rappel rope to pick their way through rock-strewn snow. This was a dangerous time and each climber moved with great care. Their backs were to the summit now and they kept their eyes down, on their feet. The wind died as they reached the fixed ropes and their hearts began to lift under the weight of their confusion. Don felt tired for the first time.

They reached Camp Six in time for the evening radio call. Don handed the set to Dougal. Chris, snowbound down at Camp Four, wanted to know if they'd managed to leave the tent that morning despite the storm.

Aye, Dougal told him. *We've just climbed Annapurna.*

MICK'S VOICE BROKE in amid the relief and happy chatter from the various camps, where the climbers hunched over their radios. He and Tom were at Camp Five. They wanted to move up to Camp Six for their summit attempt. Chris agreed, but his concern over the first summit team's prospects had given way to concern—an almost childish anxiety—for the safety of the expedition members. The weather remained unsettled, and the strength had gone out of the team. There was little chance of mounting a serious rescue attempt if something went wrong high on the face. Chris had what he wanted most—the expedition had climbed the route—and now he saw the appalling risks in a new light. There was nothing left to achieve worth even the chance of casualties. He slept poorly that night, and woke resolved to order everyone off the face.

He made his announcement during the morning radio call. Tom Frost came on the air to talk him out of it, and Chris recognized that he couldn't force anyone to abandon the route. He agreed that Tom and Mick would go for the summit while the rest of the team began to evacuate the mountain.

Chris immediately regretted his decision. The face seemed to grow more threatening by the hour. The impending monsoon warmed the ice walls and towers that threatened many sections of the route. The mountain heaved invisibly, as if brewing some violence. Chris left Camp Four with Ian Clough and Dave Lambert and the three men descended amid the falling snow: it was monsoon snow, heavy and wet. They stopped at Camp Three.

Mike Thompson was there. Don and Dougal arrived a few hours later; there were subdued congratulations. The climbers all felt the peak's menace, as if they had provoked some huge enemy and now found themselves in retreat. There was an element of horror in their growing sense that the mountain was not dead, not mindless or even fully asleep. They felt little pride in their shared achievement; instead they succumbed to an inchoate shame, which carried with it a choking fear. Don in particular was afraid and he urged Chris to get everyone off the mountain.

Dougal and Don departed and moved quickly down the route. The BBC crew ventured out onto the glacier to greet and film them. Chris and the others remained at Camp Three to wait for the second summit team.

Mick and Tom meanwhile made their way up to Camp Six. They climbed into the beginnings of a new storm. Tom was moving well, but Mick had gone slowly all day. Tom cooked that evening. The climbers slept for a few hours and woke soon after midnight to brew drinks and make ready to climb. Their preparations took three hours. It was still very cold when they left the tent.

Mick's feet quickly turned numb. He was very worried about his toes—if nothing else, losing them would interrupt his budding career as a cameraman. He turned back, leaving Tom to try to finish the route alone.

The American climbed on into the storm. It grew colder and the wind rose again. He took four hours to reach the top of the gully—one of the spots where Don and Dougal had tried and failed to dig a platform for a seventh camp. The summit had seemed close to those two then; Tom thought it looked pretty far away.

He was alone, without the comfort or incentive that a partner might provide. He imagined himself on the wall that led to the summit ridge, solitary and cold. He weighed the possibilities with an intensity that reflected the stakes. He might not live to see another sunrise if he pressed on—but if he continued to the summit and survived, every sunrise from this day forward would be different.

He conducted an experiment: he told himself that he would climb on—his mind gave the command—and then he waited for his body to decide the issue: to lurch forward or to turn back. He waited in the stillness. The empty, windblown plateau seemed a place of death. He waited for three hours, allowing his options to narrow as the morning passed and the temperature began to fall. He daydreamed and collected rock specimens and at last turned away from the summit and from his desire for it. He descended the fixed ropes in the gully and was back with Mick at Camp Six before noon.

Mick gave the others the news at the midday radio call. Chris now felt free to descend to Base Camp. He came upon the debris of an ice avalanche at the foot of a gully below Camp Three. The torrent of snow and ice had buried the tracks left by Don and Dougal during their descent to Base Camp the previous afternoon. Chris continued his own descent, and reached Base Camp before dark. He slept poorly that night and rose early to write an account of the expedition's success—a rough draft for a press release. He broke off from his work every so often, stepping out into the sun to scan the face for signs of the others. The television crew set up their cameras for an interview and he was standing in the sun answering their questions when he heard a commotion—anxious, frightened voices— he couldn't make out the words—only his own name.

IAN CLOUGH AND Mike Thompson and Dave Lambert had left Camp Three that morning. They were glad to be getting off the mountain and their relief allowed them to feel their sadness at this end to their adventure. They had decided not to wait on Tom and Mick. Those two sounded fine, and the urge to get down to Base Camp was very strong.

Ian and Mike reached Camp Two at 9:30. Dave was perhaps five minutes behind them. Ian wanted to stop to rest and eat something. Mike wanted to carry on down to Camp One—it was easy going, another half-hour. Ian shrugged and gave his assent, and they kept moving.

The worst of the ice towers that threatened this part of the glacier had toppled some weeks earlier. Still, the climbers moved as quickly as they could. Ian led the way, with Mike just behind. They were thirsty and tired and their feet hurt in their heavy boots and sweat-soaked socks but they were nearly done. There would be no more climbing here—only easy talk and packing and sorting out feelings. The lives they had left to visit this mountain awaited them in various stages of neglect and disarray. Ian was glad to be going back to his wife and child and his work at the climbing shop. His ordinary life with a bed and bodies to touch and ordinary smells seemed a vision—he saw with a charming clarity the shape and texture of his life.

He dug in himself for a sense of urgency that might help him to move quickly here. He didn't find it; he was too warm, the day's heat heavy upon him. The two men emerged from a corridor of ice—a cavern of light, carved and hollowed by the season's gathering warmth—and into the open sky once more. The sunlight greeted them. Ian saw a party of Sherpas ascending the glacier for some purpose. The enormous bulk of the mountain lay behind the two descending climbers, like an ocean or a Continent at their backs.

The explosion amid the high silence made a sound like the ringing of some huge and ancient bell. The sky went dark amidst the sound of it. Mike leaped for a trough of snow that lay behind a wall of ice. A torrent of ice blocks swept over and past him, leaving him half-buried in debris.

Ian had begun to run at the sound. He moved heavily in the snow beset by the impending dark even as he felt a curious lightness. Reasons were lifted from him, replaced by awareness of an imperative that didn't need to make sense in order to matter. He needed the sun; he sorted through memories—which single thing to take in a dream from a burning house. He came upon it as the mountain's exhalation reached him; the force of this drove away thoughts and needs and something he hadn't known was there; its departing amazed him.

The Sherpas coming up the glacier had fled downhill. They collected themselves as the light returned to the sky and their surroundings. They found Ian's body almost at once.

CHRIS SAW THEM from a distance as he walked up from Base Camp. They were dragging the corpse—wrapped in a tarp and then strapped to a ladder—across the bleak glacier. The image seemed a manifestation of the corruption implicit in change, implicit in spring as much as in any other season. His eyes rose to the ice cliffs that still stood above the glacier. The mountain had no sympathy for men's tasks or ceremonies. It made no decisions; it was mindless.

He walked on. He passed Mick Burke and Dave Lambert on their way down and kept walking; he was looking for Tom Frost and a young trekker—one of the honorary Sherpas who had wandered into Base Camp one day and stayed to help. Tom and the trekker were the last men down the mountain. Chris almost passed them in the mist, but hearing their voices and the rattle of stones dislodged by their boots he turned from his path and they rose in his sight—ghostly black forms; he dreaded speaking to them. The three men descended together in near-silence.

10

MILLIONS OF PEOPLE had followed newspaper and television reports of the Annapurna climb. The BBC reports and the film that followed the expedition featured dramatic interviews with the plainspoken climbers just down from the face. These exuberant, easygoing young men offered the public a refreshing contrast to the stuffy restraint of the old breed. The climbers were still brave and hardy, but they dressed and talked like pop stars—they seemed to be having a good time.

Chris had agreed to write a book about the expedition. He had spent hours in his tent at Base Camp recording events and impressions; he also had access to the other climbers' journals, which he drew upon to flesh out the controversies and undercurrents of feeling that had informed the expedition. The resulting book, *Annapurna South Face,* was another departure; it portrayed the climbers as authentic characters with human strengths and weaknesses. Chris and Don and Dougal and the rest emerged as personalities; they seemed nothing like the earnest automatons that had populated most previous expedition accounts.

The media coverage and the book's success made Chris a household name in Great Britain for the first time. Don and Dougal, the men who had reached the summit, were nearly as famous. The rest of the Annapurna climbers also were known to a wider world now. They were part of the circle—they were Bonington's Boys. The climbers' respective positions within the group defined their individual prospects and shaped their ambitions. They were no longer anonymous and powerless vagabonds, no longer mere climbing bums. They were the emerging climbing establishment.

This new role took them by surprise. Their response to it was informed by undertones of grief for Ian Clough and for another friend. They had arrived home from Annapurna to the news that Tom Patey—the Scottish climber who had recruited Chris to climb the Old Man of Hoy—had been killed in a rappelling accident, roping down from another of his beloved sea stacks. He'd died on May 25, 1970, four days before Ian Clough's death halfway around the world. Tom had been good for Chris. He had been inclined to mock Bonington's hopes and pretensions—had written a satirical song about them—but he was a friend. And the Scotsman's death would be felt in other, unacknowledged ways. Patey had stood opposed to big expeditions, with their growing tendency to commercialize climbing. His death was the death of a dissident; it made a gap that gave passage to tendencies he'd resisted not only by his words but also by his mode of life.

Fame meanwhile offered Chris new ways to marry commerce and climbing. He had accumulated considerable credibility in the wider world, and with that credibility came the power to mount even larger expeditions to big mountains. Chris saw the risk that such expeditions would revert to the old and outmoded system of overpowering a mountain, but he set aside such concerns for the moment. The deaths of Ian Clough and Tom Patey propelled him along the path that unfolded before him; whatever guilt or grief these losses provoked might be swallowed by some astonishing endeavor.

THE PATH NOW led to Everest and that mountain's huge and unclimbed Southwest Face. John Harlin had talked of mounting an expedition there. He'd told Dougal of his hopes when they were stormbound in their snow cave on the Eiger. Dougal and Chris had talked about the face after John's death, when the two of them were together in the hospital for treatment of their frostbite.

That was more than four years ago. The Southwest Face of Everest had since emerged as mountaineering's Next Great Problem. The face presented huge logistical challenges. A successful expedition would need to ferry tons of supplies up steep ground to the base of a steep rock section. This was the Rock Band, at 8,300 meters—already higher than all but four of the world's summits. The team would then have to lay siege to 1,000 feet of hard mixed climbing to escape the face; after that, there was more climbing to the summit.

The Japanese had visited the face in 1969 and 1970. Their second expedition had included a team of more than 100 climbers and Sherpas, with an army of porters in support, but the climbers had turned back at the bottom of the Rock Band.

Jimmy Roberts—Chris's friend and mentor on Annapurna II more than a decade earlier—had organized a third attempt on Everest's Southwest Face for the spring of 1971. The expedition was to include an all-star roster of mountaineers from various countries. Chris had turned down an invitation to come as leader of the climbing team; he was worried that the climbers wouldn't form a cohesive enough group to get up the route.

Roberts also had invited Don Whillans and Dougal Haston, and both men had accepted. The two of them climbed together on Everest as they had on Annapurna forging much of the route up the face. They eventually established the expedition's high camp near the right-hand end of the Rock Band, but by then several climbers had quit the expedition. Chris had been right; competing national cliques had poisoned the atmosphere of the expedition. The climbers who remained were too exhausted or ill to support an attempt on the summit. Bad weather had also plagued the team. An Indian climber—Harsh Bahuguna—had died of exposure during a storm.

A second international team tried the route a year later, in the spring of 1972. The expedition leader was a cantankerous German promoter named Karl Herrligkoffer. Don joined the expedition, but Chris and Dougal turned down their invitations. Herrligkoffer gave one of their slots to Chris's old friend Hamish MacInnes. Hamish had continued to cut an eccentric swathe through the fringes of the mountaineering world, at one point leading an expedition to search for the Yeti. He taught climbing and ran the Mountain Rescue Team in Glencoe; he also designed and manufactured climbing equipment. He'd always wanted to climb Everest; back in 1953, he'd teamed up with a friend to launch an unofficial—illegal, infact—vastly underfunded and somewhat harebrained expedition to the peak. Hamish and his partner had been making their way to the mountain when they got word that Hillary and Tenzing had reached the summit. Hamish accepted Herrligkoffer's invitation as an opportunity to come to grips with the mountain.

The other British slot on Herrligkoffer's team went to a rising English climber named Doug Scott, a strapping young teacher—he was thirty—from Nottingham. Doug had made his first climb with a washing line in Derbyshire, three weeks before his twelfth birthday, which came on the very day Hillary and Tenzing reached the summit of Everest. He had spent his teens climbing in the usual places—the Lakes, up in Scotland, down in Wales—with summer trips to the Alps. He had married young, at age twenty, but he hadn't by any means settled down. He lived his life as a schoolteacher and family man between low-budget trips to exotic destinations—mountain ranges in Africa and Central Asia, including climbs in Chad, Afghanistan and Kurdistan. He'd also climbed big walls in Norway, the United States and elsewhere.

Doug was an intimidating figure, slender but immensely strong, with wide shoulders and big hands. He was ambitious and he was an idealist; the combination could be maddening. He looked a lot like John Lennon, staring skeptically out from behind wire-rimmed glasses, his gaze framed by dark, shoulder-length hair and a beard. He had something of Lennon's accent and some of his attitude, too: Doug knew his rights, and he enjoyed questioning authority—he in fact liked to run things himself. He believed big mountaineering expeditions were by nature corrupt—hierarchical and unsporting—but he wanted to climb big mountains. Herrligkoffer's invitation to Everest was a chance to get in that game.

Herrligkoffer's 1972 expedition to the Southwest Face also included ten Germans, seven Austrians, one Swiss and a South Tyrolean. The Continentals were suspicious of the three British climbers. Several Germans soon accused Don and his compatriots of saving themselves for a summit attempt. The British contingent eventually withdrew from the expedition. Illness and exhaustion took their toll on the remaining climbers, who eventually retreated without reaching Don and Dougal's high point of the previous year.

CHRIS MEANWHILE HAD applied to Nepal for permission to lead his own expedition to the Southwest Face. He'd engage it on his own terms rather than tag along on someone else's expedition. Chris assumed he would have to wait in line for years, but he was wrong. The Herrligkoffer expedition was still on Everest when Bonington learned that an Italian team had canceled their expedition to the Southwest Face, scheduled for the fall of 1972. The Italians had withdrawn at almost the last possible moment; the Nepalese authorities invited Chris to step into their slot.

He accepted immediately—but he had serious reservations. The expedition would have to try and climb the face during the postmonsoon season, a time of year when no expedition had climbed Everest by any route. The late fall brought very low temperatures and high winds. Worse, the timing of the invitation meant Chris had only a few months to finance and organize a large-scale expedition.

He cast about for alternatives. Why not climb Everest by the normal South Col route—the old Hillary and Tenzing route—but do it in better form? Chris figured a small-scale alpine-style expedition would require only four principal climbers. He had set about recruiting them when he learned that Herrligkoffer's team had failed to climb the Southwest Face.

This was May. Chris quickly realized that the challenge of the still-unclimbed Southwest Face was too great to pass up, despite the huge logistic and fund-raising obstacles and the absurdly tight deadline. He now calculated that he'd need eleven climbers for the trip. That group should include six men who would share most of the leading—and perhaps have a realistic crack at being chosen for a summit team.

Chris himself would fill the first of those six slots. That left five for his friends. He began by inviting some of the Annapurna team. Dougal Haston—still running John Harlin's old climbing school in Leysin—was an automatic pick. Nick Estcourt was another. Nick had worked hard on the Annapurna expedition, and Chris knew he could rely on his neighbor's good sense to help sort through problems that might arise. He liked having Nick around; they knew each other's strengths and accepted each other's oddities and shortcomings.

He invited Mick Burke, too. Mick was newly married and starting to establish himself as a professional cameraman. He had questioned many of Chris's decisions on Annupurna, and had given him absolute hell for favoring Don and Dougal and their summit ambitions. But Mick's criticism wasn't manipulative—as Don's often was—or petulant. Mick was a contrary bugger and he had his problems with authority, but he wasn't blind to the fact that Chris often made good use of his leadership role. Mick's attacks were sometimes useful reminders of facts or feelings the other climbers were afraid to acknowledge. And Mick would do the necessary in a pinch. Beth Burke would come too; her nursing skills would be useful at Base Camp.

That left two lead climber slots. Chris filled one of them with his former mentor Hamish MacInnes. Hamish had pulled his weight on Herrligkoffer's expeditions to the Southwest Face. Moreover, he had considerable skill as an engineer, which would prove useful in creating a path through the complexities of the Khumbu Icefall—the notoriously dangerous maze of crevasses and ice towers at the start of the route.

The sixth remaining slot went to a new acquaintance, Doug Scott, who had helped arrange some of Chris's lectures in Nottingham. Doug was by all accounts an immensely strong climber—his performance on Everest that spring had impressed even the hard-to-impress Don Whillans.

That left the question of Don himself. His association with Chris—in recent years, a very public one—had lasted almost fifteen years. Their shared history and Whillan's fame in the wake of Annapurna seemed to guarantee the older man a role on the new expedition, especially in light of his two recent trips to the Southwest Face itself.

That was the popular view—an outsider's view. But while Chris felt a certain loyalty to Don, he resented Don's willingness to take advantage of that loyalty. Don as Deputy Leader on Annapurna had alienated and then infuriated some of the other climbers, including Mick Burke and Nick Estcourt and Martin Boysen. Mick in particular had been deeply angry; his own working-class background made him less willing than some of the others to tolerate Don's bullying and condescension. Mick and the other Annupurna climbers were convinced that Don had saved himself for the summit. And perhaps Don had done just that; he might have believed that Chris owed him this shot at success, that it would be some compensation for Chris's own success on the Eiger and elsewhere.

Any such debt was discharged. Moreover, Chris wasn't sure he needed Don on Everest. He had relied upon Don's route finding, his survival instincts and even his selfishness to help the Annapurna expedition succeed. The others—Mick and Nick and the rest—were more experienced now; they were ready for their shot. Mick made it abundantly clear that he didn't want Don along; Nick took the same position. Even Dougal—who had served his high-altitude apprenticeship with Don on Annapurna and then on the first international expedition to Everest— turned against his mentor. Chris understood; he had bridled at Don's stubborn and sometimes bullying ways in the Alps a decade earlier. And Chris himself also worried that Don, having been to the Southwest Face twice, might not be content taking orders from a former protégé who had never been on the face.

Hamish MacInnes and Doug Scott did what they could to press Don's case. Neither man had been on Annapurna, but they'd climbed with Don more recently, on Everest. Like others before them, Hamish and Doug had been impressed by Whillan's strength and skill in the big mountains. And they got along with him, liked having him around. Don's awkward ways made him a kind of lightning rod for the insecurities of others—he welcomed and absorbed their resentment. Some of that resentment might otherwise have settled on Hamish—whose self-sufficiency sometimes rendered him oblivious to the others and their views—or Doug, who could be overbearing at times, and whose sheer strength made him a threat to the others' ambitions.

That wasn't all. Don had saved Hamish's life back on the Bonatti Pillar. Doug had known Whillans almost as long. They'd met in the Lakes, when Doug was a boy of fifteen, already powerful enough to break the older man's rib in a pickup rugby match at Wasdale Head (Don had blackened his eye in return). Doug didn't see Don as a threat; he'd cheerfully cooked for Don that spring on Everest, where he'd watched the older man's antics with a half-amused admiration.

It didn't matter. Chris announced the team that spring, and Don's name was not on the list. It was a spectacularly public rebuff. For Don, the snub echoed other betrayals—Joe Brown leaving for Kangchenjunga, Chris climbing the Eiger with Ian Clough. Chris for his part sometimes felt the rift as another loss.

Bonington had added several other expedition members in supporting roles. His old friend Jimmy Roberts, now running a trekking company in Nepal, would serve as Deputy Leader. Kelvin Kent—Base Camp Manager on Annapurna—would run Advance Base this time. Mike Thompson wasn't able to come on this trip; Chris filled his place with Dave Bathgate, a Scotsman who was a strong climber. Chris recruited another Scot, Graham Tiso, to organize equipment—Tiso owned a climbing shop in Edinburgh—and serve as a support climber.

Ken Wilson, the contentious and respected editor of *Mountain* magazine, was coming out to cover the expedition; he could help run Camp One. The expedition needed a doctor. Chris's first choice—a friend named Peter Steele—couldn't make it, but

Brown recommended a friend named Barney Rosedale, who agreed to come.

Tony Tighe, a young Australian friend of Dougal Haston's, was planning a trek to Nepal. He offered to meet up with the expedition and help run Base Camp. Tony had drifted into the Club Vagabond in Leysin a few years earlier and stayed on; he'd ended up managing the bar. Chris had spent a day skiing with Tony in Leysin, and found him easy company. He accepted Tony's offer.

THE CLIMBERS AND their 16,000 pounds of gear, food and oxygen cylinders arrived in Kathmandu on August 23. They assembled their 400 porters and set out for the twelve-day walk to Base Camp. Chris spent much of the walk mulling over assignments for his team's various members.

He had decided that his commitments as expedition leader were too demanding to allow him a leading role in forging the route. He would hang just behind the leaders, keeping an eye on the flow of supplies and people up the face. Dave Bathgate could take his place as one of the six lead climbers. Chris sorted them into three pairs: Bathgate and Nick Estcourt, Mick Burke and Doug Scott, Hamish MacInnes and Dougal Haston.

Chris hoped to avoid the infighting that had occurred on Annapurna, and with that in mind he also mapped out the roles each team would play on the peak. The three pairs would share the first task: finding a way through the Icefall. Each pair would take turns leading on the lower part of the face, as well. Nick and Dave would then take the lead from Camp Five to Camp Six, at the base of the Rock Band. Mick and Doug would tackle the Rock Band, which had stymied every previous attempt on the face. They would then make the first summit attempt—if they weren't too exhausted by that point.

Dougal and Hamish would wait in reserve for a second summit attempt.

The plan reflected Bonington's take on the various temperaments of his climbers as well as their abilities. Dave and Nick would accept a secondary role more readily than the other pairings. Mick and Doug would probably be too weary to make the summit after their efforts on the Rock Band, but they would value the Rock Band as a prize in itself. Hamish and Dougal would have little reason to complain of their reserve role; it probably offered them the most realistic shot at the summit.

Chris had arranged for the team to arrive at Base Camp on September 15, the start of the postmonsoon season. He worried that they would encounter too much monsoon snow on the route if they arrived sooner—but arriving this late posed other problems. Their late start left them with a narrow window—a month or so—before the arrival of the postmonsoon winds that could transform the mountain into a hell on earth.

The British climbers and the Sherpas who served as high-altitude porters had to pass through the Icefall to reach the Western Cwm (pronounced "koom"); this was the enormous valley of snow that lay below the Southwest Face itself. The team spent almost a week building a route through the Icefall. Much of the work involved fixing ropes and building makeshift bridges to span yawning gaps in the glacier. Hamish and Dougal soon stepped into the role Don and Dougal had taken on Annapurna: forcing the route, making decisions and implementing them without fuss or delay. Most of the other climbers—including Chris—were sick from altitude or the change in diet.

They made each passage through the Icefall in the knowledge that the glacier was moving beneath them. The climbers passed through its shadows like thieves, hoping to escape notice. The Sherpas spent the most time in the Icefall, ferrying loads of equipment and food on the lower sections of the route. They prayed before they entered the place, but otherwise seemed not to fear it.

Doug Scott and Mick Burke established Camp One at the bottom of the Western Cwm in perfect weather on September 20. A group of twenty-five Sherpas carried loads to the new camp the next day, while Dougal and Hamish worked with Sherpas to improve the route through the Icefall, bypassing obstacles and reinforcing the crude rope-and-ladder bridges the expedition had built to span the worst gaps in the glacier. Nick Estcourt and Dave Bathgate meanwhile moved up to Camp One—but the weather deteriorated, with high winds and low clouds. No one climbed on September 23 or 24. It was just as well: a huge section of the Icefall collapsed, undoing much of their work. Chris mainly felt relief that no one had been in the area when it occurred.

More snow fell, slowing the expedition's progress up through the Western Cwm. The climbers eventually established and stocked Camp Two at the foot of the Southwest Face. Doug and Mick moved up to establish Camp Three on the face itself, but a storm drove them down in early October. They returned to the face and reached the site of Camp Four, at 24,600 feet, on October 9.

Hamish and Dougal took over the lead. They dug platforms at Camp Four for two MacInnes Boxes. Hamish had designed the box as a sturdier, lighter alternative to the Whillans Box. They took two days to ascend a huge snow gully that led toward the Rock Band, climbing with bottled oxygen, fixing rope as they went. They reached 26,000 feet on the evening of October 14, running out of rope just short of the site they had chosen for Camp Five.

The weather was perfect. Chris entertained visions of a summit attempt by the end of the month. The expedition meanwhile had to keep supplies moving up the face. Chris himself moved up to

Camp Four with several Sherpas on October 15. He planned to lead four days of carries to Camp Five. Nick Estcourt and Dave Bathgate could then occupy the camp and push the route out toward the projected site of Camp Six, a barren shelf of snow just below the Rock Band.

CHRIS CAME AWAKE at Camp Four to the roar of wind and the rattle of ice on the walls of his tent. His oxygen canister had run dry. It was midnight. He lay in the dark and listened to the sounds. He imagined the white of windblown ice swarming in the darkness outside. The wind continued through the night and into the morning. Chris put off leaving his tent in hopes that the weather would improve. He was still inside—reading *The Lord of the Rings* and brewing endless mugs of tea—when Kelvin Kent arrived from Camp Three.

Kent was a relatively inexperienced climber. He didn't know better than to be out in such conditions, and he had managed to struggle up through the wind with his load. His hands were frostbitten—he'd neglected to wear windproof shells over his wool mittens. Chris lit into him, feeling guilty even as he did so, and sent him down the mountain with a Sherpa—leaving one less man to make the carries to Camp Five.

There was no question of carrying loads today, however. The wind continued to hammer at Bonington's tent and bombard the camp with dangerous flotsam. The weather at times was perfectly clear—the sky an amazing blue—so that the wind seemed to come out of nothing, which somehow seemed to imply that there might be no end to it. Chris as the hours passed felt that this wind had a purpose; it meant to sweep them from the mountain. And yet the wind seemed beautiful to him just because it was implacable; his own cunning and self-regard meant nothing to it. He could barely imagine a world where he could be warm, feel the sun on his shoulders and hands.

There were moments of near-silence when he listened for the wind's return. It would scream across the mountain, engulfing the tents, an invisible avalanche. He thought of the dead from previous expeditions to this peak: seven Sherpas avalanched in 1922; Mallory and Irvine walking into oblivion two years later; the others since. The bodies littered the mountain, impossible to find or recover; they lay out there in this wind or buried in the glacier—much as their various lives lay elsewhere, in tatters, all projects, connections and moments abandoned and scattered. He reviewed his own career to this point: his fatherless childhood; school and the army; Wendy and the children and their various households; friendships; his travels in mountains and elsewhere. He considered his losses, beginning with his father's absence and later in some unspeakably cruel inversion of that absence, the death of his own son. And now this growing list of friends and collaborators lost to him. He could sometimes manage not to think of the ones who were dead—John Harlin or Ian Clough or Tom Patey—but he had no wish to forget them. Chris drank his tea. He read and listened and thought and waited for the wind to stop.

Three days passed, and the wind continued; it grew stronger. Hamish came on the radio the night of October 19 to suggest that the team make a temporary retreat from the face, taking apart the tents and box shelters. Already, the wind and snow had destroyed or damaged nearly half of their shelters. Chris resisted Hamish's plan; he worried that the expedition would never recover its momentum. The wind grew worse that night and he changed his mind—but in the morning he woke to perfect calm.

He made the first carry to Camp Five that day, accompanied by two Sherpas. It was miserable plodding, their backs to the stupendous view. Chris stopped once and stared across to the summit of Nuptse, where he'd stood eleven years before. He'd been twenty-six years old.

The wind returned that night but the day of fine weather had left Chris once again resolved that the climbers should maintain their foothold on the face. That way, they could make immediate progress during any further breaks in the weather. Chris himself needed a rest after four days above 24,500 feet. He asked Nick and Dave to occupy Camp Five and get started on the next section of the route.

Nick and Dave planned to move up from Camp Four on October 26. They downed sleeping pills the night before, but were awakened several hours later when a rock careened into their MacInnes Box, half-collapsing it. They pulled on boots and worked frantically in the dark and wind—it was astonishingly cold—to repair the Box framework. They patched the damaged sections, propped up a corner with a shovel and sat inside brewing and drinking tea until the sun rose. They abandoned their camp, now a shambles, the MacInnes Boxes damaged and half-swamped by drifts of new snow. Nick and Dave descended through deep drifts, their hands and feet turning to blocks of wood. The wind kicked the new snow up into their faces; at one point they found themselves dodging a hail of windblown rocks.

They were heading for Camp Two at the bottom of the face, but they couldn't see it in the whiteout. They roamed about like blind men at the fringes of the Western Cwm. Nick began to calculate the chances of surviving a night out in these conditions—the odds were not good—but Chris and a pair of Sherpas loomed up out of the gloom to lead them to shelter. Nick felt an unfamiliar gratitude. It had not occurred to him that anyone would come for them.

The wind had at last driven the expedition from the face. They would have to reclimb it, rebuilding Camps Four and Five. The route through the Icefall also was deteriorating, and deep snow made the going very difficult between the lower camps. They hadn't begun the hardest climbing—the Rock Band and the ground that led beyond it to the top of the face. And they were running out of time; winter was coming.

The wind stopped on October 27. Chris—now operating from Camp Two just below the face—made plans for the next attempt. He asked Mick and Doug to move up the mountain while the other climbers labored to restore the lower sections of the route. Chris himself accompanied a group of four Sherpas down to collect food and mail from a party making its way up from Camp One. The four Sherpas roped up, but Chris didn't bother; he simply followed their tracks, moving alone across the enormous amphitheater of the Western Cwm. He stepped out of the Sherpas' path to take a picture of them and disappeared.

He fell a body-length and stopped. He dangled over a chasm in the glacier; his legs and midsection hung in the black air. He didn't dare to move—he might disturb the glacier's purchase on his upper torso. He shouted, and felt himself slip deeper into the gap. He understood that he would disappear into the mountain. He shouted again, but faintly this time—he couldn't afford to deflate his lungs. It occurred to Chris that his body heat would soon cause the hole in the snow to grow wider. He was already cold, and this sign of nature's stark impatience terrified him.

The Sherpas edged closer and tossed rope across to Bonington; they moved cautiously to drag him back to their path across the glacier. Chris gathered himself—life had reclaimed him so smoothly that he felt deflated, even felt a twinge of odd resentment—and eventually dug out his camera to photograph the hole his body had made in the roof of the crevasse. He felt that he was taking a picture of his grave—he had nowhere to put this image. He stood unaware of his own trembling. His dead companions came to mind; were they in that black hell? No—it was empty; his ghosts were with him, shadows of shadows. He turned his mind away from death; it was like moving a chair from a window.

Chris and his group continued down to meet the Sherpas who were bringing up food and mail. Chris collected the mail and turned around to follow the track back up to Camp Two. He stopped after a time and sat down in the snow to read his own letters. The sight of Wendy's handwriting made him deeply homesick; tears came to his eyes as he read.

He reached Camp Two before lunch and spent the rest of the day turning over his most recent plans for getting climbers up and down the peak before the wind returned. He had originally given Dave and Nick the task of pushing the route from Camp Five to Camp Six, leaving Doug Scott and Mick Burke to climb the Rock Band. But Dave and Nick had been busy low on the mountain; they were all the way down at Camp One. Doug and Mick were on their way up to Camp Four—why not let them push on and make the route to Camp Six, leaving the Rock Band to Dave and Nick?

It made obvious sense—but Chris was determined to stick to his original plan. He wanted Dave and Nick to move up the mountain now and remake the route between Camp Four and Camp Five, then climb high enough to establish Camp Six at the base of the Rock Band. Doug and Mick would step in at that point to climb the Rock Band itself.

Chris announced his intention to stick with the old plan during the morning radio call on November 1. Nick was furious; Chris seemed to be going out of his way to deprive him of plum assignments. Chris was conciliatory, but he held his ground. He knew Nick would come around, and he thought Doug and Mick had more of the drive needed to get up the Rock Band; meanwhile, they would chip away at the route below it while Dave and Mick moved up the route to take over.

Doug and Mick and four Sherpas reached Camp Four late on the afternoon of November 1. The party set to work clearing up the mess left by the storm. The MacInnes Boxes were filled with blown snow that had set into a kind of friable stone. The frames of two shelters had crumpled, and boxes of gear and food were buried under more stonelike snow.

The sky grew dim and the temperature fell as the two climbers labored to clear a space to sleep and cook. They wandered about on the frozen snow, clipped to safety lines and clutching shovels and pots and packages; anything dropped would skitter across the snow to shoot down the steep slopes of the Southwest Face. The climbers' hands and feet grew numb. It was ten o'clock before they had cleared space in two boxes and made supper.

Doug and two of the Sherpas made a carry to Camp Five the next morning. Mick and the remaining Sherpas stayed behind to finish sorting out the wreckage of Camp Four. Doug and Mick moved up to Camp Five the next day, November 3. They felt winter's approach; it came at them like some vast and invisible enemy. They felt themselves shrink before it.

Camp Five was a snow-covered ledge in the sky. Mick dug a tent platform. Doug took photographs. He was tired. He stepped back to frame a shot and slipped on the hard snow, and then he was sliding in his slick one-piece suit. He knew without thinking that the snow slope ran 50 feet to a fall of some 2,000 feet. He knew he must roll onto his belly and bury the pick of his ice axe in the snow—if he delayed, his momentum would carry him past the point where stopping was possible even in theory.

He had no ice axe. He had put away the axe and had taken his gloves off to handle the camera and now he clawed at the snow with bare fingers. He could kick with his crampons but the points were likely to catch in the hard snow, send him cartwheeling over the cliff. He kicked anyway and he continued to claw at the hard snow but he was still sliding and he imagined what came next: spinning and twisting and the rushing view—a glass barrel over a waterfall. He felt no dread but rather a strange clarity; he continued to work the fall, and a change in the angle of the slope slowed him and he stopped. He was two or three seconds above the drop that now as he lay breathing, contemplating his escape, appeared in a corner of his mind as the mouth of a whale. He lay there thinking that he should be falling now. Another moment passed and he thought without joy or satisfaction, only a dull surprise: *Now I should be dead. . . .*

He stood with infinite care and found his footing; a slip could still kill him. He had the impulse to take another photograph: this one looking down to Camp Four past the slopes that appeared to him now as the beautiful web of a spider. He turned and kicked his way back up the way he had come. It was odd without his axe. He moved deliberately but without fear. He felt his boot punch through the crust at each kick, and trusted each boot to hold his weight as he raised the other to kick again. He kicked perhaps twenty or thirty steps in the snow; it was enough to build a rhythm like the one that had carried him up this face and up other mountains. The rhythmic kicking restored him to his life, brought him back into his body. Mick, busy at camp chores, had missed the whole incident. He came into view as Doug climbed.

Doug told Mick what had happened, and the telling of it in the murky, fading light reminded them both of how far they were from any safe place. Such reminders were constant now; the climbers sometimes felt like storybook characters that would not leave a house that promised to harm them. They had come to a place that belonged to winter; it had the spooky, vacant feel of a bone yard. They were amid spirits; crystals formed and clotted and disintegrated. Doug took three sleeping pills that night. The climbers woke to the shadows of a beautiful morning, very cold. The sun didn't reach their tents until two o'clock. They stayed in their sleeping bags, too exhausted to move.

Chris, still keeping an eye on things from down at Camp Two, had hoped that Doug and Mick would make progress that day in the huge snow gully that led to the Rock Band. He grew frustrated as the day wore on with no sign of climbers above Camp Five; by day's end he had changed his plans again. Dave Bathgate and Nick Estcourt were on their way up to Camp Five to join Doug and Mick. Chris decided that he would put all four climbers to work making the route to Camp Six. He could then push Hamish and Dougal through to tackle the Rock Band—thus snatching that prize from Doug and Mick after all.

Dave and Nick reached Camp Five that evening. Nick teamed up with Doug the next day to fix rope above Camp Five. Mick went along to film them; Dave Bathgate stayed behind to put the camp in order. Nick took the lead first. He soon ran into difficult climbing. His oxygen mask and cylinder disrupted his balance. He scraped and teetered up over crumbling rock and hard snow to a ledge where he established an anchor. Doug led through and ran the rope out to the foot of the Rock Band, at 26,700 feet.

Nick struggled up after him. He wanted to touch the rock that had beckoned to them for so long. The temperature was well below zero degrees Fahrenheit. There was no wind; even so Nick's fingers lost feeling. Doug had descended already; he and Mick were heading down the mountain for a rest at Camp Two. Nick turned and descended to join Dave.

Nick and Dave spent two days fixing more rope above Camp Five. Their route ran across the bottom of the Rock Band to the base of another snow gully, where they intended to establish Camp Six. The gully seemed to offer a way through the lower section of the Rock Band—kicking steps up through the snow would be far more feasible at this altitude than trying to climb the rock itself.

Nick approached the foot of the snow gully late on November 6. Dave had turned back earlier in the day—problems with his oxygen set. Nick's companion now was a high-altitude porter named Pertemba. The last reel of rope came taut 40 feet short of the gully. Nick stopped to put in an anchor. He took off his rucksack to work and dropped it in the snow; he watched dully as it tipped sideways and tumbled down the slopes he had just climbed. It was the kind of mistake they were all making now. Dave had dropped his own pack just the day before.

Nick cursed himself and now he noticed the lateness of the hour; the sun was slipping behind the mountains to the west. The temperature fell sharply. A stiff wind arrived with the day's departure as if operating on a schedule, taking up its shift. Nick and Pertemba turned and started down. The wind rose steadily until it had the force and substance of a torrent. Nick could not see, and he repeatedly lost his footing as he staggered down through the snow. Pertemba was climbing without bottled oxygen—the Sherpas often did without it—and he moved very slowly as the two men struggled back across the traverse at the base of the Rock Band.

The cold made them clumsy. Nick fumbled with the carabiners that attached him to the fixed ropes. A slip would result in a long pendulum-like fall. Rescuers would not reach them in these conditions. They would die as Harsh Bahuguna, the unfortunate Indian climber, had died on this mountain the previous year.

They couldn't even help each other. Pertemba fell behind. Nick carried on alone, hating the dark and this horrendous wind, and came upon Camp Five in the pitch black. He fell into one of the shelters and lay shaking, his face a mask of ice so that his tears of relief and remorse melted tracks on his bearded face.

Dave Bathgate had spent the past hour clinging to the shelter's framework to steady and support it. He made tea. Nick drank some and then tried to thaw his frostbitten hands in warm water—it was very painful—and eventually crawled outside into the wind and across to the other MacInnes Box. He was immensely relieved to come upon Pertemba there; Nick had been terribly ashamed of leaving him. They talked for a long time.

Nick and Dave descended the route the next morning. Chris meanwhile was on his way up to help establish Camp Six. He spent the night at Camp Four, and climbed to Camp Five with Sherpa Ang Phurba on November 10. They got a late start the next day. The fixed ropes brought them to Nick's high point, at the gully that made a gash in the lower reaches of the Rock Band.

Chris stared up into the gully, and what he saw took him aback. The gully was no easy snow plod but rather a tunnel of rock steps and overhangs. He turned his attention to a more immediate worry: finding a site for Camp Six. He found a spot with room for tents or MacInnes Boxes, on a shelf just below the Rock Band. There was no real shelter from the wind, but the site would get sun in the morning. The view was staggering. Chris looked down upon vast ranges. He grew cold in the stillness; after a moment or two the sight disoriented him: he felt he might tumble up into the sky. A sweet clarity arose like a wind off the sea; it swept his mind clean of regret and of thought for the future.

He descended to Camp Five. There was no wind this evening. He rummaged in a stack of oxygen bottles, moving awkwardly in his down suit and heavy boots and gloves, and dislodged three cylinders. The cylinders careened down the slopes. Ang Pherba looked very grave; Graham Tiso was directly below them at

Camp Four. Chris was appalled; his clumsiness might have killed Graham. There was no way of knowing until the radio call that evening.

Graham was not at Camp Four. He'd been hit in the head by a stone earlier in the day. The stone had ripped through his tent wall and opened his forehead, knocking him unconscious. He'd come awake covered with blood and had made his way down to Camp Two for stitches. Graham would be fine, but his absence meant one less climber to help maintain the flow of supplies on the face.

The wind returned the next day. Mick Burke came on the radio in the morning to remind Chris that the high camps were low on oxygen cylinders. Chris spent the rest of the day in his tent at Camp Five, working on logistics. Ang Phurba made a solo carry to Camp Six. He returned exhausted; he would need to descend to the lower camps the next morning.

Chris remained in Camp Five for a second day—it was too cold to venture out—but the next morning he made one more carry, climbing alone to Camp Six. He knew that he would not be this high on the face again—but for now he was the highest climber on the peak, perhaps in the world. The day waned and the wind gained strength, and he began to worry. His oxygen tank had stopped working and he was very tired. He had been too high for too long.

He struggled across and down to Camp Five. He was almost weeping with exhaustion as he tottered the last few steps into the campsite, where he came upon four of his friends busy about their tasks. Dougal and Hamish had arrived to begin work on the Rock Band. Mick and Doug were digging a snow hole; they had come up to carry loads in support of the leaders.

Doug met Chris with a few brusque words—urged him to hurry on down to Camp Four, where there was room for him. Chris was too tired to react. Hamish was more sympathetic; he gave Chris something hot to drink. And then Chris carried on down, stopping to sit and rest every few steps in the gathering night, too weary to be on his feet but glad for more solitude. He took in the almost liquid orange of the ending day—the light was like a dye—and finished his walk in blackness. Ang Phurba met him at Camp Four and gave him more to drink. Chris crawled into a sleeping bag and lay shivering, lapsing in and out of sleep, undone.

He woke tired and discouraged. The expedition had only a few days to finish climbing the mountain. The winds that blow ceaselessly just over the summit of Everest were descending upon them as a flood might rise to obliterate a city. There was no margin for error or delay. The expedition must keep Camp Five supplied so that Mick and Doug could make their daily carries to Camp Six in support of Hamish and Dougal—who must in turn make quick progress through the gully and on through to the top of the Rock Band.

Everyone wanted to quit. Each step called for concentration and devotion to the task at hand. They were tired and miserably uncomfortable; they were befuddled by fatigue and altitude; they were homesick and afraid. They lay in their sleeping bags in the evenings and thought of what death would cost them even as their hopes of climbing the route ebbed. Four of them had left the face already. Kelvin Kent was sick. Graham Tiso was nursing his head injury. Nick Estcourt and Dave Bathgate were recovering from their ordeal in the storm. Chris remained up at Camp Four, but he was very weary.

None of this was decisive, however. The four climbers at Camp Six—Dougal and Hamish, Doug and Mick—believed there was still a chance of getting up the route. Dougal in particular was engrossed in calculations of how to make it happen. The expedition's original plan had been to establish a seventh camp, above the Rock Band. This now looked impossible; there wasn't enough manpower to supply another camp, and there wasn't time.

Dougal, however, had an idea. He carried with him a tent sac—a lightweight shelter that a climber might use to get through a summer's night in the Alps. He believed that one or two climbers should go for the summit from Camp Six. The summit team would carry the tent sac in case a bivouac was necessary on the descent—a near-certainty. The tent sac might give sufficient protection if there was no wind. Dougal mentioned his scheme to the others and received in return their blank looks.

Hamish and Dougal set out for Camp Six on November 14. They would occupy the camp while Mick and Doug ferried supplies from Camp Five over the next two days. Dougal left first. He crawled from his box and stood looking across the heavens. The sun was a mere image, a painting on the sky; the cold here reduced it to a concept, thin and useless. Dougal was aware of his own strength; he was stronger than the others except for maybe Doug Scott. The view reminded him of something: he'd been here with Don Whillans. This desolate slope had continued to exist during the intervening time and would continue to exist when he was gone.

The others followed Dougal out and up the slope. The wind rose and grew freakishly strong as they climbed. A gust picked Doug up and carried him several feet; the fixed ropes stopped him. The four climbers squinted through blowing snow at a blue sky that seemed to recede as they moved higher. They felt drawn into the pursuit of something that moved too quickly for them. They pursued it because they wished to keep it in sight; it was too interesting for them to turn away; it seemed the thing that could confirm their most precious and precarious beliefs.

Dougal reached Camp Six, still a scattering of boxes, and dropped his load and left. They could not pitch a tent in this wind, much less climb. He moved now with his back to the wind, his mind clouded by the strangeness and beauty of his position and by the cold. He looked up into the gully—the gully he had explored it with Whillans in 1971. He remembered: They had climbed perhaps 300 feet on snow and easy rock before turning back. But the gully was bare rock this time, much harder to climb; this wind had swept the snow from it. There was no chance of getting up that; there wasn't time.

There remained another possibility. They could leave the face unfinished and move across to the Southeast Ridge, which led more or less easily to the summit. Dougal moved right, turning a corner and here the wind was still more terrible. He wore an oxygen mask and breathed from a cylinder; he could not otherwise have drawn breath here. The wind would blow them from the ridge.

There was nowhere else to go. He turned and went down. He met Doug at the top of the fixed ropes, and pointed down. Doug nodded his acceptance and turned. They passed Mick a bit further down. He filmed them on their way back to Camp Five, and then he followed. Hamish was waiting for them; his oxygen set had failed; he'd turned around earlier in the day.

The four climbers understood that they were not going back up. The expedition didn't have the time or the manpower to lay siege to the bare rock in the gully. Dougal told Chris on the radio that night.

Chris took the news calmly. He was relieved; they could go home. Nick Estcourt said he wished the four lead climbers had spent a night at Camp Six; he wished they'd tried harder to make further progress. He'd been back at Base Camp long enough to begin to forget the conditions high on the route, and he was angry and bereft. His work on Annapurna and now on this route, his friendship with Chris—he had earned a say in these matters.

Chris wanted them all off the route. Dougal and the other lead climbers descended to Camp Four in the morning. Sherpas climbed up to retrieve gear that was too valuable to be left behind, but the climbers and Sherpas were all down at Camp Two by evening. They joked and chattered, well disposed toward one another now that the work was done. Dougal felt strangely calm. It struck him that failure was easy; a success always made him think of how he'd crashed the van into that boy on the road. He had wondered after the Eiger and then Annapurna what the dead boy's family must think when they read the name Haston in the headlines. He'd been here twice and failed both times. He wanted to come here again.

Mick Burke descended to Base Camp on the evening of November 16. He needed to get his film back to Britain. Chris and the other climbers left Camp Two at dawn of the following day to walk in morning shadows on the snows of the Western Cwm. The walkers fell silent. Camp One was empty; they pushed on down.

Dougal and Hamish went first. Doug and Chris followed. The two of them entered the top of the Icefall together. The place had changed utterly since Chris had passed through it on his last trip up the mountain. There were huge new gaps in the glacier. Towers of ice had disappeared; new towers replaced them. The chaos seemed at once random and contrived. The place held Chris, despite its obvious dangers. He wandered about in one spot for an hour, taking pictures of some of the most grotesque features. Doug lingered with him. This place of ice shadows and monsters was very quiet. It seemed safe enough to them after the winds and cold of the Southwest Face.

Doug and Chris carried on, and soon came across Dougal's

friend young Tony Tighe, who was making his first trip above
Base Camp. He had no legal right to be on the mountain—the
permit didn't include him—but he'd contributed to the expedition, taking radio calls from high on the face, relaying messages
to Chris and other decision-makers. He'd been a sort of diplomat,
often restating climbers' demands and complaints in more tactful terms. His carefulness had helped smooth relations between
various expedition members. Tony had made himself useful in
other ways, getting up early to see the Sherpas off in the predawn
hours; they'd voted him their favorite of the British climbers.
Chris was grateful to him. And so he'd invited Tony to walk up
through the Icefall for a view of the Western Cwm.

Tony was delighted; he was eager to see more of the mountain. He had accompanied twenty Sherpas up through the lower
part of the Icefall that morning—they were going up to retrieve
tents and other gear. He had soon fallen behind his companions.
He was alone, but it didn't matter. The track up to the Western
Cwm was easy to follow, safe enough even for an inexperienced climber; ladders and fixed ropes protected the difficult
sections.

Chris and Doug left Tony to his adventure. They arrived at
Base Camp in time for lunch, and spent the afternoon cleaning
up and drinking tea and chatting. They were happy. The issue
was decided. They had yet to turn their minds to home and its
responsibilities.

There was a ruckus among the Sherpas. Kelvin Kent was calling
to Chris; something huge had collapsed in the Icefall.

Chris felt a buzzing in his head as he stood and crossed to
the outskirts of the camp, where Kelvin and the other climbers
were gathering. A Sherpa named Phurkipa arrived with a load of
gear retrieved from Camp One. The collapse had occurred well
above him. He didn't know if anyone had been hurt. He'd passed

Tony Tighe a few moments before the collapse, had last seen him climbing a ladder that surmounted a steep wall of ice.

It seemed impossible that the mountain should choose Tony as its victim. He'd been stuck at Base Camp throughout the expedition, while the climbers and especially the Sherpas made scores of trips through the Icefall. He knew little of climbing's risks. He was a civilian—an innocent. A party of Sherpas came into sight. Mick Burke shouted that one of them was Tony. Dougal in his relief put a hand on Chris's shoulder and murmured something: *I couldn't have taken another Annapurna.*

Ian Clough was in all of their minds. Each man had rehearsed his part in this new tragedy, rummaging for feelings that might be useful or appropriate if Tony were dead. They began to put such notions aside and then someone else shouted that the climber in the orange suit was Barney Rosedale; he had stayed behind to oversee the cleanup at Camp Two.

The new arrivals were shaken and grim. They had narrowly escaped disaster themselves. A shelf of ice had collapsed under them, leaving one of the Sherpas dangling over a 70-foot drop. The others had rescued him and had picked their careful way down and around the collapse, impressed by its magnitude. They had not seen Tony Tighe.

Mick Burke and Dave Bathgate led four Sherpas back up into the Icefall that afternoon. They reached the region of the collapse at around eight o'clock in the evening. They stopped to listen in the moonlight that illuminated the ice blocks and towers, throwing gray shadows on the snow. They were listening for Tony's voice, which they dreaded to hear.

They perhaps walked upon his grave. He might be anywhere, alive or dead, in this world shaped by tremors made in turn by the warmth of the now-absent sun. They were aware of the moon and how it cast upon them the ghost of that very sun's warmth.

They did not dwell upon the fact that Tony might be buried alive but too deep for them to reach or even hear. They imagined him caught up by some inexplicable wind, swept skyward as the ice collapsed. The glacier creaked, a terrifying sound. Mick found he was trembling.

Hamish MacInnes and Doug Scott led another group the next morning. Dougal had known Tony best; he didn't go. The second party found nothing. Every hour that passed made the loss seem less real—more like a dream of loss. They stood and listened to water run under the ice and tried to imagine what had occurred.

It was easy to do: Tony moving higher through the Icefall, alone amid the huge, confining shapes and shadows, the corners and walls—everything white and massive and cold, no sound or life but his own. He looked forward to the huge valley that lay above; he imagined vistas and sky and sun and the great Southwest Face itself. He would carry it forever. Meanwhile, there was this—the risk and fascination of it. Already he was learning things that had been hidden to him. He had no words for this new knowledge but he believed they might come. He eyed the ground that lay ahead and when the ice moved his fear gathered itself and left him—abandoned him as if to seek another host.

Doug and the others kept their voices low. It was possible to believe that Tony lay trapped in some pitch-black pocket amid this jumble, cold to the bone and ashamed of his dread, grieved beyond imagination for what he had risked and now lost. Or maybe as he fell or scrambled he had time to feel only surprise that he would not see the Western Cwm.

TONY'S DEATH, so eerily similar to Ian Clough's death on Annapurna, had the quality of a warning or message repeated. The climbers acknowledged this message awkwardly or not at all. This new death drove them back upon themselves; their talk of it was clumsy and felt largely pointless. They tried to catalogue it as a fact; meanwhile, they carried Tony like a corpse between them, feeling the weight and looking for a decent place to set it down.

And yet they crowded around death itself, calling to it and dodging like children into shadows when it wheeled to face them. Death impressed and interested them. They pretended to hide from it—creeping across a huge snowfield or skittering past a serac—but they understood that any death that wished to find them had only to seek. It was thrilling, the deaths horrible proof that this eyeless giant might catch them at their play.

Chris amid his own work on the mountain had taken Tony and his efforts largely for granted. His last-minute impulse to reward Tony with permission to pass through the Icefall—such a dangerous place—had led to the young man's death. Chris knew that his own lack of fear in the Icefall that day—he had lingered to take those photographs—was a failure of imagination; he was tired and the place was familiar.

And anyway he wasn't always afraid of death. A child deprived of comfort may crave intensity in other forms, even in loss. And Chris felt sometimes that his losses were leading him somewhere; they gave shape to his life and his story even more than the mountains themselves or his growing fame could do. He wished to absorb his losses into what he knew—to frame and accept them. And yet other notions at moments flickered in him—that his losses did not define him; that loss was part of something still larger that he couldn't understand or encompass; that he stood apart from the truth; that he turned away from some version of peace—from whatever it was that he hoped welcomed each new member of the dead.

THE OTHERS HAD their own ways of thinking about Tony's death. Dougal felt that he'd helped to kill another person; it made him want to get drunk. Mick's wife, Beth Burke, had helped look after cuts and bruises at Base Camp. She had liked being one of the boys, but she had watched the episode of Tony's death with a growing sense of helplessness; these men in their confusion and desire for guidance were like marooned children. She was glad the expedition was ending. She was eager to leave the mountain.

She walked out from the tents on the last morning and stood and stared at Everest while the others carried on with their preparations for departure. The mountain was her enemy and unlike these others she knew it. They might come back here, but she wouldn't see it again. She stood looking at Everest and thinking that it wasn't the mountain she feared; she feared people who didn't know an easier way to be happy.

The mountain was beautiful, though. She looked at it for a long time.

B ONINGTON'S EXPEDITION TO Everest's Southwest Face was widely followed at home, cementing his position as the leading British climber of his generation. He was thirty-eight years old, and his career path had at last taken shape. Other climbers recognized his organizational genius and his leadership skills. Corporate sponsors admired his ability to put on a show with the BBC and other media—even when his team failed to reach a summit. All of this made him the country's leading candidate to lead major expeditions to Everest or other high peaks.

His life in Bowden had begun to settle into a new pattern. Daniel was now five years old. Wendy had given birth to the couple's third son, Rupert, three years before, in 1969. Chris saw less than he would have liked of Wendy and the boys: he now lectured all over the United Kingdom as well as on the Continent and even in the United States. He was also writing—his Annapurna book had done well, and he now set to work on a book about the attempt on the Southwest Face (virtually all of the proceeds would go to help pay the expedition's debts). When he was home, he often climbed in the evenings with friends, including Nick Estcourt and Martin Boysen. The three of them talked about future ventures to the high mountains.

Those ventures would be informed in part by Bonington's

growing awareness of new climbing trends that undercut his recent achievements. His Annapurna and Everest expeditions had demonstrated that climbers could tackle difficult rock and ice climbing at very high altitudes—but both expeditions had relied upon the old approach, with huge teams of porters, a series of established camps and thousands of feet of fixed rope. Meanwhile, a few bold climbers were venturing into the highest ranges in smaller parties—in effect tackling Himalayan peaks as they would engage the much smaller mountains of the Alps.

These climbers aimed to move quickly up a route, traveling light and carrying a single tent or other shelter—eliminating the need to establish and stock a series of camps. This in turn meant there was no need to lay fixed rope for climbers and porters to move up and down as they ferried gear between camps. The new alpine-style ascents were also relatively inexpensive, an important point. Corporate and other funding for expeditions was mostly limited to assaults on the most famous peaks—in particular, Everest.

Some older climbers disapproved of the trend toward alpine-style ascents of very big routes. The authorities that granted permission to climb in countries such as India and Pakistan and Nepal also were skeptical. Fewer climbers and porters meant less support in the event of an accident. The lack of fixed ropes and established camps on the mountain could make an emergency retreat difficult or impossible.

Chris knew all of this—but he also knew the risks posed by traditional siege-style expeditions. Climbers moving up and down the route between camps were on the peak for much longer, exposed to the hazards of rockfall, avalanche, weather and accident. There was much to be said for getting a small team up and back down in a matter of days rather than months, putting fewer lives at risk for shorter periods. Apart from such considerations, the Everest trip had left him physically and emotionally drained. He wanted a break from the organizational and other responsibilities of leading a major expedition. And there was another point. He wasn't ready to fade into climbing history. He wanted to stay a climber, a mountaineer engaged with mountains.

He wangled an invitation to join a 1973 Indian expedition to Kashmir, on the border of Pakistan and India. He recruited his neighbor Nick Estcourt to come on the trip. The two British climbers hoped to make the first ascent of a peak called Brammah (6,416 meters; 21,050 feet). They set up a camp at 5,000 meters and sat out a week of bad weather. They made the summit in a long day of climbing, up a ridge to a dome of snow. Chris was pleased to share a high summit with Nick, who had given so much on Annapurna and Everest. It made things easier between them. Their descent to high camp was interrupted by darkness, and they spent the night on a narrow ridge, looking out to views of distant lightning. The glow of those storms appeared to them beautiful and ominous, the flickers of some far away sea battle.

Nick and Chris on the approach to Brammah
CHRIS BONINGTON, CHRIS BONINGTON PICTURE LIBRARY

CHRIS WAS PLANNING another small expedition for the following year. He'd invited Doug Scott, Dougal Haston and Martin Boysen—Nick Estcourt couldn't take more time off from work. The four British climbers planned to join four Indian climbers to attempt Changabang, (6,864 meters; 22,520 feet) a highly coveted peak in the Garhwal Himalaya. The explorer Tom Longstaff, almost seventy years before, had called Changabang the most beautiful mountain he had ever seen. The Scottish climber W. H. Murray—Chris growing up had loved his books—had later written rapturously of gazing upon Changabang in the moonlight: *a product of earth and sky rare and fantastic . . . the heart gave thanks—that this mountain should be as it is.*

The mountain in spite of its great beauty remained unclimbed. The peak's pale granite walls were unrelentingly steep on all sides, so that climbers and explorers often compared it to a gigantic shark's fin. Changabang thus offered Chris and his partners a superb technical challenge. It also provided an excuse to travel to the Garhwal region of the central Himalayas, a wild and remote district that had challenged and delighted previous generations of British explorers. Eric Shipton and Bill Tilman had forced a way up the difficult Rishi Gorge in 1934 to reach the inner sanctuary of Nanda Devi (7,817 meters; 25,646 feet), which lay five miles south of Changabang. Tilman had led the team that climbed Nanda Devi two years later. Shipton meanwhile had explored the northern part of the sanctuary, including the glaciers that led to Changabang itself.

The region held great spiritual significance for Hindus, who believed it to be a home of the Gods. Bonington and his fellow climbers during their approach to the peak would encounter many holy men, wrapped in blankets and clutching their begging bowls; these men were pilgrims on their way to the temple at Badrinath, high in the foothills.

Chris suffered pangs of guilt as the expedition's departure date approached. He was leaving Wendy and the two boys yet again. This time they would have to fend for themselves in a trailer in the northern Lake District, while Wendy oversaw renovations of a ramshackle property called Badger Hill. The Boningtons had bought the place for a song three years before. It had proven a perfect retreat; they had now decided to leave the Manchester suburbs and make their cottage a permanent home. It was something out of a fairy tale: a low, slate-roofed affair well off the main road, peering out of thickets at the end of a single-track lane, the lane patrolled by stray sheep from neighboring farms.

The expedition members left England on May 1. A telegram was waiting for Chris in New Delhi. Nepal had granted him permission to attempt Everest in the fall of 1975, just over a year away. He had applied for the slot thinking he'd like to make a small, alpine-style expedition up the original South Col route. Doug and Dougal now urged him to change his plans. They wanted another shot at the Southwest Face. They conjured up for Chris a vision of walking beneath that huge wall on their way to the South Col route. The face would beckon to them a dream they'd abandoned. Their failure to engage it would define them more than anything they could accomplish elsewhere on the mountain.

Chris wasn't convinced. He dreaded the task of organizing a second large-scale expedition to the mountain. He also questioned whether another attempt on the Southwest Face during the difficult postmonsoon season had any real chance of success. He equivocated: they would go to Everest next year, but he would not choose the route yet. For now, there was Changabang to climb.

THE EXPEDITION TRAVELED eastward up the Rishi Gorge. They crossed to the Rhamani Gorge to travel north toward Changabang. The group took ten days to get to the peak, slowed by difficult routefinding on dangerous ground. One of the Indian climbers wandered onto exposed ground and survived a fall that could have been fatal. The Garhwal porters were fractious; they complained about the cold and the rations and a shortage of cigarettes. They threatened to drop their loads and go home in a dispute over medical supplies—they wanted more pills and other medicine that they could stockpile for future needs or for use in trade.

The dispute blew over. The expedition established a temporary camp on May 17. They settled in for a few days to rest and to prepare for the next stage of the journey. Chris and Dougal set out the following day to find a site for Base Camp and have a closer look at the mountain. They spent two days making their way up to the foot of the Rhamani Glacier, where they established Base Camp in a grassy area near running water.

The West Ridge looked much steeper and more difficult than it had in photographs. The South Ridge, a series of rock towers also accessible from the Rhamini Glacier, looked even harder. Dougal floated an alternative: The team could cross Shipton Col at the bottom of the South Ridge and descend to the Changabang Glacier. This would put them in the very heart of the Nanda Devi Sanctuary—and in position to climb the mountain's more feasible Southeast Ridge.

The expedition established an Advance Base Camp at the head of the Rhamani Glacier, at 18,000 feet. Doug Scott and Martin Boysen moved up to the camp on May 22, and spent several days climbing and fixing ropes up the steep, snow-covered granite wall that ended at Shipton Col. Dougal and Chris meanwhile made an attempt on Rishikot, a 21,000-foot peak above Base Camp. They set out at one o'clock on the morning of May 23, carrying down jackets and food for a one-day attempt.

They were trying something new—treating a Himalayan peak

Chris, Doug, Dougal and Martin study Changabang
Doug Scott, Chris Bonington Picture Library

like an alpine romp—and the freedom of it made them giddy.
They climbed through the remaining hours of night and into
the morning, kicking steps in shallow snow that lay over steep
ice, using ice pitons for protection. The sun rose but they moved
in shadow, kicking shallow and precarious steps toward a line
where the snow turned gold; after a time they crossed into the
golden snow and felt the sun's warmth upon them. They paused
and gazed across and upward to clouds that obscured the summit
of Changabang. They climbed further, and as they did the sky
changed; the sun disappeared and they approached a high gray
slick of cloud. Then they were in blowing snow. It was still only
nine o'clock in the morning.

They climbed through the late morning and into the afternoon,
bugs on a wall—little routefinding, just a tilted white plane. They
were barely aware of the bulk of the mountain. It was as if they were

climbing a miracle of geometry, a random surface in the vastness of space. They might step or fall through it—like stepping through a cornice or snow bridge—and into an entirely different world. The stories they imposed upon their lives had faded until they knew nothing at all; thoughts arose and departed like the meltwater released in the shallow depths of the ice field itself. This peace of mind flickered and receded at moments and they felt themselves reach for it as you might reach for the hand of someone falling.

They moved slowly at times. The snow high on the wall was rotten, pocked and brittle. They finished the wall and stood on the summit ice field in snow and wind. The summit itself wasn't close; going on would mean spending a night out in their down jackets, with the likelihood of frostbite or worse. There were two hours of daylight left to them—they had been gaining height for sixteen hours. They turned back. They reached camp six hours later, at ten o'clock, having climbed and descended 7,000 feet.

It gave them something to bring to the Changabang climb. It was one more experience leading them down a path that had called to them from the beginning. Mountaineering had given them reputation and success and prospects but on a climb such as this one on Rishikot they could imagine that those things were distractions, that success was mostly a burden. They clung less fiercely to their lives and futures and comforts. This was true for some of the other climbers as well as for Dougal and Chris. They pursued with growing intensity and recklessness these moments where the desire for liberation from time and from fear over-whelmed their attachment to any life but one backlit by a vast and glittering darkness.

DOUGAL AND CHRIS moved back up to Advance Base Camp on May 26. They spent the next day reinforcing the line of fixed ropes that led up the wall to Shipton Col. That work cleared the way for a succession of carries, and by May 31 the expedition had accumulated enough gear at the col to support a six-man attempt on the summit.

The summit team at Advance Base Camp included the four British climbers, as well as the leader of the Indian party— Lieutenant Colonel Balwant Sandhu, known to all as Ballu—and Sherpa Tashi Chewang. The climbers planned to move their supplies down the other side of the Shipton Col to a camp at the head of the Changabang Glacier. They would climb from there to a second col—the one between Changabang and its neighbor Kalanka—and establish a top camp near Changabang's Southeast Ridge. The party could then dash up the ridge to the summit.

They set out early on May 31, rising just after midnight to climb the fixed ropes to Shipton Col. They arrived at the col in the early morning and loaded up with gear. Each man took some 80 pounds on his back. They plunged down a snow slope toward the Changabang Glacier, moving as quickly as they could with their heavy loads. They drew near the glacier at around eight o'clock in the morning. The snow had turned soft as they descended, making it harder to keep their footing. They were anxious about the risk of avalanche.

They established the new camp at the base of a rock spur that would provide some protection against snow slides. Doug spent the day gazing up at the face that the party would have to climb to reach the Southeast Ridge. Avalanches scoured the face every hour or so. Snow fell the night of June 1. The climbers spent another day at their camp on the Changabang Glacier to allow the snow to settle. The delay meant they would have to ration their food to reduce the risk of running out before their eventual return over Shipton Col to Advance Base.

The moon came out that night. They set out at ten o'clock, roped in pairs, climbing in the cold and dark to take advantage of the firmer snow. Dougal—he was climbing very strongly—led them in single file up the moonlit face to a huge basin. The deep snow in the basin slowed the party's progress and intensified their fears of an avalanche that would sweep them back into the depths that accumulated beneath them as they climbed. They reached a ridge of ice and as they prepared to climb further the slope beneath them unleashed a huge slide that carried away their freshly made steps.

Someone made a joke. Two or three of the other climbers made amused sounds and the party resumed their climb. They moved in silence, each man alone with his thoughts as the world once more dwindled to snow and night. A climber might occasionally try to acknowledge the growing void at his feet, but he would not be successful. The darkness was a shiny black stone. A person couldn't fall into that.

Dougal led a difficult pitch and anchored a rope. The others jumared up to join him, but Dougal had disappeared up into the next set of difficulties. The moon set at 3:30 in the morning. The darkness grew more complete so that it was hard to see the ground in front of them. The party came to a halt and waited, their feet growing numb while light appeared at the tops of the surrounding peaks. The climbers crossed a crevasse to reach a shelf where they set about making camp.

The six climbers crowded into two tents. The day passed quietly. They heard no sounds but the sounds they made themselves. Hearing the shuffling and coughs and talk was like hearing a person tune a piano in a wilderness. They sorted gear. They made stew in the evening and ate a communal supper—the six climbers huddled over stoves, five of them sharing a single spoon. Dougal preferred to eat with a piton he kept handy for the purpose. Later they retired to their tents. Chris shared a tent with Martin and Ballu. Dougal, Doug and Tashi had the other. The climbers lay pressed against one another in the early darkness and tried to sleep.

They rose at one o'clock in the morning and had breakfast—tea and cereal. Martin Boysen was optimistic about finishing the route. He could see reasonable climbing to the col between Kalanka and Changabang, and after that just the long Southeast Ridge to the summit. Tashi was feeling under the weather; Martin heard him mutter something about ill omens.

They were off by two o'clock. Chris and Dougal were first to leave camp. Chris took the lead this time. He struggled past an overhang. He found his rhythm, and climbed 100 feet of steep ice, fixing a rope for the others. They followed, and then the climbers waded through deep snow to the col at the bottom of their ridge. The sun rose in a clear and windless sky as the climbers stared across a spectacular vista of mountains reaching north to Tibet.

The ridge to the summit of Changabang looked more difficult from here: a knife's edge of snow, growing steeper as it approached the top of the peak. They dropped their gear and reformed into two roped trios—Chris, Martin and Ballu made one rope. Dougal, Doug and Tashi made the other. Martin led the first rope. The snow here was loose and decayed; it lay on a base of brittle ice that wouldn't take an ice piton. The climbers moved slowly, one man at a time. They sometimes straddled the ridge as if riding horseback—*au cheval*—using their hands to stay in balance. Other times they dropped to one side or another of the ridge crest and teetered across steep snow slopes that fell away into views of distant glacier. Dougal and Doug left Tashi with the others and climbed ahead. The two of them cut occasional steps in the ice to safeguard the team's descent.

The climbers were all very tired and increasingly aware of their thirst. Their discomfort reminded them that they lived in their bodies and not merely in the stories that preoccupied and frightened them. Dougal in his fatigue and in his half-felt bliss at being here looked upon his own membranes and muscles as if upon some forgotten geography. He saw his body as he might have seen a contour map of new ground, long unexplored and assumed to be empty and arid, now known to be rampant with life.

The ridge beckoned them further into the sky. They were fearfully high already; they could look down some 6,000 feet to the Bagini Glacier, a dirty-gray swathe shadowed in the remotest distance. They climbed on into the afternoon, each climber bound to others so that one man's fatigue or clumsiness slowed the other climbers down. The world seemed frozen. They moved within the confines of a moment that did not change but instead unfolded endlessly even as they themselves grew increasingly weary and thirsty and ever more quiet.

Dougal and Doug reached the summit at four o'clock in the afternoon. The others arrived an hour later. The six climbers crouched together in a cold mist, thinking of the descent. It was twenty rope-lengths to the col and then they must descend the wall to the Changabang Glacier. Other peaks appeared and vanished in the clouds that swirled and moved past like elements of some tidal body. Doug and Chris took a few pictures. They had climbed the mountain but there was no impulse to gloat or preen; there was instead a faint and obscure and somehow sweet sense of having done wrong, of deserving notice for that.

No one wished to linger here. Dougal and Doug spotted a place on the summit ridge that looked as if it might be slightly higher than the point where the party had gathered. The two of them crossed the snow to tag it. The others set off down. The descent of the narrow, snow-covered ridge was as difficult as the climb. The climbers looked upon a wintry void as they picked their way down. Gravity made them awkward—it was like an incompetent friend or clumsy child at their heels—but at moments they lost track of their suffering: night came and they sailed and drifted away from the moon, which lit the snow and echoed the sun, of which their memories in turn seemed images from prehistory, something discovered in drawings in caves. Gravity, the sun's echo, the snow, the thin air they breathed—each climber felt himself to be solitary amid this even as each was glad of the other's company.

Dougal and Doug had performed their summit errand and moved down to catch the others. Martin was moving more quickly than the rest. He descended the last difficult stretch to easy snow slopes and made a final rappel to the glacier camp to put up the tents and make tea. The rest found him at it when they staggered in.

It was ten o'clock. They were tired. They ate nothing that night. They brewed tea and drank it and chatted. The four British climbers eyed each other and pondered their experience of the past two days. The climb had been difficult, but well within their limits. And something else: they had enjoyed it. They sprawled around their campsite and made jokes and wished for nothing. They talked like boys—the kinds who dig for buried treasure and expect to find it.

12

THE CHALLENGE OF Everest's Southwest Face still lay before them. A third Japanese expedition had failed to get past the Rock Band that guarded its higher reaches. The news made Chris realize that Dougal Haston and Doug Scott were right—that his ambition and his destiny were linked with the task of climbing that face. The problems it posed occupied his thoughts on his journey homeward from Changabang in the spring of 1974.

His interest in the Southwest Face had become a fascination, which bloomed now into an obsession, one that distracted him from the more ordinary tasks of his life as a husband and father. Those family duties sustained him at moments, but they interfered with his compulsion to solve the problem, to manage difficulties that taxed his growing powers, at times consuming him entirely. He had discovered in himself tremendous appetites, including an appetite for the stupendously taxing and complex work of inventing this expedition, and now he indulged his need fully, telling himself that the work of creating a successful expedition to the Southwest Face would reinvent him, that he would return to his other life a new man and a better one.

This time he went at the problem with certain advantages. He had a year to plan the expedition—he had thrown together his first Everest expedition in a few months. What was more, he now knew the route firsthand. He had come to believe that the best way past the Rock Band lay up a snow gully just to the left of the route through the lower camps on the face. The earliest expeditions to the face had considered this gully, but recent attempts—including his own expedition—had focused their efforts on a gully that led to the far right of the face, near the Southeast Ridge. The right-hand gully had proven impossible in 1972, when Dougal Haston had gazed up into it to discover rock blown clean of snow. Worse, that gully appeared to lead to further hard climbing. Chris had concluded that the gully that lay to the left offered a more promising alternative.

He had learned from his experience with the weather. He figured the expedition should make an earlier start to avoid the winds that had wrecked their chances in 1972. This would expose the team to more avalanche risk, but the gamble seemed worthwhile—necessary. He would bring stronger shelters, as well. The wind had destroyed most of the climbers had established on the face during the first expedition.

Veterans of the 1972 expedition would provide the core of his climbing team, but he would bring a larger group this time—more climbers and more porters. That meant he needed more money, at a time when Great Britain's economic problems—the country was mired in a recession—would make it difficult to find sponsors.

Chris carried these plans and concerns back to England, where he joined Wendy and the children in their trailer at Badger Hill; the builders were still engaged in renovating the cottage. His literary agent George Greenfield set to work to find a sponsor who could put up 100,000 pounds to finance the new Everest venture—and succeeded almost immediately. Barclay's Bank agreed to put up the cash. The deal provoked a minor controversy in the press and several speeches in Parliament to the effect that such a sum could be better invested in the slumping British economy.

Chris began assembling his team. Dougal Haston and Doug Scott were already committed. Martin Boysen had been on Annapurna

as well as Changabang. He had skipped the first Everest expedition—his wife had been pregnant—but he would come along this
time. Nick Estcourt's job had kept him from Changabang, but
he would return to Everest. Hamish MacInnes, now forty-four,
would come as deputy leader. Hamish would be making his third
expedition to the face. His experience had left him doubtful of
the chances for success, but he wanted to come.

Mick Burke was skeptical, too, but he was coming. He would
be miserable if the team got up the route without him. Mick had
come a long way from his days of bartending and odd jobs in
the Lake District. He now worked full-time for the BBC, and he
and Beth had a daughter, Sara. Mick doted on the child. He had
always liked children; he was quite friendly with the Boningtons'
young sons, Daniel and Rupert. He would get down on the floor
to play with the kids during his visits to the Bonington home,
where expedition meetings often served as excuses for somewhat
boozy reunions among the climbers and their families.

Chris offered Mick two options: He could go along as a full-
time cameraman—or he could join the climbing team and do
his filming on the side. Mick chose the second option. He would
climb the route with the rest of them and tote a camera, much as
he had done on Annapurna and on the first Everest trip.

Graham Tiso and Dave Bathgate, both members of the 1972
team, turned down Bonington's invitation this time; so did Barney
Rosedale and Kelvin Kent. Chris invited Charlie Clarke to replace
Rosedale as the expedition doctor. Clarke, thirty-one, the son of
an eminent physician, was himself a successful neurologist, an earnest and engaging young man. He had made six expeditions to the
Himalaya, always with small parties. He climbed at a reasonable
standard but wasn't madly ambitious as a climber—he simply loved
the high mountains. Chris liked Charlie enormously, recognized
and valued the younger man's intelligence and maturity. Chris also

was impressed by Charlie's background and the steady confidence the younger man seemed to draw from it. Charlie seemed in some ways a younger, in some ways more blessed and perhaps less driven version of Bonington himself. Charlie seemed reliable, a person who would behave well in a crisis.

Chris recruited Dave Clarke—an occasional climbing partner, a steady sort and the owner of a Leeds climbing shop—to manage the equipment for the expedition. Chris also invited his old army friend Mike Thompson, a low-key eccentric with a quick wit. Mike had served nobly as a support climber on Annapurna. He agreed to organize the food for Everest. Mike Cheney—he worked for Jimmy Roberts's trekking business in Nepal—would take charge of Base Camp.

Chris needed more climbers. He invited Allen Fyffe, a first-rate ice climber, on the advice of Graham Tiso. Barclays Bank wanted a representative on the climb, and the bank proposed Mike Rhodes, an affable and energetic young man—he was twenty-seven—who supported a wife and three young children on his job at the bank. Doug Scott proposed Paul Braithwaite (known to all as Tut), an art school dropout who made his living as a freelance decorator. Tut was tall and absurdly slim, with long hair and a droopy moustache. Chris thought he looked too skinny to be much of a force on the mountain, but Tut's record in the Alps as well as Alaska and the Pamirs was reassuring.

Tut suggested one more climber: Peter Boardman, twenty-four, an outdoors instructor who had made impressive alpine-style climbs on difficult peaks in the Hindu Kush. Peter climbed rock as well as almost anyone in England—only Martin Boysen and perhaps one or two others could match him.

Chris invited Boardman to come down to the Lake District for a climb. Peter was a good-looking boy, six feet tall with a mop of black hair that set off his strong but regular features.

His eyes were very dark, and carried an air of intelligence—of curiosity tempered by shyness—which Chris found immediately appealing. The young man seemed modest and thoughtful; he was well-spoken, courteous and even respectful without overdoing it. He seemed almost gentle—he was careful of other people—but none of this could conceal an ambitious, competitive and deeply confident streak that Chris recognized and approved.

The confidence came partly from Peter's awareness of his various gifts, which included his abilities on rock. He had a strong upper body, with a long torso and long arms. He started up a route and it was clear that he was made differently in some way. It was strangely soothing to see him move higher; there seemed not much effort in it.

Chris asked Peter to come along to Everest. There was little question of refusing such an invitation. Peter understood—as did Chris—that this was the sort of gift or blessing other types of men had issued or not issued to climbers a generation before. The old Oxbridge elite had passed into history some time during the past decade. Chris Bonington and his boys had replaced them.

The relics of the old elite were still in evidence. The 1975 Southwest Face expedition sported a Committee of Management chaired by Lord Hunt—the man who had organized and led the 1953 expedition that put Hillary and Tenzing on the summit of Everest. The committee members were mostly adventurers from an earlier day. They weren't entirely sure what to make of Chris and his friends, including the climbing team's single representative: long-haired, blunt-spoken Doug Scott, with his North Country accent and his habit of quoting Eastern religious texts. The committee suggested Chris bring along a second doctor, so he invited Jim Duff, a British army medical officer. Finally, there was the media: the BBC wished to send four people, and the *Sunday Times* was sending a reporter.

Chris based his expedition strategy partly on the approach that John Hunt had taken in 1953. He also engaged a professional programmer with access to a mainframe computer to work out logistics and test various schemes for establishing and stocking camps on the mountain. He sent most of the gear and food overland, leaving a cushion for accidents and setbacks, and was delighted when the two trucks arrived safely in Kathmandu. Mike Cheney arranged for the local Sherpa cooperative to transfer everything to the Luglha (now Lukla) airstrip, a day's march from the Sherpa settlements below Everest. Cheney also recruited porters. He needed hundreds of them to help carry the expedition's twenty-seven tons of equipment and thirteen tons of food to Base Camp; sixty or so more experienced men would ferry supplies through the Icefall and up the Southwest Face.

The climbers assembled in Kathmandu in early August. They traveled by road to Lamosangu, where Chris divided them into two parties for the approach march. His own group included his two closest cronies, Dougal and Nick, with Mick and Charlie Clarke; also most of the BBC crew. The second group—they immediately dubbed themselves the B Team—included Hamish MacInnes, Doug Scott and Martin Boysen as well as the new boy, Peter Boardman.

Peter was impressed by his illustrious companions, and enthralled by his surroundings. He took in the prayer flags and the water buffaloes and the often sweet-faced villagers along the route. He listened to the talk of his fellow climbers—seasoned veterans of major Himalayan expeditions who seemed to take it all in stride, and who teased him endlessly about his position in the British mountaineering bureaucracy—Peter had recently taken an office job at the British Mountaineering Council. He

watched bemused as camp servants served tea from steaming
kettles to grubby, longhaired Britons who sat segregated in their
mess tent; the scene brought to his mind the imperialist explorers
of an earlier time.

The approach march took two weeks. Chris brooded over his
plans for the mountain and sounded out various climbers. He
knew very well that any decision he made regarding their roles
on the peak would anger and disappoint some of them. Dougal
Haston thought himself the best man to summit the peak, and
wasn't prepared to give way in favor of other climbers. Dougal
wanted Doug Scott for a partner, but Chris rejected that idea
for now. He wasn't ready to pair off his two strongest climbers.
The others would figure he'd picked his summit team, and they'd
be right. Nick Estcourt as usual refused to put himself forward.
He told Chris he'd accept any role assigned to him. Mick Burke,
who had his filming to do, also was content to let Chris arrange
things. Doug Scott and Hamish MacInnes seemed willing to
cooperate as well.

Any thoughts of the summit seemed premature. Chris by now
was fighting dysentery. Hamish was still getting over an infection
he'd contracted in Kathmandu. Mike Cheney was suffering from
an undiagnosed ailment; his symptoms included weakness and
severe abdominal pain.

Charlie Clarke watched the Sherpas slaughter a black goat
one evening. The scene left him thoughtful, frightened of the
mountain they were approaching—in particular the Icefall. He
listened half-horrified to the others' casual talk about Ian Clough
and Tony Tighe; people talked as if no one realized that the two
men had died—had actually *died*—on expeditions very like this
one. Charlie found it especially distressing that Dougal still wore
Tony's floppy hat.

Bonington's party reached the Sherpa village of Khumde on

August 14. Doug's group arrived two days later. The team spent several days unpacking and reorganizing gear. Chris sent Dougal and Nick ahead to scout for a good site for Base Camp and inspect the Icefall.

Bonington's group set out for Base Camp on August 18; the second group would follow a day or two later. Chris and Charlie Clarke agreed to walk up together, taking the journey in easy stages. Charlie watched a Sherpa take leave of his wife and three children, who stood with the man around a juniper fire, praying for his safe return. Charlie thought of his own family—his wife, Ruth, and their daughter, Rebecca, aged four.

Chris and Charlie spent that night on a hillside beneath the Tengpoche monastery. The next morning they walked up to receive the old Lama's blessing. He told them what he'd told Chris and his companions three years before: *If you work together and do not argue among yourselves, you have a chance of climbing the mountain.*

CHRIS'S GROUP LEFT the Lama and walked up to Pheriche, which in recent years had become a haven for trekkers, with a half-dozen guesthouses. Chris found himself distressed at the changes he saw in the area. A place such as this one would have been virtually empty of travelers a decade earlier. He cheered up on learning that an old friend—a Sherpa named Nima—owned one of the guesthouses. Nima had served as a high-altitude porter on the Annapurna expedition five years before. It was pleasant catching up with an old friend, and Nima seemed happy in his newfound prosperity.

It took another three days for Chris and his party to reach the site of Everest Base Camp. Sherpas came and went among the boulders, ferrying loads across the snow. Dougal and Nick were already up in the Icefall, having a look. The second group of climbers and porters arrived at Base Camp the next day—August 23.

The temperature rose on August 24, so that it was too warm to enter the Icefall. The Sherpas instead held a ceremony to consecrate Base Camp. The Sherpas chanted and shouted; they prayed and laughed, throwing rice and tsampa in fistfuls. They built a fire and made their offerings to their mountain, Sagarmatha—Nepalese for *Head of the Ocean*. Their good spirits and their piety moved Chris; he felt a responsibility to them even as he recognized that he couldn't keep them safe. A Sherpa presented him a tray with a bottle of rum; another, his face lit by a smile devoid of self-consciousness, planted himself in front of Chris and reached to wrap a scarf around the Englishman's neck.

Chris learned that very evening that one of the youngest porters—a deaf and dumb boy named Mingma—was missing. Mingma was helping to ferry loads to Base Camp from Gorak Shep, the expedition's staging point at the bottom of the Khumbu Glacier. The other Sherpas tended to leave Mingma to himself; communication with him was difficult. But Doug Scott—along with Don Whillans and Hamish MacInnes—had stayed with Mingma's family in Pheriche during the International Everest expedition in the spring of 1972. Doug had made a point of spending time with the boy on this trip; had even helped Mingma carry his load.

Mingma had set out to make a carry to Base Camp that morning, and had not yet returned to Gorak Shep. When he failed to turn up the following morning, Chris organized six small search parties, equipping each group with a radio. Doug took three Sherpas, and searched with genuine urgency until Adrian Gordon came on the radio to say that his group had come upon a body in a stream. Doug made his way to the body and lifted it from the water. His sense of responsibility for the boy made this tragedy particularly hard to bear. Chris ran the two miles from Base Camp, his mind playing odd tricks—his steps on the glacier were oddly loud—and arrived breathless, unable to speak. He saw Doug and crossed to him. They wrapped their arms around each other, both of them in tears, Doug sobbing in his grief and his guilt over the death of this boy. Chris tried to console him, spoke of his own first child, also drowned in a stream. It was odd and deeply painful to reflect that Conrad would have been a teenager now. Bonington's own child and Doug's young friend had been almost contemporaries, born into different worlds but now both of them gone in much the same way, only under different skies.

The climbers and porters stood and milled uncertainly in that ancient, barren wilderness, ordinarily empty of men. Most of them were young; some were mere boys, as Mingma had been. His corpse had curled and bent into a kind of question mark: where had he gone? The expedition had ventured into this vast emptiness, displacing it as a swimmer displaces water. Now one of their numbers had drowned; the emptiness had occupied him as if in turnabout. Mingma was not different from the rest of them, or perhaps his silence had made him more vulnerable. Maybe the void had mistaken him for itself. It might be that some balance or equilibrium was restored. Maybe the rest of them were safer now. Or it might be that this mountain was angry; Mingma's death might be a sort of warning. Some of the porters were frightened.

There was no talk of quitting the expedition. The boy was in fact a stranger to most of the climbers and his death made him seem still more of a stranger. The climbers and porters continued their work. They were making a route up through the Icefall, perhaps the most dangerous work of the expedition, creating a path through the shifting maze of crevasses and teetering cliffs and towers of ice. The white looming shapes were like enormous tombstones or buildings—the place sometimes had the feel of an urban churchyard. It was hard to forget that this place had buried Tony Tighe three years before. His crushed and frozen corpse was somewhere beneath them—and with it the remnants of others, Sherpa and Westerner. The climbers and the hired porters were building their path to the Southwest Face on top of a slow motion avalanche, a mass grave for the spectacularly unfortunate—for what were the odds of being born to die here?

Once here, of course, the risk was very real. They might fall into a crevasse or die under the weight of a collapse; there was also a significant risk of avalanche now, so soon after the monsoon snows. They worked in shadow and cold and at moments forgot the sun until it spilled across the ice and set it creaking and shifting beneath and around them. The heat was stupefying and also dangerous as it set about its work of undoing the ground they stood upon. They gasped and suffered from the altitude. Young Peter Boardman was relieved to see that Dougal and Nick and the others who dwelt within Bonington's exalted inner circle struggled and sweated at their work just as he did—sometimes perhaps a bit more.

Chris on August 26 led a party to consolidate the lower sections of the route while Doug and Dougal climbed ahead to make more progress higher up. Chris called across a snow slope to Mike Rhodes—the fair-haired young father of three, the Barclays Bank man—to come and help bridge a crevasse. Mike walked toward him, forgetting to clip into a safety rope, and dropped through the snow to his shoulders, his feet dangling over a space that brought to his racing mind an enormous black cathedral, roofless and empty. Someone tossed him a rope's end. Rhodes seized it and scrambled out, more astonished than terrified at his near miss.

Doug and Dougal meanwhile reached the top of the Icefall. They soon discovered a place for Camp One, an island of snow surrounded by deep moats that would protect them from slides. It stood just at the foot of the Western Cwm, the great snow basin that lay like a sea of clouds below the dark expanses of the Southwest Face. They stood and looked across toward the bottom of the face to the place where the mountain seemed to rise from the snow. It was possible to imagine the roots of the mountain—what lay beneath the snow in the still darker vastness of the earth herself. Dougal cast his mind back to the mountain unborn, still one of the infinite number of possible mountains dormant in the planet's many wombs.

The climbers and porters spent a day consolidating the upper part of the route through the Icefall. They began ferrying loads to the newly established Camp One on August 28. This put them well ahead of their 1972 schedule—Chris in fact worried that they might be too early. Huge avalanches—partly remnants of the monsoon—billowed down the walls of Everest and neighboring Nuptse each afternoon to sweep across the cwm above Camp One.

Doug and Dougal spent three days threading their way past crevasses in search of a site for Camp Two. The other climbers followed in support, building ladder bridges across the worst gaps in the route, preparing a way for the porters to carry supplies to higher camps. Sherpas—thirty to forty on a given day—meanwhile ferried loads through the Icefall to Camp One.

Mornings in the Western Cwm dawned gray and after a time turned gold; this lasted until the sun hit the high snows of the surrounding peaks, when things went a blinding white. Mist and snow arrived toward the middle of each day; climbers and Sherpas listened in the afternoon to the rumblings of more avalanches. They lay in their tents at night and wondered if Camp One were really safe. The newer hands—Ronnie Richards was one—listened nervously to the others joke about the likelihood that the camp and its inhabitants would tumble into the Icefall that lay just behind and below them.

Dougal and Doug found a spot for Camp Two at the base of the Southwest Face. The climbers spent the next week stocking the new camp and sitting out a brief storm, debating the merits and risks of various lines up the face. They settled on their original line; the others were too exposed to avalanche.

Doug and Mick Burke climbed onto the face itself on September 6, unreeling fixed rope for the first time on the expedition. Doug led most of the way; Mick filmed him. They stopped to rest. The basin beneath them was like a vast, half-frozen lake. They could imagine a country of formless power and darkness and surprise beneath it, as a sailor might imagine a world beneath the surface of the sea. Dark specks crawled across the snow in single file. These were the porters bringing loads to Camp Two, a huddle of orange tents and brown box shelters, invaders or settlers come to sully a new world with their noise and clutter. Doug and Mick climbed 1,200 feet to the base of a buttress—this was the site they'd chosen for Camp Three—and descended. They were due for a rest.

Nick Estcourt and Tut Braithwaite had moved up to Camp Two that day. They followed the ropes to Camp Three on September 7, reaching the new site early in the day. They continued to climb, fixing rope up through soft snow until the sun swept out onto the face and the heat brought them to a stop. They followed the ropes back down to Camp Three, wading now through soft, wet snow that gave way beneath their boots.

Nick and Tut spent another two days fixing rope up slabs of snow that threatened to break away and carry them off the face. The climbing wasn't difficult but the scale of the place was frightening. Occasional powder avalanches added to their sense of insecurity. They put in two more days climbing, establishing

Camp Four at 23,700 feet and then fixing rope up into the Great Central Gully that split the face.

Martin Boysen and Peter Boardman reached Camp Four on September 11 and climbed on, fixing rope on the snow slopes above the site. Dougal and Hamish arrived at Camp Four the same day. Chris had come up as well to help in the work hacking out tent platforms and setting up shelters.

The climbers were making good progress on the route. There was a sense among them that this time the summit was perhaps in the cards. Their hopes turned them inward and they were less patient with one another. Martin thought young Peter Boardman seemed unduly impressed by some of the bigger names; Peter would get busy helping Hamish set up his shelter and then ask Martin to fetch his camera or hand him a tent peg. Still, Martin liked him; everyone did. Peter was performing well on the mountain; he was surprisingly strong and clearly determined to get up the face and have his own shot at the summit.

Peter was aware of some slight condescension or coolness on Martin's part. And Dougal was remote—but Hamish was cheerful and friendly. Hamish was almost twice Peter's age; the gap made competition between them ridiculous. It had been a long time—more than two decades—since Hamish had taken young Chris Bonington up those first terrifying climbs in Scotland. Hamish had maintained a certain distance from the Bonington circle—or circus, as it sometimes seemed these days—but he was forty-four years old; he wouldn't have many more chances at getting up Everest. He had taken the lead in building the road through the Icefall, bringing to bear his engineering skills. Meanwhile, he was enjoying himself.

Chris descended the face that afternoon. The others settled in at the newly established Camp Four, their shelters pinioned to the snow slope by various anchors. Small avalanches buffeted the camp during the night; at one point Hamish was half-convinced that they would be swept, tents and all, from their perch. All four climbers slept fitfully. They woke in the morning to more settled conditions, but the two Sherpas who had shared camp with them were subdued; they didn't like the look of the freshly loaded snow slopes that lay above the camp.

Dougal and Hamish set off ahead of the others. They were both moving strongly. Hamish, climbing without oxygen—his set had malfunctioned—was pleased to find that he could keep pace with his younger companion. He carried on, struggling a little with the jumars—they slipped on the frozen rope that Peter and Martin had fixed the previous day. He was engaged in his task and he resisted for a beat the impulse to raise his head to investigate a sound and as he did look up the avalanche arrived. He kept his feet long enough to wrap the fixed rope around his hand—he didn't trust the jumars to grip the rope's icy sheath. A fog of ice crystals seemed to fill his lungs and the thick, sliding mass at his legs tore him from his footing. He hung by his hand, near drowning as the snow covered him. His mind skimmed various questions but the battering and the pain in his hand and also his need to breathe prevented him from settling upon any of them.

The avalanche passed and he lay in the snow, gasping and retching and slowly coming back to himself—this oddly helpless creature. Dougal had watched the slide from his perch higher above. He climbed quickly down to Hamish and helped him to his feet and they retraced their steps to camp. Hamish had trouble getting his breath; the powder snow had gotten into his lungs. He rested that afternoon but he slept poorly that night, still unable to breath freely even with the help of bottled oxygen. He felt very weak. He retreated to Camp Two the next morning.

The others—Peter and Martin and Dougal—went up to find

a site for Camp Five. They settled on some narrow ledges, which offered a view into the gully that led up into the Rock Band. The Western Cwm lay far below them, its enormity dwarfed by distance. Nuptse rose up from the other side of the valley; Everest's sister peak was vast and black and snow-dappled, dwarfed in its turn by the sky. The climbers could peer across and past to a view that disappeared into infinite depths—bank after bank of clouds lay crumpled and matted like a feather quilt. The climbers felt their own emptiness; they fell into their own huge blue silence. The clouds below them gently shifted, formed and reformed.

They returned to Camp Four for the night. They were far from home. They woke to cold in the mornings. The cold forced upon them a near-paranoid awareness, the keeping track of fingers and toes until the sun rose high enough to warm their shelters. The very world shifted with the sun's appearance; they glimpsed the sun's power.

Peter and Martin descended the face on September 14. They needed a rest after three days out front. Dougal remained at Camp Four. He wanted some time away from the others. He spent the afternoon reading letters and daydreaming in MacInnes Box. The wind rose at nightfall, and it began to snow. He woke to the sounds of snow moving, shapes sliding past the tent; it must be from the snowfields on the route to the old Camp Six. A great deal of snow had come down, and as Dougal listened something heavy slammed into the shelter and knocked him across the floor. He lay sprawled, overcome by a sense of his own failings, his ignorance; he didn't know what was happening or how it would end—was he falling or not?

The avalanche passed. The shelter remained moored to the mountain. Dougal dressed, putting on his boots so that he could leave quickly if another avalanche hit. There were no more—only small, hissing slides whose sounds merged with the sound of the wind that slid across his shelter like water past a stone bottom. He peered outside and saw that the slide had buried the other shelter; he was lucky to be in this one. He felt himself a sort of ghost, gazing across at the scene of the death of some other self.

Dougal sometimes felt in the mountains that his death took notice of him. He lost most of his shyness—his fear—when that happened. The notion of himself as a ghost appealed to him. He sometimes awoke believing that he had become a ghost and had talked to the ghost of the boy on the road. Dougal thought he would like to haunt a place like this—high and precarious, almost unfindable—and he felt a little that he was doing it now. He looked across the snow to the buried tent and saw a glimpse of the mistake or the moment that would finish him.

He lay alone and afraid through the rest of the night as a pagan might lie on an altar. He was not a victim. He offered himself as a flesh-and-bone prayer. He felt the blood and breath move in his body in the vast unthinking motion of this place. He left Camp Five early in the morning and descended the ropes to the others; as he lost height he felt within him the thin exultance of a ghost, invulnerable and taskless, untouchable.

He encountered Chris, who was on his way up the mountain with Ronnie Richards. Chris wanted to inspect the line the climbers were forging up the face; and he wanted some time in the lead. Chris and Ronnie continued up the ropes to Camp Four. They dug out the shelters—the damage wasn't as bad as Dougal had believed—and spent the night there. The next day, September 16, they made a carry to Camp Five. Chris was impressed by the situation, tucked in beneath the walls of a buttress, the mountain falling away beneath them into distance that was like time; it could be crossed, but at a pace they could not fix or change.

Chris and Ronnie spent much of the day digging a platform in the ice and erecting a single box shelter. The altitude was like an illness. They moved slowly at their work, digging and sweating, slaves on an alien moon. They slept that night on bottled oxygen, their faces buried in the buglike masks. The hissing of the cylinders in the apparatus echoed like the breath of some unspeaking creature, sounds of breathing in a cave.

They set off early in the morning. They were aiming for the bottom of the Rock Band, but Chris made a route-finding mistake. They wasted the morning, moving slowly higher on dangerously thin snow that was difficult to climb and impossible to protect adequately. Chris admitted his mistake and the climbers reversed two long pitches, finding their way back across and then up through deeper snow. It was very warm by now, so they retreated to camp. They fixed the rest of their rope the next morning and descended.

Doug Scott and Mick Burke greeted them at Camp Five. Chris continued down to meet one of the support climbers, Jim Duff. Jim was making a carry from Camp Four. Chris found him sitting in the snow, slurring his words; he was clearly hypothermic. Chris took Jim's load and sent him back down the fixed ropes, then turned and climbed back to Camp Five. He reached it in time for the afternoon radio call—which brought the news that Jim was missing. Nick Estcourt and Tut Braithwaite climbed up from Camp Four and soon came upon him; Jim was barely conscious, slumped in the snow just below where Chris had last seen him. The two rescuers got him back down to Camp Four, where they wrapped him in a sleeping bag and revived him with hot drinks.

The expedition was gaining momentum. Eight fresh Sherpas arrived at Camp Four that night—September 18—ready to ferry more gear to Camp Five. Chris and Doug climbed above Camp Five the next day, moving through deep snow nearly to the foot of the Rock Band. Nick and Tut joined them at Camp Five that afternoon.

Chris was now ready to announce his plans for the first summit team. He wanted the strongest pair to take the first shot; a change in the weather might make a second attempt impossible. He decided to bring Dougal up from Camp Two to Camp Five so that Dougal and Doug Scott could go for the summit together.

Dougal's climb up from Camp Two would take two days. Nick Estcourt and Tut Braithwaite could use that time to try to climb the Rock Band, which would bring them to the start of the route's final section. The Rock Band was a major plum—the hardest technical climbing on the face—but it would leave them exhausted, probably too tired to participate in any summit attempt. Nick would once again sacrifice his shot at a major Himalayan summit for the sake of a Bonington-led expedition's success.

Chris announced his plans during the afternoon radio call on September 19. He hadn't yet worked out who would make the subsequent summit attempts. He promised the climbers that he'd work on those assignments the next day.

Sunset from Camp Five seemed a benediction. A distant yellow orb sank in clouds that wafted beneath an ocean of blue, all of it framed below by black rock. Snow slopes beneath the camp fanned out into a gathering blue-black gloom, empty and quiet.

Nick and Tut left camp early on September 20. They kicked steps toward the start of the gully that led into the Rock Band. Chris slept through their departure and awoke some time later feeling ragged and weary from his four-day stint at high camp. He and Mick waited for Sherpas who were bringing up more rope. Chris and Mick didn't leave camp until the sun was already on the face, but they didn't take long to climb the fixed ropes; they soon caught the others.

Tut was leading the first pitch above the fixed ropes. He was moving very slowly on thin snow over rock. He couldn't find anywhere to put a piton, but the climbing was just easy enough to beckon him onward. Each step left him more exposed, but it was far easier to move higher than to reverse his steps on such terrain. He carried on in hopes of finding some crack to fit a piton, or snow deep enough for a snow stake. He climbed with heavy boots, lugging his oxygen and encumbered by the mask; everything at 27,000 feet was difficult, and this ground was extremely dangerous. The mask made it hard to see, but Tut found a place to tap in an ice piton. He put in three more as he balanced across a difficult traverse. His pack threatened to disrupt his balance. He was relieved when at last the angle lay back and the snow grew deep enough to take a snow anchor. He clipped himself to the anchor and brought Nick up into the snow, which fanned down from the base of the gully proper. Chris and Mick Burke followed on the fixed rope.

The four climbers peered up into the gully, twenty or so feet across, its boundaries black rock walls—a seeming corridor to the sky. Nick led into the snow at the very base of the gully. Chris felt his fear—the gully was a perfect funnel for avalanches that began on the upper regions of the face.

Tut led the next pitch. He climbed to a chock stone—a huge boulder jammed across the gully—and squeezed past it. The gully narrowed and grew steeper; snow streamed down over huge overhangs like rain from a roof with no gutters. Tut put in a piton and the others followed. Tut led out again, across more snow. He spotted a ramp and moved toward it on small ledges, searching for handholds, absorbed in his task, and his oxygen cylinder ran out—a hand reaching from behind to cover his mouth and pinch his nostrils. He struggled to wrench his mask off, a diver swimming for the sunlit surface, feeling the suck and pull of green darkness beneath and around him. He came as close to falling as seemed possible without actually falling. His preoccupation with the task of staying in balance distracted him from other tasks; he urinated as he fumbled at his mask. He got the mask off and sucked in the thin air and only then noticed the warmth on his leg. He recovered himself sufficiently to climb a short ridge of rock that delivered him to snow that was blessedly firm. He drove the shaft of his axe deeply into the snow and put a sling around the top of the axe and clipped his harness to it: his first protection in 100 feet. He'd come excruciatingly close to a fall that would certainly have killed him. He stood slumped and gasping for a while and when he could he took off his heavy oxygen cylinder and jammed it into the snow for a better anchor. He brought Nick up and then Chris and Mick.

The gully here grew wider and split in two. The main arm ran up to the left. Tut's ramp led right, below rock that had gone a hazy yellow in the high light. Nick took over the lead. He moved right to an island of rock that would take a real anchor. He built the new anchor and brought Tut up. Nick's oxygen was gone now; he felt its absence as he set out to lead another pitch.

The first bit was easy, but the holds petered out. Nick jammed his left arm into a snow bank that bordered the wall, and leaned back and right to look for a piton placement. He cleared snow from smooth rock as his goggles grew foggy. He found a crack and felt for a piton that hung from the back of his harness. He was wearing gloves and so he couldn't find the piton at first but then he had it out and was groping for the hammer in his holster—all of this taking its toll at an altitude of well over 27,000 feet. Nick placed the piton somehow; it was not a solid placement but he could weight it just a little as he moved his feet higher on the wall. He found more snow and pulled himself higher and into sunlight. He climbed another 20 feet of soft snow on loose rock, and at last found a crack that would take a good piton. His happiness simmered in him—he had never worked harder on a pitch. It was the hardest climbing on the route, maybe the hardest ever done at this altitude.

It was late. Chris and Mick dropped what was left of the rope they had carried up from Camp Five and descended. Tut followed Nick up and the two of them climbed another 40 feet to a patch of snow that looked as though it would take them to more snow: the Upper Snow Field.

They had climbed the Rock Band, the crux of the route, the barrier that had turned back no fewer than five expeditions. The top of the Southwest Face and beyond that the summit of Everest lay before them—not defenseless, but exposed.

13

CHRIS HAD ALREADY decided that Doug and Dougal would make the first summit attempt. His plans called for two four-man summit parties to follow them. He had promised to include Nick and Tut in the second summit team—the first foursome—but now he changed his mind. Their recent efforts on the Rock Band might have left them too weak to reach the summit—and the climbers who had spent more time in support roles deserved a shot at some real climbing. Chris decided to send Nick and Tut down to Camp Two for now, assigning them slots on the third summit team.

They took it well; they *were* tired, and they knew that other climbers deserved a shot at the top. And they might yet get their own opportunity, if the weather held. Meanwhile, their success on the Rock Band had secured them at least a share of whatever glory the expedition would garner. They had done well and now they could rest, if only briefly.

That left four places to fill on the second team and two on the third. Chris had promised to include a Sherpa in the second summit party. He felt the Sherpas deserved a slot in the third group as well. Pertemba, the head Sherpa, picked himself and his deputy Ang Phurba.

That left four slots for British climbers. Allen Fyfe had not been above Camp Four yet; he hadn't performed as strongly as the lead climbers. Ronnie Richards and Mike Thompson were relatively inexperienced. Hamish MacInnes was a different matter. He had now been to Everest four times, including three trips to the Southwest Face. He had paired off with Dougal at the start of this expedition, and they had climbed well together—but Hamish had not fully recovered from the avalanche. That left him out.

Mick Burke hadn't climbed as well as some others, but Chris wanted a good film record of the climb. He put Mick on the second summit team, along with Martin Boysen. Martin had come on the radio the evening before to ask about his role. He had earned his shot by his work on this expedition and on Annapurna.

Peter Boardman had pulled his weight and was still climbing well. He was a thoughtful young man, sensible and unselfish. He was new to the circle, easier to manage than some of the old hands. Chris needed recruits to flesh out the ranks of his dwindling crew. Don Whillans was out of the picture. Ian Clough was dead. Mick Burke was increasingly taken up with his work at the BBC. Hamish had always been his own man, and at forty-four he was getting old. Dougal was loyal mainly to his own ambitions, which might not always coincide with Chris's plans. Doug Scott had ambitions as well, and he had other climbing partners—his old mates from Nottingham, a rough-and-ready set who made their own circle. Mike Thompson was an old friend, but he wasn't a front-rank climber; neither was Charlie Clarke. There was Nick, but Chris had come to rely upon him more than seemed fair.

The upshot was that Chris offered the twenty-three-year-old Peter Boardman a spot on the second summit team. Peter would rope up with Pertemba. That left one slot to fill on the third team, which so far included Nick Estcourt, Tut Braithwaite and Ang Phurba. Chris wanted that slot for himself.

He made his announcement on the radio at two o'clock on

the afternoon of September 21. Each of the climbers scattered up and down the route listening grimly for his name. Charlie Clarke broke in when Chris was finished and asked to have a private word. The others signed off, and Charlie urged Chris to give up his plans to summit the peak. Charlie pointed out that Chris had been above 25,000 feet for more than a week; he was losing strength and lucidity; he slurred his words. Chris listened and promised to think it over.

Hamish now took the radio from Charlie and told Chris he had decided to leave the expedition. He needed to get lower for the sake of his lungs. Hamish agreed to assure reporters that his departure was the result of his medical condition, not expedition politics.

Chris considered Charlie's advice, and decided to give up his own summit team slot to Ronnie Richards. Chris would make a final carry above Camp Five to support the summit climbers; that done, he'd descend to Camp Two to direct operations.

Doug Scott and Dougal Haston and Ang Phurba left Camp Five on the morning of September 22. Doug was first on the fixed ropes that led through the Rock Band. Ang Phurba came next; Dougal brought up the rear. Three more Sherpas would follow later with loads, as would Chris and Mick Burke and Mike Thompson.

Doug was impressed by the difficulty of the terrain. Nick had done a superb job leading it without oxygen. Doug reached the top of the fixed ropes and climbed out of the gully. Ang Phurba arrived and Doug led another 30 feet of hard climbing; from there, he ran out 250 more feet of rope to a ridge of snow that would serve for Camp Six.

Dougal came up behind the others, happy to be here at last: the actual territory above the Rock Band now replaced the map he had carried in his head through three expeditions. Nothing, no one, stood between him and the way forward and up. It could be done: a stretch of steep rock and then some snow to the exit gully and then the top of the face; after that, a long but easy climb over to and up the Southeast Ridge.

Ang Phurba descended, leaving Doug and Dougal to their work of carving out the new site. They alternated digging, taking oxygen during their rests. The three Sherpas and then Chris and Mick and Mike arrived with their loads. The five British climbers chatted for a time. They were aware of their respective roles; for the moment it seemed right that Doug and Dougal should be the ones to finish this. Mick said he thought Camp Six would make a lovely spot for a bungalow. Chris did some thinking and announced that the six of them must be the highest people on Earth. The others conceded that he must be right: the Americans had just failed on K2, and there was no one on Kangchenjunga or Lhotse.

The load bearers departed down the ropes, near-staggering in their orange wind suits, cajoled by gravity, a hand at their backs. Doug watched them go, and felt a stab of gratitude. Their shapes blurred and shifted and faded; the jumble and span of black rock and gray snow and blue shadow framed and then swallowed them.

Doug and Dougal put up the two-man summit tent. They planned to fix 500 meters of rope the next day—a long traversing line across snow—and then return to their new camp. The day after, they'd follow the fixed rope across and then try to reach the summit.

They were comfortable in their tent. A gas stove flared up when they tried to change an oxygen cylinder. There was a moment of panic—Dougal pictured the tent in flames—but they averted disaster; Dougal turned off the stove and Doug fixed the leak. They exchanged curses and looks and crawled into their sleeping bags and slept like tired children.

Dougal led the first pitch in the morning. He moved across in deep snow that fell apart under his weight, and then climbed a short stretch of snow-slick rock. He felt at once small and oddly large, inflated by the pleasure of being at this work. The sky seemed empty but for the sun's distant bulb, a blue wreathed in orange. He occasionally glanced up at the heavens, a witness to his doings.

Doug followed him, and then led through for a single pitch of easier ground. Dougal resumed the lead. He climbed onto snow-covered rock that offered very little purchase for his crampons; the rock was loose and there were no cracks for pitons. A slip here was unthinkable. He teetered sideways toward a tiny island of snow that might offer a stance. It did. He stood in the snow and leaned to place a dubious piton in the rock. He clipped the rope to it and took tension from the rope that stretched down and moved out onto rock again. He slipped once but the piton held and he at last came to deeper snow. He sucked in oxygen, his heart hammering, and gazed up, peering through his mask—the way ahead looked easier. They ran out the rest of their rope and returned to their tent at Camp Six at the top of the Rock Band. They were tired, but by no means exhausted.

Dougal had concluded that the round-trip from Camp Six to the summit would be too long to accomplish in a single day; they would require a bivouac. They would need a tent sac—a sheath of windproof material—and a stove for melting snow. Each man would require two oxygen cylinders. They'd need three 50-meter ropes to fix on difficult ground to safeguard their retreat. They wouldn't bring sleeping bags; they couldn't afford the additional weight at this altitude. They made radio contact with Chris and the others at Camp Two; that done, they cooked corned beef hash and ate it and went to sleep.

Doug woke at one o'clock to the sound of wind pelting the tent with bits of snow and ice. He started the stove and melted snow for tea, and warmed up the leftover hash. Dougal was awake, too. The climbers put on their boots. They left camp at 3:30.

They climbed the fixed ropes above Camp Six in darkness. The wind rose and fell, tugging at their clothes and intensifying a sense that the night was a sort of ragged blanket. Dougal listened to the rattle of his breath in the oxygen mask. He watched the day begin; it gently spewed light west as snow swirled at his legs. Doug followed him up the last of the fixed rope, seeming to rise with the sun, a huge black-masked angel. He reached Dougal's stance and they took some pictures.

Dougal set off into the long Exit Couloir. He climbed knee-deep snow between patches of rock. The rope sagged between the two men as they climbed. Dougal could find no cracks for pitons and no snow deep enough for a picket. Even so, any fear withdrew in the face of these immense spaces. The climbers were drawn toward the top of the face and the summit beyond as though the top of Everest were the end of everything. Dougal thought of something Robin Smith had once told him—how the American Indians would tap their enemies with a stick in battle, not to harm but to taunt them. Dougal meant to count coup on some version of death and death knew it, awaited his coming. Death was coming out to play. The notion, giddy and ridiculous, swirled behind his eyes like a flurry of snow.

His oxygen apparatus stopped working. He found a good stance on bare rock and fussed with the device. Doug suggested taking the thing apart, and they did so and found that a piece of ice had blocked the mouthpiece. Doug used a knife to cut the ice away and then set off to lead the next section. Dougal sat in the snow watching the rope snake through his gloved hands and found that he was trembling. A broken set would have forced him to turn back, and for the first time this day he was badly frightened—not of the climb's dangers but of his desire to finish the route and what would happen if he failed. He looked up and his fear receded; Doug was climbing well.

Doug fixed rope on a difficult 60-foot section of rock. The two climbers carried on, at times lifting their eyes toward the South Summit at the top of the face, a table-sized dome of snow and ice at 28,700 feet. Dougal took back the lead for a time and sank in the snow to his waist. He waded on, using his arms to make progress. The angle grew steeper, and the two climbers found themselves half-swimming across slopes that seemed likely to slide at any moment.

They finished the worst of the snow. Doug took another turn out front. He passed a cave amid a group of rocks, and noted it as a possible spot for a bivouac on the descent. The climbers approached the South Summit and the top of the Southwest Face in a torrent of wind. Doug crawled across a section near the top, and then took in rope as Dougal followed.

They walked together to the top of the face and stood in the wind to stare across the brown of Tibet. They recognized Kangchenjunga, the world's third-highest peak; Makalu, the fifth-highest, was closer and its summit lay well below them now.

The Southwest Face was below them too. They would savor that later—now they wanted to finish climbing the mountain. The way lay along the top of the Southeast Ridge, the route first climbed by Hillary and Tenzing twenty-two years before. They knew it from books and stories. There was a traverse of some

400 feet across wind-carved snow; they must take care not to step through one of the cornices that overhung the enormous Kangshung Face. After that, the Hillary Step—40 feet of steep rock or snow, tricky in certain conditions—and then the easy summit slopes.

Dougal suggested bivouacking here and setting out again at three o'clock the next morning; the soft snow might freeze in the night, making it easier to climb. He climbed into his bivouac sheet and melted water on the stove. Doug began scraping a hole in the snow to provide a better shelter from the wind—but he didn't want to wait; he knew he would feel sick in the morning, far worse than now. He was a child on Christmas morning; he was afire to see what awaited him. He abandoned his work on the cave and set off to test the snow conditions. The snow was firm enough—reasonable—and he looked back and waved for Dougal to come.

CHRIS AND NICK and the others had spent the morning at Camp Two gazing up at the enormous backdrop of the face. They took turns with binoculars and a camera lens, and eventually spotted figures at the top of the fixed ropes on the upper snowfield. They watched the two climbers disappear into the gully that led to the South Summit. Chris thought of Noel Odell. Odell had stood on the north side of the mountain just over a half-century before; he'd watched George Mallory and Andrew Irvine climb toward the virgin summit via the mountain's Northeast Ridge. Odell had seen the two climbers disappear behind a cloud; they had not been seen again.

Nick Estcourt, peering through the camera lens at four o'clock, shouted that he'd seen Doug and Dougal at the top of the exit gully. The others took the lens from him, passed it around—surely the climbers were on their way down at this hour? But no, they were moving up, toward the summit.

Darkness came. Chris slept poorly, restless in his anxiety for his friends. He woke from time to time and lay shivering and tried to keep at bay his understanding that Doug and Dougal might be dying even now, freezing to death in the dark. He resisted as well the whispery thought that they might have reached the summit. He pictured them ecstatic in their suffering. He envied them with a force that balanced the grief that massed like a bank of clouds in the distance so that he slept again amid dreams of darkness.

Dougal and Doug were moving up the Southeast Ridge, still the afternoon. The ridge fell away to their left. Steep and weirdly shaped monsoon cornices—huge wind-built shelves of snow—overhung the abyss to their right, blocking their view. The climbers moved carefully, with a sort of rigid glee. The Hillary Step—the steepest bit of climbing on the Southeast Ridge—was covered with snow. It was Dougal's turn to lead. Doug belayed him and took pictures. The situation was very dramatic. The snow made the climbing easy but there was no real protection if it gave way under Dougal's weight.

It didn't. They were going to reach the top of the mountain. Doug felt a curious sense of déjà vu. He felt himself at home as he followed Dougal up and took over the lead, moving again in deep and difficult snow. His mind broke into two minds. One spoke to the other, making suggestions—stay away from the cornice; be careful, go slowly, not too slowly. The advice comforted him. He carried on without questioning this new state.

The climbers could see a red flag, the relic of a Chinese expedition. Dougal led again up the final slope. He waited for Doug and they walked to the summit together. Doug was surprised at how his joy flooded him. The climbers took off their oxygen masks. Doug saw that Dougal was looking at him, was smiling broadly—Dougal never smiled at you that way. They hugged each other and thwacked each other's back.

They stepped apart and looked around them. Doug took note of countless gray peaks in Tibet—high mountains without much snow—and of his own feelings. He was not relieved. His feelings overlapped those of a man who contemplates his own approaching death and decides that he will miss his difficulties.

Far away, a line of black clouds approached; lightning flickered in it. Mallory and young Irvine had disappeared on the north side of the mountain, which lay now at Doug and Dougal's feet. Had those two earlier climbers been here? If not, Doug was the first Englishman to climb Everest—Edmund Hillary was from New Zealand. Doug took pictures of Dougal and then handed the camera to him: *Here you are, youth. Take one for me mother.*

Dougal took a picture of Doug and handed the camera back. The two of them stood watching the sun sink behind clouds that then dipped to unveil it once more—explosions of light, bright intervals in a series of sunsets. The true night would soon be upon them. They shouldered their packs and took a last look around them and set off down on snow that had begun to harden in the cold of dusk. They knew that falling on this snow would be close to falling on ice; you must stop immediately or you would not stop at all.

They tried to move carefully, but staggered with fatigue. They reached the top of the Hillary Step. They had fixed a 40-foot section of rope here to protect their descent. They rappelled the pitch, the drama of the ascent already fading. The rope stuck when they pulled on it so they left it behind.

They carried on across and reached the beginnings of their

snow cave at the South Summit Col as the first clouds arrived to cover the sky. Lightning punctuated the spaces between mountains; Doug saw the shapes of various peaks in what seemed the near distance. There would be no moon to light their way down. The climbers considered the option of descending further in the dark. Dougal in his impatience walked 50 feet down the southwest side of the ridge, but wind had blown away the climbers' tracks, and his hands and feet quickly grew numb. Dougal returned and set about helping Doug make the cave big enough to keep the wind from them.

They dug until nine o'clock and then settled in for the night. Their oxygen was gone. They had run out of fuel for the stove. A handful of Everest climbers had survived bivouacs high on the peak. Dougal and Doug thought they could survive this night—assuming the weather held—but they feared for their fingers and toes.

They removed boots and gloves and rubbed each other's hands and feet to maintain circulation. It was oddly pleasant to hold another man's bare hand or foot. Doug had left behind his down suit to save weight, and he couldn't stop shivering. He hacked at the back of the cave with his axe to try to keep warm. The climbers' minds wandered; the altitude and their fatigue made them loopy. Dougal unzipped his duvet and took Doug's left foot under his own right armpit; the intimacy of this was not disturbing to either man. Dougal spoke aloud; he seemed to be having a long conversation with one of the other climbers—it was Dave Clarke. Doug noticed this without finding it odd, and meanwhile carried on a series of conversations with his own feet. He found that each foot had a separate personality. The right foot was very solicitous of the left one.

They were resolved to stay awake. Warmth was a pale ghost

of a memory. The world seemed very cruel; this was too cold. Dougal worried vaguely that time itself had frozen, like a glacier, or like one of the winterbound rivers he knew in Scotland. The climbers' childish imaginings helped to undercut any sense of achievement or anticipation.

They had thought of the Southwest Face as it appeared in certain photographs: enormous, sky-hooded, snow-wreathed and empty of man. The morning illuminated their sorrow at finding themselves complicit in the end of something staggering.

They found they could stand and move their toes and fingers. The sun at first offered no real warmth but movement warmed them and they felt their blood's return with a pleasure that was a distraction from their regret; this pleasure at last triggered another, less familiar pleasure, a sense that they were entirely unassailable, that the mountain itself could protect them now, that they were a part of its enormous presence. And still they eyed one another with suspicion—each man knew that neither was physically or otherwise reliable now. They had not slept or taken food for thirty hours. They had survived a night without oxygen at 28,700 feet, the highest bivouac in history.

They found the fixed ropes and followed them down to their tent at Camp Six. And still the others didn't exist for them. Doug looking for food came upon the radio. He picked up the device and turned it on and spoke into it.

CHRIS KNEW THEY were alive; he had watched them make the traverse back across the ropes of the upper snow slope that morning. Doug's call frightened him. Doug was so strong—stronger than the others—and he sounded half-destroyed by his ordeal. Chris was in tears when he put down the radio.

And now the others were hell-bent on climbing the mountain. The second party—Martin Boysen, Mick Burke, Peter Boardman and Pertemba—had left Camp Five that morning. Chris was afraid for all four of them, but especially for Mick, who had been at Camp Five for eight nights and was showing it.

That evening's radio call brought news that Mick had fallen behind the others and had not yet arrived at Camp Six. That did it: Chris told Martin Boysen that Mick should stay behind when the others left for the summit the next day—September 26.

Mick came on the radio less than an hour later. He'd been delayed helping one of the Sherpas with an oxygen set and sorting out a tangle of ropes. He insisted he was no more tired than the others; at any rate, he was going for the summit. Chris conceded the point—still worried but partly consoled by the fact that the decision was no longer his to make. He asked to speak to Martin. Martin shared Chris's concern but agreed that the decision was Mick's. Chris urged him to keep the group together—if one climber turned around, they should all turn around—and left it at that.

Even that was too much to ask. The climbers at Camp Five talked; they decided that anyone going poorly in the morning should turn back before reaching the top of the fixed ropes. The others would continue.

The four climbers left at dawn under a high windless sky. Clouds surged up from the valleys, and a thin haze rode the western horizon. The weather was changing; a bivouac would be very dangerous. They needed to move quickly. Martin left camp first. Peter and Pertemba came behind him on the fixed ropes. Mick came last.

Martin's crampon came off. He put it back on—but his oxygen set stopped working. He found a place to sit and he tinkered with it, growing angry and then despairing as the others caught and passed him, each making his clumsy and infuriating gestures of sympathy from the shelter of wind suit and oxygen mask. Martin eventually admitted defeat and descended, practically howling with frustration. This trip had been a misery from the start; he'd arrived two weeks behind the others and never really found his stride. He'd come here straight from a failed attempt on Pakistan's Trango Tower, a spectacular rock monolith that had given Martin and his companions many days of hard technical climbing. The Southwest Face was something quite different, huge and steep but mostly snow and fixed ropes; it wasn't what he loved. And now there was to be no reward—not the one he'd wanted—and it felt like a punishment. It brought him to tears that seemed useless even as he shed them.

He retreated to the tent and lay miserable in his sleeping bag through the long morning. He unzipped the entrance at eleven o'clock and peered up into the day; it was impossible not to be conscious of the time and it was strange to be idle in this place where each hour of daylight was a commodity to be consumed with care. He saw that two climbers had reached the top of the final gully; a third stood at its base. The wind was rising. He closed the tent flap and lay back with his anger and sadness and what he recognized as the beginnings of fear.

PETER FELT VERY strong. His strength was mixed up with his happiness at being above the fixed ropes, the clutter of the camps, the people there. The snow was firmer than Dougal and Doug had found it; the frozen remnants of their steps provided a blurred stairway up the gully that led to the South Summit. Peter glanced back and saw a figure traversing the snowfield far below.

He figured it must be Martin or Mick coming back up to watch, having abandoned the climb early on.

Peter and Pertemba climbed the steep gully and crossed to the South Summit. They moved unroped; here the sun still lit the sky above them but clouds obliterated the landscape below—only here and there summits showed, fins frozen in a white sea. Pertemba's oxygen set failed and Peter stopped to help him. They spent more than an hour clearing ice from the apparatus and managed to get it to work.

They roped up and climbed together across the corniced ridge that led to the final snow slope. They reached the summit together just after one o'clock. They had made very fast time but neither man was particularly tired. Peter felt much as he had felt on other good days in the mountains—simply happy. They stood in mist. No view. They spent a half-hour taking photographs of each other and snacking on chocolate and cake and then they left.

They descended a few hundred yards and came upon Mick, still laboring upward. Peter was amazed; he had been certain that Martin and Mick had turned back. Mick wanted to film Peter and Pertemba on the ridge above; they could pretend it was the summit. Peter told him that the Chinese who had climbed Everest from the north the previous spring had left a big red flag at the top. The flag needed to be in the shot or people would know it was a fake.

Mick asked if they'd be willing to go the top again so he could film them there for real. Peter agreed—he and Pertemba were still moving strongly—but he wasn't happy about it. Mick read Peter's tone and withdrew his request. Peter and Pertemba climbed back up the ridge for 50 feet or so and turned to parade down past Mick's camera—it wasn't a summit shot but it would make a nice image for the film.

Peter took some pictures of Mick, who wanted to continue up alone and tag the summit. Peter and Pertemba would wait for him at a big rock near the South Summit; they had dumped some gear there earlier. The three climbers would descend together.

Mick left. Peter watched him for a moment or two, almost envious, and then turned away and plunged down with Pertemba. The Sherpa had asked to rope up for this portion of the descent. Peter was surprised at his partner's speed. Peter moved quickly himself; they were men on a spree, divesting themselves of altitude, throwing it from them in fistfuls, eagerly spending the height the expedition had acquired at such cost—getting the hell out of here.

They had to stop at the South Summit to wait for Mick and it was like doing themselves harm; it felt wrong. The weather had grown worse as they descended. The wind continued to rise now and they stood shivering, waiting, until somehow it was late, four o'clock; they had waited an hour and a half. The sky was turning dark and there was no sign of Mick.

It was snowing. They couldn't see to find Doug and Dougal's bivouac site. Pertemba had lost feeling in his fingers and in his toes. They were three hours above Camp Six with only an hour of light, and they were now in a blizzard. Peter felt the night's approach as the coming of a mindless army.

He spoke to Pertemba. They would wait ten more minutes. Mick's fate now seemed in some obscure way to rest with Peter's watch; no person was responsible. Peter unpacked his stove and left it in the snow. Mick would not find it; if he did it would be useless in these conditions. The ten minutes were up and the two climbers turned down and lost the way almost immediately, then found it and lost it again. A half-hour of this and the snow let up for a moment. Peter turned to look up toward the South Summit. No Mick.

Peter directed his full attention to Pertemba. The Sherpa was going too slowly; he had little experience moving on snow in these conditions. Peter placed snow pickets—long aluminum stakes—and used them to belay his companion. They found the gully at the top of the Southwest Face and descended it, unable to see the route beneath them.

Peter at one point thought they had strayed from the gully. They had not. They reached its bottom and now they searched in growing desperation for the fixed ropes. Powder avalanches from the newly laden slopes chased and buffeted the climbers. One slide threatened to sweep them from the mountain; Peter plunged the pick of his axe into the ice and it held. He stood and resumed his search and a few moments later he found the fixed ropes in the dark, a near-miracle that brought him no joy or relief.

They set off down the ropes. Pertemba lost a crampon almost immediately but kept moving without it. Peter stumbled and fell and slid over the lip of something—bare rock—to fall 15 feet before the rope came taut and stopped him. He wasn't injured by the fall but he saw that Pertemba was fading, seemed likely to collapse at any moment. Peter would need to untie the rope that still joined them, but he didn't know if had the strength to do so; he might have to sit down and die with his friend. Peter half-dragged Pertemba toward camp, following the ropes across the last stretches of snow-covered rock to Camp Six. Martin was there, waiting in one of the shelters, afraid for them. Peter stuck his head in the tent and Martin felt enormous relief even as he saw that Peter was crying.

CHRIS AND THE others at Camp Two had resumed their vigil that morning. They'd seen two figures early in the day, moving up near the foot of the gully that led to the top of the face; after that cloud had obscured their view and they had waited, keeping the radio open all day. Martin in his tent at Camp Six told them of the rising wind, and they heard the worry in his voice. The storm came and with it darkness and still the others had not returned.

Martin came back on the air about eight o'clock to tell them of Pete and Pertemba's return and that Mick was still out in the storm. It was bad but Mick might still show up, maybe just behind the others. Or he might find Doug's and Dougal's snow cave and bivouac; in that case he'd be down in the morning.

Their hope faded and disappeared as the storm intensified during the night and continued through the following day. Martin and the two summit climbers were pinned down at Camp Six. Pertemba was exhausted and snowblind. Peter was wracked with grief and guilt, punished by his memory of Mick departing up the ridge and by notions that he might have stopped Mick or gone with him or waited longer. Martin took care of them. He went about it almost absentmindedly at first. Mick had been his particular friend, very different from Martin himself. Mick was a tough little guy; he used to shake when he climbed and you would think *he won't get up this* but he surprised you. And he made you laugh; however miserable the circumstances on a mountain, you could make the best of it with Mick. He made you feel better.

Martin after a time put Mick out of his mind and went on running things. He established the two summit climbers in their shelter and made them tea and soup. The three of them had to get down. They were low on gas cartridges for the stove; for food they had only one more soup packet. They might be stuck here for days, losing strength by the hour; the altitude would eventually kill them. Martin felt an unreasoning anger and an intense desire to be gone from this place. He felt once again as if he was being punished unfairly and he despised his own weakness—his inability to retaliate. He believed that they might all three die in this storm that by now had surely killed Mick.

Night fell again. The three climbers at Camp Six settled in to sleep. The darkness and wind were almost a comfort—the climbers' helplessness in the face of conditions seemed a respite from what lay ahead. Martin slept in the box he'd shared with Mick, and woke in the morning to quiet. The wind had stopped. Martin lay in his sleeping bag and sobbed for Mick and also for himself and the rest of them—the ones who were going home.

THE CLIMBERS IN the lower camps were convinced that Mick was gone. Dougal and Doug figured he'd been blinded by the storm—his eyesight wasn't that good in the best of conditions—and had walked off the edge of the summit ridge; it would be like stepping into a hole in the dark with only the difference that it was all white. Or he might have climbed the peak and made it down the ridge and stopped to wait out the storm; if so he'd be dead after two nights that high without food or supplemental oxygen.

Chris wanted the climbers all down. He'd evacuated Camp One, which had continued its gradual slide into the Icefall. Nick—with Ronnie Richards, Tut Braithwaite and Ang Phurba—had weathered the blizzard at Camp Five. Their summit hopes were finished; they reported huge snow avalanches down the Great Central Gully that split the face. Their camp was protected from the slides, but it wasn't yet safe for them to descend.

Camp Four was more exposed to avalanche, so Chris had asked Adrian Gordon to evacuate it. Adrian sent six Sherpas down the face and then followed them, but he took a wrong turn in the storm. Chris led a rescue party up from Camp Two and found Adrian calm but exhausted. The rescuers got him back down to Camp Two at midnight. An avalanche hit the camp a few hours later, wrecking one of the box shelters and the kitchen.

The climbers took each near-disaster calmly. They continued their systematic withdrawal from the face. September 28 dawned clear and bright. The climbers agreed among themselves that there was no point in going up to look for Mick. Chris asked Nick and his three companions at Camp Five to wait for Martin and the two summit climbers to descend. The seven climbers could then make their way down to the others at the bottom of the face.

PETE STOOD IN the sunlight outside of his MacInnes Box at Camp Six. He felt his youth amid this ancient landscape. He had nothing to say to Martin or Pertemba. He didn't want to leave but he followed them down the ropes, losing height quickly. Space swam up beneath him and receded above; it was like a descent into the depths of some great body of water, the Western Cwm the bottom of the sea. The conviction rose in Peter that he had wanted all of this—the summit, the difficulty, the loss, and now this return to an alien world. He was obscurely, darkly happy and ashamed of his happiness.

It was odd to come upon Nick and the others at Camp Five. There was still the work of descending the rest of the face and the seven of them got on with it. Dougal, unbearably gaunt, his long face a horse's death's head, walked out of Camp Two into the Western Cwm to meet them. Doug Scott still looked strong; he kneeled to take the boots off Peter's battered feet. Chris was kind as well, as if to show that he didn't blame Peter for Mick. Their tenderness swamped Peter. He felt himself a necessary younger brother to these men—Mick almost forgotten in each man's regard and care for him. He was comforted by what seemed newly familiar: Tut absurdly scrawny, Charlie Clarke in red silk underwear.

The expedition members took two days to empty the Western Cwm, making their retreat through the Icefall. They finished on September 30. The Sherpas built another fire, and there was a celebration. The climbers got drunk and danced and sang with the Sherpas in the darkness. After a while, they stopped making so much noise and sat in little groups and some of them—especially Chris and Dougal and Doug—talked about other mountains, smaller ones. They believed they were finished with Everest.

BETH BURKE GOT a telegram at home with the news that Dougal and Doug had made the summit. She went out right away and sent a telegram to Mick; she wondered if he'd get it. This was to be his last big expedition; as it was, he'd be missing Sara's second birthday. He'd said on leaving that he would never miss another one. The wording of the telegram suggested to Beth that Mick was on the mountain and probably somewhere high on the face. She slept badly that night. Sara was up too, and acting strangely—that was Thursday night.

The next morning they had a meal with a vicar. Beth felt very young and for some reason—it puzzled her—she started a conversation about what happens to people when they die.

Sara's birthday was Monday. They spent that morning at a friend's house. There were three calls for Beth. The first was a man she didn't know who told her that Mick had lost his life—*Mick has lost his life*. She said *All right, thank you* then she hung up very quickly. Her friend, whose own husband was traveling in Africa, went into hysterics at the news. Beth was fine.

The next call was Lord Hunt, who wanted to know if she'd had a call about Mick. She said yes but that it was all right, that she didn't believe it. Lord Hunt said that he was afraid that it was true. Wendy Bonington reached her a half-hour later.

And even now Beth wasn't convinced, but she turned on the television. Mick had been sending film back to the BBC and now they were telling what had happened to him. He'd walked into the clouds and hadn't come back. Beth had the thought that it must be true; it was on the television.

She went through a strange period after that. She wouldn't answer the phone and she wouldn't call anyone because if the person on the other end of the line didn't answer it felt like another loss. She got up every morning and went to the bathroom and threw up. She believed that Sara was all right, but she looked at pictures later and saw that the little girl looked haunted.

Beth meanwhile moved in a straight line or thought she did but sometimes she saw—with a dazed amazement—how badly it hurt her feelings that he wasn't coming back. It was like he'd left them for somebody better—like they hadn't meant that much to him. Once, two months after she'd had the news, a police car pulled up across the street. She saw them through a window and knew at once that they'd come to tell her they'd found him, that Mick was alive.

AND MICK, HE moves up the ridge toward this summit of dreams. The mist obliterates the view but not really; he knows what is around him. It begins with the features of this mountain, the snow he walks upon, massed strangely here at this odd borderland. He walks carefully. He can't hear much either; his breath echoes in his mask.

It doesn't matter. He knows what's out there: more of the same, more of the beauty he has known elsewhere, at home and in the mountains and in the faces of his companions—how he loves them. He thinks of Peter and Pertemba waiting for him down at the South Summit. They are representatives, appointed escorts for the return trip he must make when this is done.

He is glad to be alone now. He knows that underneath the snow he walks upon is sky; the blue he's enjoyed only in dreams and in the mountains. And this mist is merely a curtain; he can lift a corner to peek at infinity, and what a joy it is—what fun—to know that this invisible blue is the blue of God.

Mick keeps taking steps. He is bloody tired. Chris was right about that. Mick is touched to think of Chris and his concern for the rest of them. But look at this. Mick's on top.

He still can't see and now he is afraid. There's nothing to film except the flag that he can't even find. His feet are cold and his fingers have gone numb. Frostbite is a worry at this point and so is finding the ridge again; it won't be easy in this white wind. This place is empty. There is no arrangement to make and nothing to negotiate or witness. He needs to leave.

He finds the ridge—very careful here—and sets off down, aware of the several things that can happen. He can step through the cornice and fall all the way to Tibet. He won't hit anything for a while; it's just a near-vertical sheet of snow. He wonders, thinking of it—he can't feel his feet now—how does the snow stick to the face at such angles?

If he falls he'll pick up speed, no time to figure out anything. He thinks of Beth and the child but he can't be a child himself now. He squints again, looking for the cornices. It wouldn't have to be a cornice, either. He's walking on wind slab that could give way and carry him off. Or he might just fall. He can't change the snow conditions and he can't stop here. He carries on carefully down the ridge until his figure blurs and disappears.

A bit later he dreams that he opens his eyes; he doesn't know where. His grief packs his mouth and his throat and freezes his face and neck. He struggles for breath, for coherence. He made a mistake and he is ready to forgive it, but there is no apparent need. He's grateful for that but he is distracted. He is swimming in a blue, blue light—it reminds him of something—and the snow keeps falling; the flakes touch the ocean and vanish.

PART THREE

Legends

*He goes because he must, as Galahad
went toward the Grail, knowing that for
those who can live it, this alone is life.*

—EVELYN UNDERHILL,
MYSTICISM (1911)

K2, Abruzzi Ridge.
CHRIS BONINGTON, CHRIS BONINGTON PICTURE LIBRARY

A YOUNG CLIMBER named Joe Tasker stopped by the Manchester offices of the British Mountaineering Council one day in the winter of 1976. He was looking for Peter Boardman.

The two young men knew each other, though not well. They'd met in 1971 when they were both in school. The recent ascent of Annapurna's South Face had delivered thrilling evidence that the British were once again at the forefront of international mountaineering. Thus inspired, Peter had gone out to the Alps that summer with Martin Wragg, his best mate and regular climbing partner. They had knocked off the North Face of the Matterhorn and gone on to Chamonix to tackle another test piece, the Northeast Spur of Les Droites.

Peter and Martin had camped on a little rock in the middle of the glacier that led up to the base of the spur, and from that vantage point they'd watched another pair cross the glacier late in the day. Those other two had started up the route itself to bivouac on the climb. Peter and Martin had risen early the next morning and passed them around dawn, hearing voices through the flimsy walls of the bivouac tent.

The route was heavily iced. The conditions had forced Peter and Martin out onto the mountain's North Face. They had made a miserable hanging bivouac that night, and had turned back the next day, a thousand feet below the top. It was a terrifying descent, chopping holes in the ice for rappel anchors, the exposure tremendous.

They had come upon the other two climbers—Joe Tasker with his regular partner Dick Renshaw—on a ledge. Those two also were descending and the two parties agreed to join forces. The encounter cheered the four young men. They stood chatting idly, relieved at having company, until a huge block detached from the face and swept past them—it actually brushed Joe's pack—frightening them and bringing their attention back to the job at hand.

They'd finished the retreat. Joe and Peter hadn't seen much of each other since then. The two young men were from very different worlds, and climbing had led them down different paths—but those paths were about to converge once more.

PETER WAS A middle-class boy, the younger of two sons. His father was an engineer, and his mother taught school. His mother also was a writer of sorts; she kept a detailed journal of her life, including Peter's childhood. He'd grown up near Stockport, a small town near Manchester, attending the local grammar school. He had done his first climbs on a school trip to Corsica when he was fourteen years old. That was 1964. He joined a Stockport climbing club two years later, a few months after Dougal Haston and the Germans climbed the Eiger Direct.

Peter was a natural rock climber. By the time he enrolled at the University of Nottingham in 1968 he was one of several candidates for the unofficial title of England's best young rock climber. Peter teamed up with a slightly older Nottingham student—Martin Wragg—and the two of them made several trips to the Alps, where they put up a few new routes.

They put together a four-man expedition to Afghanistan's Hindu Kush in the summer of 1972. They had hopes of climbing

Koh-i-Khoaik, a remote and—as it proved—formidable objective. The four climbers left Base Camp with two days food. They were gone for five days. There were opportunities to turn back, but Peter wasn't having it. The others were led on in part by his stamina and his unwavering confidence that they would finish the route. They'd flirted with starvation, and they had come close to drowning during a river crossing on their way back to Base Camp—but they'd managed to get up the peak. They'd also climbed the North Face of Koh-i-Mondi, an even tougher route that impressed climbers back home.

Peter was ambitious as well as determined, but his drive was partly hidden. He was quiet; he had a literary bent—he read widely and like his mother he kept a journal. He enrolled in an outdoors training course in Wales, where he also studied Welsh for a time. He received his diploma in 1973, and went to work as a climbing instructor in Scotland, in the Cairngorms. He had landed his job at the British Mountaineering Council in 1975—just when Chris was choosing the members of his second Everest expedition. Peter was good at his work, meeting with climbers to sort out issues such as training and safety and access. The other climbers liked him; he was articulate and tactful, and he had an easy confidence with a hint of reserve.

And now Peter was famous. He had shared in the publicity that had engulfed the Everest climbers upon their return from the peak several months before. Chris had cemented his own position with the public as British mountaineering's leading figure; he'd launched a series of lectures and slide shows and in between his travels he would retreat to the Lakes to grind away at another expedition book. Dougal Haston and Doug Scott were doing the lecture circuit as well. The two had become close on Everest, and they continued to climb together in Alaska and elsewhere.

There were lingering questions about the Everest climb among the expedition's survivors and in wider mountaineering circles. There was talk—some of it jealous—that the huge logistical effort had made the climb at once too easy and too dangerous. The more cynical critics maintained—not entirely fairly—that much of the route was a plod up fixed ropes, dragging gear up the mountain in service of Bonington's career; that there was nothing much in it for Nick or Martin or most of the rest of the climbers—not the summit, not even much real climbing. Some of the critics added that the format of the expedition put too many bodies at risk in any given moment. Perhaps it was no wonder that two men—young Mingma and then Mick Burke—had died. The toll might have been still worse.

That was one way to see it. Others dimly saw the expedition for what it was—at once a crowning achievement and the end of an era. Each climber had his notions. Peter's own views troubled him. He was not comfortable profiting from his part in the climb. This was partly because of Mick's death, and also because Nick Estcourt and Tut Braithwaite and Martin Boysen—let alone Pertemba—were largely excluded from the fuss that surrounded Dougal and Doug and Peter himself.

Peter's discomfort also reflected his knowledge that his own generation was inventing new ways to climb. They were beginning to climb difficult routes on big mountains in groups of three or four—or even one or two. These were climbers who had grown up with images of Bonington; they had wanted to be that young man in the photos, up there on a ledge on the Eiger eating tuna with a piton for a spoon. Now their own achievements made Bonington's Everest venture seem outmoded.

The public ignored the new generation's accomplishments. It didn't begin to understand them. But Peter knew what his most accomplished peers must think of the fanfare that surrounded the

Southwest Face expedition and its central figures. He agreed with them. The crowds at Peter's own Everest lectures distressed him. The people who paid to hear him speak did not understand. They thought he was something he was not.

He returned to his job at the British Mountaineering Council to sit on committees and negotiate climbing access and certification standards. He was bored and unhappy. Occasionally, he would find himself back on the South Summit. He'd look up and see Mick's gray form fade into white and he would wonder if that was for nothing.

AND NOW YOUNG Joe Tasker stood there in front of Peter's scarred and cluttered desk looking like what he was—an emissary from climbing's cutting edge. Joe was quick-witted and sharp-tongued. He could be friendly enough but he was guarded; he meant to be nobody's fool. Some of the other climbers didn't much like him; he had a way of keeping you at a distance even when he was pressing you for information about a climb he wanted to do. His ambition was a bit too evident for some tastes; he didn't always bother to hide or modulate it.

He'd been born in 1948 during the lean years that followed the war, the second of ten children—each named for a Catholic saint—in Hull on England's Northeast coast. The mother of this brood, a birdlike but strong-willed and deeply religious woman named Betty, was losing her eyesight by the time Joe arrived. She soon lost it entirely. Tom Tasker, the children's father, also was very devout. He was a former merchant seaman. He supported the family by working as a painter and decorator, but he couldn't always find sufficient work. The Taskers sent Joe and one of his brothers to live in an orphanage for several months when Joe was seven—an episode that marked them both and remained for many years a source of distress for the family.

Joe went away again when he was thirteen. This time he went to study for the priesthood. He had liked being an altar boy, the solemnity, the sense of theater, and so he'd volunteered for the seminary, delighting his parents. The discipline there was very strict. There was a coldness to it that was hard to bear; you had to go a bit cold yourself to tolerate it. Joe wasn't the best behaved of the boys, but he did what was required to get along. It was easier or at least more interesting than home in some ways. The teachers at the seminary would read aloud to the boys during meals. One of the teachers read from a book about a rescue on the Eiger. Joe and his fellow seminarians were riveted. Already another teacher—a rough-spoken but good-natured young priest named Tony Barker—had begun taking a group of them climbing at a nearby quarry and later in the Peak District. Early on, there was a walking trip to the Alps, but no climbing. Back in England, Father Barker would give the keener boys rides in his car to see climbers like Tom Patey and Ian Clough lecture in neighboring cities. It wasn't official. Father Barker would just tell the boys he was going, and he would indicate that he wasn't averse to picking up hitchhikers. He would drive out of the seminary and there they'd be, usually Joe and his special mate, a fellow climber by the name of Stefan; they'd stand there grinning at him. The boys would go their own way at the lecture. Father Barker would ignore them until afterward, when he'd pick them up again on the road.

One time they were driving back and passed another teacher—a stricter man—walking in the rain. They had to pick him up; he'd know the car and ask questions and then Father Barker would have to tell the truth. And so they stopped for the man, who piled in soaking wet and saw the boys and wanted to know what was going on. And Father Barker looked at him and said: *You want to walk, do you?* And the fellow got such a look on him that the boys couldn't help themselves; they burst out laughing, and then the teacher laughed as well. And Father Barker began laughing in his turn and sped on, driving them back through the rain in the dark, all of them carrying on fit to split.

Joe was among the bolder climbers at seminary. He was soon soloing routes in the quarries and further afield, in the Lakes. He followed reports of John Harlin's Eiger expedition in 1966, including the dramatic and shocking news of Harlin's death. He stayed at seminary for seven years, and left in 1968, when he was twenty. His parents were bitterly disappointed; their Joe had been the oldest, the golden boy. A priest for a son: that was the blessing of blessings; now it was lost to them. But Joe later told more than one friend that he'd lost his faith—it was partly all the reading they made the boys do—and with it any interest in a life of celibacy: *One day I looked down and I said, "Mate, I'm getting you out of here."*

He spent a year or so working as a dustman—a garbage collector—to the distress of his parents. He also worked in a quarry—many of the local boys did that—but by then he was ready for more school so he enrolled at Manchester University. He brought to college his classical education and a determination to climb. He studied sociology. He had an interest in the lower orders of society. He remembered his blind mother doling out food to beggars when they came to the door of the Tasker's modest council house. Joe spent some of his time at school taking pictures of homeless men. He frightened some of his family by making friends with a newly released prisoner.

He had an intense, almost brittle manner at times; it put off some people and interested others. He said what came to his mind, and his intelligence gave force to his comments. His own eyesight was poor, even with glasses; he sometimes strained to see, and it gave him a serious, even humorless, air that would make him seem more unhappy, less generous, than he was. People said Peter Boardman would make a good politician—they meant it kindly. No one said that of Joe.

He would go to parties and drink and do hash or even acid and pick up girls; he liked having that kind of fun. But he combined such appetites with an impressive work ethic. He took pictures; he read and wrote—he was proud of the education the priests had given him. He was loyal to his family and friends, who knew him to be a kind person, considerate of others and hard on himself; he always came home for Christmas, and when he did he'd make the rounds of old schoolmates and their parents.

He continued to rock climb. He was good at it—not as gifted as Peter Boardman, but as driven. He made a trip to the Alps in 1971 and had his first encounter with Dick Renshaw; they met at a campsite and did a few climbs together. Joe wasn't much of a talker, but even he was impressed by Dick's self-containment—the way he would sit for hours on a bivouac without speaking—and by Dick's ability to deny himself even the smallest comforts. It seemed to Joe that his friend would have made an ideal seminarian. The two young men ended up sharing a ratty house in a Manchester suburb, subsisting on odd jobs and part-time teaching. They climbed difficult routes in Great Britain, and made a modest splash by getting up five of the Alps' six classic North Faces during the 1973 season. They turned a few more heads when they made a winter ascent of the Eiger's North Face in 1975.

Peter knew—every serious climber knew—what Joe and Dick had done next. The two young men had traveled alone to India in the fall of 1975—while Peter was with Chris and the others on the Southwest Face of Everest—to make a spectacularly bold attempt on Dunagiri (7,066 meters; 23,184 feet).

DUNAGIRI STOOD IN the Garwhal Himalaya, just across from Changabang. The mountain had been climbed once—back in 1939—but Joe and Dick had their eye on a new and far more difficult route. They had almost no money, so poverty as much as climbing ethics dictated the tiny scale of their expedition. Joe bought a dilapidated van for 170 pounds, ignoring an engineer's report that included this sentence: *The best way of using this van to reach the Himalayas is to drive it to Heathrow and fly.*

The two climbers stuffed the van with gear and food and set off, taking the ferry to France and then driving overland to India—6,000 miles in three weeks. They listened to Bob Dylan; Dick's classical tapes couldn't compete with the noise of the van. They lived on chapatis, sandwich spread, canned meat and—when they could find it—local produce.

Joe found himself envying the hashish-smoking drifters they encountered on the road; these people seemed unburdened by the sort of ambition he carried. At the same time, he felt shame at his inability to match Dick's spartan ethic. Joe felt a hedonist because he wanted to spend money on ordinary bread when Dick was content with chapatis. Joe also tormented himself with thoughts of his inadequacy for the task ahead. They'd had news before leaving England that another two-man expedition—the famous Tyrolean climber Reinhold Messner and his equally celebrated partner, the Austrian Peter Habeler—had climbed Hidden Peak (8,068 meters; 26,471 feet). Joe could not imagine himself in such company.

The two young British climbers, with their sloppy attire and shoestring budget, did not impress the bureaucrats at the headquarters of the Indian Mountaineering Foundation (IMF) in Delhi. It took the better part of a week to muster the necessary permissions to proceed to Dunagiri. Joe and Dick met an English trekker named Peter Roberts, who offered to come along as porter and help manage Base Camp. Meanwhile the IMF at last assigned the expedition a liaison officer, an athletics instructor named Inder Kapoor.

Joe and Dick had been gone from England for six weeks when the four men piled into the van to drive up the Rishi Ganga. They hired ten porters in the villages of Latia and Reni, where the road ended. Joe after two days of walking developed a toothache and a bad fever. The others continued toward Base Camp while a porter escorted Joe, half-delirious, back down to an army compound in the village of Joshimath. An orderly gave him injections of penicillin from a syringe stored in a glass of dirty water. Joe lay in a dark, stinking room and took his injections twice a day. His fever abated but he was possessed by a numb sense of loss that surprised and frightened him. He hadn't known how much he needed to climb this mountain.

His jaw remained swollen and sore. The doctor at Joshimath urged him to return to Great Britain. Joe agreed to do so, but instead set off to rejoin Dick. He walked alone, drawn up the Rishi Gorge by views of Nanda Devi. He turned up a valley and on the second day came to a clearing and found a note from Dick indicating the track toward Base Camp. That afternoon he encountered Dick himself, come down to find Joe and escort Peter Roberts back to civilization. The trekker had been terribly lonely with only the taciturn Renshaw for company. The two climbers parted with Peter, and walked up to Base Camp together. Joe felt his strength return as he walked. He could not repress an animal certainty that his troubles were over, that climbing the mountain would be a simple and joyous undertaking.

THEY CHOSE A route up the Southeast Spur, which included a very long section of steep rock. They had to move quickly; it was now late September. They built a shelter of stones and plastic tarp, and left some supplies there. They moved their tent up to a spot that was a two hours' walk from the foot of their route; this would serve as Advance Base Camp.

A snowstorm held them up for a day. They set off the next morning. They climbed in a gully for several hours, until falling rocks drove them out of it and onto more difficult ground; this eventually brought them onto the Southeast Ridge itself. They had made a good start, climbing roughly 1,000 feet in a day.

They carried a light bivouac tent, but they didn't pitch it; there was no wind and they preferred to sleep in the open. Dunagiri's neighbor Changabang had come into view as they climbed. They watched it darken from white into gold and orange, passing into red. The twilight was translucent, the color of water.

The climbing on their ridge seemed reasonable. They had tackled worse in the Alps, though not at this height—they were now more than 19,000 feet above sea level. They figured on another three days to reach the summit, then two days to descend by an easier route—the route of the peak's first ascent thirty-six years before.

They covered another 1,000 feet the second day, making their way up a series of granite towers to reach a small ledge. It was windy; snow flurries danced around their heads. They pitched their tent. The summit faded from their thoughts. Joe felt an unfamiliar patience; it made him think of the saints whose invisible presence had haunted his family and informed his schooling. He thought of the saints' patient suffering as he enjoyed his own comforts, his warm drink and his piece of fruitcake.

They continued to climb; everything took longer than they had hoped. Time as much as disappeared. An entire day vanished; neither climber could recall how they had spent the third day on the route. Joe at one point believed that they had climbed the steepest section, but they hadn't. They came to the start of it at the end of their fourth day on the peak. They camped there in a square pit they dug in snow. Joe made a mess trying to open sardines with a Swiss army knife; Dick had left the only decent can opener behind to save weight. They bickered and fussed about who was to blame for the mess and who should sleep on which side of the tent.

Joe took the lead in the morning. There was ice at first, but then bare rock. His crampons made climbing more difficult here but the terrain was too steep for him to stop and remove them. He pulled onto a hollow flake—an enormous and unstable slab of rock almost entirely detached from the cliff—and entered a chimney. He climbed slowly, in pain from his half-frozen fingers. He could not retreat; there was nowhere to make a rappel anchor. He was near the end of his strength when he found a ledge.

The climbers made slow progress that day, and spent a difficult night on a narrow, icy platform. They climbed more steep rock in the morning. They half-expected to finish the climb before nightfall, but they were moving too slowly now. The sunsets no longer uplifted them; they watched the sun's sinking with dull anxious eyes. They dragged the thin air into their lungs and wished for more. It was hard not to give way to weakness; not to simply give up. They bivouacked as night fell; they were now a few hundred feet below the summit. It seemed a long way.

They set off again in the morning. Joe took less than an hour to finish the route. He reached the summit and looked back for his partner. Dick was 40 meters away, lying on his back in the snow. He looked dead. He had simply stopped to lie down and stare at the sky. He stood and walked up to where Joe waited. Dick apologized. This evidence of his condition surprised and alarmed both of them.

Their spirits seemed to flicker within their exhausted bodies as they looked around them. Nanda Devi, stern and elegant, jutted through clouds to return their gaze. Joe thought of the head of some beautiful beast. Changabang's summit, domelike, also lay before them, as did the top of Kalanka. The clouds below them stretched to the horizon as the climbers looked down the Southwest Ridge, the route they had chosen for their descent.

It frightened them now. They worried that they might fall through a cornice on the unfamiliar ridge. They revised their plan. They would sleep just below the summit tonight and then descend the way they'd come.

They felt little joy at their achievement and no wish to stay on the summit. There was some relief that they would not have to go higher but their weariness and a simmering fear overshadowed it. They were short of food and they had run out of fuel for the stove. The absence of fuel meant they could not melt snow for water; without water they would deteriorate very quickly.

It was happening now. The next day saw them only part of the way down the steep rock barrier near the top of their route. The passage of time assumed yet another dimension: time flirted and poked at them and withdrew. Joe felt immensely frustrated. He felt at all times that he and Dick were in hopeless pursuit of someone. They were burdened with some message to deliver but the object of their chase was unresponsive to their shouts and pleas to wait, to relieve them of their work. This fantasy deepened a sense of failure that he could not attribute to anything else.

The climbers wandered in sun and fog performing their various tasks: setting up a rappel anchor, descending the rope, retrieving the rope, then repeating the process. They moved earthward in a stupefied wonder as if descending toward the unknown. They did not speak to make decisions. They both knew what to do.

They stopped at a tiny ledge. They didn't want the snacks they still carried. Their throats had gone as hard and dry as old bread. The two of them slept and woke and started down again. It was hard to find cracks for the pitons they still carried, whose clanking made echoes in the hollow sky. This work was difficult but they had done it many times on other mountains.

They came to a traverse spanned by a sheet of ice. Joe led it. His legs barely held his weight. There was the risk of a long swinging fall. He chopped a small ledge and stood on it to place an ice piton and climbed on; only then did he come off. He rode an arc across 40 feet; he was not surprised by it and there was no fear—this was expected—but he was surprised at the sound: the jangle of hardware, the rush of air. It stopped. He dangled from his screw and glanced down at the view—another 4,000 feet to the glacier—and scanned his body; there was nothing new, nothing torn or broken. He regained the ice and relied on tension from the peg to help him across into snow. He climbed the snow to bare rock, where he placed several more pitons.

Dick fell trying to follow him, but the anchor held. The cold and their fatigue and especially their dehydration made them incompetent. The rope grew tangled as they made their way toward their next bivouac site. Joe set up a tent and got into his sleeping bag. Dick remained outside in the moonlight. He inventoried the remaining food and made vague comments about the view. It didn't occur to Joe that something was wrong.

Dick drifted into the tent and tried to eat bits of chocolate in the dark; he gnawed at his fingers, mistaking them for the candy. He woke Joe in the morning and showed him torn fingers that had turned blue and hard from frostbite.

They waited for the sun. It appeared, and they commenced the third day of their descent. Joe set up the rappels. Dick could do nothing to help. He insisted on an early halt and the climbers suffered through a cramped, semihanging bivouac. Joe was angry at his own predicament but in the morning he looked around a corner and saw that Dick had spent the night on a ledge so small he'd been unable to get into his sleeping bag. Dick had instead crouched on the ledge in his crampons, nursing his frozen fingers and growing colder as the night wore on. Joe was pierced by shame at this fresh evidence of his own selfishness, his lack of consideration for his suffering friend.

They had lost track of time again; neither man knew how long it was since they'd stood on the summit. Joe felt a part of himself fade and die. He didn't mind what he lost. He only wanted to stop suffering; he wished to step off the wheel. His growing belief that he and Dick were meant to die on this mountain awakened in him an almost desperate craving for some form of liberation.

The climbers moved with difficulty. They stumbled more frequently even as they reached easier ground and drank in the thicker air of lower altitude. Dick seemed better, but Joe felt himself slipping away and he asked for a rest in the middle of the day. The two of them salvaged crumbs from food wrappers. They mixed oats with snow in Dick's cup and ate the mush; it was very good.

They resumed their descent. The ground became more difficult than they had remembered. They stopped for the night when Joe couldn't continue. There was room to lie down and they spoke to each other—it seemed to Joe that they hadn't done so in a long time. Dick took note of a vein of crystal in the rock, and he wondered aloud what they'd climb next. Joe knew that Dick had his eye on Changabang's West Face. The two of them had gazed awestruck at the face during the approach to Dunagiri; in their innocence they had even talked of climbing Changabang after they'd knocked off this peak.

Joe promised himself—he spoke aloud—that he wouldn't put himself in this situation again. He would not do it for a climb,

not for anything. He wanted only ease and comfort. His thirst
woke him three times in the night. He stuffed snow in his mouth
to try to stop the horrible burning there and heard Dick doing the
same. Dick went back to sleep and dreamed of an accident. He
came awake convinced that a helicopter rescue was in progress
around the corner from the bivouac site. He woke Joe to ask him
if he heard the voices.

They slept again. The sun rose. The climbers woke and ate
more of their snow-mush. They were beginning to hope that they
would survive the descent. They set off and Dick slipped, twisting
his ankle. He didn't tell Joe. Dick's fingers had begun to torment
him. He took pills for the pain. The climbers came to the top of
the gully that would lead them to flat ground. Joe looked down
and decided against it. He had spotted an alternate route that
would bring them to the glacier sooner, though it meant a longer
walk on the glacier itself.

Dick said no and set off down the gully alone. Joe headed
down his shortcut, and soon came to a cliff. He took out a length
of rope and made an anchor and rappelled the cliff and then he
slid on his backside to the edge of the glacier. He began walking
and realized that he had forgotten about the crevasses; no one
would know where to look for his body if he fell into one now. He
cursed as he peered through his scratched sunglasses, searching
for telltale shadows on the surface of the snow. He stumbled on
and nothing happened. He found a rock with a pool of water on
top. He broke through a glaze of ice and mixed water from the
puddle with his remaining bits of oats and chocolate. He spooned
the mush into his mouth. An American family took shape in the
glimmer of sun on snow and watched him eat. There was a young
boy and he was disdainful; he disapproved of Joe's greed.

Changabang hung like a mural against the sky. It looked unbelievably difficult. Joe found his camera and took a picture of it but he was finished with mountains of this kind.

Other specters joined the Americans and everyone walked with Joe as he made his way toward Base Camp. They watched him with some of the cold puzzlement of ghosts but they seemed at moments engaged by his struggle—not without feeling. Their company distracted and reassured him. He knew he was going to live—the chocolate and the oats had convinced him of that—and now much of what he saw seemed newly familiar: Dunagiri at his back and this jumble of boulders and dirt at his feet.

He walked on in a mood of extraordinary acceptance. He cared what happened to him, but only a little. The American family didn't speak to him; they spoke about him but only to one another. He heard them complain that he was slow, but they offered him no assistance. He wondered peevishly why they didn't offer to take his rucksack.

He left the rucksack on the ground and kept walking. His route across the glacier had taken him behind a small satellite peak but now Dunagiri hove back into view. He recognized the valley that led to Base Camp. He made his way down. He felt the lurching oddness of his gait. He imagined himself as a toddler in the body of a very old man. He had to stop walking and his body shook briefly with some unfamiliar joyless version of amusement. He looked up and here was Base Camp.

Dick had not arrived. He might have stopped to eat at the tent near the base of their route. Joe ate from tins of fruit and meat and lay with water and chocolate near him in the dark. Thoughts glowed and streaked as if his mind were a galaxy, a vast darkness interrupted by light that smoldered and flashed at unimaginable intervals. His sense of safety and of ease amid this wonder was too glorious to waste on sleep. He left his sleeping bag once, to move his bowels, but it was too late. He went back to his sleeping bag without bothering to clean himself up properly—he could not find the strength to undress.

Dick didn't appear in the morning. Joe began to plan a rescue. He packed medical supplies in case Dick had hurt himself in the gully—and then Dick hobbled into camp. There was something odd about him; he was talking, making explanations. His ankle was bad, and he had been unable to find his way past a crevasse until a voice—Joe's—had offered directions that proved useful. Dick was very concerned about his hands. The ends of his fingers were black.

Joe gave him antibiotics. Dick rested a day and subsided into his familiar silence. Joe hiked up to the tent at Advance Base Camp to retrieve money and the keys to the van. Dick needed to leave now; he had to find a hospital and try to save his fingers. He would send porters back for the gear.

Joe was sad to part with Dick—there was an understanding between them that might not arise again. He waited alone at Base Camp for six days, too weary to explore his surroundings. He did set out once to have a look at Changabang but his battered feet didn't take him far. A creature of some kind, an animal, made its way into the food bags after dark. One night the animal upset Joe by eating a piece of fruitcake Joe had saved to treat himself.

The porters arrived. There were only two of them—Joe had expected three—and one was nearly useless. The porters smoked hashish in the mornings. The party walked into a snowstorm one day; another day they got lost and bushwhacked for hours through thickets that tore at their faces and clothing. They arrived in Joshimath. Joe stayed in the room where he had been treated for his infection. That episode seemed like something from a dream in another life. He could not stop looking at things and at faces; they seemed as real to him as if he had been born without vision and had recovered it now. This new condition was at once exhilarating and terribly sad. He was afraid of what he might see and also afraid that he might waste or lose this gift, that he might once again become blind. He understood that the shape of his fear—this obvious metaphor—was related to his awareness of his mother's blindness and to his own damaged vision. Someone else might experience this new way of being differently, perhaps as a new way of being in the body or in relation to the world. He understood that this gift did not free him of his past but it seemed to thrust him toward the present; the newness of that was as much as he could stand.

Joe made his way to Delhi. He found Dick in a hospital there. The standard of treatment was very poor, and Dick had resolved to fly back to England—an extravagance that betrayed the depth of his concern for his hands. That left Joe to make the drive back to England. Joe took on a passenger who could help pay for gas. The van caused endless trouble. Joe traded it for bus tickets, piling onto the bus in Kabul with the expedition's fourteen pieces of luggage. The bus driver drove for days without sleeping. The passengers asked him to stop and rest and he refused; when they insisted, he pulled a knife and waved it at them. Another time, a passenger became hysterical, claiming to be Jesus Christ. Joe worried that border officials would take the young man for a drug user and make trouble for the other passengers.

Joe abandoned the bus in Istanbul and bought a ticket on the Orient Express. He traveled now with an English lady, perhaps sixty years old, and an American girl. Joe slept for much of the journey, which was itself like swimming up to light from the last stages of a nightmare. Once, nearing Paris, he woke to a memory of Changabang—that enormous wall of milk-white stone.

CHANGABANG HAD BEEN an almost spectral presence during the days on Dunagiri. Joe and Dick had labored in its shadow in the early mornings. The huge white tower had loomed across the void like a ghostly witness, knowing and unknowable, its soaring contours a reminder of all they could not accomplish or understand.

Joe after leaving those mountains spent hours trying to imagine himself on Changabang's West Face. He tinkered at his idea at first like a child might tinker at making a bomb; it was not possible but it interested him. And after playing at this for a time he lost any sense of whether it was possible or impossible. He would go back and try to climb the face.

He needed a partner. Dick couldn't come; it wasn't yet clear that he would keep all of his fingers. And so in the winter of 1976 Joe went to see young Peter Boardman, disillusioned and bored at his desk at the shabby offices of the British Mountaineering Council.

The two young men had known each other only as acquaintances, but now their experience in the big mountains had left them scarred and needful in ways they didn't bother to disguise from each other. They weren't looking for friendship or love. Each man needed someone who shared this imperative that grew and pressed upon him from inside, so that he knew he must do whatever was required or this suffering would continue and grow worse.

Joe spoke to Peter of Changabang's West Face. Peter was at once entranced; he immediately agreed to make the attempt. This venture would be nothing like the previous year's Everest expedition. It offered engagement with something entirely unknown. No expedition large or small had climbed a Himalayan route as technically difficult as this one looked to be. The idea that the two of them could do it had arisen seemingly from nowhere. The idea would not have attached itself even to Joe if he had not encountered Changabang in the context of his suffering on Dunagiri.

A successful ascent of Changabang's West Face—a wall that Bonington and his team had dismissed as impossible in 1974—would compare with any previous achievement in the world's mountains. But the climbers felt that the nature of their engagement could have nothing to do with succeeding or failing; it must arise out of and sustain itself upon blind expectationless effort.

Joe and Peter met at Joe's house and studied photographs of the wall. They saw no obvious way to climb it. They consulted Doug Scott, who had studied the face at close range in 1974. He told them he thought it was probably too difficult to climb but he wanted to come with them and try.

Joe turned him down. Doug would bring another set of ideas to the climb, another way to see the experience; his judgments and his wishes might muddy this task, this pursuit. Even now Joe could not defend the climb—not to climbers apart from Peter, not to potential sponsors or donors of gear. Joe's notion of climbing the West Face of Changabang was an indulgence of a primitive need that had no claim on anyone but himself and now Peter. The expedition stood at odds with the needs of institutions and other climbers. Joe liked it that way. He meant to insulate the expedition from agendas that would blur his unthinking desire to engage the wall—a wish that had become a part of him, so that to turn even partly away from it would be dishonorable, a blurring of his integrity.

Joe and eventually Peter understood the expedition as a pilgrimage, an act of faith that arose from a sense of their own emptiness. This emptiness made them light; it made them desperate yet sure of themselves.

They raised a total of 850 pounds: from the Mount Everest Foundation; from Peter's employers at the BMC; from the Greater Manchester Council, which wanted to support two local boys. That left about a thousand pounds to come from their own pockets. Peter continued his committee work with the BMC. Joe worked at nights in a cold storage warehouse, loading frozen food onto trucks.

Joe lived alone; his life in some ways drew its pattern from the seminary. His motives for living this way and for this climb eluded him. He wasn't sure why he chose to suffer as he did. He wondered if he should do something else. He was afraid of more pain, some ultimate failure, some blame or waste.

Joe and Peter climbed together on the weekends. Joe climbed badly; he was distracted and also weary from his job at the warehouse. Peter climbed well. They were hard on each other from the beginning; they pushed and prodded each other. They were learning about one another, trying on various definitions of a partnership. They were determined not to mind things in ways that would interfere with the two of them getting up Changabang's West Face.

Other climbers knew Peter from his BMC work. They liked him well enough, but he stood apart from them in ways that Joe did not. Peter showed an earnest and touching interest in other climbers—as if he wanted to know what they knew and yet was half-convinced that such knowledge was beyond him. Joe decided that Peter was in some ways a careful person, something of a diplomat, someone who knew how to hang back and be tactful and end by having his way.

Peter for his part had felt his life getting away. Changabang was a raft drifting by on a current. He set aside his memory and his possessions to gather his intention and to time his leap.

Joe had a girlfriend but she found out about the Changabang trip—he hadn't told her—and she left for Australia. Peter took Joe around to meet his parents as though to solicit their blessing upon the union between their son and this stranger. The couple—they were in their forties—sized Joe up and eyed him apprehensively, as if they knew him for a fanatic. Joe went alone to visit his own parents in their modest council house. He had long since ceased to notice his mother's blindness in her presence, but her sightless eyes as he said his good-byes seemed evidence that what he sought existed—a world unknown.

THEY WERE FLYING out; they had booked a flight to Delhi for August 22. They spent the night before their departure at the London home of Charlie Clarke. Charlie was the young doctor from Bonington's Southwest Face expedition the previous year. His wife, Ruth Seifert, was pregnant, but she liked the two boys, and she came with Charlie to see them off at the airport. Four of Peter's friends were there. Joe had never been on an airplane; a forlorn-looking young woman arrived to say good-bye to him.

Pete and Joe wore their double boots and down parkas onto the plane; it saved the cost of shipping them. The good-byes left them momentarily hollow, but those feelings gave way to thoughts and images of the mountain that awaited them. The images had a simple clarity that shored up the notion that Pete and Joe had not failed at the task of making ordinary lives and connections, that on the contrary they were casting themselves loose from a world that had failed them.

Things went smoothly in Delhi. The climbers met their liaison officer—Flight Lieutenant D. N. Palta, a pilot in the Indian Air Force—on August 26. The lieutenant found the climbers' obvious poverty disconcerting. Joe and Peter shopped for food and saw their sixteen pieces of luggage onto a steam train; the train carried the little party to the village of Hardwar. The climbers now found their way onto a series of buses. The first bus carried wayfarers making the pilgrimage into the mountains; other pilgrims walked the margins of the road, which wound its spectacular way along crumbling rims of vast gorges. The driver and his passengers chanted prayers and talked in tones at once matter-of-fact and hysterical of the horrible accidents that routinely occurred—eight or nine in the previous year—on this section of the journey.

Joshimath, 2,000 meters above sea level, was blessedly cool. Joe and Peter spent several days there, sorting loads for porters. Joe found it strangely reassuring to revisit the place where he had suffered so much during his illness the previous year. The sight of the place undermined an irrational but growing sense that his expedition to Dunagiri had never occurred, that he had dreamed it, that Changabang did not exist. This time he was able to take in the stupendous scenery that surrounded the town. Jagged, mud-colored mountain walls allowed views across to distant snow peaks. One night Joe and Peter went with Lieutenant Palta to an Indian film. The three men sat near a small boy who sang along with the film's music. The sound of his singing would stay with Peter. The two climbers bought nuts and ate them in the dark. A light came on. The bag swarmed with grubs. Some lie had been unraveled; they were finished with civilization for a time.

They met a trekker—this one was named Hans—who for the sake of the adventure agreed to accompany them to the mountain and stay for a few days to help with camp chores. Another short bus ride took the party to the village of Lata. They hired fifteen porters and set off into the Rishi Gorge. They climbed four days, passing through meadows alive with lupine. They crossed streams swollen with monsoon rains and run-off from the high snows. They used their hands on the steeper and muddier slopes. They glimpsed Nanda Devi one day. Peter thought this brief sight of the mountain was reason enough to have come to this place.

Four days of this, and Lieutenant Palta wanted to quit. He couldn't eat the climber's food. He was unhappy at the prospect of living alone at Base Camp while Joe and Peter climbed the mountain. Joe had no patience for the man. Peter felt sorry for him. The lieutenant was a distraction; the climbers told him he could go when he liked.

They meant to reach Base Camp that day. Lieutenant Palta stayed for that. The party arrived at the Rhamini Glacier and the view up to Changabang. Joe was surprised and grateful to discover that the mountain was as he had remembered it. Peter had not seen Changabang in the flesh before. His first sight of it brought to his mind the image of a shark's tooth.

They arrived at the site Joe and Dick had occupied the year before, for Dunagiri. Here they said good-bye to Lieutenant Palta—there were no hard feelings, only shyness and relief on both sides. They paid the porters and said good-bye to them as well. Lieutenant Palta and the porters left; only the trekker Hans and the two climbers remained. It seemed to Peter that he was no longer in India—nothing here was strange to him; he was back in the mountains.

Hans stayed for two more days. Joe and Peter saw him off. Now they began to ferry loads to Advance Base Camp on a tongue of glacier near the bottom of the mountain, some two thousand feet above Base Camp. It was a good walk with their thirty-five-pound loads. The walk became familiar to them, almost comfortable. They made the round-trip in the mornings, and rested in the afternoons. Peter annoyed Joe by making long diary entries. The diary seemed to Joe a witness in this place, which otherwise seemed to render him invisible.

They made their first foray above Advance Base Camp on September 16. They hoped to establish a camp on a ridge that seemed to lead onto the West Wall. They climbed unroped on snow and then onto a sheet of ice six inches thick. The ice made sounds that frightened Peter but not Joe. It was as if they had decided that they couldn't afford to be afraid at the same time.

They continued higher. They were climbing now, coming to grips with the mountain. They were reminded of its size—it had lost the tame quality that it seemed to possess in photographs. The climbers were not in the sun yet. Peter's toes were cold; he had tried a new arrangement with his socks and it didn't work.

They reached the ridge and now the climbers grew colder. The mountain's North Face loomed to their right. Peter felt its darkness as menace; his dread rose in him. They would try to stay clear of that wall. They made their way up the ridge in the wind and staggered into a vision; Peter felt himself bathed in the newness of it. The glacier camp had been in a hollow that cut them off from their surroundings—from views of mountains he had dreamed of seeing. Joe seemed unmoved. He carried these peaks in his memory—had seen them from Dunagiri. He associated them with suffering.

They dug a ledge for a tent on the ridge just where it joined the West Face. The new camp—Camp One—offered a view of mountains in all directions but one. The remaining aspect offered only the wall, rising skyward like a great Buddha, serene and unattached.

They returned to Advance Base Camp for more supplies and

a second tent. They ferried those things back up the ridge on September 17 and returned to Base Camp for the night. They rested and discussed their eventual descent route. They could go up and over the peak and descend Bonington's East Ridge or they could follow their own route back down the West Wall. They had consulted Bonington himself. He had advised them to descend the East Ridge. Chris had changed his mind later, but Joe and Peter had decided that they would try to descend his ridge anyway.

They made two last carries to their ridge camp—on September 19 and 20—picking their way up the ice field that creaked beneath their weight. Camp One now held enough rope and gear and food to keep them on the mountain for another fourteen days.

THEY CLIMBED AND fixed rope every day, returning to their separate tents on the ridge each night. The weather held. They made progress sufficient to tempt them higher. The going was hard. The rock was granite, sturdy and reassuring under their hands and boots; some days it seemed to give them strength.

Pete cooked in the mornings while Joe lay in his sleeping bag. Joe managed the cooking at night. They took turns leading. Each climber led four consecutive pitches. Some pitches took a long time. One climber might spend a full day or longer in the lead. His partner at the anchor would sit or hang in his harness and pay out rope that snaked slowly up into the fog that often sheathed the peak. The wind made it difficult or impossible for either man to hear the other's shouts. The rope might lie motionless in the second's hand for an hour, increasingly dubious evidence that the other climber existed. Then it would move again and the leader would finish the pitch and build an anchor and fix rope for his second to climb.

They came to a series of overhangs after two days. Peter led into them. He made slow going. He found moments of exhilaration in peering over yet another ledge or past a corner to a new place. He reached a crack and worked a sliver of a piton into it—the piton like a table knife, an alien sliver of metal in rock. He stood on the pin and the world shrunk to this scene; all moments led to this. The rock's past bled from it, staining Peter; he felt black with the rock's long unknowing. He scraped snow from rock and found a hold and weighted it. He felt inside him all he had to lose—stale things in a paper bag; he could do without them. He muscled up onto a slope of snow, aware of how it fell away past him to the abyss at his back.

Joe paid out rope in the cold. He grew angry. It seemed to him that he was always angry. Lieutenant Palta had made him angry. Peter made him angry: why should Peter climb so well and with such steadiness of mind and then fret about trivial matters—the size of the ledge where he slept, backing up an anchor that didn't need it? Joe knew his anger would make it impossible for him to properly praise Peter's lead into the overhangs and he felt shame at his weakness.

Peter got two pitons in at the top of the pitch and only now noticed that it was snowing. He shouted down to Joe. The snow was heavy. Hail began to fall. It was only midafternoon, but there was nothing to do but go down to Camp One on the ridge. The descent was soon accomplished; they hadn't climbed far in three days. The storm ended as they approached their tents. They could speak to each other without shouting. Sun blinded them.

The next morning they rose and climbed the fixed ropes to their high point. Peter grew warm as he jumared up a frayed yellow rope. He was getting used to the exposure, but at moments he experienced a ridiculous thrill—a sense of getting away with something. He felt this now and as he did the world seemed to give way and he fell; it was like being sucked out of a window. He fell backward past rock and saw glacier and he had time to think that the rope had snapped. Something stopped him. He hung upside down from his jumars; they would be biting into the sheath of the rope. A piton had pulled—not the anchor itself, but a subsidiary pin meant to direct the line of the rope. He knew the one; he had placed it himself the previous day. He'd fallen 20 feet but the wall was so steep that there had been nothing to hit.

Peter made his way back up the rope past the lowest of the overhangs. He took the lead at the top of the fixed ropes, moving carefully over a huge block. He hammered a piton into a crack in a roof and clipped a sling to the piton and stood gently in the sling. When the sling held, he felt like shouting.

Joe watched Peter climb out of sight. He held Peter's rope and thought of sitting in the hollow of a dry river near one of their campsites during their approach to the mountain. He recalled how the trees and the hollow itself had seemed to shelter him from time. He had gone to the riverbed to think and plot but he'd lain back in the dead leaves and slept away part of an evening to awake entirely calm—but he was not calm now here on this sloping shelf of snow and rock. He was an ant on a countertop; there was no hiding. He grew cold waiting for Peter to finish.

Peter climbed on. He hammered in more pitons and clipped slings to them and stood in the slings. He was aware that no other person had been here, that no one belonged here. He cleared ice from rock, reaching awkwardly and working until his hands felt almost hollow, empty of strength. He shook and gasped with effort. His grip on his ice axe began to fail. He noted features of the rock and the ice as he chopped; he was like one of those soft creatures in a streambed—he groped for material to weave himself a shell. It seemed ridiculous to have bones on the inside and only skin for protection. His thoughts wandered and returned and left him again as he worked. He didn't know what to do with his mind—it was like a helpless and troublesome dependent.

The climbing became more difficult. He placed the pick of his axe into a slab of ice and tied a sling to the axe. The sling gave him enough support to cross to the first good foothold he'd seen in two hours of chopping steps in the ice. There was no wind. He looked down but he couldn't see Joe. Peter moved across to a section of decayed rock and managed to place his last pitons. He stood in two slings and called down to Joe.

Joe heard him and followed on Peter's rope. He arrived out of breath, and offered no acknowledgment of what Peter had accomplished in leading the pitch. Peter set off again. But it was late; he made 20 feet of progress and turned back. The climbers retreated down the fixed ropes.

Peter took the lead again the next morning. This was his fourth pitch since they'd come to the bottom of the overhangs three days before. He hung from his axes on ice that seemed likely to sheer away from the rock. He came near to fainting from fatigue before reaching a gully that offered a small ledge for an anchor. Joe followed, and now it was his turn to lead. He moved quickly up onto ice, climbing on easier ground.

Joe led another three pitches the next day, climbing mixed terrain past weathered and unstable rock. The third pitch brought him to the base of a rock tower. Peter struggled to follow. He felt something—desire, a wish to be safe and comfortable—nibble and tug at the frayed remnants of his strength. He carried a sack of provisions, and its weight was like a punishment. The climbers left their supplies at their high point and rappelled the fixed ropes back to their ridge camp for the night. Peter, sliding down the ropes, felt something give way in him. Nothing worried him; for a moment he felt that he couldn't be touched, couldn't die.

It took several hours each morning to climb the fixed ropes to the previous day's high point. The time had come to abandon Camp One on the ridge and strike out for the summit, carrying their food and shelter on their backs. The prospect frightened them.

They woke too tired to climb. They spent the day in their tent. Snow fell in the afternoon; the next morning the sky had a roof of cloud. The unpromising weather convinced them to drop down to Base Camp to pick up more food for their final push.

They moved down across the ice field and onto the glacier. They stumbled and shuffled across the rocks as the mountain receded. They had fixed rope on 3,000 feet of the route. That left another 2,500 feet to the summit. It was September 28; they had been on the mountain for three weeks. Joe pointed out that it had been a year and a day since Peter had reached the summit of Everest. Peter considered the fact, and a sense of detachment—familiar and vaguely shocking—arose in him. He saw as he always did Mick walking up that ridge into white oblivion.

THEY SPENT A single night at Base Camp. They had hoped to find new neighbors; there had been talk in Joshimath of an American expedition to Dunagiri. They found no one. They wrote a note offering details of their climb so far. The note was meant to find its way to their families if the two of them didn't return from the mountain. Joe in particular felt it would comfort his people to know whatever could be known.

They left Base Camp in the morning. They walked up past Advance Base and on up to Camp One. The weather began to close in. They carried on with heavy loads up the ice field, a place already strange to them, spooky after their brief absence. They were halfway up the fixed ropes when light faded from the sky.

They stopped and melted snow for drinks. This upper section of the route was too steep to provide bivouac ledges, so they had brought hammocks for sleeping. They fussed and struggled with the hammocks. Joe had designed them with a half-dozen straps that converged to a single suspension point. He'd lined them with foam and a nylon sheath against the wind. There was a system of rods to prevent the hammocks from wrapping themselves too tightly around the occupants' bodies—but they'd left the rods up with the gear they'd already carried to the top of the fixed ropes.

The two climbers spent a miserable evening and night— struggling to breathe, fumbling with boots, suffering from cramps and claustrophobia and the cold. Snow and wind made their way into the hammocks. There was no escape in the darkness. They had tested the hammocks before leaving England, spending a night in the meat lockers at Joe's workplace, swinging in the cold light with the hams and other carcasses. This was far worse.

Peter fell asleep briefly and woke with his foot jutting out of the hammock and into the sky. The foot was numb with cold and he quickly retrieved it. The climbers had come to see their body parts as gear, indispensable, under their protection. The nights until now had offered relief from the days of struggle; tonight the climbers longed for the sun that would free them from their coffinlike shelters. They were afraid as well as uncomfortable—it occurred to both of them that a falling rock could sever the ropes and pitch them into oblivion. Peter imagined himself and Joe as two swimmers in an ocean at night.

They woke to white—clouds and snow and more cold—and lay in the hammocks until ten o'clock. Peter's voice roused Joe. Peter had removed a glove to tie his boots, and he'd lost feeling in his fingers; now he was shouting in pain as the blood returned to them. He stopped shouting and told Joe not to worry—the fingers wouldn't stop him from climbing. Joe felt something crack and some of the anger that had pestered and distracted him leaked away.

They left their miserable bivouac without taking time to melt snow for water. Their fatigue and their heavy loads made them slow. Darkness returned as they reached the top of the ice field. A storm blew up. Once again, there were no ledges. They managed to melt enough water to fill their cups once. They drank it and pitched the hammocks and clambered into them. They had not yet reached the top of the fixed ropes, but already they were dangerously tired and very thirsty.

The third day was no better. They finished climbing the fixed ropes and gained another 150 feet and that was all they could manage. They longed for a ledge, for water and food.

They woke to a storm on the fourth day. They retreated, following the ropes back to Camp One on the ridge. Joe arrived first. He fell asleep in his tent without thinking to put a pan of snow on the stove. Peter arrived and admonished him for his oversight. They groused mechanically at one another. There was no real sense of outrage, only fatigue and a creeping worry that they might not be able to climb the route.

The weather had improved during their retreat but when they peered up at the route they wondered at their own audacity. They had at times imagined that they could climb this spectacular wall if only they tried for long enough; their optimism now struck them as stupid, inappropriate. They roused themselves after a short rest and continued down to Advance Base Camp. They were too weary to go further. They spent the night there and descended to Base Camp the next morning.

They rested two days. Joe dressed Peter's fingers, which were cracked and painful. The climbers were far behind schedule. Peter assumed that he would return to England too late to keep his BMC job, but the prospect meant nothing. Neither climber spoke of leaving because the notion was so intensely alluring; to speak of it would endanger this enterprise, this way of being.

They agreed that they would need at least one more proper camp above the ice field. They couldn't maintain their strength if they had to sleep in the hammocks. They talked again about how to descend the peak if they managed to climb it. They fought over petty matters—who should cook or perform certain camp chores; Peter's tendency to sit daydreaming when there was work to bed done. One or the other would say: *Don't worry. It will be all right when we get back.*

Each climber had come to trust that the other had no wish to quit the route. This understanding gave them comfort and a new regard for one another. They were grateful to each other. Peter complained of his fingers but Joe didn't mind; that sort of weakness was a relief after Dick Renshaw's stoicism.

Joe told stories that revealed little about him. He spoke once of his past—of his parents and his nine siblings, of his position as the eldest of five sons. His seven years in seminary and his stint at university had left Joe suspicious of institutions and ideology; he was impatient of authority but he claimed to have no time for idealists and thinkers; he said he simply wanted to do things.

He believed that they must climb the route. It was no longer something he wanted and he took no pleasure in the prospect of having done it. He couldn't find or name any value in it. They would have to do it on faith. He took unthinking comfort in that familiar notion.

Peter saw that Joe was no skeptic, was rather a fanatic. Peter also knew himself for a kind of believer, but he thought himself happier than Joe. He sometimes wondered if he could compete with Joe's appetite for difficulty. His motivation to finish the route was informed by his connection to Joe. They were blurred mirrors to one another; it was difficult for one to imagine himself and his motives apart from the presence of the other.

They discussed practical matters, in particular their need to establish a higher camp where they could sit or even lie down—where they could cook and sleep. They would bring a tent lining and chop a ledge, however cramped. The season was advancing. They would carry more clothing this time. Joe found an extra down jacket among supplies they'd acquired for the porters. Peter packed the bulky one-piece suit he'd worn on Everest.

THEY PREPARED TO leave Base Camp for a third time. They revised the note they would again leave behind for anyone who might come looking for them. They set about packing. They heard voices as they prepared to leave on the morning of October 6. They emerged from their tents to find visitors. Three members of the American Dunagiri team had entered their camp. The Americans brought news that a young American woman had collapsed and died high on Nanda Devi. The girl, Nanda Devi Unsoeld, was the daughter of the famous American climber Willi Unsoeld. Joe and Peter had hoped for visitors but this news was disturbing and the men who brought it seemed old, unsure of themselves.

Joe and Peter said good-bye to them and left for Advance Base Camp. The two climbers walked up the glacier chatting about their visitors. They felt that much of their strength had returned to them. They had made a late start and soon they were walking in moonlight. The night grew chill and white. Peter shivered and felt some lining give way and his happiness filled him like blood; he wondered if Joe felt something like that.

They spent the night at Advance Base Camp on the glacier. The camp was near the slopes that led up to Shipton Col—the col crossed by Bonington and his party two years before. Joe and Peter climbed up to inspect the old anchors and ropes that lay buried or partially buried in snow. There had been another expedition on these slopes since then; climbers had crossed the col on the way to Kalanka. The ropes were badly weathered. Joe weighted one and a piton came out; he teetered and almost fell but recovered himself. These mountains were dangerous; just wandering around could kill you.

They would have to come down from these slopes if they chose to descend from the summit by way of Bonington's East Ridge. The poor condition of the old anchors and ropes meant they'd have to set up their own rappels. They put off their decision.

They returned to the glacier and climbed their own fixed ropes to Camp One. It remained their high camp for now, but they meant to establish a higher one on the ice field that lay above the great overhangs. Peter spent the afternoon—five hours of it—mending his overboots. The boots were in tatters, like much of the climbers' gear and clothing. A two-hour thunderstorm rolled through during the early afternoon; it reminded Peter of the Alps. The clouds drifted off and the climbers saw that the Rishi Gorge had turned white.

A strong wind followed the storm. The wind continued through the night. They woke late in the morning and argued over whether to climb. Joe was against it. Peter argued the point just to see where the debate would take them. They decided to wait. They did not want to spend another night out on the steep ground below their high point, this time without even the hammocks, which they'd left back up on the ice field.

The weather improved later in the morning, but it was too late for them to change their minds. Their talk sputtered and died. They puttered and read and thought and listened to the unfamiliar quiet. It was odd not to be climbing in this calm. Peter read John Steinbeck's diaries; he found them trivial and tedious and stopped reading to make marker flags from strips of cloth. The climbers would leave the flags near anchor points on the route. This was to help them find rappel anchors if they decided to descend the West Face. That seemed likely now. Their route was difficult but much of it was familiar from their repeated visits. The idea of finding their way down new ground was too frightening now that they were so tired.

They dozed off early. Pete woke at three o'clock and melted snow for tea. They were away from the tent by six o'clock. Peter carried the extra down clothing. Joe followed him. Joe's job was to dismantle the fixed ropes below the balcony, the spot where they had spent their first night in the hammocks. They would need those ropes for the Rock Tower, the last major feature on the face.

The weather was cold, but they were warmly dressed. They moved well. Joe imagined himself as a bird, a creature that visited this place by some genetic right. Peter, climbing a vertical section on the fixed ropes, tore a hole in his down suit and bits of fluff escaped. He watched them rise hundreds of feet in the updrafts that swept the face. He felt his strength, a relic of these weeks of struggle. He knew it could leave him at any time but it filled him with a brittle, joyful confidence.

They reached their old high point at midafternoon. Peter untied from the rope and wandered about looking for a ledge with room for a tent. He climbed 15 feet and then gently told himself that it was not wise to be unroped here where a fall would be like falling from the sky itself. He retreated. Joe arrived and the two of them set out to chop a platform from the ice. They anchored their tent liner to it and then Peter led an easy pitch, fixing rope for the morning. The ridge sank into shadow as he rappelled back down to the new campsite.

The new sleeping arrangement was cramped, but far superior to the hammocks. The climbers were able to cook and sleep. The new situation made them once again believe that their climb was possible. This time their belief seemed less a tactic and more of a bona fide discovery.

The ground ahead looked very difficult. Peter and Joe agreed that each climber would lead just two pitches in succession—not four, as they'd done lower on the route. Peter led his second pitch the next morning. It was much more difficult than the one he'd led the night before. He felt his fatigue again and his vulnerability, how susceptible he was to suffering. His fingers grew cold as he climbed an ice bulge. He was afraid that he'd damage them further if he stopped to put on crampons. He moved left onto rock and then climbed a narrow funnel of ice. He hammered in ice pegs and clipped slings to them, stepping in the slings to gain height.

This brought him to the foot of an overhang, a six-foot ceiling strangely disorienting as he leaned back to study it. He crawled across a narrow ledge that took him around a corner and onto the mountain's North Face, a near-vertical field of iced-over rock, barely touched by the sun. He had gazed upon this face from the glacier—even at that great distance it had filled him with dread. He'd never thought to arrive here, and for a moment he swam in a fear that seemed rooted in a sense that he had planned none of this, that some false, unloving guardian had imposed it upon him. He looked down into the void and then up to a looming 200-foot corner—vertical, slick with ice, impossible.

He retreated back around the corner to the ledge beneath the overhang. He rested for a moment and then he set off up a short crack. He hoped to climb the roof by direct aid—hammering pitons into the crack and clipping slings to them and using the slings for steps—but none of his pitons fit the crack. He wrapped his fingers around an edge and leaned back on his arms, pressing his feet into the wall. Laybacks are difficult at sea level, and this one was absurdly strenuous; he was climbing at altitude, encumbered by his gear and wind suit. He was losing strength too quickly. He inserted a fist into the crack and twisted his wrist just so. This allowed him to hang on the arm and he rested like that. He waited just long enough for a whisper of strength to return and then he finished in a rush, up and over. He grabbed at a slab of rock that moved; he knew it would take him with it and scoop up Joe further down, but his feet found decent holds and he stood in them, his chest heaving. He fended off the urge to throw up. He hammered in a piton and fixed the rope to it and called to Joe.

Joe climbed the fixed rope and took the lead now on difficult mixed ground that reminded him of winter routes in Scotland. He brought Peter up and then set off again and moved left, this time out onto the North Face. He followed a steep tongue of ice until it disappeared. He would have to climb on rock again. The rock was too steep to manage in crampons. He buried his pick in the last of the ice and then ever so carefully stood on the head of his axe. He crouched to take off his crampons and stood upright again to step across onto the rock—every movement precise, the climber aware and yet not aware of what would happen if the movement dislodged the axe—the brief chaos and the long near-silent drop, punctuated by spinning blows and lights to end in quiet.

He found his footing on the rock slab and reached back for the axe and tugged at it. The axe came back to him as if it were part of his body, as if it shared his intentions. It felt odd to have the crampons off. He made a few moves on rock and then came to more ice and drove his pick into the ice with real force. It held his weight while he stooped awkwardly to strap the crampons back onto his boots. He climbed to a cluster of boulders and at last made another anchor.

It would be dark in a half-hour. Joe had led his two pitches. He was climbing well, though. Peter felt clumsy and timid following him. He let Joe lead another 70 feet to the top of the ice; then the climbers descended to spend another night at their new camp.

They woke fearful and tense the next morning. There was little talk between them now. They knew from photographs that they must get off the North Face and back onto their West Face, where a ramp of snow seemed to lead to the summit. Joe went down to fetch some rope they'd left just below their high camp. Peter went up the fixed ropes alone; he meant to rearrange them to eliminate a couple of awkward traverses. He took out a piton and leaned sideways and was suddenly swinging toward a corner; he picked up speed and twisted to get his legs up. He was traveling so fast now that the impact might break a bone—utter disaster—but before he could make his turn he finished his 40-foot pendulum, his body punching sideways into rock.

The impact hammered the breath from him. He hung on the rope until he could breathe. Then he gathered his wits and conducted a sort of drunken inspection. Nothing broken. He looked down to where Joe had dwindled to a speck of black. There wasn't much they could do for each other. The thought somehow restored him. Peter set out again, sorting out the fixed ropes as he climbed. He stopped from time to time and looked around at what there was to see. It amazed him; the view seemed a chain of evidence that nothing was as it seemed. Any concerns he carried in one place were meaningless in another—certainly in this world with its vast mind, a mind that seemed manifest in rock that poked through snow and ice like bone though flesh. The glacier at this distance receded from the sky as space recedes from planets through layers so weightless and thick that traveling through them would be like moving through time; time would become mere geography or the other way around. Peter felt like a speck on the eye of some mind that at most times ignored him but might at any moment turn its awareness to him. His fall thrilled him in retrospect. He wanted to do it again—the fall had brushed by his defenses so quickly that he had for a moment felt his connection to all of this mystery.

He reached the top of the ropes late in the morning. Joe came up behind him. It was Peter's turn to lead, to find a way back across to the West Face. Joe put him on belay. Peter stepped onto a huge hollow-sounding flake. He all but tiptoed on the front-points of his crampons finding tiny lips in the rock until he found a spot for a piton in a crack above the block. He stood in good footholds and the sound of his hammering was like the tolling of church bells; it summoned believers to remember, to come.

He rested. Music—chanting—ran through his mind. It grew and filled his ears and skull, his mouth—he was amazed. He noticed his shadow; the sun had moved. He looked down at Joe, who hung in slings at the anchor, and past down the face to the Bagnini Glacier, from this height a swirling abstraction. Changabang's West Face—parts of it—had come back into view as he crossed the fringes of the North Face toward the ridgeline that separated the two great walls. Peter imagined himself the sun, rising and flooding nooks of the world with his awareness; whatever he failed to look upon remained in shadow. He leaned across and found a hand jam and muscled his way up to an ice slope. He buried his axe pick and teetered higher on his crampons. The wall veered above him, offering a single thin crack for an anchor. He hammered in three knifeblade pitons and fixed the rope for Joe to follow.

Peter set off to lead another pitch. He came to more steep rock and worked his way up cracks, dangling awkwardly to hammer in pitons and stand in slings; reaching down to retrieve the pegs at his feet so that he could use them again higher up.

There were no holds on this vertical ground; there were only these thin cracks for gear so that there was nothing to do but build this ladder of slings. The climbers were running short of pitons—Joe retrieved them on each pitch, but they had used many to anchor the fixed ropes, and had dropped a few. Peter made another anchor and rappelled to Joe; it was growing late and they retreated to the tent.

They climbed the fixed ropes again the next morning. Peter arrived at the start of the last rope and thought of that last anchor he'd placed—he hadn't much liked it. He weighted the rope and struggled up in a swirl of fright; it held him and Joe followed and set off to lead more thin cracks then an arête. Pete watched him wrestle his way across and up on holds too small for the toes of his boots.

Joe placed a piton and clipped a sling to it. He ran his trailing rope through the carabiner and moved cautiously up and sideways on more thin holds. He took tension from the rope that ran down to Peter and worked his way into a groove that offered some security. He rested there and then climbed to a huge boulder. He rested again. He could see a corner that led to the start of the ramp they hoped would take them to the summit. He moved to the base of the corner and built another hanging belay beneath some overhangs and brought up Peter.

Joe took an hour to find a way past the overhangs, and then made his way back onto the crest of a ridge. The ramp was perhaps a rope's length further. Peter followed, stopping once to take pictures. Joe told him to hurry.

They descended to their high camp in the growing murk. Joe went first. Peter was feeling the altitude without knowing it and he lost himself in games, in the twisted logic of dreams. He named the various knots *cows* and thought of the pitons as

Americans. He gave a girl's name to each of the carabiners that
dangled from his waist.

The tent surprised him. Joe was there; he looked frightened.
He had somehow unclipped from both of the fixed ropes while
shifting from one to another. He'd had one hand on a jumar;
otherwise he'd be gone now. Peter regarded Joe's stricken face
and could find nothing to say.

They were beginning to believe that the route's major difficulties
were behind them. One more hard pitch would bring them to the
ramp. They packed food for two days. They intended to set off in
the morning but they slept late and decided to rest a day.

They had been on the mountain for five weeks but it seemed
much longer—months. Peter left the tent in the afternoon and
looked around at the mountains that sprawled in every direction, endless, most of them anonymous. He wondered which
was Kailas: center of the universe and throne to Shiva, creator
and destroyer of all things. He returned to the tent; when he
stooped to crawl into the entrance he saw blood in the snow—Joe
must have coughed it up—but neither climber mentioned it. Joe
described the way the tent fabric brushed his face as he lay in his
sleeping bag. He said he loved how that felt. Peter realized that
they weren't afraid anymore.

THEY ROSE EARLY—three o'clock—on October 14. The wind
had risen in the night. They set out with bivouac sacks, sleeping
bags, stove and pan, food and rope. Joe went first. Peter followed.
He regarded the fixed ropes with dread. The wind gusted and his
hands grew numb as he fumbled with his jumars.

Peter caught Joe at the top of the ropes and stopped to warm
his hands. He climbed past Joe onto new ground. He climbed
in shadow and he again lost feeling in his fingers—this meant

stopping to hang in slings and shove his hands into his oversuit to restore circulation. He bridged up a chimney, his legs spanning the gap in the rock as he climbed 20 feet on vertical and then overhanging ground. He wedged a nut into a crack and hung from it, the route spinning and falling away beneath his body. The ridge he climbed divided the world into shadow and light, but the distinction meant nothing to him. He looked up and judged from the quality of the light overhead that weather was coming; he briefly wondered when it would reach them. There was a huge block at the top of the groove. He placed another nut and moved higher to squirm under the block and onto snow. He was on the ramp, at last out of the shadow of the West Face.

Joe followed him up and into the sunlight. There remained only 1,000 feet to the summit. The climbers dropped their axes and most of their gear, keeping two ropes and a few slings and pitons and carabiners. Peter started up another pitch on powder snow. Joe followed, making his own way up the snow; it was not steep enough here to require fixed rope. Joe led a difficult pitch up the lower part of a buttress. Peter led through on mixed ground; it was more difficult than he had expected. He was enjoying the climbing and he volunteered to lead the next pitch as well. Joe was tired enough to let him.

Peter continued up the buttress. A shadow climbed the rock below him as the sun sank in the sky. His arms and his body grew light as he moved higher. He felt this as a kindness, and felt himself released even from the obligation to be grateful. Joe began moving before Peter finished the pitch and as Joe climbed darkness arrived as if beckoned.

There wasn't enough snow to dig a snow hole. They scratched out a platform and crawled into their bivouac sacks. They lay still. They were 6,700 meters above the sea in this impossible place. They dozed and woke to fidget in the dark. The wind rose in the night. Peter slept again but after midnight woke to spend two hours rubbing his numb feet. The climbers packed when the sun appeared. They left camp under a thin scum of high cloud. They climbed more rock and then they were back on snow; it was easy climbing, not terribly steep. Joe led it. He was very close to exhaustion but his weariness didn't surprise or worry him now.

The day seemed to Peter unreal. There was no warmth and no color to it. He wanted to see Nanda Devi from the summit— there had been nothing but clouds at the top of Everest. Joe shouted down and told him not to worry; Nanda Devi was there, through the gray—also the vast territory that lay at its feet and at their own.

Joe waited and they walked another 30 feet on nearly flat ground to the summit. Their relief clashed with their dread of the task still ahead. They could find little to say to each other. The climbers ate chocolate and took pictures. They rested for a half-hour. Nanda Devi disappeared in cloud. Flakes of new snow drifted in silence past the two men's faces and came to rest on the mountain.

Joe roused himself to suggest that they unrope to descend to the first rappel. That way one of them could fall without pulling the other off the mountain. Peter didn't like the idea, but he was glad that Joe was sufficiently focused on the work at hand to be ruthless. They set off. They felt the storm rise at their backs. Peter allowed himself occasional glances toward the Rhamani Glacier far below. It would lead them home if they could manage to reach it.

The storm grew worse. The climbers became shapes in the snow. Speed alone could protect them. They reached the top of the first rappel and carried on down, building anchors and setting up more rappels; they had left no fixed ropes on these highest sections of the route. They were almost out of pitons now. Joe frightened Peter by building an anchor that featured a single peg, driven perhaps an inch into a crack.

The piton held them. They reached the line of fixed ropes. Joe descended more quickly than Peter and found their camp on the ledge—Camp Two—long after dark and crawled into the tent to melt snow. He had time to imagine the worst before he heard Peter's approach. Joe at the sound felt his bones grow light again. They had climbed the mountain.

They talked about it. There was this relief, and something else—they groped for it for a time, and at last grew calm enough to sleep. They woke to sun and an unfamiliar absence of urgency. They were sorry to leave this place but also eager to escape it. Joe again fixed a single-piton anchor for a rappel. He set off down. The piton flexed and Peter unclipped from it so that if the anchor failed it wouldn't take them both. Joe looked up and saw what Peter had done and made a joke; it was all right between them.

They had made a late start. They moved slowly, fumbling with the ropes. They were still 500 feet above Camp One on the ridge when night fell. It began to snow heavily. Pete had better night vision. Joe asked him to go ahead. They were tired and cold but they would rest soon, and meanwhile they enjoyed aspects of this; they flirted with a sense of not wanting it to end. They reached the tent after three hours of moving in darkness.

They descended the rest of the ridge in the morning, coming at last to the creaking ice slope that led to the glacier. Joe climbed down quickly. Peter followed more slowly. It was bliss to come off the ropes and stand on level ground. Everything was absolutely clear—the snow seemed painted on the ground—but there were no words to explain.

THEY HAD EARNED their happiness. They wanted to be among people. They spent the night at Advance Base Camp. They descended to Base Camp the next day—October 18—and found another expedition camped near their tent. The new arrivals were Italians who had come up this valley by mistake hoping to reach Kalanka; they were on the wrong side of Shipton Col.

A middle-aged American woman was with them. She introduced herself as Ruth; she had been with the Dunagiri expedition. Joe and Peter spoke to her and learned that four of the Dunagiri climbers had been killed in a fall; one of the dead had been her husband. The bodies were still lying in the snow where their fall had taken them.

Joe and Peter volunteered to attend to the corpses. They recruited two porters to help. The party set out before light the next day. The porters soon fell behind. Peter and Joe reached the bodies together. The dead climbers were still roped in teams of two. The climber tied to Ruth's husband had been nineteen years old. They found a journal in the boy's pack and kept it for his family. Joe took one rope; Peter took the other. They dragged the corpses down the hill toward a crevasse where they meant to deposit them, away from the birds.

There seemed no important difference between the living and the dead. The difference was like the difference between an acquaintance and a stranger—a matter of circumstance. The two climbers were careful as they approached the dark slot in the snow. Peter felt a child's distress at the notion of being entombed with these newly dead.

Joe slid two of the bodies into the crevasse. Peter hung back, watching; he felt ill. Joe took Peter's rope from him, pulled the remaining bodies, stiff and distorted, through the snow until he could push them in after the others. Peter suggested a prayer. Joe agreed to stand in silence for a time.

The two climbers descended Base Camp. They reached it in darkness. The porters were singing around a fire. They stopped singing when the two British climbers arrived. Ruth had been crying. She apologized; she said it was the singing.

16

CHRIS BONINGTON SPENT 1976 consolidating his status as the leading British mountaineer of his generation. He was made a Commander of the British Empire (CBE) on New Year's Day in recognition of the Everest triumph. He toured the country lecturing to sold-out crowds eager to hear his version of events on the Southwest Face. He was made a vice-president of the British Mountaineering Council. He lent his name to charities. He made appearances at business conferences to supplement his income from lectures and books.

He was no longer a poverty-stricken climber—but he was still a climber. Doug Scott called that summer. He wanted Chris to join an expedition to the Karakoram the following year. Pakistan had reopened the range to exploration in 1975, giving climbers renewed access to some of the world's most beautiful and challenging peaks: the likes of K2 and the spectacular Trango Tower and the brutish-looking Ogre.

Doug had picked the Ogre (7,285 meters; 23,901 feet), the tallest mountain in the Biafo Glacier region. The mountain remained unclimbed after six attempts. It presented a squat-looking mass of rock and ice, with an elaborate assortment of towers, buttresses, walls and gullies. Chris, studying photographs, saw the complex as a monster with three heads.

Doug had become a big-wall enthusiast; he had his eye on a line that went straight up a seemingly featureless spire to snow that wrapped like a bandage around the peak's upper reaches. Chris thought Doug's chosen route looked appallingly difficult, but he saw the potential for an easier way up the peak. And he liked the idea that someone else would be running the expedition; for once, Chris could leave the fund-raising and the organizational chores to other climbers.

The Ogre wasn't the type of mountain to make his reputation with the public, but Everest had done that—and anyway, that wasn't the point, whatever others might wish to believe. He was touched that Doug had invited him—and the Ogre was an enticing destination, a spectacular mountain. That said, it was also true that the Ogre might help rehabilitate his reputation among the young climbers who saw the Southwest Face expedition as a throwback to a bygone era—a time when sheer organizational ability mattered as much as climbing skill or boldness. Bonington's expedition to Changabang in 1974 had been a step in the right direction, but young Joe Tasker and Dick Renshaw had increased the ante the following year with their spectacular two-man ascent of Dunagiri. The success of Tasker and Peter Boardman on Changabang's West Face in the fall of 1976 would soon provide further evidence that a new generation of British mountaineers had arrived—a generation at least as creative and determined as Chris Bonington and his circle.

Bonington's triumphs on Annapurna and Everest had in fact put a cap on the era of big expeditions. They had done this largely by proving that climbers could scale virtually any mountain feature given sufficient resources and organization. The possibility of failure receded, and with it much of the reason for mounting large expeditions in the first place. Meanwhile, corporate sponsors had lost interest in funding such trips. The biggest sponsors generally required a hugely visible target like Everest—and the feeling for the moment was that Everest had been done.

Even Doug Scott had his doubts about the Everest trip that had made him a celebrity. Doug had always been a proponent of lightweight, alpine-style mountaineering. He disapproved of formal hierarchies—partly on principle; also because (as Chris and others liked to point out) the strength of his personality allowed him to dominate more informal proceedings. He had rankled at Bonington's authority on both Everest trips and on Changabang in 1974. The Ogre would be different; this was to be Doug's expedition. There would be no army of porters, no central command and no master plan. Climbers would do as they pleased.

Chris was now forty-one, and his mountaineering options were dwindling. The Ogre seemed to offer a way back to the past—climbing for the sake of climbing, without the pressures of sponsors and headlines—even as it offered a chance to continue to play a further role in shaping the future of mountaineering. His own experience and the example of younger climbers had convinced him that he could tackle difficult routes on the biggest peaks with truly small teams and succeed. The Ogre might be just the thing.

DOUG HAD ALREADY chosen the other climbers for the expedition. He had invited his mate Tut Braithwaite. Chris knew Tut from Everest but they weren't old friends. Clive Rowland and Mo Anthoine also were coming. Clive was another old friend of Doug; he worked as a builder on the Black Isle, north of Inverness. He had a huge, shaggy beard and a sharp tongue. He seemed unimpressed by and perhaps resentful of Bonington's fame.

Mo Anthoine was a bona fide character. He was a native of the English Midlands, a fireplug of a man at 5'7", with a big neck and a deep chest. He walked with a stiff, rolling gait—a sailor on shore leave, maybe looking for a fight. Mo as a young man had in fact worked his passage on ships to New Zealand and back. He'd been gone two years; during that time he had crewed yachts, worked in the asbestos mines and smuggled turquoise into Pakistan.

He had returned from his travels to start a company with Don Whillan's old climbing partner, the great Joe Brown. The firm manufactured and sold climbing gear out of the Welsh climbing center of Llanberis, where it employed a staff of two-dozen workers. Mo used his share of profits to finance small expeditions. He'd climbed the Great Prow of Roraima—a sandstone wall in the jungles of Guyana—in 1975. He'd done it with Hamish Mac Innes and Joe and Don. The Ogre invitation, which came early in 1976, found Mo preparing for an expedition to the Karakoram's Trango Tower. That trip—led by Joe Brown—would put Martin Boysen and Mo on the peak's summit that fall.

Mo was a highly competent climber. Other climbers knew him as a great wit—a talker, inclined to be vulgar, a cheerful dispenser of insults, utterly independent, dismissive of authority and disdainful of reputation. He was not a person likely to put Chris at ease.

Doug had invited Dougal Haston, too. Dougal, now thirty-six, had enjoyed his Everest fame and the sense of possibility that came with it. He had pursued his literary ambitions, drafting a novel about a pair of mountaineers—a brooding, darkly handsome young Scot and his mentor, an American modeled on John Harlin. Dougal's plans for the coming year included summer guiding in the Alps and teaching a climbing course in Canada, as well as a series of lectures to raise money. Meanwhile he ran the climbing school back in Leysin. He had cut back on his drinking—though he still indulged in occasional binges. His finances were a shambles, his bank accounts often overdrawn. He'd parted with his wife Annie after several years of hard living and mutual infidelity. He had settled into a less tempestuous relationship with Ariane Giobellina, a young woman—his junior by eleven years—who had grown up in Leysin. Ariane worked at a travel agency in town to help cover the couple's living expenses.

Dougal was no longer the *enfant terrible* he had been on the Eiger and Annapurna. The new generation climbed routes in the Alps that were far harder than his own best efforts, and made their high-altitude climbs without the support of Bonington's well-oiled expeditionary machine. It didn't matter; his writing absorbed him, and he climbed routes that interested him. It was enough. Dougal and Chris spoke on the telephone, and agreed that they would climb together on the Ogre. They would take one of the more reasonable lines to the summit; let Doug tackle his big wall with one of the other climbers. The idea of climbing with Dougal again made Chris happy; it would be a chance to revisit their friendship, which had deepened over time.

Chris drove out to Chamonix in January, bringing along Mo Anthoine. They planned to do a little climbing and meet Dougal to talk about preparations for the Ogre. Chris and Mo found the Chamonix weather too unsettled for climbing, but fine for skiing. Chris telephoned Dougal, who confirmed that he would come over from Leysin in a few days.

DOUGAL HAD NOW lived in Leysin for ten years. He had become a good skier; it was part of his identity as a complete mountaineer. He avoided the resort slopes near town, preferring to ski off-piste. His daily routine during the first two weeks of January of 1977 included a morning of work on his novel—he had set himself a daily target of 2,000 words—and lunch with Ariane. He'd ski in the afternoon if conditions were good. He got very drunk one night just after the New Year, and arrived home in the early morning with a deep cut over one eye. He told Ariane he'd fallen.

He finished a draft of his novel on Sunday, January 16. One passage described a run down the Northeast Face of La Riondaz—one of the few difficult runs easily accessible from Leysin. The face wasn't always in condition; it was forested, and required heavy snowfall to create adequate covering for a skier. The face occasionally unleashed huge avalanches. The American climber in Dougal's book triggered a slide there but managed to outrun it.

Dougal planned to ski the face on Monday. He walked Ariane to her office that morning and kissed her good-bye at the building entrance. She went inside, and then she followed an impulse to run up the stairs and out onto a balcony; she hoped to catch sight of him, but he was already gone. They spoke again an hour or two later when Dougal phoned her office. He wanted her to join him on La Riondaz. Conditions on the mountain would be beautiful: sunshine, a lot of snow. Ariane was touched, but she refused; her boss couldn't spare her.

Dougal took the lift to La Berneuse, which lay at the bottom of the face. The upper lift was closed due to avalanche hazard. Dougal kicked steps up the snow, carrying his skis across his shoulder. He was glad the lift was closed; he had the slope entirely to himself.

He was doing what he'd always done: moving alone in the mountains, putting distance between himself and the rest of the world. It took time, and he felt his breathing deepen. The work didn't stop him from thinking, but it helped. He still carried with him his shame. The shame didn't always attach itself to a particular sin or omission. The understanding that he'd killed that boy in Scotland wasn't always there; Dougal sometimes had trouble finding it. When he did it was like digging a snow cave and poking through to sky, rearing back—but that version of his shame mostly eluded him.

It sometimes seemed to him that his shame and confusion had little to do with the boy; it was nothing he could think about or face as directly as that. He carried with him voices—he'd heard them on Everest—that spoke mostly in mutters or dialect. He wasn't sure they were talking to him; it might be that they talked of him among themselves.

It was quiet here. The snow was softer now so that he had to concentrate to keep his footing. The skis over his shoulder made him clumsy. He felt lonely and he fended the feeling off with pictures, as he often did. He conjured up Whillans standing there at the top of Annapurna looking grim, still half-disappointed at the ways things turned out, still angry about it. Dougal saw almost nothing of Don these days. The older man—he was forty-five—seemed finished with serious climbing; he'd been to Alaska the previous year and he'd had his hands full getting up the tourist route on McKinley. And now he was back to plumbing. He traveled around in his van—outfitted for sleeping—to do emergency jobs between visits to friends who would give him a free bed and maybe rope up for a climb. Audrey didn't seem to mind. She was probably happiest when her man was on the road. Don was a spent force—but Dougal sometimes missed him. He missed them all: John and Ian, Tony and Mick.

John Harlin had been dead more than a decade now. He'd left his school to Dougal, which had turned out all right. Dougal had to rummage to find the American but then Harlin came into focus, confused but near stupid in his determination—his version of courage. The Eiger Direct—the Harlin Route—had killed John. It had made Dougal famous. They'd all died for Dougal; they'd died getting him up the Eiger and Annapurna and Everest. It was ridiculous. He was something like Christ in reverse.

He stopped thinking. He reached the top of the slope. He wanted to ski; the walking had excited and calmed him, had put him back in his body as if that was where he belonged. He knew the view from this place. There was no need to linger. He put on his skis and for a moment he felt tired. He closed his eyes and made an effort. He didn't know what he wanted, but he resolved to wish for it with all of his power; to conjure his strength, which he believed lay in his desire. He imagined himself spending everything he had in pursuit of some wish or need and failing. This failure seemed a vision of purity. This failure, this empty outcome, this purity was itself what he desired. His strength was of no use to him—it came between him and what he loved.

He pushed off and turned quickly once, and again; he was skiing well and his mind receded. This was bliss; it was passing too quickly. He heard something and the slope moved under him and he fell; he was carrying an urn, and it flew from his hands and shattered soundlessly, scattered black ash across snow. He rose in a fluid, spectacular cartwheel and subsided again; he was conscious of carrying his heart in his body. The earth became a moving flood and entered him; he woke and struggled and black fear rose—it seemed composed of everything he knew. The sun receded and vanished and something clanged; he felt a terrible pain. The flood of earth had turned to pitch or cinder but someone had left a door just barely ajar and not for the first time in his life he was lost entirely in a wish to thank someone. He reached for the door but something caught and his head turned as if to greet or beckon a pursuer.

THE SEARCHERS FOUND Dougal's body the next day. The slide had broken his leg and buried him under three feet of snow. He had worn a scarf. A doctor at the scene told someone that the scarf had strangled the skier.

Wendy Bonington heard the news on the radio in England. Her first thought was that Chris might have been with him; she knew the two of them were planning to ski together that week. She made calls and reached Chris at a bar in Chamonix and told him. The news was like taking a blow to the face; he felt the blood rise in his body and his mind went dark at his inability to retaliate. Instead he would have to bear the fact that he could do nothing for Dougal now.

They had been friends and collaborators; Dougal was part of his history. Chris had helped to invent Dougal—they had helped to invent one other. He wondered dimly in the days that followed whether he shared some blame for the fact that Dougal had never entirely grown up; had not managed to finish his life before ending it. It might feel like a kind of disgrace to die in that condition, a Catholic dying unconfessed. Chris felt a rising horror at the ease with which death was overtaking the members of his dwindling band and at his own inability to protect them.

They buried Dougal in Leysin, at the cemetery where John Harlin's family and friends had buried him eleven years before. Doug Scott and Big Ely Moriarity carried the coffin from the road up a path cleared in the snow; they were the two strongest men but it was still tricky; the path was icy and the grave stood up on the tier of graves just below the highest ground. Annie Haston and Ariane were both there. Mick Burke's widow, Beth Bevan, came from London. Beth was glad to see Annie, and glad for the ceremony of Dougal's burial; she told herself that she was laying Mick to rest, as well.

She remembered coming to Leysin with Annie for the first time, two nurses on holiday, the two of them walking into the Vagabond that night and right away meeting Dougal and Mick, those two boys as if waiting for them, swimming up out of nowhere and into the young women's lives. And now it seemed the boys had swum back off into the blue. They were at any rate both absent again, so much so that at certain odd moments it was possible to imagine that first encounter had never occurred.

CHRIS WOULD NEED another partner for the Ogre. His old friend and neighbor Nick Estcourt agreed to come, and took on the task of organizing the food. Tut Braithwaite assembled the expedition's gear. Clive Rowland drove all of it out to Islamabad. He was waiting to greet the rest of the team at the airport on May 27.

Chris was determined to sit back and let the others run things. Doug and Clive and Mo had all climbed in Pakistan before. Chris had not. They didn't ask his views on much and they didn't seem to like it when he spoke up. Clive seemed especially prickly. Some exchanges were awkward, unpleasant. Chris didn't much mind. He liked the freedom. He could play with the idea that he was just a climber again. It had been a long time since he'd been in the Himalaya without the responsibility to run things.

The expedition hired porters in Skardu, and crossed the Indus in a boat. The porters broke into song during the crossing. The party walked three days to the village of Askole, near the start of the Biafo Glacier; then another four days to Base Camp. Here they came upon another small party of British climbers. The party hoped to climb a nearby peak—Latok I—but had been stalled for a week by storms that dumped huge quantities of snow on their mountain.

Doug still planned to follow the line he'd shown Chris—straight up a huge rock buttress to a snowfield within striking distance of the Ogre's summit. He would rope up with his friend Tut. Chris and Nick and Mo and Clive had their eye on the mountain's West Ridge. The ridge led through a jumble of buttresses and snow gullies to the peak's West Summit; once there they could descend to a col and then climb to the higher Main Summit. The West Ridge had turned back a Japanese team the year before but it seemed to offer the best chance at getting up the peak.

The climbers recruited seven of their strongest porters to stay for a few days. The four West Ridge climbers and the porters took four days to lug supplies to an Advance Base Camp at the start of their route's difficulties. Mo and Clive then settled in at Base Camp for a brief rest. They had asked their wives to join them for part of the trip, and expected the women to arrive any day.

Chris and Nick moved up to Advance Base Camp. They began the real climbing the next day, June 15, roping up to cross the glacier. Nick broke trail through heavy snow until a slot in the ice swallowed him up to his armpits. Chris hauled on the rope and Nick dragged himself out and they walked on, picking their way cautiously to the face.

They reached the face and kicked steps up a snow gully. They were keenly aware that the gully would act as a funnel for any avalanche that occurred on the slopes above them. They climbed out of it as soon as they could. Nick moved up steep rock with adequate holds. He built an anchor and fixed a rope. Chris got out his jumars and climbed it. The sun was well up; it was ten o'clock—already too hot to climb further. They retreated to Advance Base Camp.

The women had arrived at Base Camp, cheering up Mo and Clive and stirring vague resentment among the others, who groused that the wives were distracting their husbands from the task at hand. The climbers meanwhile continued to make progress on their respective routes. Tut was Jumaring up a chimney to the first bivouac on the buttress he and Doug had chosen when his rope dislodged a stone the size of a soccer ball. Tut's feet were wedged against the ice in the chimney and the rock brushed his thigh, knocking both feet from their perch; if he'd worn crampons the impact might have taken off his legs. As it was, the stone bruised his leg very badly. He could walk, but he would be out of action for at least a few days.

Chris and Nick established Camp One on June 20. The camp was partway up a face that led to a dip in the West Ridge—this dip was the West Col. The two of them had altered their plans slightly. They would establish Camp Two at the col, traverse right to the Southwest Ridge, and make their way up mixed ground to the col between the Ogre's West Summit and its Main Summit.

Mo and Clive still intended to climb from the West Col directly up the West Ridge, which meant crossing the West Summit on their way to the Main Summit. They took a turn out front on June 21, fixing ropes to just beneath the West Col, where they meant to part with Chris and Nick. They descended to Camp One, where all four men spent the night. The two pairs would move back up to Camp Two beneath the col in the morning, and then launch their separate attempts on the summit.

Chris and Nick had trouble sleeping. Nick suffered the most. He had an increasingly painful cough. He complained bitterly of Bonington's snoring, which was as usual very loud. Morning came at last, but Mo and Clive showed no signs of rousing themselves. They said something about waiting for Doug, who might wish to join them if Tut's injury kept him from climbing.

Chris and Nick were off by 5:30. They muscled their way up 1,600 feet of fixed rope and then climbed snow to arrive at the West Col, an airy shelf heavily corniced on both sides. They made camp and brewed tea. The sky clouded up and then cleared again at evening.

They were alone with the prospect of the summit push ahead. They had a week's supply of food to see them up and then back down 3,500 feet of hard climbing on new ground. The past bound them together, but each man was sustained and defined by secret narratives, endlessly revisited and revised. Nick had his resentment and his standards of behavior and his wits. Chris had his ideals and his mounting losses and achievements. Here the two friends were necessary to one another in the most practical ways: to hold a rope, to brew tea. They allowed each other liberties. Nick today was somewhat cranky, but Chris was tolerant and subdued. He felt that his youth had at last escaped him; he sometimes feared that he would replace it with something heavy and pointless.

They set out early—five o'clock—on the morning of June 23. They climbed past crevasses and up snow that lay precariously on a slope of hard ice. They came upon a fixed rope left behind by the Japanese expedition. They followed the rope to the snow shelf that would lead them across to the Southwest Ridge. The sky at moments was blue enough to seem to stain the snow and the rock. The two climbers felt themselves figures in these pools of color; boundaries gave way and the climbers' connection to each other and to the world waved and shimmered in the high mountain light.

Chris and Nick dropped their loads at the top of the Japanese rope and returned to their camp at the West Col. They reached their tent in the late morning. They rested and tinkered with their packing. They would make another carry, this one all the way across the snow shelf to the Southwest Ridge. They hoped to find a spot for one last camp that could serve as a launch point for their summit attempt.

Chris the next morning led back across the fixed ropes and continued across to the end of the snow shelf. Nick followed and the two climbers peered around a corner at granite slabs that ended in snowfields on the South Face. A gap of sky between the Ogre and a nearby peak framed a tiny triangle of black in the distance.

Chris recognized K2. He meant to lead a small expedition there next year. Nick was planning to go with him. It was unsettling to see the mountain now. Chris turned away from it; the sight of that black pyramid undermined this moment.

They dumped their supplies and once more returned to the West Col. Chris and Nick took inventory of their supplies and found they had only enough fuel to melt water for three days. They considered descending to pick up more gas cylinders for their summit attempt, but quickly rejected the idea. Some spell had settled upon them. They were drawn on by a dubious but entrancing promise. They understood the falseness of it but the promise fed a half-skittish calm and they were attached to this calm. They lived at moments inside a brittle shell of quiet. They had woven the shell from the mountain itself—from bits of sand and fossil. Each man's experience of the mountain was solitary, but they relied upon each other. One or the other would experience a flicker of doubt—and his partner's presence would help to quell it.

They bickered in the morning over whether or not to bring the tent for their high camp. Chris said they could dig snow holes. Nick worried the snow might be too shallow. The altitude had worn on them. Neither man picked the tent up as they left the West Col.

They reached their high point quickly and set out to fix ropes across rock to the snow on the South Face. Nick led a pitch on mixed ground. Chris followed and then led higher. The climbing was very delicate. He scraped snow off rock and found dubious piton placements. At his back were mountains upon mountains; he half-turned and they seemed to rear up as if meaning to fill the sky itself. The view was a vast curtain or tapestry, seeming to assert that there was no other world but this one. The notion somehow glued him to the rock so that he felt as if gravity were suspended or reversed on his behalf.

He climbed with great care for more than an hour. He reached snow. The snow was too shallow for a picket but the ice beneath it would take a screw. They were now at the start of the snowfield that led to a rock band at the top of the South Face. The snow looked dangerous: steep and unstable.

They descended to a snow shelf and dug a cave. They were high now—6,650 meters, more than 21,800 feet. They had been above Advance Base Camp for a week, most of the time on steep ground. Chris woke Nick early the next morning. Nick wouldn't get up. He wanted to take a rest day. Chris argued the point. They'd use up more of their dwindling supply of cooking gas and lose their window of good weather. Nick agreed to make an effort. The two of them pulled on boots and started up the route. Nick moved so slowly that Chris gave in. They'd take a rest day.

They spent it sleeping and muttering at each other. Chris couldn't shake his worry that they'd missed their chance for the summit. Nick felt better the next morning but Chris poked his head out of the tent and what he saw confirmed his fears. A huge bank of dark cloud loomed to the west. He tore into Nick—they should have snatched the summit while they could—but then he quickly apologized. There was no time or strength for childishness. They needed to climb the route today or retreat; there was only one gas cylinder left.

They gathered themselves and their gear and climbed the fixed ropes to the snow slope on the South Face. A wind had come up and it grew worse. They suffered from the cold for the first time. The snow was too soft and shallow to carry their weight. The ice beneath the snow was very hard; their crampon points barely penetrated it. They placed a single ice piton at the base of each pitch. The leader ran out full rope-lengths. A fall would rip them both from the mountain. They would travel a tremendous distance. This struck Nick as an astonishing prospect; he thought of astronauts, space walkers.

They had been climbing most of the day when they reached the rock band at the top of the South Face. The sky was entirely overcast. Chris wanted to continue. He thought they could reach the summit today.

Nick was angry; he had begun to believe that his friend's ambition would get them killed this time. He wanted to go back but instead he set out to lead a truly frightening pitch, a traverse across a span of fragile ice that seemed likely to collapse under his weight.

Chris watched him disappear around a corner. Nick would kill them both if he fell now. Chris looked down. The vast space at his feet felt like a body of water. The notion was comforting. Nick's voice when it came floated down through the gathering murk. He'd found a spot that would take an ice screw. Chris climbed up to him and took the lead to run out two easy rope lengths.

It was nearly dark. The climbers stopped to dig a cave in the snow. The cave was too shallow for them to lie down. They had to sit up, their backs against rock. Nick didn't sleep. He sat miserable and shivering through the dark hours, imagining what it might be like to die of the cold.

The day's first light illuminated another overcast sky. Nick once again pleaded with Chris to descend. Chris wanted to wait; eventually, patches of blue emerged from cloud. They set out for the col at the top of the face. They were at last approaching the tower that led to the Main Summit, but the tower presented a bleak prospect. Chris had hoped to find some gully or other feature that would offer a quick route to the top. There was nothing of the kind: only hard climbing on steep rock. They were short of pitons as well as food and fuel.

Chris thought the West Summit, now off to their left, looked like a more reasonable goal. Nick agreed and the two climbers veered left toward the col between the two summits. The sky cleared as they reached it, and Chris once more changed his mind. He proposed to Nick that they should try for the Main Summit after all.

Nick was by now convinced that Chris had gone mad with ambition; that he had lost track of what could happen to them. Nick's voice shook with anger as he pointed out that regardless of the weather their supplies of food and fuel were dangerously short. Chris gave in quickly. Nick was right; Chris had in fact counted on his friend's good sense to restrain his own impulse. The two climbers dug a snow hole in the slope just below the col, out of the wind. They were comfortable, and they began to relax. The hard climbing lay beneath them.

They woke to good weather and moved quickly up easy snow. Chris was feeling strong. He moved ahead and onto steeper ground and up and onto the West Summit. Nick arrived soon after. They stared down at the Biafo Glacier—a furrowed gray-brown ribbon—and across at innumerable peaks. They looked back across the col to the Main Summit block. It didn't look much higher than the spot they occupied, but it obscured their view to the east.

It took Chris and Nick two days to descend their route. They wondered about the others—where had they been all this time? Chris worked himself up; as he came down the West Ridge with Nick he was close to tears thinking there might have been an accident.

They found Doug and the other climbers at Camp One. There was news of the Latok I expedition; one of the climbers—a man named Don Morrison—had fallen into a crevasse and been killed.

Chris had known Morrison slightly. He was too weary to absorb the news.

Meanwhile, the Ogre's main summit remained unclimbed. Doug and the others had been busy moving supplies up to the West Col and onto the West Ridge. They still planned to climb over the West Summit and down across and up to the Main Summit.

Chris despite his weariness was horrified at the thought that the others might reach the Main Summit without him. He argued that they should return to Base Camp for more food and fuel. It wasn't a bad idea—and it might give Chris a chance to recover enough strength to join this new summit attempt. Chris had his way. The six climbers descended to Base Camp that afternoon.

Nick was unhappy with the new arrangement. He'd reached the West Summit, and that was sufficient. He longed to go home; he didn't want the option to climb again. Chris felt surprisingly fit, and the idea of another chance at the mountain's Main Summit filled him with satisfaction. He was one of the boys for a change. He'd begun to lose track of his role as a celebrity, a middle-aged Commander of the British Empire. And the mountain didn't scare him much anymore. He'd been on it and most of the way up it, and that made an enormous difference. The Ogre was evolving from an imagined mountain to a real one.

Chris lay in his tent at Base Camp and flirted with images from his days on the mountain, moments of climbing that transcended any notion of doubt. He drifted off to sleep and into a dream of being up there again.

17

D OUG, MO AND Clive spent two days at Base Camp
    before heading back up the mountain. Chris and the others
lingered a third day. Tut was still limping from his accident, and
Nick had a horrible sore throat. The two ailing climbers talked
that afternoon and decided they weren't fit to climb.

Chris set off alone early on the morning of July 9. He was
still tired but he couldn't bear the thought that the others might
reach the Main Summit without him. He had an anxious time
crossing the snowfields that led to the first set of fixed ropes. Don
Morrison's death only days before on Latok I was a reminder of
the dangers of traveling alone on a glacier.

Chris reached the fixed ropes safely. The surface snow had
melted from the wall, leaving ice that made it more difficult to
work his way up the ropes. It took ten hours to reach the camp at
the West Col. There was a single tent waiting; the other climbers
had gone ahead to camp at the base of the West Ridge.

Chris melted snow for tea and went to sleep without eating. He
rose in the morning and followed a snow gully that led toward
the West Ridge. He could look up and see figures at work on the
ridge itself. The figures were climbing a stretch of sunlit rock.
He wished for bad weather. He needed time to rest, to gather the
strength he would need to keep up with the others.

He reached the camp at the base of the ridge. Doug and Mo

and Clive returned that afternoon, having made good progress. The friendliness of their welcome surprised Chris. He slept under the stars that night—there was only one tent—and his happiness returned to him. He hadn't expected this second chance—at the Ogre, at being a certain kind of climber.

Mo and Clive went back up in the morning to fix rope on the ridge. Doug and Chris dropped down to retrieve more gear from the West Col. The preparations were in place for a summit attempt, but Chris was still very tired. The sky filled with clouds that evening. Chris was secretly delighted when the others decided to put off the summit for another day.

They left camp on July 11. Their heavy packs made them slow and awkward on the fixed ropes up the ridge. Chris climbed with Doug, who took the lead for a long traverse that avoided a difficult section of the ridge. Chris followed, moving awkwardly under the weight of his pack. He slipped at a difficult spot and swung out under a piton, smacking an elbow against rock. The pain left him weak and nervous. He climbed up to Doug and then led through snow that took them back up to the ridge crest. Doug followed, and they dropped a rope down to Mo and Clive.

It was late. They had brought only a single small tent. Doug and Clive shared it. Chris and Mo dug a small snow hole. The party passed a reasonably comfortable night, and woke to good weather. Mo and Clive led up the ridge. Chris could sense Doug's impatience; the big man's drive was intimidating as well as impressive. The ground was dangerous at first—a thin layer of snow on steep ice—but after a time the climbers found deeper snow and kicked good steps in it.

Doug passed the others and led Chris up the ridge and over the West Summit with barely a pause. The two of them reached the snow hole that Chris and Nick had dug on the other side, just off the col between the West Summit and the Main Summit tower.

Mo and Clive arrived just behind them. The four climbers took turns digging to expand the cave, which lay on a bed of steep ice. Chris was convinced that the snow was safely consolidated. The others worried that it would simply slide off the mountain, but it was too late to start another cave. They took another look at the sky—still clear—and settled in for the night, hoping the weather would hold.

Chris and Doug were up early and gone by five o'clock, leaving the others to follow later. The two of them moved together on snow for a time. The slope grew steeper and they moved one at a time, belaying each other. Doug led the first pitch of rock and then the next. He anchored the rope at the top of the second pitch so that Chris could climb it with his jumars, and went ahead to look for the best way to the summit.

Chris finished the pitch and followed his partner's tracks. He found Doug preparing to lead yet another pitch. Chris objected—he wanted a turn out front—but Doug told him flatly that this one was too hard for him. It was late; they had to move fast if they were going to reach the summit and descend to the cave before dark.

Doug set off, but a tangle in the rope stopped him. He came down while Chris sorted it out. Doug led the pitch and Chris followed—but when he tried to retrieve the rope it jammed. It took Chris half an hour to descend and clear a knot from a crack; by now, he was cursing to himself. He could have led the pitch; it wasn't that hard; he hadn't come all this way to follow Doug up the mountain.

The next pitch *did* look difficult, though, and Chris left it to Doug. Doug struggled up a thin crack until it petered out. Chris lowered him from his last piece of gear and Doug made several attempts to pendulum across to another crack. He kept missing his hold at the far end of the pendulum, and each time he came scraping and sliding back across the rock to hang panting on the rope. It was stupendously difficult work at this altitude but he learned something each time he failed, and at last he managed to jam fingers into the crack at the top of his swing. That stopped him from swinging back and he worked his way up the crack to easier ground and a foothold that allowed him a rest. He finished the pitch easily after that.

Chris got his jumars out and followed the rope, retrieving Doug's gear as he climbed. The sun had slipped across the sky. He looked back for Mo and Clive and saw that they had retreated to the snow cave. There might be time for Chris and Doug to make the top before dark, but it would be close.

Chris wanted to lead a pitch. He set off up rock and came to an overhang. He put in a piton and brought up Doug, who stood on his partner's shoulders to surmount the overhang and then brought Chris up on a tight rope. Chris finished the pitch and lay gasping for breath in the snow at the start of a gully. He would have liked to lead through—he still had his crampons on—but Doug was up and away. Chris could only grab the rope and put him on belay and sit hunched and shivering while Doug once more disappeared into the jumble of rock and ice overhead. Chris thought of other climbers: Whillans barging up the Bonatti Pillar; Dougal Haston at the top of the Harlin route on the Eiger. They had been strong, too. They had been like this one. He felt a stab of pain near his ribs. His chest ached from the wheezing he had done these last weeks.

Chris lurched to his feet. He looked at his hands and the rope that moved in them. His mind wandered; he forgot where he was. He had the momentary notion that nothing was lost after all—even as he felt that he had missed something; it had gotten past him.

Doug shouted down and Chris set off. He kicked steps in the

snow until he came to a rock the size of a shed. The sky bled a science fiction purple; looking up was like being inside of a bruise. Doug was crouched on top of the rock. He had taken pictures; he was ready to go down.

Doug set up the first rappel and disappeared. Chris waited for his turn on the rope. He looked around, hoping to remember something of this. He made out K2 once again, that black pyramid. He picked out other mountains—massive Nanga Parbat and the Latok group, black teeth in the gathering night. He was alone for the moment and glad of it. He was glad he'd come back up, and glad that now there was nothing but the descent.

He heard a scream and then silence. It occurred to him—he felt a strange calm—Doug must have rappelled off the ends of the rope in the dark. Chris imagined a huge wing—its shadow rushed toward and past him, swallowing the night.

DOUG WAS IN a hurry. He had been in a hurry for days now and it had brought him to this. Night was upon them. They had no shelter and no sleeping bags, no warm clothes. There wasn't snow on the summit to dig a cave. Chris could go on about the view if he liked, but it was time to leave. He set off down the rope, and spotted some pitons Chris had placed. Doug walked sideways, using the tension from the rope to get far enough across to reach the pegs. It would save time if he could rappel from them; otherwise, he'd have to set up another rappel anchor.

The pegs were further away than he'd thought. He continued to traverse and the tug of the rope grew stronger; if he slipped, he'd swing a hundred feet or more—and as he reached the pitons his boot touched ice and he skated and fell. He swung on the end of the rope, describing an accelerating arc through the dusk. The swing itself was painless, exhilarating. He stuck his legs out as he gathered momentum and they took the impact when he at last collided with a corner. He had shut his eyes but they opened when he opened his mouth to scream.

CHRIS HAVING HEARD the scream stood for a moment and then bent to pick up the rope but couldn't—there was still a body on the end of it. Even then he was surprised to hear Doug's voice again: *I've broken my leg.*

His eyes filled. He shouted down to Doug to get his weight off the rope—it's impossible to descend a weighted rope. Doug had in fact broken both legs but he was able to haul himself onto a ledge, grunting in pain and noting with grim satisfaction that his arms and spine still functioned.

Chris as he backed from the summit into the night was thinking that Doug might yet die. There was no way to carry him down the West Ridge. He reached Doug—a figure huddled in shadow—and fumbled in the dark to rig another rappel. Another rope length would take them to a snow-covered ledge where they could try to dig a cave. Doug tried to stand. Chris heard bone scrape. Doug screamed again and fell to his knees; he paused there as if considering his next move and fell forward onto his hands. He would crawl.

He crossed the ledge to join Chris at the new rappel anchor. Chris went first this time. Doug followed, careful to keep his back to the rock as he slid down the ropes, his worse-than-useless legs dangling in space. The pain kept a sufficient distance if he didn't move the legs.

They spent the night in a ditch dug in the snow. Chris carefully took Doug's boots off for him and removed his own. The two climbers took turns rubbing one another's feet, much as Doug and Dougal had done for each other on Everest two years before. They didn't talk much. Doug was occupied with his pain and Chris was thinking about the morning. The hours passed.

The climbers were moving again before the sun hit the Ogre's western slopes.

Chris set up more rappels that took them off the summit block and down onto the col that led back across to the West Summit. Mo had come out to meet them. Doug looked up at Mo and asked if he and Clive would be going for the summit today. Mo looked down at him—*fucking lunatic*—and shook his head. He took custody of Doug while Chris carried on to the four-man cave on the col.

Doug started crawling; he found he could manage the pain if he concentrated on this task. Mo couldn't do much to help. It took the two of them another two hours to reach the cave.

The four climbers were 9,000 feet above Base Camp. They were short of food; their remaining supplies consisted of a single freeze-dried meal and some soup and tea bags. The run of perfect weather that had seen Doug and Chris to the summit was drawing to a close. These circumstances would have posed serious problems for four healthy climbers. As it was, Doug would have to crawl up and over the West Summit and then down the West Ridge to their camp at the West Col.

The climbers made plans. They would rest this afternoon and tonight and then start their descent. They played cards all afternoon; by evening it had begun to snow heavily. They ate the last of their food, and spent a restless night coping with spindrift that tried to force its way into the cave.

They woke to a howling snowstorm. Clive set out to break trail to the West Summit, forcing his way through thigh-deep snow for more than an hour. He returned with half-frozen hands; he had managed to cover only 150 feet. Mo tried later and traveled 30 feet before he retreated; by then his eyelids were frozen to his eyes and he had lost feeling in his hands. The climbers stayed put for another day, playing cards. There was no cooking to do since there was no food. There was one gas cylinder for melting snow. There would be nothing to drink when that was gone.

NICK ESTCOURT HAD watched two figures—Chris and Doug—leave the summit on July 13. He'd expected the four climbers down the next day; they had not come. The porters had arrived to pick up the expedition's gear. Nick had loaded most of them up and sent them down toward Askole. Tut had gone with them. Nick had settled in to wait for Chris and the others, and to fend off his growing belief that they were all dead.

He couldn't go up to look for them; he'd sent his climbing gear down with Tut. The days were immensely long. He remembered the deaths of Ian on Annapurna and Tony and Mick on Everest. This new disaster seemed to weave itself into those as he gazed up at the storm that hung over the peak. It was like watching a spider come upon an abandoned web. The spider spun its thread so as to crowd and then encompass the old nest. The juxtaposition of the old musty web and the new living silk struck Nick as obscene.

The notion of Chris dead confused him. Nick found that he was furious at Chris—for bringing him here and for leaving him here like this—and yet it was some kind of permission.

There had been a moment when the two of them waited with the others for Mick to come down from Everest. Nick had imagined Chris at another camp looking up at a mountain like this one and waiting for Nick but knowing him dead as they had all known Mick to be dead.

Nick had assumed that Chris would be the one to suffer in this way. Chris was the one who could bear it. He had shouldered this burden for Nick and the others and as if in return they had carried out their assigned tasks in support of his ambitions as well as their own, not understanding exactly but knowing that

Chris was their protector—or that he would at least find a way to manage things if they didn't come down.

And now Chris had abandoned that work. Nick was furious at this betrayal. Nick had done everything that his own role required. He had been unselfish; he'd worked and taken ridiculous chances and let Chris choose others for the summits—Don and Dougal on Annapurna; Doug and Dougal and Mick and even young Peter Boardman on Everest. Nick had done this because it had fallen to him but also because it made sense, it suited him. Chris had known this about him and had used it. That was fine—but this was not. Nick hadn't volunteered in any way for this.

Grief lapped at his anger. He stood up to his thighs in it, scanning the empty sky, and on the fifth night as he lay in his tent he felt his grief and his helplessness pull him down into silence, dreams of light. He heard voices, someone calling his name—and he awoke to a bewildering relief. He was going to live to old age, finish raising his children; he wouldn't do this kind of thing again; it wasn't necessary now.

He rose early and gathered the remaining porters and set about organizing his departure from the mountain. The next morning, July 20, he wrote a note—a gesture—and left it under a rock. He was in a hurry. He left Base Camp as if pursued by a former and suddenly alien life.

THEY HAD BEEN two nights in the ice cave. It was still snowing this morning but they couldn't stay longer. They'd soon be too weak to move at all. Clive left first, breaking trail through the heavy drifts, trailing a rope behind him. Doug clipped to the rope and hauled himself up the easy slopes toward the West Summit, drawing on the enormous strength of his upper body. Mo followed Doug. Chris waited until it was clear that they were not going to turn back and then he set out behind them. The last stretch of snow up to the West Summit was too steep for Doug to manage alone. Mo climbed past him and joined Clive to haul on the rope while Chris got beneath Doug and pushed.

They reached the West Summit four hours after leaving their snow cave. They immediately began the long descent of the West Ridge. They established a series of rappels but they couldn't risk letting the last man use them. They'd have to pull the ropes from below to retrieve them, and a rope could easily jam on this low-angle ground. Chris stayed behind each time to take apart the anchor. Then he down-climbed the pitch, carrying the rope. He picked his way carefully down through mixed ground or he plunge-stepped in snow, keeping his axe ready to attempt a self-arrest if he lost his footing.

The storm had abated. They could see 50 yards or so. They were aiming for the snow cave they had dug five nights before, on their way up the West Ridge. The new snow made the ground feasible for Doug. He could not have crossed it otherwise. Mo took the lead, making the route and setting up rappels. Clive walked beside Doug and tried to help him past the most difficult spots. The four climbers' personalities faded; they became more alike. There was nothing to be gained by looking ahead. Their discomfort and the difficulty of the work crowded out wishes, any thought of a future free of this burden of effort.

They reached the snow cave. They had dug the cave for two climbers. Mo got on his knees and began to burrow to make room for four. He quit after a while. The climbers piled in and melted snow and shared the remaining tea bag. The snow hole was still too small. Doug had urged them to make it bigger, but they were too tired. The snow made its way into the cave and then melted. The climbers woke in the night to find their sleeping bags and clothes were wet.

The storm continued the next day but again they had to move.

It was now July 17. Four days had passed since Doug's accident. The climbers had been without food for two days. They were now just above the most difficult section of the descent, a thousand foot pillar of rock near the bottom of the West Ridge. That would bring them to the two small tents at the foot of the ridge, above the West Col.

Their first task this morning was to descend a narrow subsidiary ridge to the top of the pillar. The ridge wasn't steep enough here to rappel. Doug tied in and set off crawling while Clive held his rope.

Doug reached the top of the pillar. The others followed and Mo set up a rappel. The climbers hoped it would take them to the top of the ropes they'd fixed to safeguard their retreat down the steepest section. The snow continued to blow past their faces, turning the world an unearthly gray-blue, stinging cheeks and noses. They wore goggles but they couldn't see much in the half-light.

Mo went first. Doug followed. He slid down the ropes quickly and straight off the ends; he couldn't see anything in this shadow-world. He skated 15 feet down a gully, his mouth open to scream into the wind. The ground wasn't vertical here but he gathered speed quickly. He had a glimpse of what was coming and turned his head from it and saw the first of the fixed ropes; his body hit something that hurt but it slowed him and he grabbed at the rope and held it in both of his clumsy mittened hands. He hung there for a moment, more stricken than relieved. He would have fallen perhaps 4,000 feet but here he was. He could not do the emotional or intellectual work to try to acknowledge or respond to the oddness of this. The storm and his hunger and the pain in his legs were enough to occupy him.

Clive followed Doug down and tied off one end of the doubled rope, leaving the shorter end free. Chris, hunched in the wind

150 feet above Doug and the others, knew nothing of Doug's new accident. He clipped into the ropes and followed the others into the storm. It occurred to him that they might all survive this. Thinking it made him aware of how physically miserable he was, everything dank and heavy as he slid down the ropes, careful to manage his speed. He caught a glimpse of Clive, a shape looming up like some sea creature in the murk of the storm. Chris thought of a walrus. He had the image in mind as he shot off the unanchored end of the rope.

He felt naked falling head first into nothing. There was no thought, only this sense of being stripped. This gave way to aversion—he wanted it stopped—and a sense of the depth of his failure flooded his body. He felt something hammer at his chest—it was like being hit by an axe handle—and he stopped falling. He hung and swayed and tried to collect himself. He had come to the tied-off end of the rope; Clive's anchor had stopped him.

He had fallen 25 feet and he felt broken. He had done something to his ribs. He didn't know what it was or what had happened. He found he could stand and move. The others reached him and the four climbers continued their descent.

The fixed ropes ended at a gap—a bergschrund—where a snowfield had melted away from the rock. Doug couldn't jump down and across to the snow. Chris had a short piece of rope and the climbers used it to lower Doug. The storm grew worse. The tents above the West Col were buried in three feet of dry snow. The climbers dug out their shelters. They found teabags and a pound of sugar in one of them. Chris examined himself in the tent he shared with Mo. He found a dent on the right side of his chest and his wrist seemed broken.

The storm continued through the afternoon. It had been snowing for five days. Chris had coughing fits that tore at his chest and throat and brought up a bloody froth that frightened him. He began to worry that he had high altitude pulmonary edema—HAPE—which would flood his lungs and kill him before they could get lower.

He paid a panicky visit to Doug and Clive in the other tent. They listened to his breathing and someone said it didn't sound like HAPE. There was nothing to do about it, anyway. The whiteout would make it impossible to find their way across the plateau to the fixed ropes. They needed those ropes to get down the final wall to the glacier. Chris went back to his tent and lay fretting, scanning himself for further symptoms that might confirm his fears.

Morning brought clear skies. The climbers descended easy rappels and crossed flat snow to Camp Two at the West Col, where they hoped to find food. Chris was aghast to discover that he was moving even more slowly than Doug. Mo and Doug got to Camp Two first. They found a trash bag that held some rice mixed with cigarette ash. There were also throat lozenges and a single candy bar.

The four climbers shared out the scraps and the candy and left the West Col. They descended a mile and a half of low-angle snow to the top of the route's last steep section. They set up their tents here. They were still some 2,000 feet above Advance Base Camp and more than 5,000 feet above Base Camp.

Chris and Mo left first in the morning. The party seemed to be picking up a ragged momentum. Each climber was like someone pushed while descending a hill, slightly out of control, careening and staggering past obstacles. Chris couldn't use his left hand. This handicap made the fixed ropes difficult. He turned occasionally to stare down at the glacier. He hoped to see Nick or Tut.

The four climbers reached the bottom of the fixed ropes. There was still a short snow slope to descend. Chris punched his crampons into the slope, but the jarring gave his chest such pain that he gave up and sat down in the snow to glissade. He had his axe as a brake but only the one good hand. He lost control almost at once, first angry and then frightened as he picked up speed, cursing and clutching at his ribs until he came at last to a sudden but surprisingly gentle halt in a snow bank.

He was back on the glacier. He stood and gathered himself, taking shallow breaths to stay clear of the pain in his chest. He tied in with Mo, who led across through deep snow and onto the glacial moraine—a wilderness of sand and jumbled rock—where the pair could unrope.

Mo went ahead. Chris followed him in a haze of discomfort and worry. He felt unaccountably anxious now that he knew he would live. He felt as if all of this were somehow his fault. He had dreamed himself into a story that someone was telling about him. He couldn't defend himself. He didn't know what he'd done wrong or how things had come to this, picking his wretched way over this difficult ground. The sun felt like a punishment. Each irregularity in the ground that met his boots was torture to his feet—to his entire frame and everything it carried or contained. He felt unbearably fragile. He felt a child's fear that everyone would be angry at him—that this time he'd not be forgiven.

MO WAS THE first to reach Base Camp. He found Nick's note and simply continued walking. He walked for two more days. That was how long it took him to cover the thirty-five miles to Askole. He staggered into the village and up a slope and Nick saw him and came running down the hill.

Mo had never seen such happiness as this: Nick running through the streets of that filthy village, looking not relieved but overjoyed. It was the first time Mo really saw him, really took him in. Mo watched Nick during the week that followed, during the journey to Islamabad and after. He was moved by how Nick took charge and fussed—how he organized a rescue for Doug, how he worried when problems with the helicopter stranded Chris in Askole for a week. Chris had of course spent the week indulging in paranoid fantasies—the others had left; they weren't coming back; they'd gone home without him—but Mo saw that Nick wasn't right, wasn't himself, until a new helicopter dropped Chris on the grounds of the British Embassy in Islamabad and they were all together, everyone alive, everything the way it had been.

18

A ND SO K2 was still on. Chris's injuries from the Ogre slowed his preparations during the fall of 1977 and into the winter. His ribs ached and his hand remained stiff and sore. He was seriously underweight. He couldn't walk half a mile without resting. He developed bone infections that winter, and had surgery on his ribs twice. It was nearly spring before he could resume his customary jogs in the rolling hills around his Lake District home, the cottage Wendy had renovated while he was away on the first Everest trip almost six years before. He gradually regained his strength, but as he ran he sometimes asked himself why he would leave this beautiful place for the rigors of yet another high-altitude expedition.

The world's second-highest peak topped out at 8,611 meters (28,251 feet), a mere 800 feet or so lower than Everest. And while more than a dozen expeditions had put men on the summit of Everest, climbers had reached K2's summit only once: the Italians had done it in 1954. That successful expedition had included fifty-two members—Walter Bonatti was one—and 1,500 porters.

Chris had invited four of his companions from the 1975 Everest expedition to accompany him to K2. The four were Doug Scott, Nick Estcourt, Tut Braithwaite and Peter Boardman. Chris had counted on Dougal Haston coming as well, so he needed someone to replace him. Peter recommended his Changabang partner, Joe Tasker.

Chris did not invite Martin Boysen. Martin had made important contributions on Annapurna in 1970 and on Everest in 1975. He was working hard to establish himself as an expedition climber, and this snub was a blow to those plans. More to the point, he had considered himself a friend and loyal supporter of Chris. He broke off his friendship with Bonington—as Don Whillans had done five years before. Martin would return to the Himalayas with Mo Anthoine and others, and evenutally devote himself to his first love, high-standard rock climbing.

Chris had no interest in repeating the original route up K2—the Abruzzi Ridge, named for the Italian nobleman who had pioneered its lower reaches back in 1909. Chris first considered the Northeast Ridge, where a Polish expedition had recently made a strong attempt. The route was mostly on snow. It seemed feasible for a small expedition—but Peter and Doug wanted to try something harder. The climbers settled on the mountain's West Ridge, almost as high and probably steeper than Everest's Southwest Face.

They would climb without oxygen on most of the route. They would fix rope only part of the way up the peak. This would allow them to work with minimum support on the route itself. Bonington's 1975 Everest expedition had employed sixty people above the Western Cwm. Chris intended to field only six climbers and two high-altitude porters on K2's West Ridge.

Chris resumed his accustomed role of team leader and fundraiser. Jim Duff had been with Chris on Everest in 1975 and on Changabang before that. He joined the expedition as team physician. Tony Riley would film the trip.

The smaller team meant there was less to organize, but there was still a great deal to do. Chris had enjoyed life as a foot soldier on the Ogre. He felt the strain of being back in command. It was hard to raise money for a trip to K2. The mountain might be more difficult than Everest—and nearly as high—but it lacked Everest's cachet.

Joe Tasker—new to Chris and his ways—didn't make things easier. Joe had ambitions as a writer. He balked at signing an agreement to put off publishing anything about the K2 trip until after publication of the official expedition account. Joe eventually signed, but only after Chris lost his temper. The experience left Joe skeptical about the merits of mixing commerce with mountaineering. He had now made two major Himalayan climbs, each with a single partner: Dick Renshaw on Dunagiri and Peter Boardman on Changabang. The K2 expedition—so small by Bonington standards—struck Joe as too big. He felt his outsider's status, too. The other climbers had been on Everest together, and four of them were just back from the Ogre. Chris for his part thought Joe, the new boy, was being difficult and a little ungrateful.

Tony Riley departed for Pakistan in April of 1978, shepherding two vans full of expedition gear. Chris and Peter flew out in early May, three days ahead of the rest of the team, to buy food and make other last-minute preparations. The two of them hadn't spent much time together on Everest. They struck up a friendship during this early phase of the expedition. Peter was at once idealistic and practical—in some ways a younger version of Chris, but on the whole more relaxed than Chris had been at that age.

The others arrived several days behind Chris and Peter. The team took a plane to Skardu; it was the same flight four of the climbers had taken on their way to the Ogre. The expedition hired porters in Skardu, and a week's walking brought them to the Baltoro Glacier. They reached the place on a gray, forbidding day. Chris as he took his first steps on the glacier felt that he and his companions had fallen into the hands of a storyteller—one who suspended certain rules, so that at any time the party might come upon a castle or a wizard. Mountains arose on all sides as the climbers walked. Chris had an eerie sense that the climbers came into the mountains' view and not the other way around.

They walked thirty miles on the Baltoro. The porters sang mournful songs around their cook fires in the gray mornings. The climbers knew the names of many of the peaks they passed— spectacular granite spires such as Nameless Tower and Uli Biaho. This knowledge did not make the mountains' shapes less strange or imposing. There was something dimly shocking in the way that the spires received the men's notice and gave nothing back.

The climbers and porters often woke to new snow on the ground. Chris began to wonder if the porters would continue as far as the expedition's Base Camp on the Savoia Glacier. He sent Doug Scott and Joe Tasker ahead with a small group of porters to size up the ground and report back. The other climbers stayed behind to coax the main group of porters higher. Chris and Nick and Peter doled out food and presided over the cooking. They resolved conflicts and responded to porter complaints about gear or the terrain or the weather. There was little common language between the British and the local men. The porters rose from their sleeping mats in the morning like ghosts, and then fell back to the ground to pray. There was an abstract and motiveless quality to their praying and to their complaints.

Doug and Joe had been delayed by their own porter difficulties. The main party caught them at the start of the Savoia Glacier, which led around to the western side of the mountain. Doug and Joe set off up the Savoia to finish their reconnaissance. Nick and Chris paid off most of the Baltis, doling out a total of fifteen thousand pounds in two hours. They kept twenty-five porters to carry supplies across the more difficult ground to Base Camp.

The party established Base Camp three days later, the second day of June. Peter had lagged behind the other climbers that day. He was glad to be on his own in these mountains. He felt his spirits rise at the site of new peaks. He imagined himself an explorer, the first to come here, a privileged visitor to some vast and empty picture gallery.

He was crossing a snowfield at the base of a mountain called Angel Peak when an enormous tower of ice collapsed in the near distance. He heard the collapse and threw down his pack without looking and tried to run in the snow but he fell. He had time to cover his face with his hat and snow swam over him; it got into his clothes and punched at his face.

It stopped. He picked himself up, surprised. He stood for a moment and bent to cough. The coughing turned to wheezing and at last subsided. He straightened to look up past mountains and their shadows to sun and the sky's blue mirror; nothing had changed but everything was new. He set out to finish traversing the snow slope but after the first steps he sat down. It was an hour before he could stand up and walk again. He soon came upon Nick and one of the porters, come to look for him. Nick was very relieved. He had imagined looking for Peter and not finding him and then having to tell the others.

The climbers sat outside their tents at Base Camp that night. The wind was a whisper. K2 was upon them—that huge pyramid of black and white, utterly silent. Nick and Chris had seen it from the Ogre a year ago. It was strange to recall that moment.

Nick had opened a climbing shop and given notice at his job before leaving home for this trip. He meant to combine the shop with freelance computer work after K2. His co-workers had sent him off with an inflatable doll. He'd produced this monstrosity a few nights earlier. The other climbers had found it wildly amusing. They'd all stayed up late and drunk whiskey and laughed until they were weak.

Nick at times thought the climbing was just an excuse to come to these places. Then at times climbing became everything. Kicking steps in snow was real; the rest was a cozy dream—or like that doll a slighting reference to the sacred. He thought of his home in the Manchester suburbs. He'd put on a party there to celebrate the shop opening and the place had been full of climbers; someone had gone headfirst through a window, right into the garden. People were doing this thing with knives; you'd put a knife on the stove and heat up hashish and put a glass over it or something and breathe in the smoke. People were smoking a lot of dope. Some people were doing mushrooms. It was fun but ridiculous. Carolyn wasn't pleased, and really she was right. He was thirty-four, getting too old for it.

He was too old for this as well. He had worried about this trip. His memories of the Ogre haunted him; the experience had raised questions that he did not wish to articulate, let alone try to answer. He had wondered whether he should come to K2 at all; once or twice he had been close to calling Chris and withdrawing from the expedition but he could not; there were too many reasons to come—there was the potential for surprise and discovery. Things weren't good at home. He'd been a difficult husband in some ways. He couldn't help but compare himself to a fellow like Peter Boardman who for all his obvious talent and strength seemed a sensible sort—young but not wild; he wouldn't put his head through a window. Nick liked Peter. They were to go together in the morning up the Savoia to seek an approach to the West Ridge.

THEY DIDN'T FIND it. They reached a saddle on the glacier and peered down into China. The view revealed that the northern aspect of the West Ridge was too steep and iced-up to serve as an approach to their route.

Joe and Doug meanwhile discovered a route that lay to the

south of the ridge. It took them through a small icefall pocked with holes that put Joe in mind of small black mouths. These holes gave entrance to huge, bell-shaped chambers; the thought of those brought to mind catacombs—vaults for the ancient dead. The route after passing through the icefall struck out across a vast snow basin.

Four of the climbers—Doug, Peter, Nick and Chris—set out the next day to find a site for Camp One. They passed through the icefall and struck out up into the snow basin, which was punctuated by a series of rock buttresses. They reached the first buttress late in the morning. Doug wanted to press on to a place on the crest of the West Ridge. Nick was for establishing a camp on the spot. They had words. Doug complained—a bit childishly—that Nick disagreed with all of his ideas. Nick maintained—with a touch of pomposity—that he was simply bringing his critical intelligence to bear on an important decision, as he might do at his workplace. Chris came up with an acceptable compromise: they would continue to a site a bit higher, near another small buttress that might provide protection from avalanche.

Peter and Doug and Joe carried more gear to the site the next morning and established Camp One. Tut remained at Base Camp with chest pains, and Nick stayed to pay off the rest of the porters. The next day the trio out front continued up the basin toward the ridge. They moved through deep snow that collapsed under foot. The sun and the altitude—they were now higher than 6,000 meters—made every step an ordeal.

They were laying out fixed rope from 600-foot reels. Doug broke trail for 1,200 feet before giving way to Peter. The scale of the landscape deceived them. The mountain's individual features proved much larger than they appeared from a distance. The climbers missed their way to a gully, losing two hours.

Chris meanwhile came up from Base Camp. Peter and Doug and Joe found him waiting for them when they descended to Camp One that evening. Chris and Joe climbed together the next morning. Chris was glad to be on the route; he had spent much of these first days on the mountain at Base Camp, working on logistics and writing media reports. He led a gully of ice and emerged from it onto a rock shelf at the edge of another snow basin. He had studied pictures of this basin at home. The angle was easy. He planned to cross it to reach the site he had in mind for Camp Two, at the start of the difficult climbing.

The slope's angle was just low enough to allow snow to accumulate, creating the potential for big avalanches. Doug had told Joe he thought they should bypass this second snow basin and follow a gully to the West Ridge itself. Joe mentioned Doug's idea, but Chris favored the basin—it was quicker, and it seemed safe enough to him. Joe didn't pursue the matter.

The two climbers crossed the snow unroped. It was technically easy, but they both felt the altitude. They were now at around 6,400 meters (21,000 feet) above sea level. They took turns breaking trail to a spot near a rock wall that offered some protection from slides; this was the site for Camp Two. Pete and Doug came up behind them, carrying loads for the new camp. The four climbers rested briefly and then returned to Camp One. Nick was there with a high-altitude Hunza porter named Quamajan. Nick and Quamajan made tea for everyone.

Peter wanted a turn out front the next day, and Doug volunteered to go back up with him. Chris—worried about losing control of the expedition to Doug—proposed that the five climbers draw straws to decide who would climb in the morning. Peter and Joe won. Doug turned churlish. He warned them not to make a route-finding mistake and he announced that he couldn't share a tent with Chris any longer; the snoring was keeping him awake.

Nick said he was used to the noise, and he volunteered to move in with Chris. Doug moved his things into Quamajan's tent.

Peter and Joe moved up to occupy Camp Two the next day. Three men—Chris, Nick and Quamajan—followed with loads. Doug stayed behind to organize Camp One. His anger evaporated amid the quiet mountain landscape. He had tea waiting for the load bearers when they returned that evening.

The stars came out for a time that evening, but gave way to heavy clouds and snow while the climbers slept. The snow continued to fall into the next day. It fell quietly. There was no drama to this storm; it struck Nick that this snow would have been the same if they had not been here to see it. The snow was a tide, drawn to the earth by the earth. The planet's purposes were not secret. The information, the data, was here—it was only that he couldn't read it.

The four climbers at Camp One waited for two days in their tents. They had done this kind of waiting before; it had become a sort of practice for them. Nick and Chris enjoyed the time together. They were old friends. They had never wanted the same things; that circumstance had helped them. They were in debt to each other for various services, but most of their achievements and losses seemed at least partly accidental. They weren't especially proud of what they'd achieved. They sometimes thought they were ashamed of their failures, but their shame was mostly manufactured. It obscured their sorrow and their surprise at their losses.

They loved some of the same things. They loved times like this—a quiet sky, snow on the ground and more falling. Nick one afternoon listened to Chris snore and wondered how long the new snow would remain on this mountain. The snow here seemed a version of eternity—effable, eternally renewed. The snow lay beneath them like a dense but shallow sky. The earth wanted nothing but it tugged at them all. Nick fell asleep.

The third day brought blue sky and a high wind. Peter and Joe roused themselves up at Camp Two and melted snow on their stove and pulled on boots. Their hands went numb in the shadows of morning. They set off to cross a snow slope that led to a gully, fixing rope as they went. For almost the first time on the mountain they were able to take in the scenery and feel themselves to be a part of it. They climbed into a new version of the world, gazed across at peaks and ranges unnamed and unexplored, unknown.

Chris and Nick and Doug meanwhile made a carry, crossing the snow basin to Camp Two. The new snow made their progress difficult. They dropped their loads and descended as quickly as they could manage. They felt the sun's warmth and the changes it made in the snow as they descended to Camp One for the night.

Chris had developed a head cold. He decided to take a rest day. Nick and Doug and Quamajan would make another carry the next morning. Chris woke in time to say good-bye to them. He lay in his sleeping bag when they had gone, feeling the sun's warmth through the tent fabric. He had learned to savor these moments of solitude on big expeditions—they always felt stolen. He heard shouts from lower down. Jim Duff had led some porters up from Base Camp. Chris roused himself and went down to help. He felt his strength returning. He could have gone higher today—he thought that perhaps he should have done so.

He made tea for the porters, and saw them off. Jim had brought the news that Tut Braithwaite was going home. Tut's chest was giving him trouble. He was worried about that—and he missed his girlfriend; they planned to marry upon his return. Chris took the news easily. He found he wasn't angry or let down. Tut's departure would leave them a climber short—the team was already small—but they would manage.

The sky was windless and perfectly clear. Chris and Jim spoke of Tut's departure and what it meant for their hopes of getting up the mountain. The crack and rumble of an avalanche—a huge one—interrupted their talking. They looked up and saw that they weren't in danger. Chris grabbed his camera and started taking pictures but Jim suddenly shouted at him: *For God's sake stop. The lads could be in that.*

DOUG AND NICK had decided to fix rope across the snow basin that led to Camp Two. The rope would help to protect them from any small slides in the fresh snow. Doug tied an end of rope to his waist and set out. He seemed anxious to be off, and Nick let him go first; what did it matter? Doug repaid him, turned to speak: *It looks like we'll be going to the top together, mate.*

Nick smiled at him and settled in to wait. He smoked a cigarette; Quamajan had one as well. They watched Doug cross the slope. The porter got up to follow when Doug was halfway across but Nick stopped him; Nick would go now. He tied himself to the middle of Doug's rope. He didn't bother clipping to the fixed rope.

The angle of the slope was easy; it was really just walking, and so he was free to look up at the route. The mountain struck Nick now as a sort of semifrozen chaos—a slow-motion explosion of mass. He was conscious of how the rock captured and held the snow in bowls and gullies high above them. He knew that things here were much bigger than they seemed. And yet the peak itself was a mere barnacle, a microbe on this massive planet. The sky's immensity disoriented Nick; he felt obscurely that he could at any moment be plucked from the snow by some hidden law of physics—some reverse version of gravity. The sun's warmth made him heavy; it bounced off the snow to bake his face. He was very thirsty. He was looking forward to tea.

He came to the halfway mark. He imagined that he was fording some enormous still body of water. There was no way out or across but to continue wading.

Everything around him moved. He moved with it, a solitary witness. The slope broke into floes that swam faster, colliding and breaking apart. Nick swam with them. He'd lost his footing and he was riding something—he must stay on top and for the moment he accomplished this.

He had wondered what he would do with the weight of his memory, his attachment to Carolyn, to the children, to questions, to his whole deluded state. His longing for all of it filled him but now here was this sparkling weightless sensation as things fell away. He fell too as the river reversed itself or turned him upside down and it seemed a long tumble into the pool at the bottom. He swept toward it within this astonishing roar, this roaring underwater quiet. He went deep until everything stopped but his falling.

A long moment but he felt the breath in his lungs; it slowed his fall. He described an inexorable, smile-shaped arc, scraping the sandy bottom of the pool. The surface flickered and receded as he rose to it.

DOUG HAD REACHED the other side of the snow basin when the avalanche occurred. Nick's weight came on the rope at Doug's waist and tore Doug from his steps and toward the slide. His surprise and his interest were intense. It was his first time in an avalanche. It occurred to him that he could die in it, and the notion gave him an almost warm feeling; he thought it wouldn't be so hard to die. He piled into a deep snow bank and stopped. The rope attaching him to Nick had snapped.

He dug himself out of the snow. He stood and pushed back up through snow to his original stance. He looked down across to where Quamajan still stood on the other side of the snow basin. The Hunza was looking down at his hands. He had burned them trying to hold the other end of Nick's rope. Nick had gone with the avalance over the ice cliffs at the bottom of the basin, a drop of more than 5,000 feet.

Joe and Peter had watched the slide from the fixed ropes above Camp Two. They had seen Doug start across the snow earlier. They hurried down and found him. Doug told them Nick was gone. Doug was still in tears when he turned on his radio and told Chris. *Nick's copped it. The whole bloody slope went . . . didn't have a hope.*

Chris told Doug to come down with the others. He told him to be careful, but there was no danger now. The avalanche had swept the slope clean. The climbers descended the basin on firm, consolidated snow.

CHRIS AND PETER shared a tent that night at Camp One. They talked about Nick—his jokes and his carousing, his stubborn intelligence—until Chris lapsed into silence. He had lost his closest friend. He had begun to grow old together with Nick and he realized now that he had expected much more of that. Wendy would have to tell Carolyn Estcourt who would tell her children, the little girl and the two boys.

He could find no meaning in it. He tried to stop thinking of Nick. He thought of his own childhood—of how the mountains had looked to him in picture books. They had aroused in him notions of escape, of possibility. The pictures had suggested to him that things could be utterly different, that he could leave his story, reinvent it.

He had sought in the mountains not merely a new identity but also a new way of being. He had wished to move among these places like a visitor, a fairy-tale child who escapes the streets and houses of the city for a wilderness of snow. He had managed something different. He sometimes felt himself bloom into fullness in the mountains, into a man he could admire and into a life he could love. The deaths of his friends and collaborators seemed a cruel confirmation of his notion—and a perverse fulfillment of his wish—that life might assume new aspects in these places.

Such notions flickered and collided amid the grim scenery of his grief. He felt the hard ground under his tent. He felt empty and abandoned, furious and stricken, frightened, without resource. He wanted the night to end. He wished it might go on forever, to delay what was to come.

What amazed him was the inexhaustible nature of his memory. He could skitter anywhere he liked, crossing continents of time to recover fields of blurry data. He was a boy in a library; he plucked books at random from the shelves to find that he had read them all. There was no comfort in his recollections, only this sense that he knew more than he could use. He'd traded or lost something precious, but he didn't know what. This ignorance was disastrous. And it was shameful because he believed that he chose not to know. He saw himself as he was, shivering in his sleeping bag in this awful place, his back to Peter's huddled figure. He was appalled.

The climbers rose in the morning. Each saw his bewilderment reflected in the haggard faces of the others. Chris and Peter wanted to stay and try to finish the route. Doug and Joe wanted to go home. The four climbers agreed to discuss the matter down at Base Camp. They packed their gear and left Camp One under gray skies.

Their way took them past the huge cone of debris that lay over Nick's body. Chris thought of ants at the seashore. The climbers stopped and looked at the rubble as if courtesy required them to do so. Doug had worried that the birds would get at Nick but there was no chance of that. Still they lingered. No one else knew of this; no one else could look after the fact of Nick's death.

Chris called a meeting at Base Camp later that day. The remaining climbers gathered in a MacInnes Box, a relic of the Everest trip three years before. No one knew how to talk or behave. They spoke of other matters until Chris raised his voice to ask whether they should stay and try to finish the route.

Doug said he thought it was wrong to continue here while families and friends in England coped with the news. He had no interest in continuing the climb. Jim Duff agreed with Doug. Tut said he was willing to stay on in support of the others if they decided to remain. He didn't think they would; he couldn't imagine himself or the others walking up and down past Nick's body for the month it would take to finish the climb. Joe said he didn't know what was right. Tony Riley wanted to complete his film, but that still left only two climbers—Chris and Peter—in favor of staying on. The group agreed to end the expedition.

Chris had second thoughts—he called another meeting that afternoon—but the rest of them had already moved on. They were thinking of the return to England. The team agreed that Chris and Doug would leave in the morning. The two of them would tell the local authorities of Nick's death, and send porters back from Skardu to collect the expedition gear. Chris and Doug would fly on to Islamabad, where they could at last telephone Wendy with the news. She would try to reach Carolyn Estcourt before the news got into the press.

Chris and Doug set out in the morning with Quamajan. They moved quickly, covering ground and taking satisfaction in the work. Here the two Englishmen weren't at odds. They were walkers bearing sad news. Their collaboration was coming to an end of sorts. Doug had limited patience for Chris and his style of leadership; he preferred to mount his own trips and run them as he saw fit. Those trips were smaller but that was how Doug liked it—and that was where climbing was going. You didn't need Chris now; you didn't need a lot of money or hundreds of porters. You could just ring up some friends and go.

It was a relief to Doug and Chris both that they didn't need each other any more. They suddenly understood themselves to be friends, as if they hadn't quite seen that until now. One day they crossed a river together. The water was very cold—exhilarating. Chris when he climbed the opposite bank looked over at Doug's tall figure, and was comforted by the sight of him. His love and gratitude toward Doug seemed to arise from and nurture his growing understanding that Nick was lost to them.

They reached Skardu in five days. They reported Nick's death to the District Commissioner, who treated them with great tact and found them seats on a plane to Islamabad the next day. Chris telephoned Wendy from the embassy there. He listened to the buzzing on the other end of the line before she picked up. She had called him just months ago with the news about Dougal. Wendy picked up and he heard her voice but he couldn't speak.

TOM ESTCOURT WAS seven years old when he woke up one morning and decided he didn't want to go to school. He went looking for his mother to tell her he didn't feel well. She wasn't in her bedroom and on his way downstairs he met his brother Daniel coming up. Daniel was nine. He was crying. He saw Tom and told him: *Dad's dead*.

Their mother was downstairs. She was crying too, sitting on a beanbag chair they kept in a corner.

Tom remembered leaving his father at the airport. That had been a bad day, too. Tom had cried in the car on the way home but he'd been singing as well. He remembered the words: *Don't cry, don't cry, there's a silver lining in the sky*.

PETER AND JOE and Tut and Jim waited two weeks for the porters. Joe thought with growing dread of the return to England. He remembered Ruth Erb—the widow whose husband he and Peter had buried in a crevasse with three other climbers after Changabang. He remembered how she had lingered in the mountains, reluctant to return to her friends and family, as if she feared their faces would confirm her loss.

The porters came. It took eight days to walk out to Skardu. The rivers were swollen and crossing them was dangerous. Islamabad was only another hour by plane, but no plane came. A plane would take off in Islamabad each day and the wind would rise and the plane would turn around. They'd been waiting for a week when it came. Tut and Jim managed to get seats. Joe and Peter waited three days for another flight. They talked of returning to K2. They'd failed to climb the West Ridge or even to come to grips with the mountain. Already it felt to both of them as if they'd never been there; as if they'd never touched or even seen K2 at all.

Nick had been dead for a month.

19

CHRIS RETURNED TO Great Britain bearing his burden of grief and guilt and also a sense that he had not returned whole, that he had left something of his past on the peak. He had pronounced the snow basin safe. He saw it in memory, easy ground.

The deaths had begun to blur. There were so many of them; the dead threatened to fade into the enormous backdrop of the mountains that had killed them. He couldn't carry them with him; he had to turn at least partly away from them to function. His friends continued to die—it was if he had set in motion some machine; it lurched on, doing its work in this mindless and horribly damaging way.

How could he mourn properly? If he gave his attention to one death, he neglected the others—and also the living, including Wendy and the two boys. It was better to trail his dead behind him, at a reasonable distance. But they were like a pack of children, needing him, unable to care for themselves. He sometimes felt something similar about the survivors—the other climbers, the families. They looked to him for something. They didn't seem to blame him, not entirely; still, he felt he'd incurred some obligation to them all—the living as well as their dead—and he had no clear sense of how to meet it.

He didn't know how the others managed these losses. They talked sometimes of feeling invincible after a death. Some of the married climbers would return from a disastrous expedition and fall into bed with women who were not their wives, conducting brief but intense affairs that made their family lives miserable for a time and left them hollow and ashamed. Bonington in the aftermath of a loss clung to his marriage and his family life. He fended off his grief in other ways—even as he wept for his lost friends the next journey would take its earliest shape, a sleek and glittering form that darted from tree to tree as if in a forest of secrets.

He went to see Nick's widow, Carolyn Estcourt. Jim Curran—a climber and filmmaker who also had been friendly with Nick—came along in support. The three of them met at a restaurant and got tearfully drunk. Curran took appalled notice of the strangers who interrupted to ask for Chris's autograph. Chris looked deathly ill but he was almost absurdly gracious, signing and taking time to exchange a few words with each new intruder. He seemed unable to defend himself. Or perhaps it was a relief to turn momentarily away from the two friends who looked to him in their loss.

The next night an abcess on Chris's chest burst—he had developed a serious infection, a lingering souvenir of his injuries on the Ogre the previous year. Surgeons removed part of a rib a week later. Chris took the summer to recover, pondering his immediate future. His circle of climbers was dwindling, and its surviving members had their own ambitions. Chris for the moment was too weary, too heartbroken, too encumbered to follow them, let alone lead.

It had been fifteen years since he'd climbed the Eiger's North Face with Ian Clough. Chris had since done what he'd meant to do; he had made a career of climbing. Along the way, he'd lost more than seemed possible. There were the dead—even apart from his own child, Conrad, there were all of the climbers: John Harlin, Ian Clough, Tom Patey, Tony Tighe, the Sherpa Mingma,

Mick Burke, Dougal Haston, Nick Estcourt. Climbing also had damaged or destroyed his friendships with Don Whillans and Martin Boysen.

He couldn't weigh such losses against the moments he'd gained, the happiness that at moments appeared like some oblivious guest, brushing past his objections and leaving him giddy, slightly lost. But there were other factors to consider, other connections to protect. His two surviving children were growing up. Daniel was eleven; Rupert was nine. They were frightened and angry. They had known Nick as a friend to the family and a support to their father. They'd admired and loved Nick Estcourt as they had known and loved Mick Burke before him. The string of deaths proved that their father himself was not safe—that he was willing to risk their happiness as well as his own.

Chris signed a contract to write a book about other adventurers—polar explorers and astronauts and sailors as well as climbers. That would keep him busy for a year or so. And he had an eye on China. There was talk that the country would open its borders to western climbers. China held a galaxy of peaks, mountain upon mountain unexplored and unclimbed—but the borders remained closed for now. And if they did open, it wouldn't be like before. He was finished with big expeditions—too many people on the mountain, too much to lose.

THE OTHERS CARRIED on. They had mountains to climb, careers and reputations to make. Doug Scott and Joe Tasker had been back from K2 for only three months when they left for an alpine-style attempt on Nuptse, Everest's huge neighbor. They were turned back by heavy snow low on the mountain—a failure hard to bear on the heels of the K2 debacle.

They hoped for something better on Kangchenjunga, the world's third-highest peak at 8,586 meters (28,169 feet), situated

at the eastern end of the Himalayas. Doug Scott and Peter Boardman had made plans to attempt the mountain in the spring of
1979. Joe had agreed to go with them. They would climb without
supplemental oxygen—bringing only a small amount for emergen-
cies—and with just one or two porters in support. They'd invited
Tut Braithwaite as a fourth climber, but he'd refused; he was still
suffering from the aftermath of the chest infection he'd contracted
on K2. Joe suggested a replacement: Georges Bettembourg, a
Frenchman whose achievements included an alpine-style ascent
of Broad Peak (8,047 meters; 26,401 feet) in the Karakoram.

Peter was just back from New Guinea, where he'd climbed the
remote Carstensz Pyramid with his girlfriend, Hilary Collins. He'd
met Hilary at a party the winter after his return from climbing
Everest; that was three years ago, in 1976. Peter had been newly
famous, fending off his guilt over Mick Burke and preparing for
the Changabang expedition with Joe. Hilary had been teaching
school in Derbyshire; she'd invited him to give a slide show at the
school upon his return from Changabang that spring.

They'd fallen in love very quickly. They shared a wish to
understand the world and their place in it; they were the kind
of young people who look for meaning in their lives without
cynicism or even much self-consciousness. They went climbing
sometimes—Hilary was a climber, too—and they talked, often
staying up late together to review what they had seen or learned
or felt during their hours apart.

Hilary had accepted a teaching job in Switzerland while Peter
was on Changabang. She left England after his return, but they
settled down together in 1977, when Peter came to take over
Dougal Haston's climbing school in Leysin—much as Dougal
had taken the job after death of John Harlin. Peter often took
Hilary along when he guided clients on routes near the school.
The couple made occasional trips together, traveling to Africa

and Asia to explore and climb. They wrote each other long letters when Peter went off on expeditions, but the letters weren't sufficient. The two of them would put certain of their respective experiences aside to sift through together when Peter returned. It was as if they had not fully lived their time apart; they must relive it together.

The failure on K2 had stayed with Peter and with Joe and Doug. The three friends badly wanted to succeed on Kangchenjunga, but they had set themselves an immense challenge. Climbers had reached the mountain's summit only twice—first in 1955 (that was Joe Brown's first Himalayan expedition), and again in 1977 by Indian climbers. The successful expeditions had been large-scale affairs, making heavy use of supplemental oxygen.

Recent climbs on other mountains offered hope that a small party could succeed on such a big peak. Reinhold Messner and Peter Habeler had climbed Everest without oxygen the previous year, but they had relied on help from large support teams, and they had climbed the peak by way of the relatively easy Southeast Ridge. The three British climbers and their French companion would have minimal support on Kangchenjunga—and they had their eyes on a new route, the mountain's North Ridge.

There were other reasons to worry about the feasibility of their plans. Kangchenjunga was a dangerous peak even by Himalayan standards. The approach alone held potential horrors; it would take them across terrain frequently swept by enormous avalanches. The first expedition to approach Kangchenjunga—in 1905—had lost three porters and a climber to an avalanche low on the peak. Another avalanche had killed a Sherpa in 1930, during the third attempt on the mountain.

The mountain occupied a remote corner of the Himalayan range. It stood on the border of Northeast Nepal and the region of Sikkim, recently annexed by India. The climbers flew out to

Kathmandu in March of 1979. They met up in Dharan with the Sherpa Ang Phurba; he had climbed on Everest with Doug and Peter in 1975, and on Nuptse with Doug and Joe in 1978. Ang Phurba would oversee the forty-eight porters who would carry the expedition's supplies to the mountain.

The party began their approach on March 18. They gained a high ridge and followed it for four days, meandering in small groups past farms and villages. Peter thought of his Hilary and the distance between them. He was walking into solitude. The climbers saw the mountains through clouds—there was the multipeaked bulk of Kangchenjunga, seventy-five miles distant but unmistakable through the haze.

Peter knew something of the mountain's history. The Tibetans had named it Kangchenjunga—Five Treasure Houses of the Great Snows—after its five distinct peaks. The men who had climbed the mountain in 1955 and the members of the second ascent party in 1977 had refrained from stepping on its highest point. They deemed this a courtesy due to the spirit that animated the peak—and to the local people, who believed that an ascent of Kangchenjunga would lead to floods, landslides and other misfortune.

Doug usually walked alone. The other three climbers often walked together. Georges Bettenbourg proved opinionated and disarmingly direct; he was also prone to horseplay and to hypochondria. His English was not fluent. His pronouncements often lacked nuance, which made it difficult to take offense. He was married but he shocked Peter by maintaining that it wasn't always necessary to be faithful to one's spouse. Doug made pronouncements of his own, informing the others that each of them had an allotment of only three trillion heartbeats: they should make the most of their time. Doug had recently become a vegetarian.

He held forth at length on Eastern philosophies—sometimes in oppressively authoritative tones.

They walked for eight days and came to a campsite on the Tamur River. They were anxious about the coming trial. They diverted themselves by climbing the boulders that stood near the water, working hard to outdo one another. Georges decided to play King of the Hill at the top of one of the boulders. He gave Peter a playful shove; Peter lost his balance and slid fifteen feet, landing awkwardly on his left foot. There was a snapping sound that seemed to come from his ankle.

The others—in particular Georges—looked on horrified as Peter tried to stand. The ankle wouldn't support his weight. He was furious; the injury seemed likely to make all of his planning and effort pointless even as it brought home to him the depth of his desire to climb their mountain. He couldn't tell if his ankle was broken, but it seemed likely that he would be unable to climb, let alone carry loads.

He decided nonetheless to stay with the expedition in hopes that he would recover enough to be of use on the route. The group hired porters to carry him up to Ghunsa, the last village on their approach march; that was another four days ahead. The porters produced a basket meant for carrying produce to market. They converted the basket to a makeshift chair for Peter. A porter would hoist the basket with its passenger onto his back, taking the weight on his forehead via straps, and would struggle along until relieved by one of his fellows.

The other climbers walked with Peter and his entourage of porters for a time, but it was slow going and the trail was too narrow to accommodate even a small crowd. Doug and the others soon pulled away. Peter found that it was odd, being carried; in many places a slip by a porter would have sent him tumbling down the steep slopes of the gorge formed by the Tamur River.

He wondered how he had managed to find himself in the hands of these strangers. He wondered what they must make of him. What could he make of them? His role as a burden made him anxious but it allowed a strange and reassuring intimacy with his bearers. Nima Tenzing, the expedition's assistant sirdar—he helped Ang Phurba oversee the rest of the porters—had been on eighteen expeditions, including seven to Everest. Nima walked behind Peter's little group, advising them and acting as Peter's protector. Peter listened to the old man whisper prayers throughout the day; prayer seemed Nima's ordinary habit.

A family traveling to Ghunsa walked with the expedition. The family included a lovely young girl called Dawa, who wore a green cloak and smiled at the climbers. Some days her smile was like a question: *Why leave this?* A group of policemen traveling to Ghunsa with their wives also walked with the climbers and shared the expedition's campsites.

Joe dreamed one night that one of the four climbers—himself or one of his companions—had been killed in an avalanche. He woke and recorded the details in his journal. Joe and Doug each dreamed that Peter climbed Kangchenjunga. They were anxious to tell him about the two overlapping dreams, which together seemed to constitute a good omen.

The climbers paid off their porters and hired new ones in Ghansa, the site of an ancient Buddhist monastery. The village had once been a prosperous trading community but now it seemed bereft; tattered prayer flags flapped in the wind and the inhabitants had neglected the religious monuments. Doug set up a medical clinic for the villagers. Many of them had developed eye troubles and respiratory infections from spending the winter months in their smoke-filled huts. The climbers lingered in the village for two days before setting out on April 2 to complete their journey to the mountain.

Peter's ankle was better. He left Ghansa before the others and hobbled along under his own steam. The party passed through Kangbachen, a tiny gathering of ten houses, the last habitations on their route, and walked on past the settings of legends—a sacred waterfall where saints had bathed, a cavern where someone had hidden the key to heaven.

They came to the Kangchenjunga Glacier and made their way up the rock-strewn slopes at its margins. They knew the world would grow smaller once they engaged their mountain, but now they were free to look up from their walking and lay their eyes on other peaks: Jannu, Nepal Peak, many more lacking even names. This profusion humbled the climbers. They could not hope to accomplish anything of note; their obsession was merely eccentric. They made camp. The porters—there were girls among them—danced in circles. Georges amused the porters in turn by performing cartwheels and by walking on his knees with his legs locked in the lotus position.

The expedition reached Base Camp at 16,000 feet on April 4. The site was a grassy shelf suspended below low-angled rock slopes. Doug found a tent peg: a relic of the 1930 expedition.

The proposed route followed the Kangchenjunga Glacier to a hollow between the North Ridge and a mountain called Twins Peak. The climbers established Camp One on the glacier on April 6. The site seemed reasonably safe from the avalanches that threatened the surrounding area from both sides.

Joe and Peter lay in their tent that evening and listened to the grinding of the glacier beneath them. They occasionally heard the hollow crack and echo of an ice tower collapsing on the slopes above their camp. They had both been reading *Goodbye to All That*—Robert Graves's memoir of his youth, including his service in World War I. They talked about whether shellfire would have sounded like this to the men in the trenches.

On the Kangchenjunga Glacier

They rose on April 7 and set out with Doug—Georges was ill down at Base Camp—to find a safe site for Camp Two. Their route crossed an icefall to a snow basin. They stopped every so often to rest and to inspect the towers of ice that rose to their view like frozen Gods. The three climbers knew they were near the place where the avalanche had killed the Sherpa in 1930. No one had been here since that tragedy. They moved deliberately, probing the snow with the shafts of their axes. They knew the stories. They felt themselves entering—trespassing upon—older narratives, as if no time had passed. Nothing human had happened here for almost half a century; whatever had occurred here during that empty time was no part of history. The previous expedition was an old thing come to light in mint condition. This unnatural find oppressed and excited them at once.

They chose a site for Camp Two. The site offered a view of the 3,000-foot wall they must climb to reach Kangchenjunga's North Col—their jumping off point for the North Ridge itself. They dropped their loads and returned to Base Camp.

The climbers devoted the next several days to ferrying gear between the lower camps. They spent a last night in Camp One on April 13. They were less frightened now at the creaking of the glacier. Even the occasional explosions from the surrounding walls failed to arouse much interest until Georges's shouts brought Joe and Peter from their tent just after dark. The climbers stared briefly at a huge tide of white cloud that rushed and billowed toward them in the near-distance. They retreated to their tents and zipped the flaps against the wind and waited. The tents shook and the sky rained debris, but then camp was quiet again. The slide had run itself out before reaching them. Something in Joe had gone dead as they waited; he only noticed because now it ticked back to life.

The four climbers moved up to Camp Two on April 14. Sherpa

Nima Tenzing walked with them. The Sherpa carried a bag of holy rice. He tossed handfuls of the rice at the most dangerous-looking features along the route. Peter saw Nima arrive at Camp Two in the evening—the climber's last before setting out for the wall that led up to the North Col. The Sherpa gazed up at the route, a seemingly endless series of towers gone blurry in the evening shadows, a scene mysterious as the surface of a jungle pool. Nima turned and swept his arm across the view. The rest of his rice skittered in the half-frozen snow that lay around the camp.

THE CLIMBERS APPROACHED the wall the next morning. They were quiet. The mountain's enormous scale threatened to swallow them. They walked for two hours to the gap where snow had melted from the base of the wall. This wall would offer the route's most technically difficult climbing, but it was free of the glacier's objective hazards. Doug and Peter left their loads and returned to Camp Two. Georges and Joe stayed to climb five rope-lengths of mixed rock and ice, fixing rope as they went.

Doug and Peter took their turn the next day and made more progress. The two of them were back at Camp Two on April 17. The sky was cloudless and as they lay in the sun a huge slide swept the route that led from their camp to the wall. The avalanche deposited 10 feet of snow over tracks Georges and Joe had made on their way to the bottom of the fixed ropes that morning.

The climbers finished fixing rope to the North Col on April 20. They left Camp Two the next day. They hoped to establish a camp on the North Col that evening. That camp would put them in position to follow the North Ridge to the summit. Once established on the col, they hoped to make a one-day foray up the ridge to learn what they could of its difficulties. They would then retreat to Base Camp to rest before returning to set out for the summit.

They moved heavily laden up the fixed ropes at the bottom of the wall. The wind rose and it began to snow. Small avalanches surged past them as they hung on the ropes. It was foolish to continue in these conditions. They retreated to Camp Two for the night and continued down to Base Camp the next day to rest and wait for better conditions.

They stayed at Base Camp for four days. They slept and talked and ate—gorging on fruit, eggs and potatoes—as snow continued to fall on the mountain. They were out of range of avalanches. The fear left their bodies for a time but gradually returned as the hours and days of their rest slipped away.

Peter brooded about the risk of climbing so high without supplemental oxygen. Messner and Habeler had suffered hallucinations and other side effects on Everest. This route was almost as high, and considerably more difficult. Once they regained the North Col, it would take them another two miles up and across the North Ridge. It was a long way to travel at such heights.

The climbers sniped at one another. Georges fussed about his liver or made optimistic chatter that annoyed Joe. Doug shirked cooking. He made remarks about people's diets, and quoted more philosophy at them; he was reading the *I Ching* and *The Tibetan Book of the Dead*.

The climbers left Base Camp on April 26. They spent the night at Camp Two below the wall that led up to the North Col. Joe woke up feeling ill. The others decided to give him a day to recover. Peter was impatient. He was sick of delays and rests, eager to be at the climbing and also eager to have it behind them.

The four of them returned to the wall on April 28. They moved clumsily with their burdens, breathing heavily—gasping at times—as they hoisted their bodies up the fixed ropes. Doug and Georges went first. They took off their packs to climb the last section of the wall, an overhanging rock chimney that led to a final snow slope. They hauled their gear up after them, dislodging debris. Peter looked up into a sky that seemed to rain rocks. He lurched sideways as the missiles exploded around him; one hit his arm, and the impact staggered him. The shower passed and he found his footing and drew off his gloves to find swelling and a frightening gash. He felt sure that he'd broken a bone. His despair welled up like blood, black and thick.

Peter gave Joe an angry message for the others—they might have killed him with their carelessness—and started back down the ropes. He forced himself to calm down as he made his way back to Camp Two. He dressed his wrist and spent the next day resting and watching the North Col through binoculars. Once he caught a glimpse of his friends. He wondered if they'd go for the summit without him.

His arm was not as bad as he'd imagined. He set out to catch the other climbers the next morning. Nima Tenzing and Ang Phurba followed him; they were carrying supplies for the camp on the col. The three men set off up the ropes at the base of the wall; almost immediately, a small powder avalanche poured over them. The snow carried a fist-sized rock that struck Nima in the back. The injured Sherpa retreated, bruised and shaken.

Peter and Ang Phurba climbed to the col, where they found the others at work consolidating their new camp. The camp stood on top of a huge ice tower, which creaked and groaned beneath the tents. Georges saw Peter's look and hurried over to assure him that the tower would stand at least long enough for their purposes.

The climbers woke the next morning to sun and cold, and to the feeling that they had at last come to grips with the mountain. The smaller peaks that had loomed above them on the glacier now stood far below, diminished spectators; the climbers could look upon these other mountains without the prospect of obliteration.

The Ridge was safe from avalanche. Everest's East Face—the fearsome Kangshung Face—shimmered and glowed in the distance, a mere seventy miles away.

Joe's headache had returned. It was very bad; he would have to go down to try to recover in the thicker air of the lower camps. He took his leave with reluctance, full of concern that his companions would finish the climb without him.

The three remaining climbers on the col hoped now to discover what sort of climbing the North Ridge would offer—whether it would be more difficult than they hoped. They set out up frozen snow that took their crampons well. Georges was very eager this morning; he led the others up the windswept slopes and onto new ground. The climbers enjoyed a sense of the past falling away. Something untouched lay before them, receding as it beckoned. The present seemed a shabby thing compared to the empty ridge above them. This ridge merged with the sky without even the notion of seams; there was no evident distinction between the snow on the ridge and the sky from which the snow had fallen and to which it would return, drawn by the light that spiraled everywhere around them.

The climbers had loosed the ties that bound them to the earth and its inhabitants and even to each other. Peter had no thought of what was behind or beneath him. It would not have surprised him to vanish into the thin air that he greedily sucked into his lungs at each step. His movements were labored and yet there was a lightness of step to his plodding. The view grew wider to include the purple hills of Tibet. The sight calmed Peter. He was aware of his companions now and of the fact that their presence helped to lay the foundation for the delight that flooded him at moments, receding only to return at these moments of calm.

The party came to the base of a rock buttress that stretched 600 feet up the ridge. They had named the buttress; they called it the Castle. The climbers dropped their loads of food and gear at its foot. A gully of snow split the rock to within a hundred feet of the roof of the Castle. They had climbed 1,800 feet on the North Ridge.

A storm rose as they descended the snow above their tents at Camp Three on the col. They carefully noted and followed their own crampon marks from the morning. They took this precaution to avoid falling through one of the enormous cornices that overhung the face beneath the ridge.

They reached the North Col in an hour. They lay in their tents and talked of the weather, which seemed to deteriorate in the afternoons. This pattern might cause them trouble later. They'd want a full day of good weather to make the round-trip from their eventual high camp to the summit.

Peter went out in front of the others in the morning. The wind was strong; occasional gusts made him stop and cling to the slope. The climbers waded through new snow to the base of the Castle, where they dug a snow cave that would serve as a base for the final stages of the climb. It would shelter their gear and food and protect them from the wind. They dug until the cave was enormous, and settled in for the night. They spent the hours of darkness dozing and melting snow to make tea. All three climbers were deeply lethargic. They were approaching an altitude of 25,000 feet. They felt the cold more than they would have felt it lower on the mountain.

The weather was reasonable in the morning—clouds but not too much wind. Doug led into the gully that split the Castle. Georges and Peter followed, kicking steps in snow that seemed dangerously unstable. Peter took note of a layer of ice just beneath the surface; the ice could serve as a chute for the snow that lay on top of it. The gully grew steeper. Doug at last came to rock and managed to place a piton.

The three climbers convened at Doug's anchor to discuss their next move. All three men felt ill. They carried on anyway, up low-angled ground to a view of cliffs and huge snowfields. The snowfields culminated in a triangle of black and white, the summit pyramid. The climbers turned back. They spent the rest of the day fixing ropes down to the cave at the base of the castle.

They rose late the next morning. Doug and Peter argued over who should cook; in the end, Georges made breakfast. The three of them pulled on boots and crawled outside to follow the fixed ropes back to their high point. The wind was very bad. They couldn't see past the whistling particles of dust and ice that stung their faces. They stopped and considered, shouting to be heard. They climbed higher, heading across to a notch that would take them to the other side of the ridge. That would get them out of the wind, which had climbed to hurricane force; Peter estimated that it blew at eighty or ninety miles per hour.

They struggled up to the notch. They passed through it to huddle on a slope that offered shelter from the gale. It took three hours to chop a ledge in the ice and pitch their tent. They were nearly exhausted. The summit lay a mere 1,200 feet above them. They would hang on and make their attempt in the morning.

They woke in the darkness to the sound of wind—a wall of it rising from depths they couldn't imagine. They clung to the tent's framework; they hoped to prevent the wind from destroying their shelter. They took turns at this work, each man holding the tent poles until his fingers grew numb in his mittens. The climbers used their breaks to pursue the awkward and painful work of getting their feet into half-frozen boots. Doug poked his head out of the tent entrance and saw that the wind had pulled the tent anchors from the snow. The tent was drifting across the ledge, carrying the climbers. They'd soon slide from their perch; they'd be dragged off a cliff in a bag.

They packed their sleeping bags and abandoned the tent. They stood outside in the tearing wind and collapsed its framework. Peter used a knife to rip the fabric, and the three climbers stooped to retrieve the rest of their gear through the hole. The wind took the empty tent. They climbed back up to the notch in the crest of the ridge and then onto the snow and scree of the vast field they'd named the Great Terrace.

They moved swiftly through the darkness, their minds and senses dulled by the cold and the wind's brutal thrashing. They reached the fixed ropes at the top of the Castle and descended the buttress. The darkness faded into light but the wind continued as they slid down their series of ropes, taking care in their hurry not to neglect some crucial task; they all knew of climbers who had died from such mistakes in far easier circumstances than these.

They piled into their snow cave at eight o'clock in the morning. After a time they were settled enough to take stock of their condition. They were all very tired. Doug had frostbite on one of his hands. Peter's big toes and his nose were affected. Georges's eyes hurt; he was in the early stages of snow-blindness.

The climbers left the cave and carried on down the snow slopes to the North Col and then down the wall beneath it. They yearned for the grass and running water of Base Camp. They longed especially to be free of the wind. Peter looked up as they crossed the glacier to Camp Two. Clouds raced past at such speed that the mountain seemed to rotate into them. Kangchenjunga rode in the sky, spinning in his vision like a toy.

JOE HAD SPENT the days since his descent recovering at Base Camp, worrying about the others and wondering if they would reach the summit without him. He had watched clouds race across the sky and he knew no tent could stand up to such wind. His friends would be dead if they couldn't get to a snow cave.

He was sick of this—the competition and the dread. He had muddy thoughts about why he persisted: it made no real sense to him. He had made five expeditions to the Himalayas in five years. Nothing much changed; only his need to climb these mountains grew stronger. He sometimes believed that he was performing penance for sins of sloth committed in some previous life. His confusion itself felt blameworthy to him. He did not understand how he came to this—how ordinary desires fell away, leaving this need to climb.

The previous day he had walked back up to Camp Two with Ang Phurba. They meant to climb the wall today and try to catch the others. Joe had slept late this morning and now Ang Phurba roused him to tell him that his three friends had returned.

Joe emerged from his tent and saw them. They weren't carrying much; that meant they had left the gear behind on the peak. They hadn't reached the summit; he hadn't missed his chance to climb the mountain with them. His joy at this was tempered by fear and also by regret that he had missed whatever they had endured on the ridge during the storm.

The four climbers and the Sherpa made their way down the glacier to Base Camp. Doug and Peter and Georges had been on the mountain for more than a week. They were nearly exhausted, but they had explored most of the North Ridge. Peter in particular was confident that he could climb Kangchenjunga. His worries had fallen away during the storm. The nature of climbing made sense to him for the moment. The uncertainty and confusion that often beset him gave way to this calm.

Georges and Doug felt something similar, but they woke at Base Camp the next morning feeling haggard and uncertain.

Doug told the others he felt like going home. He was good for at most one more go at the mountain. Peter felt differently—he wanted something to set against the failure on K2. He told Doug he feared that they might never again be so close to success on such a route on such a mountain.

The climbers gave themselves three days to rest. They did this partly in hopes that the mail runner would arrive during that time. They pined for connection to a world that at times seemed frighteningly distant, almost abstract. Doug mused aloud that they should wait for the runner in case one or more of them did not return from this last summit attempt; their families would be glad to know the climbers had read these last letters.

They sat through a perfect day—the first potential summit day, twenty-four hours without high winds. The mail runner arrived on May 8, their third day at Base Camp. They retreated to their tents with the month-old letters and read them with a private and animal greed. Each word suggested to its reader that the rest of the world existed, that the reader was known to those places, that he was perhaps more than he felt himself to be amid this landscape. They welcomed this suggestion even as they recoiled from it.

The climbers walked back up to Camp Two the next morning. They spent the rest of the day resting and writing letters. Nima Tenzing would carry the letters down to Base Camp the next day. Ang Phurba planned to stay with the climbers and carry a load as far as Camp Three at the col. The climbers had assembled ten days worth of supplies for this second summit attempt.

They climbed to the North Col on May 10. They meant to climb the next day to the snow cave at the base of the Castle. There seemed little prospect of shelter higher on the route; this meant they might need to climb and descend 4,000 feet on summit day. The climb at times seemed like a debt they should pay or try to pay. There was at such moments little pleasure in it; it was a necessity or perhaps a duty.

They rose early on May 11, and climbed to the snow cave. Their legs were heavy; they took a long time. The cave had settled in on itself, so they had to dig out more room. Georges had suggested that they rest in the afternoon and set out for the summit that evening. The idea seemed laughable now. The climbers resolved to take a rest day, though they knew it would be difficult if not impossible to recover strength at this altitude. Doug reminded them all that the rest day—May 12—was Joe's birthday. Joe had forgotten.

The day came and passed. The four climbers lay in the sun in the morning before the sky filled and snow began to fall. One climber or another left the cave to check the sky every few hours during the evening and into the next morning. They saw clouds each time and more snow. They resolved to take another rest day—but as the new day wore on their impatience surfaced and they decided they'd had enough waiting. They set out for the summit late on the afternoon of May 13 amid wind and cloud. They knew this was unwise. Each climber took comfort in the fact that the others were making the same choice.

They were on top of the Castle by eight o'clock. The moon appeared briefly and disappeared again as they set out across the snow and scree fields of the Great Terrace. Peter and Doug fell behind Joe and Georges but after a time came upon them behind a boulder, melting snow for a drink. The altitude had addled everyone. Peter was convinced for a moment that there should be more climbers—he almost asked where the rest of them had gone.

They carried on for a time, struggling to maintain their bearings in the dark and the wind. Joe and Doug stopped and began to dig in a shallow bank of hard snow. Georges had gone ahead.

Peter followed him higher to look for a better place to dig. He caught up with Georges, and they found a snow hole at the base of a low rise of rock, which the climbers had named the Croissant. Peter used his axe to carve out more room. Georges meanwhile was determined to press on for the summit. His idea was that they could stop at this snow hole on their way down. Pete followed him out of the shallow cave and they set out. The other two climbers were nowhere to be seen.

Peter and Georges lost the route in the dark. They came to a steep rock barrier. The wind was worse. Peter retreated onto an unstable patch of snow. His anxiety grew. He told Georges that he thought it was time to retreat.

Georges was reluctant to lose the height they had gained. He maintained they were no more than a few hundred meters below the summit. They waited for light—it was by now almost morning—but when dawn came the two climbers saw that the clouds were heavy and thick again. Georges at last agreed to retreat. The two climbers descended to their snow hole at the base of the Croissant.

Doug and Joe had spent an uncomfortable and anxious night in their snowbank, wondering what had become of their companions. They rose early and set out and came upon Peter and Georges soon after dawn. The four climbers took stock of their situation. They were all desperately weary. The slopes where they stood were still socked in by cloud. They decided to descend.

They staggered off across the Great Terrace and once again worked their way down the fixed ropes to the snow cave below the Castle. They spent the rest of the day—May 14—in their sleeping bags, listening to the wind and feeling themselves grow weaker. Georges's impetuous dash for the top had exhausted him. He was determined to descend all the way to Base Camp. The others talked of retreating as far as the North Col to pick up more food; they could then come back up for another try. That plan would mean retracing their steps on the ridge yet again—when what they wanted was to be done with this mountain.

They went to sleep without deciding on a course of action. They awoke to clear and windless skies on May 15. Doug announced that he was not going down. He would make another attempt on the summit from here. Joe and Peter said they would join him. Georges would not. The Frenchman packed and departed for Base Camp as the others prepared to set out for the summit once more.

THEY BEGAN CLIMBING at 8:30 in the morning. Joe took the lead briefly, but he was too tired to break trail through the new snow. Doug took over and led the others to the Castle and then up the fixed ropes.

The windless day was a surprise, almost a shock; it was as if the landscape itself had altered in the night. They crossed the Great Terrace. Doug took the trouble to build a rock cairn that would help them to find their way down in a storm. They climbed six hours to the snow hole Peter and Georges had dug. They hacked at its walls until there was room for three men to lie down in a row. They cooked dinner—freeze-dried turkey—and took sleeping pills and settled in to rest.

There was still no wind. The sounds of their voices when they spoke were unfamiliar to them in the quiet. The intimacy of the cave felt oppressive. They were aware of their flesh, clumsy and impermanent. They had come to this odd place to discover that nothing was what it seemed. They thought of the people who lived in the world as the dead might think of their survivors: dear but alien and largely ignorant.

Joe thought of the tramps and the garbage men he'd known in Manchester. He had become like them. He and his companions had stripped themselves of all but essentials. This condition was a type of poverty and as such a version of liberation. Joe was shivering—he didn't know whether from fatigue or excitement or the cold. He wondered dimly if perhaps they had gone too far. Doug's fingers, slightly frostbitten during the retreat from the first summit attempt, were very painful. He mentioned the pain and Joe gave him some pills. Peter was asleep. Joe considered his friend's face in repose. Peter looked calm but very tired.

Doug and then Joe fell asleep. The three climbers woke to another windless morning. They set out at eight o'clock and climbed out of shadows and into the sun almost immediately. They moved quickly toward rocks at the start of the feature they knew as the Ramp. They stopped climbing so that Doug could take off his boots and warm his feet. They resumed climbing. Peter led for a time and then Joe. The climbers labored up through snow, resting every twenty steps or so. They had never been this high without breathing bottled oxygen. All three were moving surprisingly well. They aimed for the Pinnacles, a cluster of towers that marked the convergence of Kangchenjunga's West and North Ridges. The Pinnacles were another 500 feet—the summit wasn't far from there.

They felt their hearts rise. The other peaks in the region were spread beneath them. The topography had a simplicity that swept away their fears and regrets. Doug's feet were cold again. They stopped and Doug once again took off his boots. Joe unzipped the front of his snowsuit and Doug put his feet against Joe's stomach until he felt the blood in them again.

Peter took the lead once more, moving up unstable slabs of snow. He crossed to a section of black rock that required careful climbing. He was in shadow now but moving toward sunlight and what seemed to him a roofless city, pillars of cloud supporting the sky. This notion asserted itself in the context of nightmarish physical effort; each step was very difficult.

The sun tinted the Tibetan hills a pinkish orange. Kangchenjunga's summit block, a low brown triangle, offered no acknowledgment of their achievement or their presence; it wanted nothing of them. The three climbers came to the place where the mountain's North Ridge ended, merging with the West Ridge. Joe Brown and George Band had come up from the west to stand on this spot in 1955, almost a quarter-century before. The air was still. The ground here was easy. They were safe for the moment, but sunset would come in three hours.

They set off up the final stretch of the West Ridge toward the summit. Doug ranged far ahead of Joe and Peter. He would stop to wait for them and to confirm that they wished to continue in the dwindling daylight and then he would again race ahead. He disappeared around a corner only to pop up once more on top of a huge block. He shouted down that the summit was 10 feet away. Joe and Peter hurried to join him.

The evening remained windless. The three of them kept their distance from the very top; they would honor the taboo against standing upon the mountain's highest point. Doug took photographs. He seemed reluctant to leave, but the climbers couldn't linger. The snow went red around them as they hurried down. They took care with each step—a climber who slipped here would die. Dark clouds, lit from below by blue and orange light, moved across the sky; someone took another picture as the evening subsided into night. And now at last the wind returned, blowing the snow before it. The climbers put on headlamps and continued down. They crowded into their cave at nine o'clock. They had climbed Kangchenjunga and they were safe for the night.

Joe and Pete talked quietly. Doug fussed with the stove. There was still the descent to the North Col and then to the glacier and across to Base Camp; after that their lives awaited them. They had been afraid to die on the mountain; now they feared a return to a world where such matters were misunderstood, where people thought that dying mattered more than it did. They were afraid to leave behind the clarity of intention that had possessed them here. They were afraid not to know what to do. They felt uplifted and unworthy at once—they were drunk with confusion and joy and anxiety. They had come here and retrieved something. They worried that they couldn't protect it, that they hadn't changed, that they would forget.

The morning was difficult. They were tired and it made them frightened. They spread out during the descent but every so often they bunched up again to cope with the dizziness that overtook them now. They were terribly thirsty. They stopped to brew tea at the big snow cave below the Castle. They drank the tea quickly and continued down. The wind made them cold. They reached the North Col and assembled bundles of gear. Their legs threatened to give way beneath their bodies as they heaved at the bundles, pushing them over the cliff to career down the wall to the glacier.

The wall of ice below the col was melting. It was miserable, clumsy, wet work getting down the fixed ropes. The climbers were not so afraid now but they felt that it would be squalid—embarrassing—to die now. They reached the bottom of the wall and walked through heavy wet snow that came almost to their waists. They tried to crawl on the snow, dragging their packs behind them and sinking into the stuff, chafing their faces in it. It was maddening, ridiculous. Joe looked up and saw Nima Tenzing and Ang Phurba; the Sherpas had come up the glacier to meet the climbers.

There was a brief reunion—smiles, happy banter—and the Sherpas continued on past to collect some of the gear that lay scattered at the base of the wall. It was snowing. The climbers descended to Camp Two and soon the Sherpas arrived to cook for them and give them the news from the radio. Climbers had made the first ascent of Gauri Sankar—a famously difficult mountain on the Tibet-Nepal border. A Sherpa named Ang Phu, who had climbed with Peter and Doug on Everest four years before, had died on Everest's West Ridge. They were too weary to make anything of this news. They needed to sleep. The snow had stopped falling. There was a new moon—the third since they had come here.

THEY WALKED DOWN the glacier to Base Camp the next day. Doug went ahead; he seemed happiest alone in pursuit of his destination—his new task. Joe and Peter walked together. They talked quietly, taking in the thicker air. Georges came out to meet the two of them. He brought fruit juice and he embraced them both in turn, cheerful and—Peter was glad to see—seemingly at peace with his decision to retreat.

The climbers shared a bottle of whisky in the sunshine. The

Joe Tasker and Peter Boardman
CHRIS BONINGTON, CHRIS BONINGTON PICTURE LIBRARY

grass was an extraordinary green. The girl Dawa had come up to Base Camp with a friend; they brought wood and eggs to sell. Peter found it difficult to meet Dawa's smile.

He took a walk the next morning after breakfast. He came upon a herd of blue sheep—bharal. He walked behind the herd for a time. He had climbed almost 2000 feet when the sheep at last scattered. Peter stood for a moment before turning back. He thought of Kangchenjunga. His mind's eye lit upon moments already half forgotten.

The climbers left Base Camp the next day. It was May 20. They reached the edge of a forest in the afternoon. They left the glacier and entered the woods and it was like stepping into a new story. They felt the quiet that occurs only among trees—a quiet flecked with birdsong and insect sounds and the rustle of leaves. This new quiet entranced them. They stopped to rest and lay on the ground near a stream. They listened to water running over rocks. Peter had felt a sense of déjà vu at certain times on the mountain and he felt it again here. He was a ghost already, haunting places he remembered as a ghost remembers—without access to the body and what it knew. There was only this echo, painful and sweet.

The climbers fell asleep. Hours passed. The sun dipped lower in the sky. The early afternoon light in the woods didn't fade; it gave way to something thicker: a coverlet drawn across the climbers' sleeping bodies.

Peter awoke to a sense of peace and a conviction that this last sleep was a gift from Kangchenjunga. He was grateful. He wished only that he could remember what he'd known upon waking; already it was gone.

20

J OE TASKER HAD opened a climbing shop in the Peak District, in Derbyshire. The four Kangchenjunga climbers met there in the summer of 1979 to sort through photographs from the trip. Georges and Doug were making preparations for another attempt on Nuptse, where Joe and Doug had failed the previous year. Peter returned to his climbing school in Leysin. He guided clients through the summer and made plans for his next expedition, a four-man attempt on Gauri Sankar (7,134 meters; 23,405 feet), which lay on the border of Tibet and Nepal.

Peter as a boy had attended a Don Whillans lecture. He remembered Whillan's description of a 1964 expedition to Gauri Sankar, which Whillans had made the year after he'd climbed the Central Tower of Paine with Bonington. The trip had featured a nightmare approach through leech-infested jungles patrolled by roving bandits, as well as extremely difficult climbing in very cold weather. Whillans and Ian Clough had made two attempts on the summit. They had narrowly missed being killed by collapsing ice towers during the first attempt and had almost died in an avalanche during their second retreat.

Climbers had at last reached Gauri Sankar's summit while Peter and his companions had been on Kangchenjunga. Still, the mountain remained an enticing target—a huge complex of vertical rock, avalanche-swept gullies and sharply defined ridges. Peter had his eye on the unclimbed West Ridge.

He was to serve as expedition leader. None of his three companions had been to the Himalayas. Tim Leach, an architecture student, was seven years younger than Peter. He was a very strong rock climber and passionately committed to alpine-style climbing. Guy Niethardt made his living as a climbing guide in his native Switzerland. He'd climbed with Dougal Haston and had spent many a night at the Club Vagabond, where he'd polished his English and even picked up a North Country accent. The fourth climber was John Barry—the same John Barry who had been with Bonington and Whillans and the rest in Patagonia sixteen years before.

The Gauri Sankar expedition was scheduled to leave Europe in mid-September. Peter finished his guiding and said good-bye to Hilary in Leysin and flew to England for final preparations. He felt increasingly disoriented by events. His book about Changabang—*The Shining Mountain*—had won the John Llewelyn Rhys Prize for young British authors; meanwhile, his father had been diagnosed with pancreatic cancer. Peter spent the last days before his departure packing and visiting his parents, including a final afternoon picking apples in their suburban yard near Manchester. He carried away a vision of the two of them waving good-bye to him from the front door; he studied the image and stored it carefully away like some artifact. He was on his plane on the runway at Heathrow before he allowed himself to acknowledge that his father might die while he was gone.

The climbers spent a week in Kathmandu—arranging for porters, signing insurance contracts and lining up permits. The ten-day walk to the mountain took them past terraced fields and villages. They encountered a couple with a badly burned child; they gave the couple money and urged them to take the boy to a hospital. The hospital was three days' walk away. The climbers didn't think the boy would survive.

They woke the next morning to a view of their peak and their chosen route, the mountain's West Ridge. It was a long, meandering line with huge notches that promised difficulties. They climbed up through jungles that—as Whillans had testified—swarmed with leeches. Peter would peel off his wet socks to find a dozen or more of the creatures busily draining the blood from each foot.

The climbers entered a remote hanging valley rarely traveled by westerners. They came to Lamobagar, a village of some 250 souls, half of them Tibetan refugees. The Tibetans lived well apart from the main village, in a collection of stone huts around a temple—a gompa. Peter and John followed the sound of drumming to the Tibetan settlement that evening. They came upon a group of twenty or so girls engaged in an oddly rough dance. The girls giggled as they careened around the small courtyard in front of the temple. A bearded lama waved the two Englishmen into the front room of the gompa, where a group of fifteen or so men sat drinking the local chang—a powerful brew made from barley. Peter and John drank with them. A sad young man with big teeth asked the two visitors for film and cigarettes, and for an umbrella. It was raining hard when the Englishmen left the temple to search for their tents in the dark.

The next morning they returned to the gompa with the other members of the expedition. A lama blessed them and told them to be prudent; he also urged them to make their Base Camp a holy place—to refrain from killing animals there. The climbers left the village, passing another lama who shuffled up to them muttering phrases they could not decipher. They gave him money and continued on their way, turning up the Rongshar Gorge.

Peter looked back once and saw an old man standing with

his hand resting on the shoulder of a boy. The man shivered in the morning cold as he watched the foreigners enter the valley; it had served as a path for his ancestors during their trek into Nepal from the eastern regions of Tibet. The stories said that those ancestors had seen their new home in a dream and had come here to seek it.

The British and their porters climbed muddy paths along cliffs that rose above the river. They came to a valley Peter knew to be the birthplace of Jetsun Milarepa, the eleventh-century Tibetan poet and saint. They passed a spot where porters had abandoned Whillans and his fellow climbers in 1964; the porters had fled after an encounter with armed bands of Tibetan robbers. The path to the mountain now followed the Chumalagu Chut, a tributary of the Rongshar. The members of the 1964 expedition had dabbed red paint on the trees to mark their path. Some of the marks were still visible.

Peter and his companions camped in the jungle on the night of October 7. They peered up past shafts of bamboo to a sky speckled with stars. They crossed a river the next morning and climbed into open country, catching further glimpses of their mountain. It seemed to Peter that this was a truly wild place, better suited to wolves than to men.

The expedition reached 16,000 feet amid swirls of falling snow. This was the site they had chosen for Base Camp. The quality of sounds changed as they made their camp. Peter felt as if he had been swimming out to sea against the tide and now the tide had shifted; it carried him away from shore and into a fog that hid the world.

The climbers had gained almost 9,000 feet of altitude during the final three days of their trek. Tim Leach, the youngest of the party, was feeling the change in altitude more than the others. He stayed behind while they set out to approach the mountain, still hidden by a subsidiary ridge. Snow fell and low clouds made it impossible to pick out a route to the top of this ridge. They turned back without seeing their mountain, but caught a sort of glimpse of it that night. The clouds disappeared after sunset and the mountain's huge double-peaked form blocked the stars, creating a silhouette that stared down at them like an empty mask.

The three fit climbers had a real look at the mountain on October 11. They carried loads to the site of their Advance Base Camp, at the start of the West Ridge, which rose overhead to carry on for two miles and more of rock steps and ice arêtes. The crest of the ridge looked frighteningly narrow and exposed; it fell away sharply on both sides.

The climbers and porters spent several days hauling loads to the new camp. Tim wasn't able to help; he was still suffering from the altitude. His condition grew abruptly worse on the evening of October 15; he became incoherent and his vision began to deteriorate. Peter and the other climbers helped him down to a lower camp the next day. They were vastly relieved when the thicker air revived him.

The climbers returned to their task, at last coming to grips with the ridge itself—a mix of loose rock, poorly consolidated snow and friable ice, with huge cornices overhanging the void on both sides. Tim recovered after a few days, and was able to join the others on the ridge, but the dangerous conditions forced the climbers to proceed slowly.

They had been on the mountain almost a month when a gust of wind blew John Barry from a belay stance. He fell 200 feet, colliding with snow and rocks, convinced that the rope would snap when he came to the end of it. He was surprised when he stopped falling. He hung bewildered for a time and then found his jumar and climbed the rope, ignoring the pain in his limbs and the blood that welled from his hatless scalp. He had wrenched his knee and perhaps broken his wrist and had suffered a mild concussion. He was soon lucid again, but he was too sore and shaken either to climb or to descend the ridge alone.

John's injury meant the expedition was once again down to three active climbers. They left John with Pemba, a high-altitude porter, at their high camp and set out to explore the upper reaches of the ridge. Peter led up a rock tower and over it and onto snow. The nature of the ridge—the steep snow falling off to either side, the huge cornices that overhung so much space, the blurred glacier far below—distorted his spatial awareness. His fatigue and a sudden manic joy compounded his confusion. The view seemed to veer toward him like a flying creature; its wing brushed his face and the creature carried on past and then circled back into the country that lay ahead of him. He might have been in space, in the desert, at sea. He was far from the familiar and yet he felt strangely at ease.

The three men climbed a 1,500-foot step in the ridge and arrived at a flat section that was like crossing an ancient bridge. Cornices overhung both sides of the ridge and the snow at the crest was deep and unstable. A step collapsed beneath Peter. He looked down against his better judgment and saw through the snow to Tibet. He could imagine the entire edifice collapsing and taking him with it. He imagined himself caught in tons of falling snow, an animal caught in a flood or a forest fire. He moved quickly and with great care, a barefoot thief crossing a room. He wished not for safety but only for this awful fear to leave him. He reached rock and clung to it with almost no relief but rather with a rising sense of desperation.

Tim and Guy followed him. Peter said something and turned back, leaving them to continue up the ridge. He moved down in a world of mist; if he fell he would disappear into it. He descended to the high camp where John and Pemba waited.

Tim and Guy arrived later. They had climbed two more pitches. They had soloed a section of the ridge on the way down; the wind had blown a fixed rope out of reach. A step had given way under Tim and he had nearly fallen; here the mishap seemed hardly worth mentioning.

John Barry started out with the others the next morning, but his injured hand was useless. The final sections of the ridge would be too difficult for him. He turned back. The remaining three climbers and Pemba reached the previous day's high point and continued. They fixed more rope; the ridge became still more exposed as the West Face of the peak fell away. Peter at one point sat straddling the ridge, bemused and again disoriented. The Tibetan sunshine bathed his left side; the wind and snow of Nepal came at him from his right. He felt himself part of an abstraction, a painting or quilt.

Peter and his three companions descended to their high camp late in the day. They would leave for the summit in the morning. Tim and Peter were away first, Guy and Pemba followed them. Tim came to the section he'd soloed two days before; the rope was still out of reach and he climbed the pitch with no protection. Peter started to follow but he stopped; he was certain that he would die if he tried to cross without the security of a rope. He shouted for Tim, who cursed and retraced his steps to put Peter on belay.

Tim led three pitches of mixed rock and ice, placing no protection between his anchors. Guy took over for a time, making a very difficult and exposed traverse. Peter took his turn at the lead, kicking his crampon points into frozen snow. It was dark when he finished the pitch. The ridge was behind him. He was standing at the edge of the plateau that supported the mountain's South Summit—the lower of the peak's two summits, and still unclimbed.

There was no question of trying to reach either summit tonight. The party dug holes on a shelf just below the plateau—three holes for four climbers—and lay in them as if in canoes. They had run out of food and that made the cold harder to endure. Peter had one of the trenches to himself but he rose in the night and joined Guy; it was warmer that way.

They rose at dawn and set out across a vast white field. They walked on low-angle snow, roped together, into a world both new and impossibly old. No person had seen this. Pemba threw a few grains of ceremonial rice into the air. Peter smelled jasmine. There was a buzzing in his head as if some circuit had given way; something in his mind would not accept this vast stillness. An odd feeling arose in him. He imagined icy water in an empty room, enough to cover the floor and rise to the open windows.

The South Summit was there at the top of a wide gentle slope. The four climbers approached it together and stood shyly just below it, uncertain of their rights. They had promised not to stand upon the very top. The sky was clear and they felt themselves surrounded by a vast and empty sea, as if the mountains were not mountains but rather frozen waves of stillness.

The climbers looked across to the North Summit. There was no question of trying to reach it. They would not have the strength to return. They stayed on their summit for fifteen minutes. The wind drove them off; this wind and the luminous, ghost-blue horizon put Peter in mind of some unending winter.

They climbed back down to the West Ridge in the gathering dark. They took almost five hours to retrace their route to the high camp, where John was waiting with soup.

The next morning they began the climb down the rest of the ridge. They moved together between steeper sections that required rappels. Peter and Guy tied on with John. Tim and Pemba made a second rope. The five men's concentration flickered and faded with their strength.

They spent another night on the ridge, and made their way down to Advance Base Camp in the morning. They stopped there long enough to drink tea and eat baked beans and Spam. They carried on, dragging their legs through the soft afternoon snow. Tim outpaced the others. His three companions paused above Base Camp to look down upon the tents and prayer flags in the fading light.

They left the mountain on November 15. The river had dropped. The leeches didn't trouble them. They spent a night at Pikhutu, where they had encountered the couple with the burned child. The same family had passed through the village earlier in the day on their way home. The child had survived.

Hilary's most recent letter to Peter had warned that his father's condition was now far worse. Peter considered this on his flight back to England. The approach of the death of his father seemed oddly parallel to this journey of his own, flying across mountains toward the place where the dying man waited. He looked down and considered the view: an arc of endless mountains. He had made six visits to the Himalayas in seven years. His explorations had begun to teach him the shape of the range. He was twenty-nine years old. He meant to spend his life filling in the spaces between the mountains he'd already seen. It was comforting to look down and see that there were enough mountains to occupy him for many lifetimes. He sat back in his seat and ate an orange, a parting gift from one of the Sherpas.

Peter returned to a rainy England. He drove each night with his mother to the Manchester hospital where his father lay dying. The older man's eyes were sad but he would smile at Peter as if to reassure him. Peter steadied himself by thinking of mountains he knew. One night he showed his father a color poster of Kangchenjunga. His father stared at it, said it was *lovely . . . beautiful.*

Peter's father died the next day. He had written in a last letter that he had been amazed by the kindness of his family and his friends. Peter reminded himself that his father's death was one of countless deaths. The notion calmed him. He saw again in his mind's eye the mountains in their endless ranks. His ambition receded. He had at times created a version of the mountains in his mind but they outstripped his invention. They did not belong to him; he belonged to them—he was bespoken.

HE WAS GOING back to K2. Joe Tasker was going too. Joe had stayed home during the fall of 1979 to work at his climbing shop. He also had begun preparations for a return to the mountain that had killed Nick Estcourt the previous year. Doug Scott was coming. They'd asked Dick Renshaw—Joe's partner on Dunagiri in 1975—and he had agreed to join them.

The Dunagiri climb had helped prove that two climbers could get up a hard Himalayan route alone. Joe and Peter had upped the ante on Changabang's even more difficult West Face the following year. The Kangchenjunga climb in 1979 had proven that a small team could succeed on a difficult route at extreme altitude. This second expedition to K2 would take the next step: the four climbers would attempt an even higher mountain by an even more demanding route. They planned to attempt K2's West Ridge again, but this time with a team half as big as the one Chris Bonington had assembled for the task in 1978. They would take a different approach to the ridge, avoiding the slope that had avalanched Doug and Nick.

The expedition was set to leave England on April 30, 1980. Doug and Georges and their team were off climbing Nuptse's North Buttress. Peter was back in Switzerland after his adventures on Gauri Sankar's West Ridge. They had left Joe to raise most of the money for K2. He'd come up with 12,000 pounds, much of it from two companies: a brewer that hoped to sell nonalcoholic beer to Pakistanis, and a firm that had recently designed a freezer called the K2.

The climbers were forming attachments that tugged at them as they made their plans. Doug and his wife Jan were raising two small children. Peter had made plans to marry Hilary. Dick Renshaw and his wife were expecting their first child in August. Dick called Joe in the spring to ask if the climbers would be back in time for the birth; Joe said he thought they would.

Joe had become deeply involved with a young woman named Maria Coffey, the willowy, dark-eyed sister of another climber. They'd met at a party at a climber's house in Wales, a few months after his return from Kangchenjunga. Maria was thoughtful and intelligent, with roots like Joe's—working class, Irish Catholic. She knew many of Joe's climbing friends. She had known and liked Nick Estcourt, and remained friendly with his widow, Carolyn.

Joe and Maria became lovers six weeks before Joe was scheduled to leave for the second K2 expedition. They talked about the first one, two years before. Maria was horrified to learn that Joe had been willing to continue that climb after Nick's death. Joe maintained that she had no right to judge him on this matter, but she held her ground. The idea of his return to the mountain that had killed Nick and shattered his family bewildered her. It was all the more difficult knowing that her relationship with Joe wasn't settled. Joe was coming off of another romance; he'd told Maria that they would have to wait and see what happened upon his return from K2.

Joe and Peter and Dick left England on schedule at the end of April. Joe's friend, the filmmaker Allen Jewhurst, traveled out with them; he wanted to accompany the climbers on the approach to the mountain. The party flew to Karachi and then sat on their gear in the back of a truck for three days as the vehicle bounced its way across the Sind Desert to Islamabad. Here they collected Doug—just down from Nuptse—and met their liaison officer, one Major Sarwat of the Pakistan army. The major was a devout Muslim and a very correct man, determined to abide by the conventions governing his role. He was also touchingly earnest in his desire to be of use to the expedition. Joe thought him humorless and prickly, and worried that he would cause trouble.

The party had assembled at the Islamabad airport for their flight to Skardu when two Hunza men approached them. The pair introduced themselves as Gohar and Ali. They wished to accompany the expedition to the mountain. Gohar was a striking figure, well over six feet tall. He wanted to work as a high-altitude porter; he claimed to be the cousin of one of the porters on the 1978 K2 expedition. Ali asked for a position as cook.

The climbers were reluctant to hire the two men without certifiable references but the pair managed to talk their way onto the crowded plane. Peter gave in to an impulse to include them on the team. Gohar would perform camp chores and carry loads on the lower sections of the route. Ali would cook.

The climbers hired porters in Skardu and set out for the mountain. They traveled nine days to the Baltoro Glacier, and then three days up the glacier itself. There was a short delay when the porters complained that the expedition had not supplied enough socks or sunglasses. Otherwise, the march went smoothly until the second day on the glacier, when Gohar fell into a crevasse.

He fell 20 feet and lodged in a funnel of ice, where the crevasse narrowed before opening out into the abyss. Dick Renshaw climbed down to Gohar, and the porters hauled the two of them out. Gohar wasn't badly injured but his accident revived the porters' fear of glacier travel. It was snowing, so the porters in their ragged clothing were cold as well as frightened. They made another day's march to the end of the Baltoro at the base of K2 but they refused to carry further. The final stage of the approach to Base Camp required crossing the Savoia Glacier. A porter had died on the Savoia the previous year.

The porters would not be cajoled or bribed. The climbers would have to ferry their own gear to the foot of the West Ridge. This setback delayed the start of their climbing by more than a week. Bad weather slowed them further.

They had planned to climb the mountain capsule style. That meant they would fix a rope to stock the first camp, then pull that rope up to stock the second camp—and so on, up the entire route. This was a compromise between an outright siege—which would require maintaining a line of fixed ropes all the way up and down the route—and a purely alpine-style approach.

It didn't work. The team made slow progress. Doug proposed that they finish the route alpine-style, but Dick refused. They might be trapped by a storm high on the peak, and he didn't want to risk frostbite to his hands, already damaged on Dunagiri. Pete and Joe agreed with Dick; Doug's suggestion was too dangerous. The group reached another compromise. They would abandon the West Ridge for the second time in three years. They would try an alpine-style ascent of the Abruzzi Ridge—the line taken by both successful expeditions to the peak. Those expeditions had both employed siege tactics, so an alpine-style ascent of the ridge would be a significant achievement.

Their first attempt on the Abruzzi ended at 19,000 feet. A storm held them tent-bound there for three days. They retreated to Base Camp when the storm ended. Doug was overdue in England. He decided to leave the mountain. The others were determined to stay for another attempt.

They drew upon their respective recollections—of Everest and

Kangchenjunga; of Dunagiri and Changabang; of Gauri Sankar and K2 itself—to make this decision to stay. They had learned that if they could manage to carry on long enough they could climb these routes; it was simply a matter of beginning and then continuing to work until it was done. Something might eventually stop them but for now there was nothing. They were tired but they were not exhausted. They had come to a point that all three of them recognized: nothing at home seemed to matter as much as staying to finish the climb. They knew this notion to be a hallucination but they gave themselves to it. They knew that accepting this lie was part of their work and the work seemed necessary to them.

The three climbers saw Doug off and settled in for a few days at Base Camp with Gohar and Ali and Major Sarwat. The two Hunza men were cheerful and efficient. The major had taken to heart the expedition's goal. He spoke encouraging words to the climbers. He oversaw Base Camp, making small improvements. He tinkered at building a stove. He kept himself clean and dapper even as the climbers became increasingly disheveled—their bodies and faces filthy, their clothing falling to rags, their eyes vacant or fierce by turns.

THE THREE CLIMBERS returned to the mountain on July 2. They moved slowly. They had been here for six weeks. Their strength was fading, but they did not expect to encounter much difficult climbing on the upper sections of the Abruzzi. Joe and Peter figured the three of them could climb the route in less than a week. They carried on their backs everything they needed for the attempt—there would be no porters, no lugging of gear between camps.

They found the climbing harder than they had expected—nothing extreme, but consistently challenging. The weather broke again.

They sat out the worst of it and climbed when they could, often moving in high wind and heavy snowfall. They spent four nights at 23,000 feet, making twice-daily radio contact with Major Sarwat. The major passed along regional weather reports that rarely seemed to apply to the mountain.

They set out again when the weather improved. They had camped below the Black Pyramid, a steep section of dark rock that reared up hundreds of feet to the start of an ice field. The rock had few cracks or features, so it was difficult to climb and to protect. They managed it, leaving fixed rope in place for their retreat. Dick then led the others up the ice, which proved dangerously brittle; it splintered when he struck it with his axe. Joe saw evidence of previous expeditions—frayed ropes, bits of gear and cloth. He could not imagine how the climbers of an earlier generation had managed this section.

The climbers carried fragments of stories. An American climber and three Sherpas had disappeared high on this route in 1939. Another American had died during a rescue attempt in 1953. Joe and Peter felt as they had on the glacier beneath Kangchenjunga the previous year—not haunted by past climbers and their stories, but possessed by a sense that no time had passed since those early disasters, or rather by a notion that time had collapsed into itself, muddying the laws of sequence and of narrative. It was as if the three of them had fallen from some map of the past and into the actual territory of it—as if the past were ongoing.

They made a fourth camp at 24,700 feet on a shelf on the ridge. Dick had never been this high. They were moving well given the altitude. They could look down 9,000 feet to the Godwin Austen Glacier. Base Camp was invisible in the distant glacier's immensity. They felt themselves to be voyagers from an already remote outpost. The climbers had come to a place that puzzled more than frightened them. The four men who had disappeared here in 1939 had broken their orbit and sailed into space.

The three living climbers knew that another two days—perhaps three—would see them to the top of the mountain. Then they would have to try to get down. The good weather persisted for another day. They climbed without oxygen and they suffered greatly from the altitude now. There was nothing to be done about it. They moved up easy snow, skirting a cornice to reach a short section of ice that surprised them; it was very steep. Peter led the ice. The climbers arrived at a shoulder that rose easily to the base of the huge summit pyramid.

They made their fifth camp here, below the pyramid. They gazed up and picked out a way to the top. The route led up to rock and across to a gully of snow, then up the gully to a final ice cliff and easy ground. For now they looked across to Broad Peak and down upon the rest of the surrounding mountains. The climbers were not terribly far from the summit; it seemed for the moment as though they could turn around and go down now and it would hardly matter. This was just another vantage point, another place from which to view parts of the planet. The sky looked like the beginnings of space to them. They were very high. They knew themselves to be inhabitants of one planet among many—the earth was not the center of things.

They slept heavily and woke in the morning to snow and high winds. They had been on the route for ten days. Their reserves of food were running low and they worried about altitude sickness; if they stayed here too long they might become too weak to move. They would become names in stories.

They could not climb in these conditions. They considered retreat. The snow piled up outside of their tent as they talked. The major radioed a forecast of clouds but no wind or snow the next day—July 12—with clear skies for July 13. They resolved to carry on. It was still snowing when they awoke the next morning but they set off in hopes that conditions would improve. The ridge narrowed as they climbed and soon they were moving carefully across steep snow, afraid of triggering a slide that would sweep them from the mountain. They reached the gully. It was 400 feet wide—an obvious funnel for avalanches from the ice cliff above it. Joe imagined a vast white wave heaving out of the mist and breaking upon them. Any avalanche here would carry them for a time and fling them into space.

The snow in the gully was deep. They moved as quickly as they could, gasping in the thin air but afraid to stop for a rest. Each climber felt a superstitious need to show his attachment to life. It might help to move as quickly as they could: some powerful witness might take note of their efforts, might be moved to intervene on their behalf. The climbers' fantasies distracted them from the knowledge that pressed at them here—that death was real and that they were not prepared for it.

They crossed to rock at the far side of the gully. The snow came down harder now. They climbed higher, searching for a place to pitch their single tent. They sought protection from the avalanches that would come; the mountain would shrug off much of the new snow during the night. Peter found himself back in snow that came to his thighs. Dick and Joe trailed after him but it was hard to keep up. They were vastly tired. The climbers came upon a rock ledge below a wall. The risk of avalanche seemed less grave here than on the slopes that surrounded them—slopes that at moments seemed alive, as if the climbers waded through a sea of snakes that slithered and hissed at their boots.

They pitched their tents and melted snow for tea. It wasn't enough, but they were tired. They quit while they were still thirsty. Peter and Dick lay down in their sleeping bags with their heads at the tent's narrow entrance. Joe lay with his head at the back of the tent. The snow continued to accumulate on their shelter. Joe felt the snow fill the gap between his side of the tent and the rock outside. He worried that the snow would smother him in his sleep. The others were anxious, too.

The three of them talked about their situation. They were 1,500 feet below the summit. They hoped to reach it in the morning. But this snow might make it impossible to climb or retreat in the morning. They might be stuck here while the altitude continued to wear at their bodies. Their talk died and they lay still. They felt themselves at the very border of some mystery. Sounds seemed to drift in from a world remote from even this remote place. They did not take sleeping pills. They might need to come awake quickly.

Joe drifted into a sleep like a tide that every so often cast him up. He half woke several times—each time to a sense that he had fallen asleep in a tunnel or cave; or else on an unfamiliar beach or road—and then he woke fully to darkness and squalor. The tent had collapsed as if to merge with the mountain; a river of snow flowed over the climbers. They were buried in it; they were like the villagers who died in mudslides. Joe tried to heave himself upright. He could almost move his head and shoulders—but snow hammered at his neck and forced him back; here was some astonishing powerful brute without mercy or malice. He knew death was upon him and he had no description for it. He shouted for Peter and then for Dick but now he felt Pete's foot pressed against his own elbow. The foot didn't move. The snow pounded at Joe's head. He wondered if the pounding would tear the tent from its position. A bag of three bodies would slide down the mountain to tumble and smash for 10,000 feet, the corpses sliding across one another in a bloody, splintered jumble to end as a mindless pile, rags and innards from a butcher's bin. Joe stood aloof from the possibility. It struck him as sordid. He was grieved that no one would find them or know what had happened. There would be guessing and questions; the remnants of the dead climbers would lie undiscovered. He was aghast at his own incompetence—his inability to meet this dire outcome in some satisfactory way.

Nothing happened for a time. It was dark in the tent. He thought of a river near his home, the river now nameless to him. He slipped in and under and swam along the bottom. He touched mud and debris. He couldn't see and the darkness seemed to reflect his mind; it derived from his mind rather than from his circumstances, which he suddenly recalled. He was sheathed in this tent, buried under snow in this vast mountain night. He went back to sleep.

AND WOKE AGAIN. The snow had set around him; he couldn't move his body. The slide had stopped. He couldn't draw a deep breath. The weight on his chest prevented it. It was still very dark. His fear awoke, shards of light through a web.

He remembered a small knife in the pocket of his wind suit. He could move one arm and he used it to find the knife. He tried to open the blade and nearly dropped the thing; at this a wave of terror nearly swamped him. He waited and the fear subsided. He forced himself to move his hand again. He moved it very deliberately. He opened the blade. He stabbed at the tent where the fabric pressed against his face. The quality of the air changed. He was able to wonder what might happen now—whether he could get out and what he would find if he dug up the others.

But they were digging for him. Joe heard voices and felt the weight on his chest give way. The voices grew louder and now he could reply. Peter and Dick finished digging him out. Joe sat up in the tent and began to pass out gloves and flashlights. Peter told him to stay in the tent and gather what gear he could find. Peter

and Dick cleared snow from the ledge and worked the tent back
onto solid ground. The avalanche had moved the shelter so that
Dick had hung over the abyss, suspended by the tent fabric.

Joe found boots and inner boots and handed them out to the
others, who pulled them on over wet socks. He was sitting up
now. He looked around for more gear and here was the sound
of hissing snow. He took more blows to his head and pressed
himself into the bank of snow at his back and felt the slide bury
him. He imagined the others swept into the void; this time there
would be no one to dig him out. The slide stopped. A vision of
death by suffocation rose up to appall him. He felt unbearably
alone with this prospect. He shouted for the others.

Tears rose in his eyes when they shouted back. Peter had tied
himself to the anchor after the first slide. He'd managed to throw
his arms around Dick to keep him from going over the edge in the
snow that ran through their camp like a river in flood. Peter and
Dick dug Joe out for a second time. The climbers moved quickly
to depart. There was no question of continuing up the mountain
now. Their task was to get down. They must descend 9,000 feet,
wading across open slopes of deep new snow where any step
might trigger an avalanche. They had worn their clothes to sleep
and so it was a matter of boots and gloves and stuffing food and
gear into their packs. They needed to be gone from this place but
they had to wait for the light even while new snow continued to
build on the slopes above and below them. They were too afraid
to set off across freshly loaded slopes in the dark.

Dawn came. Joe led them down. He kept to rock as much as
he could. His crampons caught and skittered. The climbers were
roped together and Joe knew that if he fell here he would kill
everyone; he knew the others knew it too. He stepped back off
the rock and into snow that came up over his knees. He pushed

through the snow with a childish sense that this was unfair; they should not have to do this. He felt bitterness rise in his chest even as he prayed that the snow would hold the climbers' weight and that they would be spared more slides from higher up the mountain. The danger of avalanche grew more severe as they descended. Joe was aware that he might be stepping in snow that would later find and bury him. There was also the chance that a patch of snow would break away under his feet. Dick and Peter might be able to hold him but probably not.

They had come here knowing that the mountain had buried Nick. And now they were doing something far more dangerous than anything Nick had done. Joe worried that he was piling up a debt that would come due and claim him; he could not believe that a debt of this magnitude would be forgiven. A mountain would decide the matter. He thought of school, the seminary—men and boys praying to a patchwork vision.

They descended in cloud and falling snow. Nothing was familiar to them. They found the great gully they had crossed the previous afternoon. They crossed it again. Snow collapsed under their feet; some huge beast stirred in its sleep. Joe stayed in front looking to pick a way down. He was moving more strongly than the other two—he had lost their names for a moment. He stared through the mist and snow in hopes that a familiar rock or feature would appear. The ground here wasn't steep.

Peter and Dick moved ahead after a time, forcing their way through deep snow. Joe was tired now. He worried he would not be able to stay with them. He sat down in the snow. He heard the voices of the other two and crawled to them. Peter had found the campsite the party had occupied two nights before.

They had descended a mere 900 feet in six hours. It was nine o'clock in the morning but they were finished for the day.

They had brought their battered tent down with them and they pitched it now, coping with the torn fabric and bent poles. They were too tired to dig a platform; so the floor of the tent lay at an angle. The three climbers shivered in their sleeping bags; they were almost dead with fatigue. They had lost their spare gas cylinders and much of their food; now they used most of their remaining gas to light the stove and melt snow for drinks. They needed to drink more but they slipped into a collective daze and then drifted off to sleep. They came awake during the afternoon to recall the events of the previous night and then dozed again. They drifted, featherlike. They were slipping away, becoming ghosts who shimmered and disappeared and reformed without reference to time. They had no opinions and no knowledge. They forgot their predicament and even talked of coming back here, back up on the ridge.

Joe at moments would awake to this nightmare. The snow was still falling but they had to leave in the morning. Their bodies would deteriorate quickly if they stayed high any longer, especially without fuel to melt snow. They spoke to Major Sarwat on the radio that afternoon. The transmission was fuzzy. Major Sarwat seemed to think the climbers were regrouping for another assault on the summit. Joe felt himself near tears; not even the major understood their predicament.

They left in the morning without their tent. They were too tired to carry it. They hoped to reach the glacier before dark. Snow continued to fall. They came to a difficult section of rock. Peter went first. He picked his steps carefully, taking tension from the rope as he scraped snow from rock and struggled to keep his footing on the steep ground. The others followed. Snow covered everything. Their crampons skidded and caught on the rock that lay beneath it. The climbers used their hands for balance. Their gloves grew soaked and their fingers went numb. Dick was very worried about frostbite. The three climbers kept moving, miserable and frightened. Joe reminded himself that they had failed decisively—there would be no need to return to the route. They could go home if they could get down.

It took six hours to descend another 800 feet. The light was fading. They were near the site of their fourth camp, but the snow had buried everything. They poked and dug until Dick uncovered a frozen piece of someone's excrement. They found the tent and excavated it and huddled inside; they were not safe but they were for now free of the obligation to move.

Joe made the evening radio call to the major, who had a surprise for them. Georges Bettembourg's voice came on the air. The Frenchman was in the area to climb Broad Peak, and had come by to visit his friends. Georges was his usual self, cheerful and enthusiastic, carrying on in his ridiculous accent. The climbers on the ridge were very glad to hear his voice. They settled in for the night. They hoped to finish their descent to the glacier the next day.

Joe took a sleeping pill. That night he dreamed of a battlefield. Tents and buildings collapsed; he could make out shapes of people inside the tents. He stood watching an American colonel. The colonel held a pistol to each head and calmly fired through the tent fabric.

The climbers woke in the morning and continued down. They were now back on the crest of the ridge, safer ground but slower going than open slopes. They lowered themselves on fixed ropes—their own as well as ropes left by previous expeditions. Dick dislodged a block of snow that knocked Pete off his footing. Pete slithered 15 feet before an old rope caught him.

They peered through cloud into the valley. It looked far

away—but now in the growing dark they came upon their friends Gohar and Ali. The two Hunza had come as high as they could; they stood shivering in their light garments on a ledge at the start of the technical climbing.

Joe was the last to reach level ground. He lost his footing; Gohar rushed forward to receive him. Ali joined them and the two Hunza encircled Joe with their arms. Joe felt their concern for him as a kind of shock and he felt himself surrender to the notion that they were his protectors. He wept at this welcome.

The two Hunza carried the climbers' packs the last 300 feet to the glacier. They had erected tents. Ali made supper for everyone. The climbers ate and thanked him and found their sleeping bags.

Gohar brought them tea in the morning. Ali had found a very small flower in the otherwise barren litter of the glacier. He picked the flower and offered it to the three young Englishmen. The little party crossed the glacier together. The climbers limped along, giddy without their packs; the Hunza carried everything.

The sky had cleared when they reached Base Camp. Georges had waited and he smiled broadly as he ran toward them. Joe once again found himself in tears, glad for the sunglasses that hid his weeping from the others. He carried on into camp where Major Sarwat, clean and trim, hurried across to shake his hand and the hands of the other two—the major so blind to their egotism and to their earlier condescension, so delighted, so happy to have his boys back that Joe was happy and ashamed. Tears rose yet again to his eyes. He could not stop this weeping—he had not understood.

THEY RESTED. IT was Ramadan. Major Sarwat was a good Muslim. He fasted during the daylight hours: he would sit with the others at lunch and eat nothing. Joe had come to respect and admire the major and rely upon his presence; it was as if the major could protect him.

Time had become a vast ocean; Joe felt his life restored to him. He drifted, turning his thoughts away from the ordeal. His tears continued to come: when he was busy sorting through gear or talking with the others; when he was eating or reading. He would turn his head and there it would be, this mix of sadness and relief and love. His heart had a crack in it like a crack in a vase full of water. He felt it dry up in his chest during the afternoons but it filled up again at night. He awoke each morning to the same sense of bleeding—of a loss that was daily renewed. The mountain country was exquisitely beautiful but its desolation frightened him. He wrote to Maria in England. He told her that he and Peter and Dick were thinking of going back on the mountain.

They didn't talk about it during those first days. It was mid-July, past time to leave. Peter had guiding commitments in Switzerland. Dick's first child was due in August. Joe needed to get back to his climbing shop, Magic Mountain. A friend was running the shop for him but the friend had other obligations. The three climbers had lost weight. They were skittish and weepy—all of them, not only Joe. Three days passed before someone spoke of returning to the ridge.

They had sent for porters, who would arrive at the end of July. There was not much to feed them so the climbers would have to pack up and leave as soon as the porters arrived—but there was still time. The climbers' bodies had adapted to the altitude during their weeks of moving up and down the mountain. They had placed fixed ropes on the difficult sections. They believed they could get to the summit in five days.

They left camp on the fifth day after their return. They took three days to reach Camp Three. Here it snowed again. They spent four nights at Camp Three waiting for the storm to end. Their food reserves dwindled. Dick—the most ascetic of them—had done nearly all of the packing at Base Camp while Joe read and Peter wrote in his journal.

They woke on July 28 to better weather and climbed to the broad gully and crossed it. The gully was safe now: avalanche or wind had swept away most of the new snow. The climbers camped on the final ridge below the summit. High winds confined them to their tents the next day. They were hungry now. They had been climbing for eight days on five days' worth of rations. They woke at two o'clock in the morning on the ninth day knowing that if the weather were good they would finish climbing the mountain.

They looked out of the tent. It was snowing. The night clouds grew thicker as they peered into the dark. They made tea and packed. They left camp when the sun rose. They moved carefully down and down, light-headed with hunger and loss and relief. They reached the bottom of the route at nine o'clock in the morning. Gohar and Ali had once again come up to meet them. Joe turned away from them to look up at the mountain but it was lost in cloud.

The expedition departed K2 the next day. The three climbers walked down the path in a dream. Joe believed that the mountain had emptied him of shame and regret; he was a man without a past. He had had no wish to return to life as it was lived by men.

Maria met him in the crowd at Heathrow. She took him home. She held him in bed that night and her hands felt the bones where the flesh of his buttocks had been.

HE HAD BEEN home a month when the two of them took a cottage in the Lake District for a weekend. Joe slept twelve hours that first night in the country. One afternoon he drove with Maria to a village. He wanted to visit the parents of one of the four climbers he and Pete had buried after Changabang. Joe had kept in touch with the couple. He told Maria in the car that he hoped someone would do the same for his own parents if it came to that.

The middle-aged people were pleased to see the young couple. They brought out tea and cake and asked Joe about his plans. He told them and they said they hoped he would be careful.

PART FOUR

Ghosts

Over all the mountains is peace. . . .
Only wait—soon
You too shall find rest

—J.W. VON GOETHE

Everest, Northeast Ridge.

CHRIS BONINGTON AND a chatty, bespectacled young climber by the name of Al Rouse woke up on a remote mountain col in Western China on the morning of June 19, 1980. The two men were members of the first European climbing expedition to visit China since the Communist takeover in 1949. They planned to spend the day making the first ascent of a 6,200-meter peak. They had decided to call the mountain Sarakyaguqi, after the closest village.

They kicked steps in firm snow for 750 meters up the peak's North Ridge. They climbed in a bitingly cold wind under a severe blue sky. It took four hours to reach the summit. They peered west into a rising haze across a sea of virgin peaks and identified the shadow of K2; it broke the skyline like a headstone. Peter and Joe and the others were there; they might be on the summit now.

The peaks here offered spectacular opportunities for mountaineers, but Chris and Al had a relatively modest agenda. They were part of a small British team invited by the Chinese to make a reconnaissance of a largely unknown peak called Kongur (7,719 meters; 25,325 feet).

Al Rouse was new to Bonington's circle, but he was a contemporary —and sometime rival—of Joe Tasker and Peter Boardman. Al had begun making difficult rock climbs in his early teens. He had moved on to big mountains in the company of peers such as Brian Hall, Rab Carrington and Roger Baxter-Jones. He had joined with those three to make a splash in climbing circles two years earlier, with an alpine-style ascent of Jannu (7,710 meters; 25,295 feet), a peak just west of Kangchenjunga in Nepal. Rouse and Hall had followed that up by joining Doug Scott and Georges Bettembourg to climb the North Face of Nuptse (7,861 meters; 25,790 feet) in 1979.

Al was very smart—he'd studied mathematics at Cambridge— and notoriously argumentative. His personal life was chaotic. He and his climbing friends shared cheap flats that deteriorated into crash pads; they traded girlfriends; they scrounged for cash and spent it on booze and hash and cigarettes—but their loose ways were deceiving.

Rouse and his peers were very young, but they were serious men. They were passionately committed to a strict climbing ethic, which rejected anything suggesting a siege-style approach to climbing a mountain. Al wasn't entirely impressed by Bonington's achievements on Annapurna and Everest. Still, Al wanted to be famous himself—he made no bones about that. He under- stood that Chris was an important figure, and a useful person to know—the sort of man who could get you invited to climb in China. He liked and admired Chris, and was flattered by the older man's interest in him.

It was also true that Chris had taken to the new way of doing things. He had climbed with small teams in recent years, on the Ogre and K2 and elsewhere. His desire to run big expeditions had died along with so many of the friends he'd recruited to take part in them. The fixed ropes and the oxygen offered a margin of safety if a climber were injured or the weather went bad, but the same accoutrements meant putting more people at risk for longer periods of time. It was just too dangerous, all those men ferrying endless amounts of gear through icefalls and across glaciers and avalanche slopes. It was more fun to climb big mountains the way Chris and Don and the rest had climbed their great routes in the Alps two decades before.

This trip to Kongur didn't really count. It was a mere reconnaissance, undertaken to explore approaches to the mountain—an echo of the British establishment's first trip to Everest almost sixty years before. Like that earlier expedition, this venture was a sizable affair. It included a cadre of scientists to document the local flora and fauna and study the altitude's effects on the climbers. Charlie Clarke, who had served as medical man on Bonington's 1975 Everest expedition was a member of the scientific team. There were also Chinese interpreters and guides to help them find their way across China.

The climbing team itself was tiny. It included only Bonington and Rouse and Michael Ward. Ward, approaching sixty, had served as expedition doctor on the team that made Everest's first ascent in 1953. He'd lately been instrumental in convincing the Chinese to grant British climbers access to China and permission to explore Kongur itself.

Chris and Al planned to return the following year—the spring of 1981—to make a proper attempt on Kongur's summit. Peter Boardman and Joe Tasker would come with them. Chris would lead the climbing team. Michael Ward would return as leader of the overall expedition. Charlie Clarke would return as a member of the Base Camp team. Chris and Wendy had become close to Charlie and his wife Ruth Seifert. Ruth was a psychiatrist, an attractive, warmhearted, outrageously outspoken woman who had become close to many of Charlie's climber friends. The couple's London home served as a kind of London Base Camp for climbers on their way to and from Asia and elsewhere; it was a spacious, cheerful townhouse overrun by dogs, children and a stream of scruffy houseguests who lugged gear-stuffed duffle bags.

Chris, Al and Mike had spent the first weeks of the Kongur reconnaissance investigating the approaches to the mountain. They had ranged through unexplored country, crossing glaciers and climbing subsidiary peaks. The ascent of Sarakyaguqi was Al's last real climb on the trip—he wrenched his ankle quite badly on the way down.

Chris and Michael Ward continued to explore. They eventually concluded that next year's expedition should approach Kongur from the west. The mountain sprawled across the landscape, huge but rather squat. Al thought it looked easy, and said so. Chris wasn't so sure. Kongur was very high and it was very big. They had not managed to get a good view of the ground near the summit.

THEY SPENT TWO months in China, and arrived back in England on August 1. Chris spent much of the following winter organizing the return trip, which was to include a total of ten men. The team would include the four climbers as well as five scientists, counting Michael Ward and Charlie Clarke. The tenth slot went to Jim Curran, who was to film the expedition.

Curran, thirty-seven, had directed several previous climbing films, including a film of Joe Brown's successful expedition to Trango Tower. He'd become friendly with Chris during the past several years, often roping up with him to snatch a climb when Chris lectured near Curran's Bristol home. Jim also was a friend of Don Whillans, and was very close to Al Rouse. Jim and Al routinely climbed or drank together. Al often confided his personal problems—which usually involved climbing politics or romantic entanglements—to the older man.

Jim was a good climber, but not in Al's league. His real strengths—apart from his filmmaking—included his ability to stay friendly with the various factions that tended to form on expeditions. He was enormously charming—tough-minded but witty and self-deprecating—and he posed little threat to the leading climbers' status or ambitions.

The second Kongur expedition was to depart England in the spring of 1981. Joe Tasker and Al meanwhile planned to attempt the first winter ascent of Everest as members of an eight-man climbing team. The Everest expedition spent most of December and all of January trying to make a route up the West Ridge of the peak. The climbers suffered greatly from the cold and from illness. Joe and another climber, Aid Burgess, established Camp Three—a snowcave at around 7,000 meters—and wanted to press on. Joe was bitterly disappointed when the remaining climbers, sick and exhausted, refused to come up behind them in support.

Joe and Al returned to England barely two months before the Kongur expedition was to depart. Joe spent the intervening time hustling to lectures, going to parties with Maria and working on a book about the Everest trip; he managed to finish the book before it was time to leave for Kongur. He was tired and still very thin—so was Al Rouse—when the expedition members flew to Hong Kong on May 13.

The team spent their first days in China seeing sights, giving lectures, and attending banquets. They eventually traveled by truck to the Karokol Lakes. The team established Base Camp on May 29; the camp lay near a meadow, a surprisingly lush place set amid millions of acres of glacial debris. The climbers could stand and look across the Koksel glacier—a sea of ice towers surrounded by highlands barren of trees and swept by low clouds. A smaller peak hid Kongur from them.

The party made several training climbs on neighboring mountains that gave views across to Kongur's slopes. The climbers identified two possible routes to Kongur's summit. The more direct route led up the mountain's steep South Ridge and across to a subsidiary peak called Junction Peak; from there, they could continue up another ridge to Kongur's summit pyramid. The alternative route would take them up the easier Southwest Rib, but would require a longer traverse to Junction Peak.

Chris woke early on June 4. He felt very weak. Charlie Clarke diagnosed lobar pneumonia and dosed him with antibiotics. Chris retired to his sleeping bag. He felt for the moment too miserable to worry much about his prospects for climbing Kongur. The other three climbers established Advance Base Camp the next day in the Koksel Basin, at the start of the technical climbing. They set out on June 6 for the Koksel Col on the South Ridge. They hoped a closer look at the South Ridge would help them choose between it and the Southwest Rib.

Al had developed a bad cough and he was not climbing strongly. He turned back. Pete and Joe continued up the South Ridge. Their crampons gave them purchase on the ice-glazed rock, which eventually gave way to frozen snow. They kicked steps easily along the edge of the ridge, feeling the altitude as they gained height. They aimed to take sixty steps between rests. That figure dwindled to forty, then twenty.

Peter was climbing strongly. Chris and other climbers had come to believe that Peter was the strongest of the pair—perhaps of them all. Joe kept up with him through some seminarian's version of grit and ambition that included an element of self-hatred or at least a desire to suffer, to know what he could bear. The effort gave him some peace—set him above certain judgments—and so he welcomed these difficulties, these mortifications. The other climbers sometimes worried that Joe would push himself too hard; that he would continue moving up a route until his physical strength was gone.

The day waned as Joe and Peter moved higher on the South Ridge. Pete in particular wanted to know what was coming.

They couldn't see as far as the summit today, but what they saw of the South Ridge looked like something they could climb. The weather grew worse; more clouds rolled in, and the two climbers at last turned back. They tried a short cut that took them across new ground. The snow at their feet merged with the fog so that they had to feel for the ground with each step. They lost their way for a time. Joe made a rappel down into the murk and was surprised to find himself on the glacier. He shouted up to Peter, who quickly followed. Peter's rappel was oddly like rising through clouds into a world of sunlight—the glacier drenched with it. He reached the glacier and unclipped from his rappel brake. He looked up through brightness, half-expecting to see the mountain, but Kongur was hidden in white.

Al Rouse had come up the glacier to place wands that would help the climbers find their way if they had to retreat down the glacier in a storm. He greeted Joe and Peter and the three climbers descended together and spent the night at Advance Base Camp. They planned to explore the lower reaches of their alternate route, the Southwest Rib, the next morning. It snowed heavily the next day, so instead they packed up some of their personal gear and walked down to Base Camp.

Chris was still recuperating from his illness. The next day the three healthy climbers set out to climb a small mountain near their camp, but the weather turned bad again while they were still low on the peak. They figured they would need four or five consecutive days of reasonably good weather to climb Kongur. They had begun to wonder if they could realistically hope for such a window.

The four climbers convened at Base Camp the next day to hash out their strategy. They decided to have the Chinese porters ferry gear to Advance Base Camp in the Koksel Basin. The climbing team would move up to that camp; they could use it as a launching pad for further forays onto the South Ridge and for a reconnaissance of the Southwest Rib.

Al didn't want to use the porters. He argued that relying on them to make carries would spoil any chance of making a purely alpine-style ascent. The others thought his qualms were ridiculous. The climbers would in fact be making an alpine-style push from the Koksel Basin, at the start of the real climbing. Joe pointed out with some heat that climbers used trains to get to the base of climbs in the Alps; surely it was all right to use porters to hump a few loads to Advance Base Camp. Al withdrew his objections, but the others were left with a sense that he looked down upon their enterprise—that he had somehow seized the high ground. There was a growing feeling that Al's scruples and his constant chatter made him a pest.

Chris moved on to a discussion of partners—whether they should draw straws or rely on logic to decide which climbers should rope up together on the peak. The younger climbers hesitated. Chris—given his age and his recent illness—was likely to be a liability to his partner, but no one was eager to acknowledge that fact.

Al spoke up at last. He suggested that perhaps Joe and Peter should not pair up since they knew each other so well. They might tend to operate as a unit; their joint views might dominate the group's decision-making. Pete volunteered to climb with Al. The two of them knew each other the least. Al had been with Chris on Kongur the previous year, and with Joe on Everest a few months ago. That settled that.

The four climbers left Base Camp the next day, June 13. Chris let the porters carry much of his personal gear, but he still moved slowly. Charlie had pronounced the infection gone, and the notion of a relapse high on the route was too appalling to contemplate. Chris concentrated on trying to keep pace with the others.

The little party reached Advance Base Camp in the late afternoon. They stood upon a snowfield that crossed a short stretch of ground to a gap between two opposing ridgelines. Chris had the sense that he and his companions stood on a cloud.

Joe and Chris went up to the South Ridge in the morning. Chris was relieved to feel his strength returning. Joe had a headache. The climbers took turns breaking trail through knee-deep snow to the base of the ridge, and climbed to a campsite below the expedition's high point. Pete and Al came up behind them. Pete wanted to continue climbing. Chris thought they had gone far enough for one day. Joe said his head still hurt. The climbers made camp.

Al chattered away in the tent he shared with Pete. He hadn't brought a book; his lightweight ethic precluded such luxuries. Joe and Chris were quiet in their tent; they were happy to read in peace.

The climbers woke to wind and snow the next morning, but the sky cleared later. They roused themselves and climbed two hours to the previous high point. Pete pushed on a bit further but after a time the others shouted to him to come down.

Chris and Joe were settling into a partnership on the mountain. Joe had resisted the older man's authority on K2 two years earlier, and Chris had resented him for it. They got along now. Chris admired Joe's toughness and intelligence and ambition. He recognized Joe's essential kindness, and he saw that Joe liked him in turn. Joe these days found Chris a surprisingly sympathetic character, more open and relaxed than the reserved and somewhat touchy Bonington he remembered from their early meetings. And the older man's achievements impressed him; Joe recognized Chris as someone who knew what it was to build a new life, to elbow past old fears in pursuit of new experience. Joe knew that Chris knew something of what it was like to layer the present over the past, to invent a life large enough to overshadow the slights and failures of one's history.

Pete cast a skeptical eye on the growing affinity between Joe and Chris. He believed that they were both dragging their feet on the mountain—that they left it to him to supply the momentum that would give them a chance to climb the peak.

The climbers talked about what to do next. Chris and Joe and Peter wanted to stay with the South Ridge. The ridge seemed to give some protection against avalanche and it offered reasonable but interesting climbing. Al wanted to have a look at the Southwest Rib before deciding. The others sometimes wished that he would take direction, defer to their collective experience. They agreed to return to the Koksel Basin and go up for a closer look at the alternate route. They descended toward Advance Base Camp, and lost their way for a time in a whiteout—the afternoon fog blending into snow—before arriving at the camp in the early afternoon.

They started up the Southwest Rib the next morning. The angle was easy but deep snow made the going difficult. They slogged to 6,300 meters, catching glimpses through fog of peaks and valleys and some of the ground that stood between them and Kongur's summit. They made camp and discussed their plans for the next day. They could stick to the Southwest Rib, but they were increasingly concerned about avalanche risk. They could detour across open slopes to the ridge that led up to Junction Peak—but those slopes had the look of the one that had killed Nick Estcourt. They put off the decision.

It snowed that evening as they lay in their tents. The snow and their situation recalled to Joe and Pete their horrendous night on K2 the previous year. Joe told Chris the story: eleven days on the mountain, food running short, the avalanches that buried the tent. Pete meanwhile told Al the same story.

Chris and Joe after a time heard the others moving out in the night; they were digging a snow hole that might protect them from a slide. Chris and Joe resisted the urge to join them, but eventually put on their boots and went out to dig their own shelter. All four climbers got wet digging in the fresh snow and they spent an uncomfortable night in their new caves. The sun came out briefly the next morning, but more snow began to fall as they prepared to climb higher on the rib. The snowfall triggered another debate. Peter wanted to stay and wait for the snow to stop, then try to gain more height. Chris and Joe wanted to go down. Al left it to the others. The climbers went down.

They spent three days at Base Camp, resting and preparing for a summit attempt. Their experience on the Southwest Rib had convinced them to return to the South Ridge. They left Base Camp on June 23. They took a day and a half to reach Advance Base Camp at the bottom of the ridge, and carried on to get a head start on the climbing. They pitched their tents on the ridge late on the second day, and in the morning they climbed unroped to their high point.

The South Ridge grew steeper here. The climbers aimed for a tower of rock that seemed to pose their next serious challenge. The weather for once was good. They had no confidence that it would last, but meanwhile the views were spectacular—a jumble of jagged white summits, most untouched by men; the mountains seemed fantasies of mountains.

Pete led up the ridge, moving quickly up easy rock, stepping off the crest to avoid patches of deteriorating snow. He came to the rock tower, the bottom sections smeared with ice. He placed an ice screw and a knife-blade piton for protection and climbed on the front points of his crampons. The sky behind him vanished; the world shrunk to his body and this gray wall. The angle eased and he chopped steps in the ice with his axe. This brought him to a small rock buttress, where he knocked in another piton.

Al had begun the morning tired, but he was feeling better. He swarmed up behind Peter, and the others followed. Al led past rock to a ridge of snow, where Peter resumed the lead. It was difficult to find protection in the snow, and the occasional patches of ice were too soft to hold screws. The climbers were aware that any sort of avalanche here would peel all of them off the mountain.

Pete was tired. His mind drifted as he continued to break trail through the snow. The others had no notion of this; they let him lead on. It was as if they were climbing the mountain because Peter insisted they climb it—as if they believed that he remembered something they had forgotten in their weariness. He climbed on snow that collapsed underfoot. He dug and kicked to make firmer steps for the others. He came at last to better snow and then to the top of the South Ridge; from there the main ridgeline stretched like a spine up over Junction Peak and on toward the summit of Kongur.

They had climbed 900 meters that day, to a height of 7,300 meters. The altitude was increasingly debilitating. The climbers pitched their tent and set about preparing their freeze-dried supper. Chris and Joe barely touched their food. The four climbers collapsed into their sleeping bags and slept deeply. Chris and Joe awoke hungry, but the party had brought almost no breakfast food. They were saving the freeze-dried meals for their remaining nights on the ridge.

The party made a late start. Chris and Joe broke trail. They moved across snow slopes below the ridge crest. The sun disappeared behind other mountains and plunged the climbers into shadow. Their unease seemed to swim up from vast depths to reach this place. Nothing made sense to their bodies; short of dying they could not adapt to this place. The weather closed in. They couldn't see to navigate. They pitched their tents again and settled in to wait for better conditions.

Chris mistook some lemonade mix for curry powder. The resulting concoction was horrible; once again, he and Joe weren't able to eat much. The wind blew hard in the night. Peter woke in the predawn hours and heard it and quickly sat up to gather his boots and gear. He finished packing and sat listening. He wanted to be ready if the wind collapsed the tent.

Morning came, and now the climbers could make out the summit pyramid of their mountain. It looked surprisingly difficult—steep and long, a mix of rock and snow; it amounted to another mountain for them to climb. They packed their tents in the rising wind.

They waded through snow for hours and at last came to the top of Junction Peak. They stopped here in the late afternoon to study their objective further. The next barrier was the long ridge of snow that led onto the summit pyramid. The snow would give tricky and dangerous climbing.

They dropped down off the ridge and dug a snow cave big enough to hold them all. The cave was cold but utterly quiet. They could have been anywhere. The blank hours passed. A storm might arise in the night and trap them here. They might run out of food and grow too weak to leave; it happened at these altitudes. No one came to this mountain; the climbers' bodies might never be found. They drifted in and out of such fantasies, a little aghast at themselves for making up such stories, for finding them interesting.

Chris was the first to climb out of the cave in the morning. He ducked back inside to report that the sky was clear but the wind was terrible. Peter argued for pressing on. Chris and Joe were worried about food. They were already hungry. There wasn't enough food to see them through a long storm. They also worried that there might not be enough snow higher up to dig a cave close to the summit. The climbers would certainly die if they were forced to spend a night in the open with the wind like this.

Peter won the argument. The party set out late in the morning to make a run for the summit and then back again. They had perhaps ten hours to climb the rest, some 600 meters on difficult and unfamiliar ground. Joe and Chris left camp ahead of the others. They climbed in crampons, up hard snow and across the slopes that ran down from the crest of the ridge, growing steeper as the climbers gained height. They could look down upon a drop of 6,000 meters. It was like looking down from the window of a commercial airliner. They were unbelievably high. The distance to the glacier receded into abstraction; it seemed to them about as real as the possibility of their own deaths.

Chris led a steep gully. Joe followed and led past him on shallow snow. They continued to swap leads as they picked their way past rock and ice towers that interrupted the ridge. They tried to identify and skirt cornices that might collapse under their weight. Chris led up a short rock tower that made him think of a huge fang. The rock offered big holds at first, but then forced him out onto difficult slabs with little protection. He gazed down past his feet to rock and then vast snow slopes. He stood there in his heavy boots and crampons, drawing the moment out. He felt somehow protected—absurdly, exhilaratingly safe in his red wind suit and his various down garments. Joe, also swathed in red, directed a silent gaze upward from the tower's base. Chris glancing down could see the blue patches of material at Joe's legs and wrists. He thought of the consequences a fall would bring upon them both.

Chris found a place to build an anchor. Joe followed him up and led past to peer over the top of the fang. He called down in a curiously flat voice; there was no way forward. Al and Pete had come up behind them. Those two traversed on steep snow around the base of the fang to a col on the ridge. Chris and Joe followed them and arrived at the col as Pete climbed up loose, brittle rock and out of sight.

The rope came tight to Al. He shouted and got no reply and set off, cursing; there was no way of knowing what sort of ground Pete was on or whether he had found a place to make an anchor. Chris and Joe gave Al a minute and then followed, moving roped together. The ground was easy but there was no hope of stopping if either man slipped. There were no good handholds and there was too little snow to perform a self-arrest with an axe. They caught up with the other two. The four climbers stood in a kind of loose huddle, suddenly aware of their surroundings and of their dangerously committed position.

They shook off this awareness and gazed across at the summit. Peter pointed to a snow gully at the base of the pyramid. They could dig a snow cave there and go for the top tomorrow—but they hadn't brought sleeping bags. The others didn't speak. After a time, the four climbers turned and set off down. It was easier now that they knew the ground. They reached their snow cave in good order. They piled in and settled into the quiet and lay with their questions, too weary to speak.

They waited until morning to discuss their options. Peter wanted to climb the mountain now. They could bring their sleeping bags this time. They could dig a cave in the snow bank he'd spotted the previous day. Chris was worried. The party was very low on food. He and Joe were very tired. The two of them thought that the climbers should all go down to Base Camp for a real rest. They could collect more food and then storm back up to finish the route. Chris also confessed his concern that he might lack the strength to make a second attempt if they tried now and failed. Al agreed with Chris and Joe; he wanted to go down.

Peter was angry—he knew he could finish the route now. The four of them packed and set off along the ridge. They climbed back up and over Junction Peak and made a long traverse through deep snow across the plateau to the Southwest Rib, which they had decided to use as a descent route. They arrived at the slopes above Advance Base Camp late in the day. Michael Ward had climbed up to meet them and to hear their news.

The party spent the night at Advance Base. They woke in the morning to gaze up at their mountain. The weather high on the peak looked bad. They were spared any sense that they might have reached the summit if Peter had won the argument the day before. They were relieved that there was no occasion for second-guessing. They felt vaguely pleased with themselves as they made their way down to Base Camp. They looked forward to Chinese food and British liquor.

Jim Curran had assembled his gear to film the climbers as they approached Base Camp. Jim was appalled by their appearance. All four figures were hollow-eyed and gaunt, more specters than men. He was staggered to hear that they meant to return to the route.

THE CLIMBERS HAD no thought of leaving the mountain—and they couldn't afford to remain at Base Camp for long if they wanted to make the first ascent of the peak. A Japanese team had permission to climb Kongur from the north. The Japanese might arrive as soon as July 14—now less than two weeks away. The British climbers rested for three days. They left Base Camp on July 4 with enough food and fuel for ten days on the mountain. The weather at base had been poor, but the sky was clear as they set out; perhaps they would be lucky with the weather.

They were going to climb the Southwest Rib—the route Al had favored all along—and not the South Ridge. They had found the descent of the rib straightforward and had decided that it was the easier route. Joe still liked the South Ridge—it still seemed safer from avalanche—but the others overruled him.

They found their new route deep in snow. The going was harder than they'd hoped. The ground was otherwise easy—it wasn't steep—but they felt the altitude more than they had on their previous attempt. Chris moved slowly and stopped for frequent rests. This evidence of his weakness depressed him. He offered to descend, to let the younger men climb the mountain without him. Peter snapped at him, told him not to be a fool.

The party reached the snow caves they'd dug during their early reconnaissance of the Southwest Rib. Peter wanted to keep climbing; they could dig new caves higher up. Chris and Joe disagreed, overruling Peter yet again. The party stopped for the night. The next morning's weather was reasonable but the wind rose in the afternoon as they climbed higher. The rib grew steeper. Chris wanted to stop again but this time Peter had his way; he convinced the others that they could reach their old snow cave near Junction Peak. That would save the work of digging a new one.

Peter and Al went first. Al couldn't stop coughing. He left the trail breaking to Peter. The weather got worse, making route finding difficult. They had left wands; someone would occasionally glimpse one through the blowing snow. Joe and Al eventually switched partners so that Joe could spell Peter at the soul-destroying task of breaking trail through the deepening snow. Peter at one point found himself standing on a cornice with a terrifying view down the South Face of the mountain. He retreated onto solid ground as quickly as he could, feeling as if someone had splashed cold water in his face.

Peter and Joe reached the cave near Junction Peak at nine o'clock that evening. Al and Chris caught them twenty minutes later; they had struggled even to follow in the others' tracks. Chris in particular felt that he must have a day of rest before going higher.

The next morning brought clouds and some wind. Peter thought the weather looked reasonable but Chris pronounced it bad. Joe and Al didn't bother to look outside. The four climbers decided to wait a day and then climb to the gully at the base of the summit pyramid. Peter all but promised that they would find sufficient snow to dig caves there. That meant they could leave the tents behind. Chris wasn't so sure.

The climbers set off the next morning, July 8. Chris made nervous jokes about the risk they were taking. He still wanted to bring tents, but in the end no one had the strength to carry them. The ridgeline that led from Junction Peak to the base of the summit pyramid was covered with deep snow. Joe led through unconsolidated drifts that he found frightening; these slopes seemed very likely to avalanche. Chris belayed him from the ridge crest; he would leap to the other side of the ridge if Joe fell. Joe was sick with weariness. His fatigue dulled his fear. He looked back after a time and saw that Chris had abandoned his stance—was just walking behind him on the other end of the rope. They would go together if the slope avalanched.

Chris took over the lead at the start of steeper ground. He led through on rock caked with a thin layer of brittle snow. He moved with great care into deeper snow at the verge of a huge drop. He might have wandered onto a cornice; it might collapse under him. He went down on all fours for a time to distribute his weight more evenly.

The ground was not technically difficult but the climbers carried heavy packs and they were clumsy in their layers of warm clothing and their bulky footwear. They felt sick and their limbs were almost unbearably heavy. The growing exposure took them aback at moments. They were like dancers who strike a pose and then catch someone's eye; they felt themselves teeter and sway.

Pete and Al went ahead now. They moved cautiously up the ridge. Chris took notice of an enormous wall of cloud approaching the peak; it had the look of something wicked. The climbers reached the bottom of the summit pyramid. There was very little snow, less than Peter had promised. They scraped at the snow and ice and wound up lying head to head in narrow slots in the ground. Chris called the slots snow coffins.

The storm had arrived while they were digging. There was too much snow and wind to move. The hours passed in a silent procession with little change to mark them. The climbers drifted in and out of a sense that it hardly mattered what became of them.

Chris felt the walls of his snow coffin give way in the night. He dug the snow out in the morning and climbed back in. The storm continued for another three days. Time blurred. Each new night's darkness came as a surprise. They were hungry, though. They worked their way through their food and felt themselves grow weaker. Each man at moments imagined himself already dead on this mountain. Their bewilderment at times blended with a sense of relief. It was almost pleasant to be in their slots where for days on end almost nothing was required of them. They had achieved some kind of liberation. This was easy.

CHRIS POKED HIS axe through the roof of his little cave on the morning of July 12. He saw gray mist; still, they could not stay here any longer. He packed and then emerged into sun. The sky above the low fog was clear. The day was cold and windy but there was no threat of further snow. They could climb again—and he was thrilled at the thought; he had forgotten that he'd come to climb the mountain. He shouted for the others. He was impatient for the first time on this expedition—not anxious, only eager. They should go. They should leave now for the summit. He felt his lost youth rise up in him.

The climbing ahead looked difficult. Pete and Al roped up and went before the others. The two of them swapped leads on awkward and dangerous ground with mixed climbing on snow and rock. Pete's hands lost feeling after several pitches. He took off his mittens; his fingers had turned dusky blue at the tips.

It scared him. He asked Joe and Chris to move past into the lead. The party climbed a ridge of snow and broken rock until the ground opened up and they could follow snow to the top of the mountain. They had climbed 150 meters in five hours. The way to Kongur's summit lay open before them.

Pete took off his boots and rubbed his feet. The others waited. He put the boots back on and the climbers continued. It was a vast relief to simply walk, but already something slipped from them, faded. Their former difficulties were like snapshots, inadequate. Their memories seemed well-meant lies. It was better not to think of it.

They continued to move toward the summit. They felt their bodies' suffering. Until now they had chosen to believe that it did not matter if they suffered. Here they allowed their bodies a certain modest importance; it would be good if this discomfort would stop. Chris felt his love for his companions even as he acknowledged his weariness; he had stored both feelings in the same place and they came into his view all at once. His eyes filled as he continued to move his legs and lift his feet; he was a certain kind of machine. He wished only to continue to breathe, to inhale and to spill his exhalations back into this sky.

Joe called down to him. Chris looked past him out across snow to the summit—perhaps 30 meters. Joe untied from the rope and went ahead with the film camera. He stopped in the snow just below the top and filmed the others as they walked past. He filmed them on the top and then realized that the film would reach England before he did. His mother would see it and worry that he'd been killed. He ran around to get himself into the picture. He had forgotten that his mother was blind.

It was very cold and windy. They stayed ten minutes. The sky above receded into space, a deep blue; clouds billowed below them like feather quilts across the folds and tops of other mountains. They climbed down into deeper snow and Chris and Joe and Al began digging. Peter with his frozen fingertips couldn't dig. Chris and Joe finished digging their cave before Al finished the one he meant to share with Peter. Chris and Joe didn't offer to help Al. Peter blew up at them. Their happiness and their gratitude and their knowledge of the work ahead, the descent, made Chris and Joe contrite. The climbers made tea in their caves. It was two o'clock in the morning when they drifted off to sleep.

THE SUN WAS shining when they awoke. The wind had dropped. It was still very cold. They came out of their caves into the daylight and stared across to Kongur's Northeast Summit. They had judged it to be lower than their high point—the Central Summit—but now they weren't sure. Pete said they must climb it; after all of this they must be absolutely certain. The others agreed. The four of them left their packs and moved in pairs across snow slopes, back up over the huge hump of the Central Summit and across to the Northeast Summit. It wasn't higher. They turned back, relieved for some reason that their original judgment had been right. They retraced their steps and reached their snow cave below the true summit in the afternoon.

It was late—past four o'clock—but they wanted to get down, past the dangers of the summit pyramid and the upper sections of the ridge from Junction Peak. They needed the food they had left in the snow cave at Junction Peak. The night might bring bad weather. The climbers might be stuck up here for days. They had been here for too long.

The descent was dangerous. They were tired and frightened, and tired of being frightened. Their wish to be safe and to rest made them hurry; they were inclined to believe what they wished to believe. Peter was just ahead of the others when he came to a section steep enough to require a rappel. He tossed the ropes and leaned back on them, and began a traverse. The rope caught a rock overhead and tugged it loose. The others saw it and shouted and saw the rock hit him.

They watched him disappear down the rope; his brake hand had come off and there was nothing to slow his fall. Joe in his mind's eye saw Peter slide off the end of the rope. The vision was familiar, as if he had seen it before in a dream.

A moment passed and Peter's voice floated up. The rock had knocked him unconscious for a moment but his rappel device had somehow caught the flesh of his hand. That had been enough to slow his descent, and the pain had revived him. The others hurried down to him. Peter had blood on his face and he was unsteady on his feet, but he could move without their assistance. The four climbers carried on down the ridge, looking for their snow cave at Junction Peak. Peter and Al went out front again. Joe and Chris followed them as the sun sank lower in the sky; they were racing it now.

It grew dark on the ridge but the moon was enough to guide them. Chris had never been so weary. He could take a few steps but then he would stop; after a time he could take a few more steps. He longed for a place where he could lie down and sleep. Joe moved deliberately behind him. He didn't hurry Chris, who was dimly moved by such patience, such intelligence. They reached the snow cave. Chris in spite of his horrible thirst went to sleep without waiting for tea.

The morning was better. They were getting close, now. They made their way up and over Junction Peak and then through deep snow across to the Southwest Rib and then down. They were too weary to consider the avalanche risk. The descent was a dream.

Chris wanted to sit down but if he did he would sleep and he could not face the prospect of waking up to more of this.

Michael Ward and Jim Curran met the climbers above Advance Base Camp. They had imagined their friends lost in the storm that had shrouded the peak for three days. The party spent the night at Advance Base. The next morning they descended to Base Camp to be received by the rest of the team, including the smiling porters. Liu Dayi, the Chinese liaison officer, was smiling as well. His relief at their safe return was evident and very touching as he wrapped his arms around Chris and whispered the Englishman's name: *Ah, Bonington, Bonington.*

A yak arrived in Base Camp that afternoon; it carried champagne sent by the trip's sponsors. The expedition put on a feast the next evening. Their celebration lasted far into the night; an almost hysterical edge crept into the repeated toasts, the laughter and the shouting in the huge darkness of their valley.

THE JAPANESE HAD arrived and begun two separate attempts on Kongur from the north. A large group laid siege to the East Ridge. Meanwhile, a smaller party—three climbers—hoped to make an alpine-style ascent of the North Ridge. The three men set out for the summit on July 16. They carried enough food for nine days on the mountain.

A local man, a shepherd, looked up a week later and saw three figures on Kongur's North Ridge through a break in the fast-moving clouds. The three figures were climbing snow near the top of their ridge. The shepherd watched until clouds rolled across his line of vision. He turned back to his flock. No one saw the climbers again.

22

THE KONGUR CLIMB was a prelude. Chris had promised his family never to return to Everest. Mick Burke's death in 1975 had been especially hard on the Boningtons' two young sons, who had come to know Mick as a kind of playful uncle or older cousin. But the Chinese decision to open their borders to foreign climbers meant that the British could approach Everest from its north side for the first time in more than thirty years.

Everest's northern slopes had been the scenes of seven failed British expeditions between the two World Wars—including George Mallory's last expedition in 1924. That expedition had ended when Mallory—the most celebrated climber of his generation—had disappeared with his young protégé Andrew Irvine high on the mountain's Northeast Ridge.

The Chinese had eventually made the first ascent of the North Col route, which intercepted the Northeast Ridge about 1,000 feet below the scene of Mallory's disappearance. No one had ever tried to climb the complete Northeast Ridge itself. The ridge was a daunting three miles long, dividing the mountain's sheer East Face—the Kangshung Face—from its North Face. A complete ascent of the Northeast Ridge would require climbers to negotiate a series of steep rocky pinnacles at about 8,000 meters before joining the North Col route near the summit.

Al Rouse had applied to the Chinese for permission to try the

Northeast Ridge. He had since decided that Bonington should lead the expedition. Chris had the sponsor—Jardine Matheson, which had backed the two Kongur trips—as well as credibility and contacts with the Chinese. The idea was that the four Kongur climbers would return to China the following year—1982—to make an alpine-style ascent of Everest's last unclimbed ridge. They had spent hours on Kongur discussing their prospects.

As it turned out, Al didn't go. He wasn't wanted. He never understood exactly why. He hadn't delivered a stellar performance on the second Kongur expedition. He'd been sick during the early days of the trip. He'd annoyed the other three climbers with his somewhat fussy concern for the finer points of climbing ethics. He'd annoyed Peter still more by hanging back with Chris and Joe when Peter wanted to push ahead.

It didn't help that Al and Peter had a history—for a time, they'd competed for the title of England's best young rock climber. And now Al was making inroads in the expedition game, threatening to replace Peter and Joe as British mountaineering's latest young prodigy. Al's privileged background and his Cambridge education hadn't exactly made him a snob but he was something of a showoff. He sometimes had the air of a precocious child, one proud of his achievements. His sheer appetite for argument could be obnoxious.

There was something else, too. Al had angered Chris before the second Kongur expedition by publicly making light of the mountain. The young hotshot had been perhaps a little embarrassed to be part of an establishment expedition. He'd indicated during a press conference that Kongur would be easy—a mere walk-up: *The really surprising thing will be if we need to use a rope.* Chris believed that Al's remark had caused some people to dismiss the expedition and its considerable achievement.

Whatever the reasons, Chris drove down to Al's home in

Sheffield and gave him the news. Al was genuinely devastated. He had considered Chris a friend. He'd defended him when other young climbers dismissed the older man as a throwback. Al experienced this rebuff as a public humiliation and a serious blow to his ambitions as a Himalayan climber.

Chris also left Jim Curran off the Everest roster. Jim had filmed the Kongur expedition, but he'd asked Joe Tasker to carry a camera and shoot some film during the second summit attempt. Joe had taken to the work, and had convinced Chris to let him make the film of the Everest expedition.

Al and Jim were neighbors in Sheffield, and around this time they came across their mutual friend Don Whillans. Don—now forty-eight—was getting used to his own status as an outsider. The younger climbers who dominated high-altitude climbing weren't eager to invite him on their expeditions to the world's great ranges. It was hard to blame them: Don was still cranky and demanding, and he was increasingly unfit.

He had managed to wangle an invitation from Doug Scott to join a trip to Shivling (6,543 meters; 21,466 feet) in the Garhwal Himalaya the previous summer—while Al and Jim were on Kongur. The other climbers had complained to Doug about Don's slowness (he was vastly overweight, and his knees troubled him) and his selfishness (he still couldn't be brought to help with the cooking). Doug and Georges Bettembourg and two other climbers had managed a beautiful route on Shivling's formidable East Pillar, climbing it in perfect alpine style. Don had attempted the mountain's West Face with another group, which had turned back in high winds. He had returned to Audrey—they lived in Wales now—and to his oddly rootless life. He roamed the countryside in his van or on his motorbike, turning up at climbing clubs and at friends' houses—Jim Curran's place in Sheffield had become a favorite stop—to drink to excess and scramble up an occasional route. His friends found him a trial—though some found him to be surprisingly good with children—but they tolerated his visits. Many did so for old time's sake or because they were too kind to send him on his way; others, including Jim Curran, genuinely enjoyed his company.

Tonight Don sat and drank with Jim and Al and the three outcasts talked mostly about climbs, and about the fickle nature of climbing careers and reputations. Al was feeling particularly shaky that evening. He had recently suffered through the end of a long-term relationship, and he had been drinking far too much, dreaming of climbs that would recoup his reputation and his shattered ego. Don listened for a while and then offered young Al Rouse his version of sympathy over Al's banishment from the Bonington circle: *Aye-aye, lad—welcome back to the 'uman race.*

THERE WAS TALK later that Chris ought to have kept Al on the team and added another pair of climbers. That would have made a total of six climbers—an opportunity to establish a different expedition chemistry. And it would have created a stronger team with greater reserves. The Northeast Ridge was a tremendous undertaking for four climbers—far more ambitious than anything Chris had yet attempted.

Chris for his part looked forward to the simple delights of a small expedition. His liking and admiration for both Pete and Joe had deepened on Kongur. This was true in spite of the differences in their ages; Chris would be forty-seven on Everest, roughly fourteen years older than Joe and more than sixteen years older than Peter. Bonington took Joe's advice and offered Al's spot to Dick Renshaw. Chris hadn't climbed with Renshaw, but Dick had performed well on Dunagiri with Joe and then with Joe and the others on K2 in 1980. It helped that Renshaw was the most self-effacing of climbers, offering the sharpest possible contrast to Al's flamboyance.

Charlie Clarke and Adrian Gordon also were coming. Charlie had provided medical care on Everest in 1975 and had organized the food for both Kongur expeditions. Adrian Gordon had managed Advance Base Camp on Everest in 1975; he would play a similar support role this time. Sponsor Jardine Matheson was sending along a small trekking party. The trekkers would accompany the expedition to Base Camp and explore the surrounding area before making an early departure.

Chris planned to climb Everest's Northeast Ridge using tactics similar to those that had succeeded on Kongur. The climbers would establish a series of low camps, and then make a dash for the summit carrying bivouac gear. They would not rely on porters past Advance Base Camp. They would hump their own gear, which meant they couldn't stock the higher camps with oxygen or carry up enough rope to fix much of the route. The lack of oxygen would make them more vulnerable to exhaustion or altitude sickness. The absence of fixed ropes meant that a rapid retreat might prove impossible. Those dangers would compound as they climbed into the increasingly thin air on the higher sections of the ridge—where they would face the most difficult climbing and be furthest from the hope of rescue if something went wrong.

The months leading up to the expedition's departure were frantic for Joe. He was finishing his second book, an account of his climbs to date. Peter's success with *The Shining Mountain* had galled Joe, who had contributed material to the book and thought he deserved a mention on the cover. Joe had taken just two months to write his own first book, about the winter Everest expedition, writing longhand with almost no revisions. He was writing this second book—*Savage Arena*—the same way. He sometimes scribbled for eight hours at a time before quitting to drive somewhere to deliver a lecture.

The writing came easier this time. He was writing about himself and his motives, about climbing with Dick and Peter and others in circumstances that had left him battered and temporarily happy. As he wrote he felt his bewilderment at finding himself compelled to undertake such difficulties. He also felt a rising sense of what it might mean to be an artist—of how much he would have to leave behind to say anything entirely true.

Meanwhile, there was packing to do for the Everest trip—and there were parties. The parties these days were fantastic; the decadence felt earned. People knew that something big was happening. The women were in love with the men and the men knew it. They all went to the parties to forget what was missing from their lives—and what they were likely to miss if they continued to live like this—and to tell themselves and each other that their sacrifices made them extraordinary. They traded gossip, too; they sorted through each other's lives like family members do; if you had a problem everyone knew all about it.

Joe went to watch all of this. He would drink some mushroom tea and stand in a corner for a time and watch the others through the smoke and noise of the party; it was as though he had stepped outside of his new life to take pleasure in its shape, or as though he were trying to learn something about these people who populated it.

Maria was still with him. She would watch him as he sized up the other partygoers, and she would marvel at his determination to understand and perhaps outdo them. Joe was always telling her he'd like a holiday. She didn't believe him. He would sometimes rest. He would lie on the couch and everything in him would give way, go completely slack: his hands and feet, his limbs and torso, his face and his neck and shoulders. Maria would see him that way and think of an animal. Other times he was completely alert, taking everything in, a curious but deeply skeptical child. And when Joe would go away for a trip she would go back to her teaching job and sit in the faculty room listening to the talk and she would remember Joe and the parties—the faces and shouts and bodies—and she would think *My God, this is so boring.*

Peter and Hilary had married after his return from K2 in 1980. He told her now that this trip to Everest would be his last major expedition for a while. He needed to make some money. He was thinking he might write a novel. He loved being home, and he was tired of the deaths—losing friends and burying strangers. He had come home to Hilary after Nick's death in 1978 and had poured out his sadness and his fear. When he returned from expeditions he would learn about a divorce or an illness or an accident, and he would grieve for others' losses as if they were his own. He wrote in the afternoons and into the evenings and stayed up late to talk with Hilary. They talked about what kind of life would make sense for them. They wanted to have a child. There might be an answer in that.

THE CLIMBERS ARRIVED in Lhasa on March 8, 1982. The Chinese guides who supervised their travels gave them a tour of the Potala Palace. The climbers followed their guides up steep flights of stairs and through dark passages to emerge a thousand feet above the city on a roof drenched in sunlight—the courtyard of the Dalai Lama's former living quarters. The Chinese also took the climbers to Jokhang Temple. Pilgrims circled the Temple clockwise, prostrating themselves and chanting. The Temple's interior held several thousand people; the air smelled of butter, smoke and incense, sweat and animal skins.

They left Lhasa in a small caravan of trucks to travel the Chinese-built road to Everest Base Camp. The trucks wound through terrain almost startling in its absence of any obvious glamour. The landscape's huge features seemed to lack features of their own; they were simply folds in the earth. The air grew cold as the trucks bumped along the road so that the road seemed to heave beneath them. The travelers stopped to visit monasteries, aware that the Red Guard had destroyed thousands of such places during Mao's Cultural Revolution. Monks still lived in these remaining retreats, but the small men with their robes and curious calm seemed reduced to relics. The climbers felt themselves tourists on some ancient battleground; they trod as it were on corpses and tattered objects, once precious to now-absent owners.

They traveled some 250 miles to Xegur, the last town on their journey. The expedition members spent two days there, resting and acclimatizing before the drive to the Rongbuk Glacier and Everest Base Camp. Chris and Charlie and Adrian Gordon had all come down with the flu; they were glad for the halt.

Xegur had been home to a pair of monasteries, and one of them survived. The guides conducted a tour. Charlie Clarke was struck by two 20-foot figures at the monastery entrance: a black demon on the left, a red dragon on the right. Inside the gates were trees that seemed sprung from the monastery itself; the region was otherwise treeless. The walls supported huge frescoes. There were golden Buddha statues and there were thousands of vases—gifts from China some centuries before, when China was a mere neighbor to the Kingdom of Tibet.

Charlie Clarke and David Mathew—a member of the trekking party—stole away from the guides to cross a bridge and climb to the ruins of the second, northern monastery. The hill had once been terraced to hold the dwellings of 6,000 monks. There remained only scattered standing fragments of frescoed wall.

The trucks left for Rongbuk Base Camp on March 16. The big mountains soon came into view. The expedition reached the

ruined Rongbuk Monastery, where British mountaineers had
stopped to receive the blessing of the high lamas a half century
before. Here Chris and his companions could at last gaze upon
the North Face of Everest, known to them from countless books
and photographs, from paintings and even models.

A group of Tibetan boys helped cut a track through two iced-
over rivers the next day. The expedition reached Base Camp, a
rocky and in some ways an ugly place, that evening. The camp
was strewn with the litter of previous expeditions, including a fair
amount of broken glass and human excrement. It was growing
dark. The wind rose and the temperature fell as the expedition
members worked to unload the trucks.

The climbers rummaged for food and pitched a mess tent. It
was a miserable evening. They were cold and hungry and intimi-
dated by the place and the conditions, and by their notions of
what lay ahead. Base Camp was at 5,200 meters, and most of the
climbers were ill with headaches and nausea. Their discomfort
blended with their anxiety to create a malaise that seemed likely
to persist. The expedition proper hadn't quite begun, but already
it was difficult to pretend that they were engaged in something
reasonable.

They planned to spend two weeks below 6,000 meters to
acclimatize. Joe and Peter led some of the trekkers on a hike up
the Central Rongbuk Glacier on March 19. Chris and Dick led
another group up the East Rongbuk Glacier; they established a
temporary camp at 5,650 meters, on the way to Advance Base
Camp. Charlie Clarke and Adrian Gordon remained at Base
Camp. Charlie noted that Joe and Peter looked tired when they
returned from their hike. It was still very cold and windy; they
had all expected spring by now.

There was a farewell banquet for the trekkers on March 22.
The cook was laid low by altitude sickness—the air at Base Camp

held only half as much oxygen as the air at sea level—and the meal was not a great success. The trekkers left for home in the morning. That left the four climbers and their support team: Charlie and Adrian as well as the liason officer, the interpreter, the cook and two drivers.

The next chore was to establish Advance Base Camp at 6,500 meters on the East Rongbuk Glacier. The climbers would rely on yaks to carry gear to Advance Base. Charlie and Adrian would oversee the process of stocking the camp once the yaks arrived; the animals and their herders were due at Base Camp on March 29. Chris estimated Charlie and Adrian would make three trips between the two camps over the next month or so, taking into account rest days and bad weather. The four principal climbers would spend the month acclimatizing—moving up and down the lower stages of the route—and making progress on the Northeast Ridge itself.

The climbers took three days to make their first trip to the site they'd chosen for Advance Base. The spot had served as Camp Three for British expeditions attempting the North Col route before World War II. The walk up the glacier gave the climbers fine and intimidating views of their own route up the Northeast Ridge. The mountain had begun to seem real to them; the sleeping gray creature they had viewed from a distance resolved into stone and snow. They pitched their tents each night near the shadows of strange ice formations—thick sails of ice that at dusk seemed carved from the mountain itself.

They returned to Base Camp on March 28, and rested the next day. They were beginning to acclimatize. An American team was attempting Everest's regular North Col route. The Americans stopped by to drink and talk in the evening. Peter wrote in his journal that his own expedition was a happy one. They were like

The 1982 British Everest team:
Chris, Charlie, Adrian, Joe, Peter, Dick

members of a certain type of family. They knew one another well enough to squabble, but they had adopted the same virtues.

The yaks arrived two days late, on April 1. Five of the expedition members—everyone but Dick Renshaw—left for Advance Base Camp the next day, again moving up in easy stages. Dick stayed behind to wait for the next mail delivery. He would follow the others in a day or two.

The yak herders stopped to rebuild a section of the path demolished by a recent rockslide. Joe and Peter filmed the work while the other climbers continued on their way. Charlie and Adrian heard the rattle of rocks on rocks a moment later and ran for cover. Charlie hid behind a boulder that took several direct hits from the hail of stones that scored the earth around them. He was frightened at this evidence of the danger of this place, and struck by how easily his companions dismissed the incident.

The party reached Advance Base Camp on April 4. Dick Renshaw caught up with the others by walking up from Base Camp that day—ten miles and an altitude gain of 1,200 meters. He was empty-handed, however; the mail hadn't arrived. Adrian and Charlie helped unload the yaks and then set off down with the animals and their herders to fetch another load.

Peter felt ill the next day. Chris and Dick walked across to the Raphu La, the col that overlooks the mountain's fearsome Kangshung Face. The two climbers brought wands to mark their route over to the col, which would bring them to the start of their ridge. It would be easy to lose their way in fog or a snowstorm. They walked in crampons on windblown snow. Chris was relieved to find that he could keep pace with Dick.

They reached the Raphu La and looked down to the Kangshung Glacier, some 1,200 meters below. They raised their eyes to the horizon and found the outline of Kangchenjunga. Jannu's exquisite form lay to the right; it brought to their minds Al Rouse and his achievement there.

Chris returned his gaze to the beautifully fluted, frighteningly steep snow of the Kangshung Face. The sight undermined his sense that the Northeast Ridge was something real. He could not always accept this scale; his mind's eye reduced it to something as artificial and flimsy as a stage set.

Chris and Dick left the col and worked their way across snow slopes, hoping to identify the most efficient route to the crest of their ridge. The ground wasn't steep. The snow took their crampons well. They identified a gully that would take them onto the ridge crest. Huge cornices overhung the gully, but the cornices looked stable. The two climbers returned to Advance Base Camp. They passed slots that opened into huge underground caverns, and skirted an area threatened by avalanche.

The wind the next day was too strong for them to go up to the ridge. They stayed in camp. Pete and Joe had put up four tents: one for each climber. The four men spent the afternoon building windbreaks and a stone table; they also erected a tarp over the mess tent. They reviewed their plans, which called for them to establish two or three camps—ideally, snow caves—on their way to the foot of the pinnacles that barred the final section of the ridge. They would make an alpine-style push from the highest snow cave to the summit, carrying food and tents and making one or more bivouacs, much as Chris and Joe and Peter and Al had done on Kongur. They hoped to do without fixed rope low on the route. They agreed that they might need it on the steeper sections higher up.

The four climbers set out for the ridge on April 7. They had been on Everest for three weeks. Their acclimatization was coming along and they were pleased to be getting to the real climbing at last. They carried their personal gear and some food, along with rope and snow pickets and pitons. They reached the ridge crest, which gave Peter and Joe their first view of the horrifying drop down the Kangshung Face. Chris suggested that this would be a good place for their first snow cave. The climbers left their gear and went down. They knew the ground now so they climbed un-roped to the glacier, where they roped up again as a safeguard against hidden crevasses.

They took the next day to organize Advance Base Camp and prepare loads to carry up the mountain. They returned to the ridge on April 9 and dug their first snow cave. They soon hit ice that required long sessions of digging and chipping. They dropped back down to Advance Base that afternoon; the next morning they carried more loads up to their new cave. Chris and Peter returned to Advance Base to pick up still more supplies. Joe and Dick spent the night in the cave and made further progress on the route on April 11.

The climbers reunited at the snow cave that evening. Chris puttered with the stove near the entrance while the four of them talked over their options and plans. They argued about tactics and chores: how close to the crest of the ridge to climb, when to retreat for a rest, who should brew tea. Chris was happy to be with the younger men—moved by their easy acceptance of him. He had known Peter for seven years now, and he'd become close to Joe on Kongur. He was impressed by Dick Renshaw's quiet determination.

The snow cave was warm; water trickled from the roof. The wind rose outside and the climbers enjoyed a sense of comfort and safety. They were cozy here. No news of the world could find them. They had almost no duties.

They didn't want to leave the cave in the morning but they made their way weak and miserable out into the cold. Peter led off and Chris followed, moving slowly, once more doubting his ability to keep up with his companions. Chris blurted his fears to Peter, talked of doing what he could in a supporting role. Peter as on Kongur the previous year told Chris to stuff it. There was lots of time; they all had these ups and downs; it was a long expedition.

The world meanwhile had changed around them. The ridge curled behind them as they toiled up the slopes just below its crest. They were dimly aware of a sparkling montage of shapes, all part of a larger whiteness lit by what seemed an interior blue. The glittering waves of the glacier broke far below: distant breakers that seemed to rise and freeze out of a still deeper blue. They kicked steps in steep snow, moving unroped over seemingly endless and more or less frozen slopes, the snow pockmarked in places by the working of the sun. They fell into the grip of their weariness. Chris would take fifty steps and lean on his axe; he would take another fifty steps and rest again.

The climbers' fear blurred and receded only to surface at moments as if for reassurance that no new danger or catastrophe had arisen. There was nowhere in life that was right or comfortable. This beauty was not entirely faceable: it encompassed the vastness of eternity and the proximity of their deaths. This place offered a picture of where they were going and it could not be more inviting or more alien. Peter had a notion that they could keep climbing forever, that indeed they would do just that. They would continue to kick steps in half-frozen snow for an eternity of moments, each moment like this one, a welter of fatigue and fear and bliss.

They hoped to dig another snow cave near the ridge's first steep section. They had been climbing for almost six hours when they came upon a promising snow bank for their cave. They dumped their ropes and gear and descended to the cave at the start of the ridge. The climbers had no appetites; it was difficult to eat. Joe had a cough that was bringing up traces of blood. That night he suggested that the climbers should carry only light loads the next day to the site they had chosen for the second cave. This would leave them more energy for digging. Even Peter was tired; he was beginning to face the route's difficulties and its length. He wondered if this ridge might impose some new limit on him. This possibility awoke his fear; if he retreated it pursued him, occupying the spaces he abandoned.

The climbers returned to their high point on April 13. They dug in snow and frozen dirt for two hours and hit rock. They cursed at this but continued digging rather than start anew; a different place might be as bad or worse. They pried away rock and clods of frozen dirt but the work was slow.

There was room for only two men to dig. Chris descended to Camp One. Peter followed him after a time, moving quickly down the steep snow. He was accustomed to such ground from his work as a teacher and guide in the Alps. And yet it crossed his mind that a fall here would kill him. He forced himself to attend to his movements, even as he pushed himself to move quickly enough to catch Chris. He'd promised Wendy that he would look after her husband on this trip. Peter was married himself now. The thought overtook him as if from behind. He felt suddenly older, and after a moment he found he had slowed almost to a halt. He gathered his wits and moved quickly again down the slope, seeing Chris in the near distance.

The two of them reached the first snow cave together. Dick and Joe arrived some time later. The four climbers that night slept like animals in their den. Chris woke once in the night to the murky cold and a feeling that he had abandoned his life.

Morning was cold and clear—a fine day for climbing. They set out to carry one more load up to the second cave and enlarge the cave further. After that they would descend to Advance Base Camp for a rest. Chris found that he could barely lift his feet in the snow. He turned back after a time, fighting a sense of failure and hating his weakness, filled with remorse at abandoning his load in the snow, at leaving the others to finish the work.

The others took two hours to reach the site of the second snow cave. They chopped and dug through the afternoon. Peter noted matter-of-factly that he was suffering hallucinations—nothing dramatic, just oddities of thought or vision. Yellow curtains parted as he chopped and the sun's rays hit a bedpost or a painted bookshelf. It worried him that his feet were cold. Snow fell as the climbers worked. They left the cave and began their descent. The steps they had kicked in the morning had begun to blur and fill. They plunged their axe shafts into the snow, aware of the potential consequences of a slip on this steep ground. They stopped to brew tea at the first snow cave and then carried on down to the glacier and a proper rest.

Charlie and Adrian had come up to Advance Base Camp with

the yak herders and their animals. They brought mail. Chris was crushed to find nothing from Wendy. Charlie and Adrian stayed for two days to pamper the climbers, feeding them soup and fresh bread. The climbers meanwhile studied the Northeast Ridge through a telescope, focusing much of their attention on a pair of buttresses above the second snow cave. A snow gully seemed to offer a path through the first buttress, but the second one showed no apparent weakness.

The climbers packed gear and food on April 17. They rose late the next day and climbed to the first snow cave. They ferried more gear to the second cave on April 19, and spent the night there. The cave was still too cramped for four men and their gear. Dick and Joe set to work the next morning to enlarge the shelter while Peter and Chris ventured further up the ridge.

They moved up firm snow, and then over low-angle rock slabs to another snowfield that grew steeper as they climbed. They stopped to rope up at an islet of rock, standing on it like seabirds. There were no cracks for pitons so they buried a flat piece of metal—a dead man—in the hard snow for an anchor. Peter led into the gully that split the first buttress. He climbed slowly now, relying on the front-points of his crampons. Chris sat on the rock, holding Peter's rope and watching him move higher; seen from below he resembled a man slowly climbing an invisible ladder. The ice at Peter's feet glinted and shimmered, the light reflecting from the ice to fade into the reds and blues of the Asian sky.

Chris looked about him, taking in the view. He could see the North Col, now far below, and he could gaze across to the purplish brown of the Tibetan hills. Huge peaks lay scattered at random—some close enough to invite a wary nausea at their bulk, others far enough away to blend into a memory, seeming almost to belong among the ghosts of mountains from his past. It was as though mountains from his past had achieved a kind of mass that attracted and merged with aspects of his present. They would not fade entirely; they haunted him in this gentle way. He wondered idly what a woman would make of this view. He glanced up at Peter's lean figure, pressed to the snow as he reached high with his axe. He thought of his own mother's legs, her white feet on a kitchen floor of forty years ago. He was surprised to encounter her memory now.

Peter ran out most of the rope. He reached rock again and placed a piton. He fixed the rope to the piton and shouted down. Chris clipped his ascender to the rope—it would hold him in case of a slip in the steep snow—and followed. Chris reached Peter and led past him, still mostly on snow. He climbed 50 meters in an hour, moving slowly, taking time to judge the snow's condition. He came to a ledge of bare rock and found a crack and tapped in a knife-blade piton for an anchor. Peter followed quickly and led through in his turn. The ground grew less steep. They reached the top of the first buttress, which ended just below the crest of the Northeast Ridge.

It occurred to Chris that he'd never roped up with Peter before. He mentioned this and Peter corrected him. They had climbed together near Bonington's home before the Everest trip in 1975. The intervening time seemed very long. Mick Burke had been alive seven years ago; so had Dougal Haston and Nick Estcourt and others now gone.

Joe and Dick took over the climbing the next day. They found an easy way through the second buttress—mixed ground at low angles, some loose rock but no other difficulties. The mountain's snowfields and gullies and slabs were becoming real to the climbers. These features emerged one by one from the vastness of Everest so that it became possible to love and fear the mountain in its particulars. The blackness of the mountain became apparent in a particular rock's blackness, bright against the snow.

The snow thawed and froze; clouds appeared and vanished. All around them was the evidence of change. The rock absorbed the light and grew warm in the afternoons. The rock would become dust and blow away, take flight to form the beaches of Africa or Thailand—even as the sands of other deserts arrived here, brought by the interminable wind.

Chris and Peter followed Joe and Dick through the second buttress, carrying heavy loads on the newly fixed ropes. Peter in particular was struck by how the ground changed from day to day as they crossed and recrossed it. Nothing stayed the same even for a matter of hours and yet there was no apparent agent for all of this change. He felt that he could spend his life as a witness here. It was like staring at something—anything—for hours, and getting glimmers of some spectacle, vast but empty, unfolding in stillness. The sights here struck him as postscripts to his father's death and to his own marriage. Those occurrences had hinted at this—at the profound instability of experience, of matter itself. He had refused to face it. He had instead come here as if to seek audience with some unseen interlocutor who—it struck him now—had nothing to add.

He looked up and across the North Col to a sea of peaks. He saw more than he could believe or accept, and he knew that from here the views would become increasingly difficult to encompass. He must travel light; he must stop thinking and wishing. He didn't believe he could do it; his preparation was inadequate. He knew he was stronger than the others; he would end up alone on this ridge unless someone surprised him. He thought of Joe and his years in the seminary and allowed himself the hope that Joe would finish it with him.

Chris lagged behind, but the others arrived almost together at a shoulder above the second buttress. The climbers were near the magic 8,000-meter mark, higher than all but fourteen of the world's summits. It was snowing heavily. Peter wanted to press on but Joe was tired. The three climbers descended, passing Chris on his way up into the rising storm.

Chris dumped his load hastily at the high point and turned to follow the others. He was vaguely frightened, worried about losing his way. He was relieved to come upon his three young comrades at the top of the fixed ropes. They were milling about, fussing with the anchor, frightened and upset. Peter had come close to killing himself. He'd leaned back on the rope, and the anchor—a single piton—had pulled. He'd somehow managed to keep his balance; failing that he'd have fallen a vast distance. It was very like his accident the previous year on Kongur—the time he'd been hit by the rock and had nearly gone off the end of the rappel rope. He'd been lucky then, too.

The others watched as Peter once again clipped into the rope and leaned back. The new anchor held. He reached the bottom of the pitch. His companions followed him. The party now had to cross a series of snow-covered rock slabs. Peter wanted a rope here but Joe ignored him and walked across without a belay. Peter shouted at him but then gave up and followed. His fear made him awkward. He looked for Joe, meaning to berate him, but felt himself grow calm. He saw this scene—the four of them in scattered poses here—as in a painting or a film, and in a flash of clarity he saw that it was thrilling, all of this. He felt an unreasoning love for his three friends.

The four climbers descended to the second snow cave. Everyone was quiet as they settled in for their rest but in the morning they were eager to talk. Peter accused Joe and Dick of showing a dangerous lack of motivation, of push. He believed they were leaving too much to him; it was like Kongur again. The others listened calmly. There was talk of descending to Advance Base Camp for a rest. Dick argued that they should stay high for now.

They talked all morning and arrived at a plan that suited Chris. They would retreat all the way down to Base Camp for a real rest. They would then send two climbers with a tent back up to the high point just below 8,000 meters. Those two climbers could spend a day or two digging a snow cave while the other two ferried loads to stock the new camp.

It was snowing again in the morning as the four climbers began their descent. The new snow made the slopes dangerous. Joe and Dick roped up. Chris and Peter had left their rope at the high point. All four climbers moved with care, afraid that their movements might dislodge a slab of unconsolidated snow. The snowstorm gained strength as they descended the ridge. Dick led them from wand to wand for a time, but then lost the way; he took them in circles until someone spotted another wand. They stumbled into Advance Base Camp, completely used up and looking forward to seeing Charlie and Adrian—their friends would fuss over them and make tea—but Charlie and Adrian weren't there. They had gone down to Base Camp. They had left behind the mail, including three letters from Wendy for Chris. The climbers settled in happily to read and drink and talk and eat.

They woke the next morning to sunshine, but when they looked up they saw more new snow on the mountain. They had been right to come down. They packed to make the long walk down to Base Camp. Chris left first. He walked alone across the glacier for a time and then disappeared as suddenly as if seized by some invisible predator; he had plunged feet first into a crevasse. The breath left his body as he lurched to a stop, caught by his armpits so that his torso and legs dangled like an insect's above the void. He was just able to drag himself out. He scrambled across to the safety of bare rock, aware but not aware that he had come very close to dying. He put aside the implications of this latest brush with death; he needed his strength for the climb itself.

Mr. Chen and his interpreter Mr. Yu came out from the huddle of tents at Base Camp to greet the climbers and to shake their hands. Charlie and Adrian had gone off to climb a small peak in the neighborhood; they were spending the night at the ruins of the Rongbuk Monastery. A truck arrived at Base Camp in the afternoon; it carried a party of Americans who meant to ski around Everest. The two parties mingled, exchanging news and speaking of mutual acquaintances, making mountaineering gossip.

The Americans left and the British climbers settled in for their rest. Peter found himself unable to read or to think beyond the difficulties that awaited him and his friends. He was increasingly aware of the order of their task—there was so far to go on the ridge—and he was saving himself for the job. He had no patience for anything else, for distractions; he had no interest in food or photography or chatter. He knew—he remembered the second time on K2—the climbers might simply run out of strength before they could get up the route. This possibility disturbed him. He was comforted by his belief that the others could be trusted to behave well upon their return to the ridge.

The climbers had been reading and hearing scraps of news about the Falklands War. They found themselves speaking in military metaphors. They were in some ways no different than soldiers, believing that they were willing to die in pursuit of some purpose they could not properly define. This seemed absurd and even dishonorable in light of the commitments they had made, promises whose fulfillment required them to remain among the useful living. The news of the war upset them obscurely. It seemed a waste, a dangerous sideshow—but then what was this?

Peter wrote in his journals. They seemed to promise a future self to read them. Dick carved a swan from a piece of mahogany he'd brought from home. Joe worked on notes for the expedition film and took long naps. Chris read and slept. He would close

his eyes and be gone and wake in a dazzled puzzlement, amazed
to return to this place.

They stayed at Base Camp for three days. A low ridge hid Everest from them. This ridge had once held a cairn to commemorate
the loss of George Mallory and Andrew Irvine but the cairn
seemed to be gone now. The climbers could imagine at moments
that the mountain wasn't there.

23

THEY TOOK A day—April 29—to walk back up to Advance Base Camp. They set out for the ridge the next morning. Charlie and Adrian came along to help carry the big 16mm camera; they would turn back at the start of the route, after Joe filmed some climbing shots. The wind blew strongly; at times the climbers were forced to crouch low and clutch their axes. Chris was still very tired. The rest at Base Camp seemed to have done him almost no good.

They spent the night in the first snow cave. They climbed to the second cave on May 1. Here they drew straws for the next day's pairings and assignments. Peter and Dick won the role of climbing to the shoulder just below 8,000 meters and staying on to dig a third cave there. Joe and Chris would carry gear up to the shoulder as well, then drop down to spend the night at the second cave and bring up more supplies the next day.

The four men climbed the fixed ropes on the first and second buttresses. The wind picked up in the afternoon, and clouds rose to envelop them. Peter reached new ground and moved on alone, eager to see what was next. He peered around corners and eventually identified a safe route across to the start of the First Pinnacle. He turned back and met Joe coming up. The two of them found a site for the third cave. It was just over the crest of the ridge, at the top of the Kangshung Face. Chris arrived and dropped his gear. He and Joe left to descend to the second snow cave, leaving Peter to start digging a third cave. Dick arrived last. He had run out of steam near the top of the second buttress. He put it down to a bad day—the sort of day even the strongest climber might experience up here.

Chris for his part found that even descending was difficult; each step was a misery. His doubts had grown during the past two days. He didn't think he could keep pace with the others. He reached the second cave after Joe and immediately burst into tears. The tears calmed him but the intensity of his disappointment shocked him. Joe finished making tea and offered Chris a cup and told him to forget it—he'd feel better in the morning.

The next day Chris was up and out first. Joe soon passed him but when Chris reached the crest of the ridge he turned to survey his own progress and saw Joe coming up behind him again. Joe had reached the third snow cave and come back to help Chris with his load but had somehow missed him. He had realized his mistake and was retracing his steps. They greeted each other and walked together up to the third cave. Peter and Dick had made it more spacious than the others—with room for gear and climbers and even a pair of alcoves for cooking.

Dick dropped down the ridge the next day to pick up rope at the second snow cave. He meant to return with the rope and then spend the afternoon carving out still more room in the third cave. The others meanwhile set out to make further progress on the ridge. The summit of Everest came into their view, a distant triangle behind the looming Pinnacles. The top of the mountain was in fact two miles away, an enormous distance to travel at these heights.

Peter reached the start of the First Pinnacle in two hours. Joe and Chris followed at a slower pace. Joe dumped his load at the base of the pinnacle and returned to camp. Chris held Peter's rope while Peter set to work on the pinnacle itself, leading up snow to rock and then onto precarious mixed ground that offered no real protection. Peter ran out the entire rope but could find nowhere to build an anchor. Chris tied a second rope to the first, and Peter climbed still higher, knowing that a fall at this point would pull Chris from his stance. Chris shivered and stamped as Peter climbed on. Almost three hours passed before Peter at last hammered in a piton for an anchor. Chris climbed the fixed rope as Peter moved up easier ground, dragging another rope. Chris followed again. They carried on up the ridge, Peter still leading. He enjoyed this climbing; he was unafraid, eager to see what came next.

It grew late, and they turned to descend. Peter realized that he was now very tired. It had begun to snow. He had trouble keeping his feet as he followed Chris down the ridge. The two climbers eventually found themselves back in the third cave, coughing and retching; the smell of milk powder in the cave made them ill.

Dick and Joe took a turn in front the next day. Chris and Peter followed with rope and tents. Everyone moved very slowly now. Chris turned back at the foot of the First Pinnacle; he couldn't force himself to undertake the long heave up the fixed rope. Dick reached the high point first, and he led the first pitch. He used both ice tools on the steep ground, kicking steps that collapsed into each other to dissolve into a shallow sea of powder snow. He moved sideways across a thin crust of ice. He worried that he might find himself on a cornice that could give way to send him swinging through space on the end of his rope.

He built an anchor. Joe followed on the fixed rope. Dick was preparing to put Joe on belay so that Joe could lead the next pitch when something odd happened. It felt at first like a sort of physical hallucination. Dick's left arm and leg went numb. His left cheek and the left side of his tongue lost feeling a moment later. He told

Joe what was happening to him. He spoke calmly: he might have been telling Joe that something tasted funny. Joe advised him to descend immediately. Peter was coming up the rope; he could belay Joe on the next pitch. Dick descended to the third snow cave. He found Chris there, making tea. Dick already felt better. He was almost embarrassed at making a fuss, though for a moment he'd been scared.

Joe meanwhile led up good snow to complete the second pitch of the day. He and Peter dropped the ropes and a tent and descended to the cave. No one knew what to make of Dick's episode. They were all too addled and weary to pursue the matter or to make plans for the next day.

They moved very slowly in the morning. They needed to go down for a rest. Chris had begun to wonder whether he would have the strength to get this high on the route again. He left some of his camera equipment at the cave as an incentive to return.

The four climbers waded down the ridge once again. This time they were in new snow that seemed very unstable. Dick lost a crampon on a low-angle section. Chris stopped to push the crampon onto Dick's boot and shoved with such force that both men fell and tumbled down the slope. The soft snow stopped them and they lay cold and wet, laughing at the lunacy of it—they might have died so stupidly. Peter watching them was obscurely moved; they had all of them let go of some inner compass.

They were all close to exhaustion when they staggered onto the glacier. They lurched across the open ground at a pace so slow that Charlie Clarke—he had come out from Advance Base to set up the camera and film their return—was amazed and then frightened for them.

He was still more worried when they told him of Dick's episode. Charlie said he'd want to examine Dick at Base Camp but he knew from their descriptions that Dick had suffered a stroke. The only question was what to do about it. Charlie watched the others with concern that afternoon. Chris was very quiet. Peter was serious and tense. Joe was unusually relaxed, clearly enjoying his work on the film. It occurred to Charlie that Joe for all of his prickly reserve had a capacity for happiness, a cheerful streak.

The party descended to Base Camp on May 7. The glacier was melting; it was summer. Each man descended apart from the others, walking to the sound of running water. No one spoke of Dick's situation. They reached Base Camp and Charlie took Dick off for his inspection. The others read mail and old magazines; they would talk seriously in the morning.

Charlie meanwhile told Dick that he'd had a small stroke—it wasn't uncommon at these heights. It might be very dangerous to return to the ridge. Dick spent the night mulling it over and decided that he was fine; he'd go on with the climb. But Charlie found him first thing in the morning and told him that he couldn't go back up—he'd be risking the others' lives, too, if he got sick up there. Charlie sent Dick off to take a walk and went to inform the others.

Chris took in the news and immediately made his own announcement: he wouldn't be coming back up on the mountain, either. Peter and Joe argued the point until Chris lost his temper; he came very near tears again as he told them that they must listen to him—he was forty-seven years old; he'd reached his physical limit; he was out of control on the mountain; he couldn't possibly keep up with them on the ridge. Joe and Peter stopped insisting; they knew he was right.

Dick turned up later in the morning. He'd shaved and he looked very young, a bit lost. He grew briefly tearful when Chris offered his sympathy. Dick had decided to leave the expedition. There was nothing for him to do here. He wanted to get home to his wife and to their son, the child born two years ago just after Dick's return from K2. Dick would stick around for a few days so that Charlie could keep him under observation; after that, he would return alone to Hong Kong and then home.

Joe found Charlie that afternoon and asked him to look at his stool; there was blood in it, and he had a persistent ache in his gut. Charlie wondered if Joe had an ulcer. It was also possible that he had swallowed the blood. He was coughing incessantly, and his throat was raw and bleeding. All of the climbers had sore throats from gasping for breath in the thin, dry air on the ridge. They huddled in the evenings over a makeshift humidifier, towels draped over their heads.

Their little expedition had settled into a grim guerilla warfare, reflected in the look of their Base Camp—the squalid mess shelter and scattering of tents amid rocks and shadow. The valley was barren, a frigid quarry at the end of the world. The climbers looked forward to the nights, when they could forget their surroundings. They would gather in the tiny mess shelter and talk. They were lonely; they all missed their homes. Peter had received a letter from Hilary; she had survived an avalanche during a day of ski mountaineering near Leysin. She would need to sit and tell him about it—he would need to hear her—when he returned.

Chris during the next days felt relief at his retreat from what had come to seem the impossible task of climbing the Northeast Ridge. He had in mind for himself a more realistic challenge, one that would allow him to make a further contribution without requiring his presence on the ridge itself. The pinnacles ended just where the North Ridge joined the Northeast Ridge for the finish of the old North Col route. Chris proposed to mount a climb with Charlie and Adrian to the North Col, at the bottom of the North Ridge. The three of them could establish a camp at the col so that Pete and Joe could drop down the North Ridge once they'd climbed the pinnacles. That way they wouldn't need to retreat back up and over the pinnacles—a staggering prospect—to get off the mountain.

Chris was afraid for them. It had begun to seem that the climbers had all underestimated their chosen route; perhaps it had been a version of madness to come here this way, only four of them to take on Everest's last great challenge.

Joe was feeling better after a couple of days of rest. He concluded that the blood in his stool had originated in his throat. He took Peter aside to say that he was coming back up the ridge; they would finish it together.

Dick took a stroll one afternoon to take photographs. He walked some three miles, mostly downhill, feeling fit. He turned back and began to climb—and immediately sat down; his vision had gone blurry and he couldn't catch his breath. He rested for a time and then struggled slowly and painfully up to Base Camp to tell Charlie, who diagnosed another stroke. Dick had to get to a lower altitude immediately. He couldn't travel alone; Charlie would have to escort him back to civilization. The two of them left Base Camp on the morning of May 10. Charlie promised to return as soon as Dick was safely on a plane to Hong Kong.

The others felt this departure as they might have felt the shadow of a cloud. It was too bad but their minds and bodies were otherwise engaged. Joe and Peter spent the following days in conference. They studied pictures of the route and tried to estimate distances between its various features. At times they imagined finishing the ridge but they put aside this fantasy as artificial, a distraction.

Joe turned thirty-four on May 12. The remnants of the expedition celebrated his birthday that evening. The party was a farewell party, too. The climbers would leave for Advance Base in the morning. The cook made a cake. Joe relaxed a bit; he was funny, more like he was sometimes at home. Adrian was nervous about climbing with Chris to the North Col. Peter teased him, telling him to cheer up; he pointed out that Adrian's hitherto undistinguished climbing career was taking off—he'd soon be one of the first Englishmen since the war to reach Everest's North Col.

Chris watching his companions felt happiness seep into his body; it mixed with his anxiety to make him lightheaded even before they opened champagne. The champagne made a mess; most of it flew from the bottle—it was the thin air. Someone took a photograph of Peter and Chris, faces momentarily unlined and forgetful, wreathed in smiles and lit by shock at the explosion of liquid and sound. Someone opened another bottle; this time they caught the champagne in a plastic bucket.

Peter and Joe walked up to Advance Base Camp the next morning. Chris and Adrian walked with them. They all knew this ground well now. They were well acclimatized, and they reached Advance Base Camp that afternoon. Its desolation, its ravaged atmosphere, struck them anew. Peter and Joe decided to take a rest day. They spent most of May 14 in their tents—writing, reading and sleeping. It was good to be inside; the wind blew hard and it snowed. Peter allowed himself to imagine five days of sun, maybe enough to do the route and get down.

They planned to reach the second snow cave the first day and continue to the third snow cave the following day. The third day they would traverse the pinnacles to reach the junction of the Northeast and North ridges. That would leave them in position to reach the summit on the fourth or fifth day. After that they could reverse their route or come down the North Ridge to meet Chris and Adrian at the North Col. It was a long time to spend at such a height, but they thought it might be just possible.

The climbers all rose early on May 15. The wind rose in the morning but the sky was clear. Chris and Adrian made breakfast. Peter and Joe stuffed last-minute odds and ends into their packs.

They put on crampons and roped up, leaving their good-byes until last. They agreed again to make radio contact that evening. No one said anything to call attention to the magnitude of the two climbers' task. Everyone pretended that this was ordinary—and in a way it was. This was how they climbed mountains now.

Peter and Joe turned to leave. The wind picked up snow and blew it past their departing figures. They felt their friends' eyes upon them. It was a relief—it always was—to start walking, to forget the others, to feel the ground change under their feet as the ridge rose up to meet them.

CHRIS HAD HIS own project—getting up to the North Col— and he turned to it with a kind of relief. Chris and Adrian left camp soon after Peter and Joe. Adrian's inexperience on technical ground was a problem. The two climbers were brought up short by a wall of steep ice, and retreated to Advance Base Camp. They got out the radio that evening and reached Peter and Joe, who had arrived at the second snow cave in good time. Chris and Peter agreed that the two parties would make contact again the next evening.

Chris and Adrian set out in the morning to make another stab at finding a route to the North Col. Chris gave Adrian a scare, leading him across a slope shadowed by a huge and unstable-looking ice tower. Adrian was game, though; he was moving more strongly than Chris, and he led the easy ground, breaking trail through sections of deep snow. Chris led the steeper pitches. The two of them reached a point near the North Col late in the day; they made radio contact with Peter just after 6:30 that evening. Peter and Joe had reached the third snow cave. They would go for the pinnacles the next day.

Chris and Adrian planned to rest the following day at Advance Base Camp. They would try to reach the North Col the day after that—

May 18—and would wait there for Peter and Joe. Chris told Peter his plan. They scheduled further radio contacts for three o'clock and six o'clock the following day.

Chris and Adrian set off to descend to Advance Base Camp. They were tired, and the ground was steep. Adrian lost his footing and slid several feet in the snow before the rope between them came taut. Chris held him, but they were tense and afraid as they continued. They moved more and more slowly. They were too tired to cook when they reached camp. They found their tents and went to sleep.

Chris woke in the morning to a day without clouds or wind. He found his way out to the mess tent around ten o'clock and peered through the telescope at the route. He began his survey of the Northeast Ridge in the vicinity of the third snow cave. He saw nothing there, and so followed the ridge along to the bottom of the First Pinnacle, then up past the expedition's previous high point.

There they were. They were far along the First Pinnacle. They had made an early start or climbed quickly—perhaps both. Their figures were small but sharply defined in the dry air. Chris could see them perfectly. He made out the arms and legs in their orange wind-suits. Two tiny figures; they put him in mind of plastic soldiers he'd brought home for Rupert and Daniel. The sight of Joe and Peter moving together on the enormous ridge made him want their lives. He loved what they were doing and he loved them for doing it.

Chris and Adrian watched the two figures for the rest of the day. The figures moved slowly now. The ground was new to them and apparently difficult and they must be tired. They were climbing at a height of more than 8,200 meters—higher than all but five of the world's summits. Chris tried and failed to make radio contact with them at three o'clock. He could still see them on the ridge, moving toward the Second Pinnacle. There was a peculiar discomfort in watching them. He might have been with them had he been stronger. His relief at being finished with the route had evaporated. He wanted to be with Joe and Peter, to know what they knew.

He tried to reach them on the radio every half-hour with no success. The sun dipped behind the mountain just before nine o'clock. Chris looked up once more. One figure stood near the crest of the ridge at the col beneath the Second Pinnacle. The second figure climbed very slowly toward the first.

Chris considered the circumstances. Joe and Peter had been climbing all day. They needed a place to spend the night. They would have to dig a snow cave or carve out a ledge for their tent. Either task might prove difficult if the snow on both sides of the ridge was very steep or too soft. The mountain became a black wall set against the deep blue of the night. Chris imagined Joe and Peter in a cave on the east side of the ridge, above the Kangshung Face.

PETER AND JOE had intended to cross the pinnacles in a day. They wondered now how they had imagined this to be possible. This was their third day on the ridge; they had been climbing for fourteen hours today and now they moved very slowly.

They stopped at the base of the Second Pinnacle. There was no snow for a cave. They scraped out a platform for their tent in the dark and spent the night wrapped in their sleeping bags. It was very cold, but there was not much wind. Joe had mostly left off worrying and remembering, but now he thought about his mother and his father. He mentioned this to Peter, who didn't reply; perhaps he was asleep. Joe woke some time later and lay listening to the silence.

They rose before light. They had no notion of dates. They packed slowly and were away at last in hopes that their strength would return as they moved. The night had done them no good. The crest of the ridge was impassable here. They moved back onto the East Face; here all was steep snow, very exposed. They roped up and moved together; they had to cover ground as quickly as they could.

Peter went ahead. He lost track of time and grew confused as to his whereabouts. The slope fell back and then reared up again. He knew he was going very slowly. He felt himself wading against a tide. The snow under his boots was frozen and still; even so, it seemed to flow under him in an imitation of perfection—of silence. He stood on the snow like some baffled maker of miracles, unsure of his role in making this happen. He felt the rope at his waist and turned to look for Joe, to solicit his company.

JOE LIKED CLIMBING. He liked even this punishment. He stopped and teetered in his tracks in the snow. He had lost for the moment any notion of the future; the summit of the mountain had ceased to exist. His weariness was a great blanket thrown across his head and shoulders. He had felt something like this before—the claustrophobia that came with great fatigue, obliterating any notion that he was of a piece with the greater world, with the immense chamber of light that surrounded him here like the room that surrounds a goldfish in a glass bowl.

He had sometimes thought of God as a sort of older cousin, someone who for the sake of some distant connection would protect him from the most terrible shame or suffering that could befall a person. His physical misery filled him with dread in part because it undermined any such idea; it seemed to indicate that such fantasies were not merely incorrect, but contemptible. His weakness frightened him. His body was a cage but also a home to him; if it failed or collapsed he would be released into this immensity.

The notion worried him here in this place that looked like heaven had looked in his many imaginings. He thought he could remember praying in his room at seminary and seeing something like this: the white ridge that led up into a sky that was almost the color of the snow; the white slope that fell away more than twelve thousand feet to the invisible glacier.

He did not have to lift his head to see any of it now. He stared down at the place where his shadow turned the snow dark. He felt his weariness recede—long enough for a single breath—and he made an effort to use this reprieve to concentrate, to move, to perform his favorite action in life.

He shifted his weight onto his left boot and bent his right knee and kicked a new step in the snow. He stood upon it but the step was too shallow; the snow beneath his boot collapsed and he began to slide.

He had imagined falling. He had played with stories about it; had dreamed of it. He was curious and in his fatigue he let this unfold, wishing for a hint of a revelation but meaning to put an end to it, assuming that he would know when. This all happened very quickly; time picking up speed, moving water gathered into a narrower avenue at some brink.

He rolled onto his stomach and dug his axe into the snow and it stopped him. He lay there for a moment and then he began to shake; he had rescued everything he knew but it amounted to nothing—his mind was empty.

He tried to rise and found he could not stand; his strength had spilled from him with his knowledge. He lay and waited for something to happen to him; he felt a great curiosity and with it some of his strength, a faded echo, returned to warm him.

He lay still, feeling this new warmth flicker and fade into more emptiness. He heard Peter's voice; it echoed like words in an empty cathedral.

CHRIS ROSE ON the morning of May 18 and left his tent.
He went to the telescope that stood in the dirt at the fringes of
Advance Base Camp. He saw no one on the ridge. There was little
wind and the sky was clear.

They could be out of sight behind the Second Pinnacle,
which dominated the ridge for several hundred meters. But
the snow on the East Face was very steep. They'd want to
cross back to the near side of the ridge as soon as they could.
This would bring them back into sight and might restore
radio contact.

Chris and Adrian left Charlie a note that spelled out the situation, and set out again for the North Col. Chris stopped every ten
minutes or so and lifted his binoculars to gaze at the mountain.
His view of the ridge was excellent from here. Still there was no
sign of Joe or Peter.

His fear had gathered itself and now it rushed at him. He
remembered looking up from a list in a shop when Rupert and
Daniel were small. He remembered the wretchedness that had
seized him then—the sense that he had let those two stray from
his protection. His ambitions collapsed now and he was left with
only dread laced by the sweetness of his wish to see Peter and
Joe, to hear their voices.

Adrian broke trail again. The snow had blown over their steps
from two days before. They reached their high point near the
North Col at six o'clock. They stopped here for the night, digging
a platform at the edge of an enormous drop. The evening view
swam across glaciers and up to the black of the Northeast Ridge.
The night sky remained empty of cloud. There was no wind. Chris
didn't want to be a fool; he felt his fears recede.

Chris and Adrian reached the North Col in the morning. They
were pleased with themselves. They congratulated one another
and made camp. The col provided a perfect view of the Northeast

Ridge and also across to the tents and fixed ropes of the American team at work on the North Face.

There was no sign of Joe or Peter. They had been out of sight for almost two days. They should have come back into view. Adrian saw figures moving around Advance Base Camp late in the day. He thought perhaps Joe and Peter had descended the ridge—but there were three figures, not two. Chris got out the radio and reached Charlie Clarke, who had walked back up from camp with two porters.

Chris told Charlie of his worries. Charlie remembered Kongur. He'd almost given up on Chris and the others during their second summit attempt, but they'd returned. He thought of Nick, waiting for Chris to come down from the Ogre. He remembered Mick Burke on Everest—how Peter had waited for him.

May 20, another perfect day: summit weather. Adrian scanned the ridge in the evening and spotted a tent. It sat on a line that ran down from the Third Pinnacle to the North Face. Chris allowed himself to hope. They would arrive, both of them, all but done in; there would be explanations, tears of joy.

The next morning there was no movement near the tent. And now in the light of morning Chris and Adrian acknowledged that it was the wrong shape and color. A French expedition had visited the north side of the peak the previous year; the tent might have belonged to them.

Joe and Pete had now been missing for four days. Chris began to experiment with stories that might explain their disappearance. It seemed unlikely that both of them had collapsed; they were so strong, particularly Peter. One of them might have fallen—but then where was his partner? Chris began to imagine that they'd fallen roped together; Joe or Peter might have slipped and pulled the other to his death. Or a snow slope might have avalanched and carried them down the East Face.

Chris and Adrian left the North Col the next day. They left behind the tent and radio, with food and cooking gear and a note for their two friends. A wind rose as they descended. They were very tired. They unroped on the glacier and Chris went ahead. Charlie was at work with the two Tibetans who had come up to Advance Base Camp to help with the packing. He came out of camp to meet Chris.

Chris spoke before Charlie could: *They've had it.*

He was just trying it out; it was partly a question.

Charlie said: *I know.*

They fell into each other's arms and wept for their loss but also in fear of what lay ahead. They would need to tell the story; they would be required to explain and they knew this to be impossible.

PETER WHEN HE turned to look for Joe saw the body in the snow and for an instant it was a vision of peace; he wished to lie down himself and call an end to this effort, this illness. In the moment before he knew he must act he stood and listened and heard only the sound of his breathing. He liked being here.

An empty beat of time, and now he was afraid and sick at heart but only dimly; his fear and his sickness were insignificant in the context of his desire to be of use to the person who lay in the snow. Peter retreated in his own steps, following the strand of rope to where Joe had fallen, and kicked a platform for himself and squatted to examine him. Joe seemed to be asleep and Peter felt the pull of sleep and also a reluctance to disturb his friend. Joe lay on his stomach, his axe still clutched in his mittens, his head turned to the side; he had settled into the snow so that it looked as though he had been dropped from a significant height.

Peter took up some of the slack in the rope and used it to make a series of loops across his own chest; he left perhaps a dozen feet of rope between himself and his partner. He sat next to Joe and was tempted to lie down but instead he put his hand on his friend's shoulder and gently shook him. Joe opened his eyes revealing to Peter an expression blank and distant yet somehow urgent and appealing, as if wishing to share—to receive or to convey—some understanding. The urgency faded and Joe rose to his hands and knees, and looked into his friend's face again, Joe's eyes friendly but shot through with blood, and this time smiled and spoke with a lucid muttering that calmed but did not reassure Peter: *I fell asleep.*

Peter's throat was dry; it was not worth the effort to talk. He patted Joe's arm and stood up on his narrow snow platform and put on his pack, careful not to drop it. He had plunged the shaft of his axe into the snow as an anchor. He gripped its head with his left hand; in his right he held coils of the rope that now stretched between them. He stood waiting to see what Joe would decide. He watched his friend as if from a vastly remote vantage point—the summit of this mountain, perhaps, still very far away.

Joe stood and swayed briefly but now Peter had lifted his axe and set off. He kicked still deeper steps than before and kept the rope taut between them. Peter stopped after each new step to half-turn to see if Joe would follow. They came to gently sloping ground on the crest of the ridge and Peter stood and listened and again there was only the sound of his breathing. He sat down and watched Joe follow his last half-dozen steps at a pace that seemed slower than glacial—occupying eons. Peter had a pleasant and curious sense of his own permanence; he could sit here forever and watch this unfold. He peered down and across the unclimbed East Face; its beauty made him dizzy. The sun's glare on its snows dazzled and nearly blinded him. No creature across all the span of time had stood here and seen this but it was known—all of it—to all of them. The world held no secrets.

Joe reached Peter and knelt in the snow for a moment and fell forward with no apparent effort to stop what was happening. Peter watched him like a man watches something through a window and again felt a brief spurt of envy but roused himself and stood and moved across to roll Joe over onto his back so that Joe's face was to the sky, so that he could see and breathe. The rope between them grew tangled as Peter went about his work. He put something under Joe's head. He thought he should put up the tent and light the stove to make tea, but there was a wind and he lost interest; the notion of doing such things seemed far-fetched, an idea from a fairy tale. He remembered the comfortable feeling of listening to stories as a child, later reading and then writing other stories; it struck him now that the stories were all the same. Peter spoke to Joe, not to comfort him but rather to accompany him—to engage and retain Joe as a companion.

JOE DIDN'T RESPOND. He was asleep. He was dreaming. In his dream he had fallen again only this time he didn't roll over and sink his axe into the snow. He just pawed at the snow with his axe as he'd seen beginners do, as if it didn't matter what happened to him. He made to shout for Peter—not for help, only goodbye—but stopped himself; Peter might turn to see and the sight would almost certainly trouble him. And anyway there wasn't time; Joe wanted to laugh at how everything moved so fast, so fast; he was a waterfall thundering into the sea. He tried again to shout but was prevented. He lapsed into silence and saw in the distance lightning: silent flickers, shapes of backlit clouds.

He felt lonely already but he heard a voice very close and opened his eyes and saw Peter looking down into his face. Peter looked stricken, but there was no need for that; Joe was unutterably weary of such goings-on. He frowned gently and made to shake his head and closed his eyes again. He had been right: He understood nothing.

There was nothing to understand.

PETER REMEMBERED A parent leaving him at someone's house when he was a child—the sense of betrayal and of possibility. He remembered a day in New Guinea with Hilary when he had seen the world as sheer wonder. He had believed then that there was nothing else to know or conclude—only this bliss of existence. He thought of his father, and then of Mick Burke walking up that ridge—it was just over the summit from here—seven years gone. Mick had been up here all that time. He wasn't far. Peter felt a flutter of despair. He felt his solitude—he wanted to talk to Chris and Charlie and the rest, to tell them about Joe.

He wanted to tell Hilary. There had been her letter about the avalanche near Leysin. He pictured her standing up in the snow, her heart hammering the blood through her body, the heat of a dying day on her face. The image was unbearably beautiful; its beauty rose up to smite him with the understanding that it was not Hilary he loved but the life in her—there was nothing to her or to any of them but that life and the wildness of it.

Peter stood and blinked until his vision cleared. Chris would be looking for them. He didn't want Chris to know about this. He felt ill and sad again.

He needed to make a decision. He needed to think—but for some reason he could only imagine, and what he imagined, what he saw, was a familiar figure in red, his own figure, climbing back down the ridge. He wanted to go down but even more to go backward in time. He thought of his first climb with Chris. He hadn't known then what would come of it. Mick hadn't known. Nor Joe. They had all of them covered their ears and hummed some loud tune because they had wanted this. Peter wanted it even now.

He couldn't leave Joe yet. He should have begun his descent of the ridge but instead he stood there and swayed, a sapling in a breeze. He felt the sun on him. There was still no wind. He would find his way down to Chris and Charlie in the morning.

He sat down near Joe's body. He rested, leaning back into the snow, and thought. He remembered various objects—he kept picturing his cassette player. He was cold but it didn't trouble him much. Joe's departure had become more difficult to believe. Peter's grief lifted as fear lifts in a nightmare when the narrative becomes less plausible. He thought he should do some work.

There seemed to be no work for him to do here. This discovery came as a relief to him. He remained sitting in the snow and after a time the sense of being in a dream lifted and he felt the fear of his death upon him like an animal upon an animal. He leaned away from it and turned his face and closed his eyes. Nothing happened. He felt calm again but he didn't bother to open his eyes.

He opened them in darkness, very cold. He stood again as if to leave. There was no reason to wait for morning to begin his further descent of the ridge. There was nothing to pack or remember. He liked this freedom. He took a few steps in no particular direction and the rope to Joe came tight and Peter stopped, surprised. He sat back down and settled into the snow and looked up at the sky and tried to fall asleep again.

He couldn't yet. He was shy in the presence of his grief, of what he now understood to be the emptiness of things and stories. And yet he thought vaguely of his or someone else's unborn children. He imagined them finding him here: skin dried and drawn up on his bones, hair gone white. It wasn't ugly but it frightened them. He wished to comfort them, but he had only himself to comfort. He set about it.

He thought about what he often thought about when it was hard to sleep: random moments, certain faces, kicking steps in snow. He lay in the snow now and tried to remember it all. He called to mind one time in particular. The day was very warm; the rock was some kind of granite. He'd come up a shady corner and onto a slab, still in shade, but now a short scramble took him into the sun. He smelled the warm rock. He drifted. He remembered more granite: a perfect little hand crack that took him to a little tree. Someone had wrapped nylon slings around the trunk to make an anchor: yellow, red, green; the colors hurt his eyes but he didn't look away.

C HRIS BONINGTON, AGE fifty, emerged from a tent on the South Col of Everest very early on the morning of April 21, 1985, to gaze about him in the oddly familiar darkness. It was not yet two o'clock, but he'd been awake for three hours; it had taken him and his companions all this time to melt snow for tea, to pack and dress in the cold and dark at 8,000 meters. Every task, every movement, was awkward; crouching half out of their sleeping bags, rummaging through stuff bags, pulling on half-frozen boots, careful to keep hands and feet from freezing.

Now he stood and watched the other shapes. There were six climbers in all; each headlamp made a small world so that they were like the stars of some galaxy, bound together by what passed for proximity in the greater darkness. Chris felt almost entirely alone. This was his fourth visit to the mountain, but it was not at all like the other times.

A Sherpa led the party toward the looming bulk of the mountain's Southeast Ridge. Chris followed. He soon fell behind. He felt the familiar heaviness of high altitude, compounded now by his age; it was difficult even to walk here. Once the others stopped to rest or to keep him in sight, only to resume walking as he approached. Chris understood their impatience but he felt profoundly alone until one of the Norwegians—it was Odd

Eliassen—noticed and came back to offer to climb behind him. Chris had slumped in the snow; now he stood and followed the other climbers' steps in snow that grew deeper as the party moved higher on the ridge.

The sun rose as they approached the crest of the ridge. Hillary and Tenzing had spent the night here some thirty-two years ago; the next day, they'd knocked the bastard off. That was Hillary's phrase; it was a ridiculous one, but perhaps only in retrospect. Chris could make out the Northeast Ridge and the pinnacles. A British expedition was on the ridge now, hoping to do what Pete and Joe had failed to do three years before; perhaps they'd find the bodies.

The Southeast Ridge was steeper than Chris had expected to find it. The climbers carried on for what seemed a long time. The climbing wasn't technically difficult, but the going was extremely hard. Chris was pleased when the South Summit came into view. Dougal and Doug had made their bivouac here, just down from the summit ten years ago. Chris peered down at the gully those two had followed up, and then down the higher reaches of the Southwest Face. He had never seen the face from above and its scale shocked him. He felt vaguely pleased at what he and his companions had achieved.

HE WAS SURPRISED to be here. He'd left Peter and Joe on the Northeast Ridge three years before and he'd thought himself finished with Everest. He'd gone home and once again he had promised Wendy and his two young sons that he would not return to the mountain.

He'd tried to keep his promise. He'd done expeditions to smaller mountains, including a trip with Al Rouse the previous year; with Peter and Joe both gone they had managed to patch up their friendship—that was a comfort, though Al had seemed troubled; he was still so young, his ambition almost frantic.

Chris had even turned down the first invitation to join this expedition. Arne Ness, a wealthy businessman from Norway, hoped to put the first Norwegians on the summit of Everest via the first ascent route—the yak route, people called it now. The Southeast Ridge—the South Col route—was a far cry from the Southwest Face or the Northeast Ridge. Still, it was Everest. The Norwegians had renewed their invitation, and Chris had accepted.

The typical BBC viewer might assume that Chris Bonington—Great Britain's best-known mountaineer—had climbed the world's highest peak several times. The fact was he'd never been to the top himself, and at fifty there wasn't much time; if he made the summit today, he'd be the oldest man ever to get up the peak. He was by no means sure he could do it, but he wasn't afraid. He didn't feel much danger. This was not like other times, though he was climbing this morning with an old friend.

Pertemba Sherpa, thirty-seven, had been with Chris on Everest in 1975. Pertemba also had broken a promise in order to come here. He'd told his wife he would not enter the Icefall again. He had agreed to come on this expedition on condition that he could manage the Sherpas from Base Camp—but he'd eventually broken down and asked to accompany Chris on his summit attempt. Chris was delighted; it was right that they should climb this mountain together.

There were two Norwegians and two more Sherpas in the summit party. The Sherpas' loads included spare bottles of oxygen for Chris and for the Norwegians. One of the Norwegians pointed out now that the party was low on oxygen; they might run out during the descent. Chris didn't care; he found that the summit mattered enormously to him. Pertemba was likewise very determined.

The six climbers carried on up the Southeast Ridge. The climbing was very exposed but the slope was gentle until they came to the Hillary Step. Chris stood looking up at it. Doug Scott had taken a marvelous shot of Dougal leading the step when they'd come up from the Southwest Face and across to this ridge in 1975. A Norwegian—Bjørn Myrer-Lund—led up the step now, moving first in deep snow and then finding rock to his left. The Norwegian reached the top and fixed a rope for the others.

Chris came last. He was very tired again. He didn't think the rope would be enough to get him up the step; for a moment he felt an almost childlike disappointment.

Doug appeared. The big man actually floated. It was disconcerting to see the big frame and the familiar searching eyes. The apparition regarded Chris with skepticism and a wary admiration. It was the look of a younger but in some ways wiser brother. The vision had a voice; it spoke to Chris in quiet, reassuring tones.

Chris found himself at the top of the Hillary Step. He was alone. Doug was gone. The other climbers had gone around a corner to the summit. He walked in their tracks. This was ground known to Doug and Dougal and Peter and almost certainly to Mick. It was odd that Doug had been the one to show up today; it seemed like a job for one of the dead.

Chris was aware of the dead—all of them. He had never ceased to be shocked by the ruthless nature of experience—how much was difficult and surprising, how much was unknowable. He had wondered at times whether death might simply deliver a person to a new set of difficulties.

The Norwegians and the Sherpas were waiting for him on the summit. He could not bear their congratulations, their evident good will. He looked at Pertemba and then away from him and across to Tibet, and then east to Kangchenjunga. The view across vast distances to other mountaintops implied the existence of an entirely different planet beneath the clouds, a world of cities and jungles unlike the world he had taught himself to imagine.

He didn't know what to make of it, this wild and empty view. He turned his head and looked down at the top of Nuptse. He'd stood on that summit looking up at this one as if from the opposite side of a bridge; that was twenty-four years ago. The connection between that young self and the self who stood here on the summit of Everest disrupted all notions of time or of meaning.

He had wished for something like this. He had wanted to be the man he had become. His youthful self had somehow invented this moment, had invented him. He was the boy's creation. He sometimes wondered if only when a moment passed did it take on a shape that you could believe or love—whether you had to have the story to have the life. He was fading, ephemeral. They were permanent, the dead; they had gone into the story.

He had two living sons at home. He loved their sweetness, but it sharpened his grief for what was lost to him and to the others. He understood something of the nature of death: how it filled and refilled the well of loss, an endless trickle and flow of unlived time. And yet time itself flowed from and into death, a sunlit river that emerged from and ended in darkness. Hamish and Don were old now, but even they were young in his recollection.

This was not nostalgia. He had come to fear the past and its power to find him out. And yet he returned to these places as if to seek its notice, as if he meant to show himself to his past, to live the moments he had escaped or bungled or forgotten. He meant for this place to burn off his shame and his sorrow or to burn them into him, to punish him for the sin of his joy, which even now filled him with desire for more of this.

He thought of the dead again, the stories they had become. His strength left him and he slumped beneath the weight of his dear ones' absence. His hands touched the earth for balance and the weight lifted. He crouched sobbing in the snow as if in prayer.

His thoughts came clearly to him. He had undertaken much for reasons he could not remember or credit now and also because he had wished to understand. He wished himself emptied of such desires—relieved of his wish to know more than he did. He renounced his need for explanations. He clung only to his joy and to his grief; they were the same and he could not renounce them—he could not.

And for a moment those too were lifted from him: he knew only the snow and sky and all that lay beneath.

POSTSCRIPT

CHRIS AND WENDY Bonington still live at Badger Hill. Chris received a knighthood in 1996. He continues to climb on the Lake District cliffs near his home, as well as in the Himalayas and elsewhere.

Martin Boysen lives in England. He continues to climb at a high standard.

Paul (Tut) Braithwaite lives in England, where he owns Vertical Access, an industrial rope access company.

Joe Brown lives in Wales, where he has put up countless new routes during the past several decades.

Charles Clarke and Ruth Seifert live in London. Charlie practices neurology, and participates in climbing and sailing expeditions. He is the president of the British Mountaineering Council.

Maria Coffey lives in Canada. She is a writer, and with her husband she runs Hidden Places, an adventure travel company.

Jim Curran lives in Sheffield, England, where he writes books, paints mountain landscapes and climbs gritstone.

Hamish MacInnes lives in Glencoe, Scotland. He has been active in writing, filmmaking, exploration and climbing as well as the development of mountain rescue techniques and equipment.

Dick Renshaw lives in Wales. He is a sculptor.

Hilary (Boardman) Rhodes lives with her husband in Switzerland, where she teaches school, climbs and practices yoga.

Al Rouse became the first Englishman to climb K2, reaching the summit on August 4, 1985. He died during the descent.

Doug Scott lives in England's Lake District, five miles from Badger Hill. He is cofounder and operations director of Community Action Nepal, a registered charity that supports community development projects in Nepal.

Don Whillans died in his sleep, of a heart attack, at a friend's home on August 4, 1985.

Climbers found Peter Boardman's body in 1992, just above the Second Pinnacle on Everest's Northeast Ridge.

Joe Tasker's body has not been found.

SELECT BIBLIOGRAPHY

Alvarez, A. *Feeding the Rat*. Thunder's Mouth Press, 2001.

Anker, Conrad and David Roberts. *The Lost Explorer: Finding Mallory on Mount Everest*. Simon and Schuster, 1999.

Birtles, G. B., ed. *World Climbing: INFO Sections from Mountain Magazine Issues No. 1–64*. Dark Peak, 1980.

Boardman, Peter. *1972 Nottingham University Hindu Kush Expedition*. Nottingham University, 1973.

———. *Sacred Summits: A Climber's Year*. The Mountaineers, 1982.

———. *The Shining Mountain: Two Men on Changabang's West Wall*. E. P. Dutton, 1982.

Bonington, Chris. *I Chose to Climb*. Victor Gollancz, 1966.

———. *Annapurna South Face*. Cassell & Company Ltd., 1971.

———. *Everest South West Face*. Hodder and Stoughton, 1973.

———. *The Next Horizon*. Victor Gollancz, 1973.

———. *Everest The Hard Way: The First Ascent of the South West Face*. Hodder and Stoughton, 1976.

———. *Quest for Adventure*. Hodder and Stoughton, 1981.

———. *Kongur: China's Elusive Summit*. Hodder and Stoughton, 1982.

————. *The Everest Years: A Climber's Life*. Hodder and Stoughton, 1986.

————. *Chris Bonington: Mountaineer*. Diadem Books, 1989.

————. *The Climbers: A History of Mountaineering*. Hodder and Stoughton, 1992.

————. *Chris Bonington's Everest*. Weidenfield & Nicolson, 2002.

Bonington, Chris, et al. *Changabang*. Oxford University Press, 1976.

Bonington, Chris and Charles Clarke. *Everest the Unclimbed Ridge*. W. W. Norton & Company, 1983.

————. *Tibet's Secret Mountain: The Triumph of Sepu Kangri*. Widenfeld & Nicolson, 1999.

Brown, Joe. *The Hard Years*. Victor Gollancz, 1967.

Bruce, C. G. *The Assault on Mount Everest*. E. Arnold & Company, 1923.

Bury, C. K. Howard. *Mount Everest: The Reconnaissance, 1921*. E. Arnold & Company, 1922.

Child, Greg. *Mixed Emotions*. The Mountaineers, 1993.

————. *Thin Air*. Patrick Stephens, 1988.

Coffey, Maria. *Fragile Edge: A Personal Portrait of Loss on Everest*. Chatto & Windus, 1989.

————. *Where the Mountain Casts Its Shadow: The Dark Side of Extreme Adventure*. St. Martin's Press, 2003.

Conefrey, Mick and Tim Jordan. *Mountain Men*. Da Capo Press, 2001.

Connor, Jeff. *Dougal Haston: The Philosophy of Risk*. Canongate Books, Ltd., 2002.

Curran, Jim. *Trango: The Nameless Tower*. Dark Peak, 1978.

————. *K2: Triumph and Tragedy*. Hodder and Stoughton, 1987.

———. *Suspended Sentences from the Life of a Climbing Cameraman*. Hodder and Stoughton, 1991.

———. *High Achiever: The Life and Climbs of Chris Bonington*. Constable and Company Limited, 1999.

Gillman, Peter. *In Balance: Twenty Years of Mountaineering Journalism*. Hodder and Stoughton, 1989.

Gillman, Peter, ed. *Everest: The Best Writing and Pictures from Seventy Years of Human Endeavour*. Little, Brown and Company, 1993.

Gillman, Peter and Dougal Haston. *Eiger Direct*. Collins, 1966.

Gillman, Peter and Leni. *The Wildest Dream: The Biography of George Mallory*. The Mountaineers, 2000.

Gray, Dennis. *Mountain Lover*. The Crowood Press, 1990.

———. *Rope Boy*. Victor Gollancz, 1970.

Graydon, Don, ed. *Mountaineering: The Freedom of the Hills 5th Edition*. The Mountaineers, 1992.

Harrer, Heinrich. *The White Spider*. Rupert-Hart Davis Ltd. 1959.

Haston, Dougal. *In High Places*. Cassell & Company, 1972.

———. *The Eiger*. Cassell & Company, 1974.

———. *Calculated Risk*, Diadem, 1979.

Herzog, Maurice translated by Nea Morin and Janet Adam Smith. *Annapurna: First Conquest of an 8,000 Meter Peak*. E. P. Dutton, 1952.

Houston, Charles, M.D. and Robert H. Bates. *K2: The Savage Mountain*. McGraw-Hill, 1954.

Hunt, Sir John. *The Conquest of Everest*. E. P. Dutton, 1953.

James, Ron. *Rock Climbing in Wales*. Constable & Company, 1970.

Jones, Chris. *Climbing in North America*. The Mountaineers, 1997.

Kauffman, Andrew J. and William L. Putnam. *K2: The 1939 Tragedy*. The Mountaineers, 1992.

Macfarlane, Robert. *Mountains of the Mind: Adventures in Reaching the Summit*. Vintage Books, 2004.

MacInnes, Hamish. *The Price of Adventure: More Mountain Rescue Stories from Four Continents*. Hodder and Stoughton, 1987.

Mantovani, Roberto and Kurt Diemberger. *K2: Challenging the Sky*. The Mountaineers, 1997.

Norgay, Tenzing with James Ramsay Ullman. *Tiger of the Snows: The Autobiography of Tenzing Norgay*. Putnam, 1955.

Norton, E. F. *The Fight For Everest 1924*. Longmans, Green & Co., 1925.

Noyce, Wilfred. *To the Unknown Mountain: An Ascent of an Unexplored Twenty-Five Thousander in the Karakoram*. The Travel Book Club, 1962.

Patey, Tom. *One Man's Mountains: Essays and Verses*. Victor Gollancz, 1971.

Perrin, Jim. *The Villain: The Life of Don Whillans*. Hutchinson, 2005.

Pye, David. *George Leigh Mallory: A Memoir by David Pye*. Oxford University Press, 1927.

Reid, Robert Leonard. *Mountains of the Great Blue Dream*. North Point Press, 1991.

Roberts, David. *Moments of Doubt*. The Mountaineers, 1986.

Roper, Robert. *Fatal Mountaineer: The High-Altitude Life and Death of Willi Unsoeld, American Himalayan Legend*. St. Martin's Griffin, 2003.

Roskelly, John. *Nanda Devi: The Tragic Expedition*. Stackpole Books, 1987.

Scott, Doug. *Doug Scott: Himalayan Climber*. Diadem Books, 1992.

Scott, Doug and Alex MacIntyre. *The Shishapangma Expedition.* Granada, 1984.

Tasker, Joe. *Everest the Cruel Way.* Eyre Methuen, 1981.

———. *Savage Arena.* St. Martin's, 1982.

Tenderini, Mirella translated by Susan Hodgkiss. *Gary Hemming: The Beatnik of the Alps.* The Ernest Press, 1995.

Ullman, James Ramsay. *Straight Up: The Life and Death of John Harlin.* Doubleday, 1968.

Unsworth, Walt. *Everest.* Cloudcap, 1989.

Wells, Colin. *A Brief History of British Mountaineering.* The Mountain Heritage Trust, 2001.

Whillans, Don and Alick Ormerod. *Don Whillans: Portrait of a Mountaineer.* Heinemann, 1971.

Younghusband, Sir Francis. *The Epic of Mount Everest.* E. Arnold & Company, 1926.

Acknowledgments

I OWE THANKS to the climbers and writers, living and dead, whose lives and work have enriched and inspired my own. They include the principal characters in this book, as well as the writers whose work is included in the bibliography.

I am grateful to the many people in Great Britain who offered me hospitality as well as insight and information; many of them also read and commented on versions of the manuscript. Al Alvarez took me swimming in Hampstead Heath, cooked me an excellent breakfast, and told me a fantastic joke about tomatoes as well as great stories about the postwar British climbing scene. Al also put me in touch with Jim Curran (see below) at an early stage of my research. Chris Bonington devoted two mornings of his busy life to answering my questions with great care; he also took me climbing one afternoon (he led, of course) and tried to help me find other climbing partners while I was in Great Britain. Joe Brown offered me a chair by the stove on a rainy Welsh afternoon and patiently fielded my questions. Joe provided important insight into his relationship with Don Whillans, as well as the course of expedition climbing during the past half-century. Charlie Clarke shared his memories of Peter Boardman, Mick Burke, Joe Tasker and others over an unforgettable dinner in London. Ruth Seifert delighted, amused and instructed me. I also enjoyed meeting Millie Dickson, the small child who wandered into the Clarkes' home from the house next door, drawn by Ruth's goodheartedness. Jim Curran put me up for two nights in a room where many a climbing great (and at least one duffer) has slept off a well-earned hangover. Jim interrupted last-minute preparations for an important showing of his art to ply me with food and drink as well as thoughtful and at times hilarious commentary on the history and nature of British climbing and climbers. He showed me (at my insistence) his paintings (I saw no etchings), gave me copies of his books and films, and introduced me to his delightful friends, who also fed me and who laughed at my jokes. Doug Scott was absurdly patient with me. He let me follow him around for three days (!), and delivered bracing insights about mountaineering, mountain people, spirituality and Bob Dylan. Doug also shared his fond memories and impressions of Dougal Haston, Don Whillans and others in their circle and put me in touch with friends who provided further help. Joe Tasker's family—especially his sister Mary McCourt and his brothers Paul Tasker and John Tasker—gave me shelter and other assistance and shared impressions of their beloved brother. I believe I learned much about Joe's exceptional gifts and spirit through meeting Mary, Paul and John as well as several of Joe's other siblings (Francis, Teresa and Margaret) and his parents, Tom and Betty. Paul and Mary also provided copies of official expedition reports, newspaper and magazine clippings, letters, photographs and other materials related to Joe's climbs and other achievements. They introduced me to Joe's fellow seminarian Monseigneur Ricardo Morgan, who shared memories of Joe's time at seminary. Finally, Mary took me to meet Joe's first climbing mentor, Father Tony Barker; Father Barker spent a morning recalling with great vividness Joe's early experiences in school and among mountains. Martin Wragg gave me perfectly good driving directions to his home in the Peak District (it's not his fault I got lost), explained the bandage on his head (rockfall in Canada), regaled me with memories of his early and somewhat hair-raising adventures with Peter Boardman in the Alps and the Hindu Kush, and offered an astute and loving analysis of Peter's character.

Dave Bathgate told me stories about the 1975 Everest Southwest Face Expedition. Paul (Tut) Braithwaite shared memories of the Alps as well as Everest, the Ogre and K2. He also offered insight into the lives of various climbers. Martin Boysen shared his recollections of the young Chris Bonington as well as Mick Burke, Doug Scott and others, and recalled his experiences on Annapurna, Changabang and Everest. Maria Coffey provided inspiration and insights through her own writing and offered thoughtful and revealing answers to my questions about Joe Tasker's habits and frame of mind during the final years and months of his life. John Harlin III took most of a morning off from writing his own book to share his memories of his father and discuss with great openness and sensitivity the man's life, character and reputation. Hamish MacInnes offered his recollections of climbing with Chris Bonington and others in Scotland, the Alps, the Himalayas and elsewhere. Hilary (Boardman) Rhodes spoke to me at length and shared passages of her own writing with me, providing a moving and illuminating portrait of her friendship and marriage with the late Peter Boardman. Our conversation gave me essential perspective on the evolution of Peter's life and hopes. Hilary also supplied information about Peter's family background, with generous help from Peter's brother John Boardman. Mike Thompson told me funny and illuminating stories about climbers, including details about Don Whillans's later years.

Henry Barber encouraged my efforts and told me some hilarious stories about the '70s British climbing scene. Ed Webster shared his recollections of British climbers and his own hard-won knowledge of the Everest region. Ed read a late version of my manuscript, helped with photo research and offered generous encouragement as well as advice that saved me from a dozen or so editorial pratfalls.

I am grateful to Margaret Body of the Boardman Tasker Trust, Alex Messenger of the British Mountaineering Council and Margaret Trinder at Chris Bonington's office; all three fielded various queries and helped me track down climbers or their survivors.

Frances Daltrey at the Chris Bonington Picture Library did a wonderful job finding photographs. She fielded almost two years worth of my e-mails and phone calls, and did so with a bracing mix of tact, skill, courtesy and good cheer. Beverly Davis helped introduce the book to my friends in Louisiana. Shawneric Hachey of 15thminute.com created the book's website (theboysofeverest. com). John Hendren went way out of his way to help promote the book. Peter Kadzis went above and beyond the call of friendship to encourage my efforts and help promote the book. Hilary Roberts at the Writing Company made important administrative and editorial contributions, shepherding the manuscript through countless drafts with extraordinary patience and skill. Carol Pickering also provided timely and skillful editorial assistance. Katie Fagan photographed me for the book jacket and website.

The editorial team at Avalon Publishing Group have been true friends to my work and to the greater cause of books and stories. I can only mention a few of them here: Yulia Borodyanskaya handled foreign rights with grace and aplomb. Wendie Carr worked hard to publicize the book, and handled my many inquiries with exquisite patience. Sarah Coglianese provided generous and tactful marketing advice. Shaun Dillon fielded my endless requests with great patience. Linda Kosarin told me stories about her accomplished and adventurous father, and fought to acquire just the right cover photograph for the book. Michele Martin provided encouragement and support. Jamie McNeely oversaw production with impressive grace and skill. India Amos designed the book. (Nice Job, India!). John Oakes generously supported efforts to publicize the book. Mike Walters helped with scheduling and other issues.

I am enormously grateful to family, friends and others who read and responded to various drafts. They include Al Alvarez, Henry Barber, Gary Belsky, Chris Bonington, Paul Braithwaite, Ellen Brodkey, Charles Clarke, John Climaco, Maria Coffey, Jim Curran, Michael Finkle, John Hendrin, Mike Jewell, Peter Kadzis, John Manderino, Lawrence Millman, Jean Nathan, Bob Porter, Annie Proulx, Hilary (Boardman) Rhodes, Mike Sager, Jay Schwamm, Doug Scott, Ruth Seifert, Paul Tasker, Ian Turnbull, Ed Webster, Abner Willis, Charles Perry Willis Sr., Elizabeth Faison Cooper Willis, Harper Willis, Jennifer Schwamm Willis and Martin Wragg.

This book owes a great deal to the friendship and professional talents of dozens of people who have been associated with the Writing Company, including former staff as well as current freelance associates and clients. Their ranks include John Bishop, Michaela Cavallero, Ellie Chatto, Sean Donahue, Shawn Hachey, Nate Hardcastle, Diane Harris, Beth Helfont, Mark Klimek, Bob Lightfoot, Nat May, Ned May, Carol Pickering, Hilary Roberts, Mike Robbins, Eric Schurenberg, Taylor Smith, March Truedsson and many others.

Thanks also are due to many friends in California, Louisiana, Maine, New York, Wyoming and elsewhere. I love you all.

Michael Jewell continues to teach me about climbing, compassion and friendship. Ian Turnbull and Jay Pistono also have helped to teach me how to have fun and stay safe in the mountains. Steve Longenecker took me climbing when it counted most.

The late Harold Brodkey took me and my work seriously from the start. The late Neill Jeffrey was amazingly kind to me and mine.

Oz and Mona Hanley never waver.

Will Balliett, Publisher of Carroll & Graf, encouraged and sustained this venture from its earliest stage through its completion, often taking precious time from other pressing obligations. I cannot imagine a better collaborator or a better friend to me and to my work.

I wish to express my deep gratitude to my father and mother (Charles Perry Willis Sr. and Elizabeth Faison Cooper Willis) and to my brother (Charles Perry Willis Jr.) and sister (Elizabeth Anne Willis McFarlain). They are all my beloved teachers.

Patrizia Levi, Susan Kohaut, Jeri Sides and the late Judy Mello Schwamm also have been my teachers.

Jennifer and Harper and Abner remind me that the universe wants me to be happy . . . which must explain why I am smiling as I write these words.

INDEX

ABOUT THE AUTHOR

CLINT WILLIS IS the author of *Epic: Stories of Survival from the World's Highest Peaks*, as well as more than forty other anthologies on adventure, politics, religion and war. His writing has appeared in hundreds of publications, including *Men's Journal, Outside* and the *New York Times*. The American Society of Magazine Editors nominated

PHOTO: KATIE FAGAN

his three-part series on investing for a 1997 National Magazine Award in the category of personal service.

Clint has been a climber since he was ten years old. He lives with his family in Maine. Please visit theboysofeverest.com, where you can check out Clint's other climbing books, part of his thirty-volume Adrenaline Books series.